I present this to [the] Public Library [with] great pleasure — it is a book about a native son of Minnesota about whom you can be very proud.

Norma Kipp Avendano
October 1999

WAIT FOR ME

Norma Kipp Avendano

San Diego, California
1994

First Edition
  1st Printing 9/94
  2nd Printing 7/96

Copyright © 1994 by Norma Kipp Avendano
All rights reserved by author
Printed in the United States of America

Cover Design by Alex Selamat & David Marlow

Every effort has been made to trace the holders of copyright, and the author trusts that any inadvertent infringement will be overlooked. At the same time, she expresses readiness to make any necessary corrections in subsequent editions.

"In the Garden" copyright 1912 C. Austin Miles.
"La Paloma" music by Sabastian de Yradier, Spanish folk song p.d.
"Hiawatha's Childhood" Henry Wadsworth Longfellow p.d.

Published by
Interaction Publishers,Inc.
El Cajon, California

Library of Congress Catalog Card Number: 94-79453
ISBN 1-57336-900-4

ACKNOWLEDGMENTS

To those who over the years have said, "You should write a book", here it is.

To those who have given encouragement, I appreciate it.

To those who have given aid, I thank you.

To Music and Memory *Semper Fidelis*.

WAIT FOR ME

Bewitched

Semper Fi

On the Outside

Prologue

Today was her birthday and Norma knew her mother and sisters would remember. Through the kitchen window she saw the postman leaving mail across the street. She expected that he would be leaving birthday greetings for her when he finished on the other side, rounded the cul-de-sac, and turned onto the forty-eight hundred block of Aberdeen Street, stopping at 4840. Smiling she waited, her hands busy with dish washing, and soon he came, taking a large manila envelope from his bag and pushing it into her box.

She reached for a towel, drying her hands on her way to the front door. Going to the mailbox. A lifelong habit. She removed the envelope and stared at the return address, puzzled. *The White House, 1600 Pennsylvania Avenue, Washington, D.C.* No mistake; it was addressed to her. She withdrew a cream colored document bearing an embossed presidential seal in gleaming gold and below a message in stark, black script.

The United States of America
honors the memory of
Harry E. Kipp

***This certificate is awarded by a grateful nation
in recognition of devoted and selfless consecration
to the service of our country in the
Armed Forces of the United States***

It was signed by Lyndon B. Johnson and arrived on June 30, 1965. Eight weeks and one day after Harry died.

Haply I think on thee, and then my state,
Like to the lark at break of day arising
From sullen earth, sings hymns at Heaven's gate
   For thy sweet love remembered such wealth brings
That then I scorn to change my state with kings.

William Shakespeare

WAIT FOR ME
PART ONE

BEWITCHED

The rural mail carrier always sounded his car horn when he rounded the curve in the road if he had mail for the Clintons. This last Saturday in February, Norma was home to hear the signal. She raced through the house and down the front porch steps to reach the roadside just as old Mr. Lowrance stopped his dusty black Ford beside the mailbox. With a questioning lift of his eyebrows and a toothy smile, he gave her an airmail letter then quickly drove away, his car tires scattering loose gravel from the unpaved road.

Quite a few letters had passed from his hand to hers over the past years. Letters from Aunt Ruby, Aunt Edna, Aunt Jean, and even a pen pal from Oslo, Norway. But never a letter like this one from Captain Harry E. Kipp, USMC, "B" Btry., 12th Defense Bn., FMF, % Fleet Post Office, San Francisco, California. Passed by a Naval Censor.

She noticed at once the correct letter form, spelling and punctuation for she was an honor student in English. A senior in La Fayette High School and class historian. But the words of this stranger, this Harry, took her breath away and stirred feelings of excitement she had never felt before. She kept his letter and its contents for her eyes only, reading it over and over in private when her parents, younger sisters and brother were asleep. As days passed, she didn't have to read the words; they were stored permanently in her mind.

Captain Kipp.....Harry....was not like the boys in her classes at school; he was a man, and a Marine. And he was, after all, she reminded herself, Aunt Jean's Marine--or had been until she married someone else. With that marriage over Aunt Jean had decided she wanted Harry again. But he wouldn't answer her letters. She thought Norma might convince him of her love if she would write and tell him-- would she? After much pleading, Norma finally wrote--two months ago--but her attempt at playing Cupid backfired. Harry had not written to Aunt Jean, as they hoped, but to Norma, and he hadn't even mentioned her reason for writing. She couldn't deny the pleasure his letter had brought even though it caused uneasiness as well, because now she was in the middle. And what in the world could she write to Aunt Jean?

12 February, 1944

Dear Norma,

    Although Jean had told me that you might drop me a line, I was nevertheless quite surprised and very pleased to receive your letter. The doubt you expressed about my not knowing you was well founded for she hadn't even told me your name, but what I learned from your letter and picture was a pleasant revelation. To be graduated from high school before reaching your seventeenth birthday is no mean accomplishment, and to become as lovely as your picture tells me you are is nothing less than a magnificent achievement.

    Your wish to become a nurse is a worthy goal to shoot at and I wish you success in realizing your aspirations. Might I hope to enjoy the privilege of your services in the event I should ever need them? or even though I didn't really need them? But since you are so proficient in chemistry you will probably be a laboratory technician who does not personally attend patients. I knew there was a reason for my dislike of chemistry other than I was too slow on the uptake to understand the elusive movements of the molecule.

    It *has* been a long time since you saw Jean. You must have been a cute little tyke at that time. I haven't seen her either since nearly four years ago. Little wonder that she married someone else. Would you wait that long for just an ordinary Marine?

    Your hobbies are very akin to mine. I too enjoy movies and like to write letters. In that we are on common ground, but I must admit that sewing holds very little fascination for me, that is if I am the one doing it, but I do find pleasure in watching a good housewife sew.

    Perhaps you believe that I deliberately delayed answering your letter, but that isn't the case. You see, I am in a very remote corner of the world and mail reaches us much more slowly than it takes to reach the States from here. Your letter arrived just yesterday. I hope that soon there shall be another (with a picture in it) and more to follow. I would enjoy looking at my pinup girl in two different moods.

    Good night, Sweets, won't you write again soon?

                                                      Yours,

Capt.H.E.Kipp. USMC   Harry.

Bewitched

Harry's remote corner of the world was in the jungles of Cape Gloucester on New Britain, one of the Solomon Islands, and mail hadn't been delivered to Marines in the thick of battle. With the fighting ended, his letters began arriving in Norma's mailbox with increasing number and passion.

27 June, 1944

Dearest Norma,

Today your letters of 19 March and 1 May arrived which makes four that I have gotten from you, and still leaves two unaccounted for. I am eagerly looking forward to their arrival.

Your pictures (I mean *you*) are heavenly. Now I do want to be two persons. Not so I could love you and someone else too, but so that both of me could love you. Looking at you lends meaning to the story of Mark Twain who, when he first saw the picture of Veli, looked at it long and earnestly, then said, "This girl shall be my wife." I said those same words of you to your picture, Norma, and heaven knows I meant them.

In my last letter I tried to explain my feeling for Jean, and why. I hope you will understand and forgive me, and realize that even though I had never known of you or never been thrilled by your loveliness, it would still be the same. It will be difficult, but tomorrow I shall tell her.

You cause me to believe that you exercise great care and much thought in writing to me. Norma, please don't compose letters to me. Just record your thoughts as they occur to you. Talk to me 'Just as if you were here'. (How I wish you were!)

Must close. I can't write tonight. Your picture distracts me. I gaze at it continuously, marveling, hoping, imagining, fascinated-- wondering if I can possibly ever be happy without you. Will write again when I recover a bit. In the meantime, I'll be dreaming of you.   Love,
Harry.

16 July, 1944

Dearest Norma,

I was very happy to receive your long and pleasant letter. To me it is sort of extra special since you wrote it on your birthday anniversary. I feel flattered in knowing that you even thought of me on such a gala day.

So, you like long letters! Well, confidentially, Sweets, I do too if they are from you. Let me warn you now though, there may be times in the more or less near future when my letters may be short, infrequent, and slow in reaching you. Will you remember then that I am doing the very best I can for you, in writing, as well as in other ways? Mmmm! how nice it would be to know that everything I do, I'd be doing for you! I want to feel that way now, but I know I'm reaching for a star. All the letters you've written to me, seven of them, have reached me but not quite in the order in which you mailed them. Want to know something? I've read and reread each one of them more than seven times. And each time I read them, I enjoy them just a little bit more. They and your pictures assure me that you are sweeter, lovelier than any girl I've ever known.

It seems that my name has found its way into your diary. To me that is a signal honor, but you do know that I am aspiring to a far greater achievement: to find *my* way into your *heart*. Norma, tell me, what did you really mean when you said, "In fact, you're too convincing!" ?

Perhaps by now you know that I wrote Jean how I felt about her. It wasn't easy and it made me feel like a hard, ruthless, unfeeling creature, for I do believe she still loves me, but you understand, don't you, Norma, that I could never have the complete faith in her that is so essential for a husband and wife to have in each other to make marriage the beautiful relationship it must be if it is to survive? There is something I can't express, something unsavory about the whole affair which I would give anything to be able to forget. Norma, you have no reason to feel even the slightest sense of guilt in the breakdown between Jean and me. It would never have been otherwise.

Am sorry I can't send you a picture now, but you did ask me to describe myself and threatened me with your anger should I fail to comply. Remembering what you told me of your terrible temper, I hasten to tell you (and this hurts) that I am not at all handsome, am only five feet seven inches tall, weight 170 pounds, have straight blond hair, blue eyes, and worst of all, have a childishly affectionate disposition. Now, *you* tell me your reaction.

As for your reserve in the letters you write to me, of course I understand. How could you write in any other way? You haven't even seen a picture of me, have never heard my voice, and know so

Bewitched

little about me. There is something I want you to know. Perhaps you will think me very naive and impulsive, but I am sincere in the protestation of my love for you. I do love you. Norma, I want you to be my wife just as soon as I can possibly come for you. And when this war is over I want to take you with me to California, to Panama, Puerto Rico, Honolulu, Manila, Shanghai or any other place I may go to. I want to see your surprised expression at the strange customs of strange people. I want to see the dream in your eyes as you gaze at the unbelievably beautiful tropical sunset. I want to feel your hair as it brushes my cheek when I wake in the morning. I want the comfort of your presence when I feel blue. I want you so terribly that I tremble each time I look at your picture. I've never felt like this before. I can't understand it, but it's true. That is why I expressed the hope that you would change your mind about embarking on a nursing career. I know that now you can do nor say anything except to express surprise at my bold proposal but, Norma, I want you to know how intense my desire for you has grown. Won't you tell me frankly, honestly, if you would marry me when I come home, should you find that you could care for me?

You have already sent me three pictures and I have the one from Jean, but I would like so much to see you with your new haircut. Do you think I'm being greedy? But you must know that I am greedy about anything concerning you.

Considering everything I've already said more than you expected to hear, I'll say "Good night, Sweets". Will you answer just as soon as you recover from the shock?

Love,
Harry.

Shocked? Yes. And her astonished eyes sought his words again. There they were, plain as day: *I want you to be my wife*. She buried her face in trembling hands to think. His words of love had been getting bolder by the letter and they had made her blood tingle and her heart race. But a proposal? She hadn't expected this. In his eighth letter! He was serious. *If he was serious.* Or is he playing a game, a wartime game when needs are great and immediate, to be quickly forgotten when situations changed or something better came along? Didn't hundreds of addresses flutter from the hands of soldiers passing in convoys through La Fayette on Highway

27 every month? And wasn't it a patriotic duty to cheer up the boys far away from home? All the war songs and movies said so. Her friends, one by one, were getting engaged, some even marrying as their boyfriends went off to fight the war...and wasn't Harry ten thousand miles from home and lonely? But his letters? How she loved his letters! And his words; at each declaration of his love she felt less resistance, more yearning. How could he write so convincingly if he were not really feeling the love he professed? And why was he able to write exactly what she wanted to read? Was he reading her mind? Was she a foolish, needy girl overreacting to flattery? and he sensed it? Was it only flattery? or was it real? Was there enough to build a marriage on? Marriage. Such a serious step. Suppose, if she said she'd marry him, he would write and say, "Ha! I fooled you!" ? But would he? Hadn't Aunt Jean written that he was the most honorable man she had ever known, even after he had told her good-by?

But she couldn't be thinking of marriage; she would be going into the Cadet Nurse Corps in September. It had all been arranged months ago when she lost hope of getting a scholarship to attend college. All those dreams of becoming a teacher and taking college prep courses, working for good grades to make it possible vanished when Daddy said she must go to work and help support the family. A scholarship would be impossible to earn if she must work along with school her senior year. She decided to enter a government paid program in nursing when she graduated. Through interviews and letters of recommendation, she had been accepted; her future was set. On June 30, her sixteenth birthday, she started work at the hosiery mill on the second shift and in September she began her senior year of high school. What did she care about being labeled a 'mill hand'? It was only temporary although it meant rushing from school to work to bed to school to work to bed every weekday and studying all weekend. Everything else took a back seat; she begrudged anything that took time away from those responsibilities. And she had put off writing to some Marine in the Pacific in Aunt Jean's behalf until Christmas vacation.

But that dutiful letter had brought something wonderful to her life. Like something she might read in literature. In her bleak life, reading had become her deliverance and she had read all that the county library had to offer. The written word impressed her more than anything and writers were her heroes. She set her measure by them, but even her teachers, whom she admired above all others, fell short. She lived in a dearth of refinement until she opened a good book. It was not surprising that the captain's letters were like an arrow striking a ready target.

Bewitched

She'd never had a boyfriend; Daddy had forbidden it until she finished high school. His edict had caused no problem since none of the local youths interested her. They were like children compared to her literary heroes. Even last summer, while visiting Great Aunt Ola and Uncle Bill on Lookout Mountain where she had met two young men, she had obeyed his law. Mama said it was Norma's obligation, as the oldest of five, to set a good example, and she agreed. Honor thy father and mother, the Bible commanded. And she did. Although these two men, each in his twenties, wanted more than friendly fellowship and singing in the choir with her, that is all they got. Neither had so much as held her hand though each had managed by overt maneuvering to occupy the pew on either side of her during the week-long revival meetings. Still, within a month of her return home, she had received their proposals of marriage. Touched by the offer of their hearts and respect for the gentlemen they were, her refusals had been gentle. She told them she was too young to marry and she had other plans for her life.

Now, at seventeen, she had Harry's proposal. And she was still young, with plans for her life. Her head knew it, but what about her heart? Why did it soar every time she thought of him, touched his letters, read his words? Why did she live for the mail deliveries? And was the plan she had for her life as important as she thought?

She wrestled with indecision during July and August, questioning him and herself, presenting her doubt and reservations while he insisted, lovingly and passionately, that their love was the most real thing in the universe and she must believe that. But there was her commitment to the Cadet Nurse Corps. August was coming to an end and her decision had to be made this month, this week, this day. On September fourth, she was due to begin nurse's training in Erlanger Hospital in Chattanooga. Her parents were asking why she wasn't already packed. She must either decide to marry Harry and drop out of the program or say "No" and begin training. She couldn't do both. If she began training and dropped out, she--or someone--would have to reimburse the government for the money spent on her. It would be irresponsible to begin in September and stop in October if Harry returned then, as he predicted, and if she married him. And she wanted to marry him; he was everything she wanted in a husband.

Today was the day. She would make the choice. At sunset, her time of day, she climbed to the top of the hill behind her house to look down on the place where she had lived for most of her life and gave her heart and mind free rein. Sitting there, wrapped in the fading twilight, she let her spirit travel to where Harry was and she knew the answer. Not a single doubt remained. She ran down the hill, to her room, to her stationery. Putting pen to paper, she joyfully began to write.

August 27, 1944

My Dearest Harry,
    Yes, yes, yes, I will marry you! Just as soon as you can come for me. I want more than anything in the world to be your wife, forever! I love you with all my heart!
Your Norma

And then she wrote another letter, a resignation from the Cadet Nurse Corps. She sealed both letters, stamped them, laid them on her desk to be mailed. For the first time in weeks she slept the sleep of the blessed.

Peace lasted only until she told her parents of her resignation. She hadn't thought they'd be upset, rather the opposite, that they'd be glad she would still work at the mill and pay board. She was wrong.

"Lord a mercy! What is ever'body gonna think about you?" Mama's tone matched her drooped shoulders. "You had a chance to make somethin' of yourself, a chance other girls would of given their eye teeth for, and you gave it up, just gave it up."

Daddy shouted in her face, his eyes blazing, "What about them people that vouched for your character *in writing*? I guess how we feel don't matter none, but what about them? You know what you're doin', don't you? I'll tell you what you're doin'. You're throwin' your life away, and for what? To be a mill hand. I thought you was smarter than that."

"Well," Mama declared, "Nobody's gonna think you're smart now."

Norma studied their angry faces, remembering that her being a mill hand hadn't bothered them when she gave them a fifth of her wages for board. And her friends' parents paid for their schoolin' while she had to pay for hers.

Daddy renewed his lecture, "I've taught you kids a man's word is his bond. Now everbody's gonna think your word don't mean nothing or that you're a liar, or crazy. Crazy." He considered the word. "That's it, you must be crazy." He threw up his hands and stomped out of the room.

They hadn't asked her reason. Like always, they decided. If she told them, they'd *really* think she was crazy. She knew she wasn't, except crazy in love with Harry, and he already thought she was somebody. She was right not to tell them her reason. If Daddy knew, he wouldn't allow her to write much less marry a man she'd never seen, a man known to Aunt Jean, Mama's younger sister, twice divorced, a cocktail waitress in Savannah, Georgia near an Army camp, and a woman who wore a two piece bathin' suit on a public beach. And Mama never missed a chance to tell of Aunt Ruby's foolishness in marryin' a soldier she'd written to in World War 1--a marriage that ended in divorce, as everyone predicted, the first in the family and a disgrace to them all. No, she wouldn't tell them she planned to marry Harry. She'd just let them think she was happy being a mill hand; and she *was* happy plannin' for her home with him, startin' a quilt top and buyin' a hope chest on credit to put it in and a beautiful blue dress for an autumn weddin'. He'd been overseas for four years; they'd have to let him come home soon. Maybe in a month or two at the most. She wouldn't have long to live with their displeasure.

In the South Pacific it was D-Day--September 15--and Harry went ashore as an artillery commander in the First Marine Division's bloody assault on Peleliu, a two-by-six mile island of coral rock. In the first week of vicious fighting the division seized all of the terrain of strategic value at the cost of 3946 casualties. Norma, safe in Georgia--though in disfavor with her parents--knew nothing of this. Harry had not given even a hint of the upcoming campaign in his September fifth letter written just before he boarded the landing craft.

>Dearest Norma,
>
>I know you dislike short letters and you've warned me of your ferocious temper, but I fear that for lack of time this will have to be short. If I should, because of my brevity, cause your wrath to fall upon me, how in your opinion could I best get back in your good graces? Might an extra diamond for your ring help a little?
>
>Oh, Norma, my lovely little darling, what wouldn't I give to be near you to prove how dearly I love you, how I want and need you. All I want in this world is to devote my life toward making you happy. Don't ask me why. I can't explain it. I only know that I think and dream only of you, that my heart strings are completely and inextricably tied up in you. I knew it the instant I looked at your picture. There can't ever be anyone else in my life. You've just got to marry me; there is no other way to happiness. Norma, think of it--a heavenly honeymoon in New Orleans, San Francisco, Niagara Falls, anywhere you are inclined to choose, then travel, interesting people and places, gay parties, and our own cozy home to come

back to, the fun of shopping for silver, linen and china, burning the breakfast toast, and waiting for your old man to come home from work to show him your new dress, and some day sewing tiny clothes for someone coming to our house. That is my picture of our life together. Do you like it? Well, you will, and you'll wonder why you ever hesitated to embark upon it. Will you want me to go shopping with you when you shop for new hats or scanties? How I dread it!

Must close, sweets. Please always remember that you are the the one I want to come home to, won't you, 'cause you are going to be my sweet little wife.

Harry.

October came and went and the new blue dress remained unworn. Norma completed the quilt top and began another. She bought towel sets, sheets and pillow cases and embroidered along their hems. And she bought a dove gray suit for a winter wedding.

7 November, 1944

Knock-knock-knock,

Two more lovely letters from you arrived yesterday. Gee! Hon, they're simply saturated with sweetness. They reflect the beauty and dearness of your personality as your pictures portray the loveliness of your gorgeous person. And please don't let yourself believe that what I say might be mere flattery. I mean every word of it. I can't say anything nice enough to express my adoration of you, even though you have been mean again. You cut off an interesting part of another picture, didn't you? Now really, Norma, must you torment me so?

Perhaps I should explain the presence of money in this letter. I hope you won't stand on convention too adamantly. We do understand each other well enough to disregard some of the little common customs, don't we, sweet? Won't you get something for yourself and pretend I got it for you? There is absolutely nothing to be purchased here and I want so much for you to have a Christmas present from me--something to remind you of me once in a while until I can come to take you in my arms. You will accept it in the spirit in which I give it, won't you? Norma dear, it's just a little present for my bride-to-be...

Bewitched

With Harry's generous monetary gift, Norma bought a war bond for their country and for herself a music box. And every night, when she lifted its mirrored cover, the melodious sound of "The Blue Danube Waltz" played along as she wrote to Harry.

...and besides, you may as well get used to accepting money from me since I will expect you to pay the grocery bills and all the other expenses incident to the keeping up of our home. The house will be yours to rule, to manage, and to keep. Think you'll like the job? It gave me a delightful feeling to learn that you are already buying and making things for our home. The towels are swell. And the pillow cases--look at them, Norma, and dream. One day not far away, you and I will rest our heads on one of them and I'll hold you so close to me and tell you over and over how sweet you are and how much I love you. And if I should then call you *Louise*, and you punished me for that by making me go without kisses for a minute or two, as you have threatened to --well, perhaps I could endure it for one minute, but at the end of two, you'd be the widow of a man who died for lack of affection!

Yes, dear, we can talk about our babies or anything that concerns us. Why shouldn't we know each others' interests and desires? You are so enchantingly frank, and I love it. When we are alone in the sanctuary of our own home where no one can see or hear us, we can discuss our most sacred intimacies with unrestrained frankness and with no sense of shame, can't we? I'd like it that way.

I'll bet you are a proud little peacock with your new gown and negligee. I'd love to see you in them. I once saw something in a magazine that struck me as being perfect. It was a sleeveless gown, peach colored and reached to just above the knees, and it had little lacy frills along the top and bottom. Mmmm! It was deliciously seductive and, I think, not at all impractical. Will you wear one like that for me during our honeymoon?

Good night, my sweet. I'm going to squeeze the feathers out of my pillow tonight, 'cause that's how much I love you.

Harry.

2

19 November, 1944

Sweetheart,

Tonight I am dreaming of you; dreaming that you are sitting alone under the stars, so still and quiet, your head slightly bowed, your hands clasped in your lap, waiting. I see you, I am coming, tiptoeing up behind you. I stand there, my eyes drinking the sweetness of your lovely person, my body trembling with eagerness until without turning your head, you sense my presence. I touch your shoulders, you close your eyes as you yield to my pressure while I gently draw you back and cradle you in my arms, kiss your lips, brush my cheek against yours, and thrill to the warm softness of your breasts pressed close to me. Norma darling, no other girl has ever made me dream like that. No other ever can. You are more that a beautiful dream to me. You are the overpowering obsession in my life. There is no barrier on earth great enough to keep me from coming to take you for mine alone, to keep, to protect, and to love forever. I see your bright eyes and sweet smile in the rainbow colors of sunset, I see your adorable face in every fleecy cloud in the sky. I feel the glowing warmth of you in the magic stillness of a moonlit tropical night. Norma, my beloved sweetheart, I'll never know a moment of rest or calm until I hold you safely in my arms. Wait for me, darling! We'll be happy.

I like the simile you used in describing your rings as fitting closely together "like you and me". Something about the suggestion made my heart beat hard and fast. No, sweet, you have never said a thing I didn't like or that I considered bold. It pleases me when you tell me things frankly and easily--things you wouldn't mention to anyone else. I already know that you are vibrant and responsive, and that you love with eager warmth and passion. I wouldn't want you to be any other way. The worst thing that could happen to me would be to marry some anemic woman whose veins carry thin, lifeless blood. I want *you*, and I *need* you. But don't let me frighten you, sweet, that kind of love can be beautiful and tender too when it is based on understanding, consideration, and trust.

No, dear, I can't be with you in January; it will probably be June or July or possibly even August before our prayers are answered. But don't stop going to church, rather go *every* Sunday and pray that God will give us strength to wait patiently until our dreams and plans are realized Pray that He will constantly remind us of that which we want so earnestly. Substitutes, however convenient they may be, can never supplant the real thing, Norma. Let us cherish it and guard it jealously. This long separation, though it is painful to our hearts, does serve to build faith in each other and to strengthen our devotion. Oh, Norma darling! Don't you see what I am trying to say? I have no fear of Japs or bombs or torpedoes or bayonets--the only fear that haunts me is that you may grow tired of waiting for me. I love you so much. Harry.

28 November, 1944

My Lovely One;
Something tells me you will not be too pleased with this letter; it may be quite dull because I am very tired tonight. Again we've been on the go since Sunday morning and now I am so tired and sleepy that I feel numb, but not so numb that I don't tremble a little when I look at your lovely face and see the sweet promise in your eyes. How many times I sit and stare at your picture and say to myself over and over again, "She will be my wife!" I really do believe that we were predestined for each other for I remember when I was just a bit of a kid in the big pine country of northern Minnesota I used to read, on cold winter nights, of the delightful ways of plantation life and of the charming Southern Belles to whom all men paid homage, and somehow I knew then that my wife would be from Georgia. And now the sweetest and most charming of all Southern Belles has promised to be mine. Norma darling, I know I don't deserve to have you, but I want you. And that's for sure!

Several times you have almost offered apologies for not writing interesting letters. Please don't feel that way, sweetheart. Your letters are the most priceless things I possess and (something I have never done before) I've saved every one of them. I'm sure you don't realize how eloquently you say the things I like most to hear, by just telling me of daily events, your experiences, thoughts, desires and dreams in your own sweet natural way. Your letters tell me that you are interesting, lovable, stirringly vibrant, and what's even more important that you are true and devoted. You are everything a man could wish his wife to be. I hope you never change.

One other thing, sweets, please don't worry about my safety. I'm as safe as you are and I will be for at least a couple of months. After that, if you must worry you may, but just a little bit, because I have a charmed life. If it were intended that anything unpleasant should happen to me, it would have happened long ago. We are not supposed to tell anyone when we go into actual combat until after we are aboard ship and on the way to make a landing on Jap territory and that letter doesn't get in the mail until several days or possibly weeks after we leave our base. To let you know that there will be no letters for a long time, I'll end my last letter before leaving by saying, "Good-by for a little while." Will you remember that?

Honeychild, I have *two* pictures of you in which your knees show. In both of them you are sitting on a low stone wall. And your knees *are* exciting. Mmmm! Just wait until I get my arms around you. Then you'll know what I mean. And if you want to drive me completely batty then tell me again that you are wanting to sleep in my arms with my shoulder for a pillow. Don't you know that the very same thought is causing me to stay awake and toss around in my cot for hours every night? I can't wait (but I've got to) until we awaken on Sunday morning, knowing that we don't have to get up. We'll thumb our noses at the clock, grin at each other, and snuggle closer. I'll hold your head in my hands, kiss your sleepy eyes and warm lips, and hug you, and hug you so tight there won't be enough breath in your body to say, "Harry, don't--please don't--please!" Yes, my darling, I'm a wolf, but I'm your wolf and I'll never howl at anyone else. And be sure, Norma, that my love for you is as understanding and tender as it is fierce and passionate, and it is sufficiently flexible to fit your every mood. Oh, Norma! You heavenly, wonderful darling, I've never loved anyone so much in every way as I love you. I could write of my love for you until the end of time and I still would not have finished trying to describe it. I will write of it until I can make you feel it with my kisses and caresses. Good night, my love. Think of me and love me as I love you.   Harry.

Bewitched

27 December, 1944

My Lovely One,

    I thank you for your beautiful Christmas presents--three wonderful letters. They made my Christmas merrier than anything else I could have possibly got out here. In the letter you wrote on the 9th, you said you were always happier at night because you know that soon, in your dreams, you will be in my arms. That is a beautiful thought and it made my heart skip a beat, but the thought that thrills me most is that soon, in my arms, you'll be dreaming.

    Norma dear, I didn't scold you for feeling blue and telling me about it. I do want you to be happy, sweet, but I don't, by any means, mind knowing that you dream of our own little Mary Lee, and that you sometimes miss me. That is another way of telling me that you love me and honey chile, your love means more to me than anything else in the world. You know that, don't you? Lovely Norma, keep it burning bright and strong for me! I know you are as true and loyal as you are sweet and lovely. I know it as surely as I know God guided our paths to meet. As surely as I know that you, and you alone, can make me happy. Norma, I love you more each day, and the more I think of you, the more I love you.

    No, sweet, I don't mind answering your questions: I like to sleep under all-wool blankets in the winter provided there are sheets between me and the blankets (your shaven legs will give me all the scratching I'll want) but I prefer the lightness of goose down or eiderdown quilts (not to the scratching of your legs). Do I like you best in dress or sport clothes? I can't answer that. I love you in either. I do like tailored suits in the daytime and you are so very cute in them. Remember the "V" picture? No, I definitely do not like very red nail polish, nor lipstick, nor thin eye-brows, nor long fingernails. Would I approve of my wife going bare-legged? Well--most places, perhaps not. I was at Pearl Harbor when it was bombed. Will I be angry with you if you wear a dress I don't like? Only when you expose too many of your lovely charms for wolves to stare at and get ideas. I'll never be angered by such trifles as hanging clothes in the bathroom. I'll build you racks or put up lines so you won't have to hang them under the shower or in front of my shaving mirror. Okay? As for laying out my clothes for me after my bath, if you do that I'll know you either love me very much or think me pitifully helpless.

I'm sorry it is so cold for you there. Wish we could make a trade, about twenty degrees of your cold for a like amount of our tropical heat. Some day when the war is over, and people go in for living again, we will go on our second honeymoon--to Honolulu where the caressing balmy breeze brings the scent of lovely flowers to beautiful Waikiki, where the big yellow moon is so close you'll want to touch it, where we can stroll under the palms, slowly, silently, arm in arm, and glory in our nearness and love, a love as strong and mysterious as the great purple-hued Hawaiian mountains. That will be our trip to the Garden of Eden, a place especially created for pleading guitars and soul-stirring love songs, a place for you and me. The weeks there will be something lovely for us to remember always. Would you like that, dear? This is not just a dream. I promise you this sincerely after the war is over.

Harry.

29 December, 1944

My Darling,

This is an anniversary that I shall observe with thanksgiving and reverence until the last day I have on earth. One year ago today you wrote your first letter to me. How well I remember the strange joyous sensation that went through me the moment I touched it. Somehow I sensed that it would mean more to me than anything that had ever happened to me. I held it in my fingers and gazed at it for a few minutes. During those minutes I saw, as in a vision, a smiling beautiful creature, lovelier than a rose in June. I knew that at last my one great love had come to me, and there was a song in my heart. Beautiful, beloved Norma, I had to tell you this today.

Your devoted Harry.

3 January, 1945

Hello Sugar;

I know you are feeling a little--shall I say *uncomfortable* -- tonight, and maybe just a wee bit cross, but won't you let me come over anyway? I'm lonesome and I want to talk to you and tell you, "I love you." Do you realize that this year, perhaps before it's even half past, you will no longer be Miss Clinton, but Mrs. Kipp? Does the thought of that make you happy? It does me, sweet, and thrills me too. Then we can tell each other of all the dreams we've had -- and we can make them come true. And Norma *you* can be my baby, my only baby, just as long as it pleases you, and if later on we should have a dozen babies, you will always be my honeychild.

Why don't you stop trying to make me believe that you are not perfect? One of your hips is higher than the other! Maybe my eyes are at fault (and I know they're not) but your hips are lovely. You needn't envy Betty Grable; the only thing she's got that you haven't is a press agent, and for that I'm glad. I wish I could devise some way to keep you hidden from the world until I can place a plain gold band around your finger with the words 'Eternally Norma and Harry' engraved on the inside. It makes me feel very selfish and mean, as if you were depriving yourself of many pleasant times because of me, but I can't help being happy to know you don't accept invitations from other men. In that respect I'll never fail you either. Your love is so precious to me that I wouldn't risk losing it for anyone or anything in the world. I know I shall never again feel the least bit of love or desire for any other woman. I live now only for the moment until we are man and wife and are tight in each other's arms, and I can feel your heart beating with mine, and hear you whisper, "Harry, I love you, I love you." When that moment comes we will be in our heaven of rapturous ecstasy, and from then on it will be 'Eternally Norma and Harry'. Beautiful Norma, you are more than my sweetheart, my darling, or my bride-to-be. You are to me what every man, in his innermost soul, wants most. You are *my woman*.

   Harry.

27 January, 1945

Hello Sugar!

Gee! It's nice to be with you again. I miss you so when I'm away from you. Come, and sit on the sofa with me, curl up your legs and lie across my lap, rest your head in the crook of my arm-- so. Comfy? Now, close your eyes. Mmmm! So sweet! Here I am making love to you, and you may not even know it. You have undoubtedly already looked at the picture of the man who aspires to be your husband and having seen how unattractive he is, you may have been prompted to throw the whole thing into the waste basket unread. Well, I warned you. The description I gave of myself gives me no claim to modesty, but it should give proof that I was honest and truthful with you. Oh, well, knowing the worst at the start is not the worst way to start. And eventually you were bound to discover the ugly truth anyway. I'm not really as sleepy looking as this picture indicates, if that's any comfort to you.

How I'll enjoy being your husband! You even make dish washing a pleasure. If it will be like that, you'll always find me waiting for you by the kitchen sink after every meal. Couldn't we have a couple of extra meals when I'm home all day? But I shouldn't say things like that until I know that you still love me and want to be my wife in spite of the fact that you now know what I look like. I *am* apprehensive about your reaction. Norma, dear lovely beautiful Norma, often in my bewilderment, I beg God to tell me how I can, and why I should, be so fervently, so utterly in love with you. My longing for you is so strong and ever-present that each day of separation from you seems like an eternity of torture. I have never known real happiness; I never shall until you are my own dearly beloved wife--Mrs. Harry Kipp, if it will please you to be called that.

I can't write any more tonight. I'm too anxious about your verdict. Until I know, I'll be hoping and praying that you still love and want me. Your devoted Harry.

    The small studio portrait of Harry, sent by his uncle, had traveled from New York to the South Pacific then to Georgia almost circling the earth by the time it reached Norma's eager hands. His Marine Corps winter green uniform bore on the left breast five service ribbons, two on the top row and three on the second. Beneath were Expert Rifle and Pistol medals. His face, a three-quarter view, was in repose with only the faintest beginning of a smile on a generous mouth. He looked like a Roman God except that his thick blond hair was straight with a part on the left above a broad forehead and full brows. A well-shaped head rose from his neck and shoulders like that of a monarch and from deep blue eyes came a mixture of appraisal and curiosity, a man who viewed the world with interest and without reservation. For whom had it been made originally, Norma wondered. But no matter; now it was hers and at last she had a face to go with his words. How she longed to touch his cheek and trace the outline of his lips and tousle that neatly combed hair! Would his mouth then break into a full smile and would his eyes twinkle when she nibbled at his beautiful ear lobe? And would he stroke her head when she pressed it against his great chest, and then tilt her face upward and press his full lips upon hers? Her fingers caressed the picture and she spoke to it,"Oh, Harry, dearest Harry, don't be anxious about my verdict. You look like a prince to me, a stern-faced Prince Charming. I can't wait to make you laugh...and of course, I still love you. More than ever!"

27 February, 1945

Hello Beautiful!

It has been so long since I've seen you and I'm starved for your loving. Never mind cooking dinner--come here. Mmm! Happy sugar? I am. You are so very sweet! And so nice and little, five feet four, twenty-three inch waist, thirty-two inch hips, but honey, tell me more-- bust? thighs? calf? I'm glad you're small because I like small women, especially blue-eyed, brown-haired women, and Honeychild, you are the cutest and most lovable of all.

Perhaps I would understand women better if I'd had sisters but I feel that I understand you well enough to be sure you are the only one who can make me completely happy. I have known women for whom I've had a feeling of tender spiritual love, others have filled me with passionate desire, but you are the first, the only one, who has given me both. And you have given me something that no other woman has ever given me--an easy, frank freedom to express any and every thought in my mind without the slightest sense of embarrassment. Honeychild, I can't imagine myself telling any woman I've ever known that I pretend my pillow is she, that I dreamed she slept in my arms, or that I would like her to wear short night gowns for me. I think I feel that way about you because you are the only girl I have really wanted to be my wife, because you are the one with whom I will actually live the delicious little intimacies that we now dream of. If any other girl had ever told me that her shaven legs would scratch me when we are in bed close to each other, or that she dreamed of sleeping with me in only pajama tops, I would think her vulgar and immoral, but when you tell me things like that it pleases me and makes me love you more. It makes me feel as if we are already living our married life and learning things about each other that we, and no one else, should know.

Yes, I remember that in my first letter I wished you success in becoming a nurse. I am ashamed of myself. Lord how I lied! I knew then what I wanted you to be: the woman who will always be by my side in our journey through life, who will make me happy just by being near me, and who will be the mother of my children, the adorable little vixen who will tantalize me by letting her dress slide up a little above her knees while there is a sly, mischievous look in her eyes. Somehow, I knew you would be that to me.

Yes, I do like the word *woman*. It has so much more meaning than 'girl'. To the world you shall be my dear lady, but in my heart you will always be my woman.

Harry.

4 March, 1945

Dear One,

The mail clerk brought me two more heavenly letters from you. How do you make your letters so sweet, hon? But you don't have to *make* them sweet, do you? Coming from you they just couldn't be otherwise.

You asked if I'd like short letters often or long ones just once in a while. Of course I like long ones, but I want letters from you often, even if they are only long enough to say, "I love you, Harry, and I'm still waiting for you." While I can be sure of that, then all's well with the world.

Did I ever tell you, Norma, how I discovered that I could never be happy without you? No? You want to know, don't you? Well, at Cape Gloucester, where your first letter and picture reached me, I used to go up to the top of a high hill each morning to look for signs of Jap activity. It used to be a lonesome watch and pretty scary at times. When your picture came I took it up there with me. I'd look at it when it was light enough to see, and talk to it. After a few days I wasn't lonesome anymore, nor afraid. It seemed as if you were there with me, and I didn't think of myself; my only care was that nothing should happen to you. One morning, reaching the top of the hill, I discovered that I had left you in my tent. My first impulse was to run down the hill to get you. I thought, "I left her alone down there!" When reason returned to me I realized there was something in my heart that wasn't there before. It was the little seed, the little drop that grew bigger, stronger and stronger, until now it runs through my body like a hot river. It will never cool, Norma, as long as I know you wait for me.

Norma darling, you mustn't feel badly when I say, "Good-by for a little while." Even though it may be soon, I feel happy and confident that everything will be all right. At other times in the past I used to wonder a little and my thoughts were not too cheerful, but this time it's different because I know your spirit is with me and I'll always sense your presence. It will seem as if I can reach back and touch your hand and feel your reassuring answering pressure. Don't you see, dear, that God didn't bring us together just to be torn apart? One day soon we'll be sitting hand in hand before our fireplace, silently dreaming as we gaze into the dancing flames while some little body near us in a little white crib stares in uncomprehending wonder at the new toe he has just discovered. Believe in that, Norma, and it will come true.

Your Harry.

23 March, 1945

Hello Sugar!

Guess what I've got. A hot, toasted cheese sandwich! Want a bite? Mmm! It's good, isn't it? Let's let that be our dinner. Then we won't have to clean the kitchen or wash any dishes and that way we can have the whole evening just for loving. Oh, Norma darling, I want you in my arms tonight--now--close to me, close! close! to kiss and caress you, to feel your hair on my cheek, your breath on my throat, your breasts crushed to me so tightly that I can feel your heart beat, your love and mine flowing in a single stream, and you murmuring, "Oh, Harry, I'm so happy!" How often I love you like that in my dreams! Soon dear, it will be a dream come true. Do you sometimes want that to come true?

Honeychild, why did you even dream that I would not treat you as an equal and talk things over with you? We're partners, aren't we? And if I don't talk about everything of interest with my wife then who else can I go to? Never worry, dear, we'll be very happy. And of course you can have a sewing machine. To hear it hum as you make things for our home will be music to me. We'll plan our house and build it exactly the way we want it and we'll have all the things in it that will make it a home, Norma. It has been so long since I've lived in one.

Am writing in the mess hall (dining room to you) and one of the cooks just now brought me a cup of coffee. If they keep on feeding me, this may turn out to be a very long letter. Do you like coffee? I mean are you especially fond of it? I am. When we stand long watches we drink as much coffee as we can to keep us from getting drowsy, and now it has become a habit with me. Usually I have a cup or two before I go to bed and then I can't sleep. That seems silly, doesn't it? But it isn't really, because that gives me more time to pretend you are with me and that I am making love to you, and that is much nicer than just sleeping.

Norma, it has been a long time since you mentioned anything about Marsha and Houston. Do you still see them often? You used to tell me so many things about them that I became rather interested in their welfare. Do you still correspond with Jean?

Gee! It must be nice in Georgia now, in the springtime. It would be so nice to be with you, looking at the man in the moon, seeing him wink as he looks down at us knowing what is in our hearts.

I must say "Good-by for a little while". Don't worry, dear. I'm not afraid because I am taking you along and everything I do will be right because you are with me.

Harry.

3

Good-by for a little while. Norma hated the words; she had prayed never to read them, that Harry would come home before he had to write them. Their coming signaled something about to happen in the Pacific war zone. She didn't have long to wait. On April first, April Fool's Day and Easter Sunday, when she was returning home from a sunrise service in Chattanooga with her Sunday School teacher, a news bulletin interrupted the radio program of early morning hymns. *United States Marines have invaded Okinawa, largest of the Ryuku Islands on Japan's southern doorstep.* She sank into the car seat, her body paralyzed but her mind

Bewitched 25

active with scenes of troops wading ashore under enemy fire...Harry is there, it screamed. She knew because he had written their code words; but he had also written that he wasn't afraid because he was taking her with him. *Please, God, protect him,* she prayed, *and please, help me, too...*

She tried to keep her thoughts off the battlefield and onto his words, and in the daytime she succeeded, keeping busy, trying to be calm and cheerful in her letters to him. At night, her suppressed fears ran rampant; so much that she dreaded to go to sleep. And without sleep, hardly eating, her strength came only in the belief that God would protect him. Harry was right; God had not brought them together only to be torn apart. She believed that God was her ally, her only ally except for Marsha and Inez. They were the only ones who knew of her plan to marry Harry and they were the only ones who shared her terror of Harry's jeopardy. Dear Marsha, her best friend from school and dear Inez, her companion at work.

Norma packed away the white eyelet pique suit she had bought for a spring wedding and waited for letters which never arrived, but her letters to him never stopped. She worked, ate, and slept with a prayer on her lips. She went to church, believed that God would spare Harry; and she waited, feeling very much alone. Then suddenly on April 12, she was one with the entire nation in shock, fright, and grief by the unexpected death of President Roosevelt. The country was without a leader for four hours until Vice-President Harry Truman assumed the presidency. His first act was to declare a month long period of national mourning. In Europe Soviet troops were shelling Berlin, advancing to join American troops at the Elbe River. In Italy, Italian patriots killed Benito Mussolini.

On the last day of April, Norma woke with a feeling of doom, absolute doom. At the mill she went from task to task in a feeling of overwhelming dread under an unshakable weight. What did it mean? Was it an omen of death? If Harry were killed, how would she ever know? Who would tell her? Who in Harry's world even knew of her existence? Had the censors noticed her address and remembered it? Suppose they were killed too? Did his uncle in New York know about her? Would she have to live the rest of her life never knowing what happened if no more letters came from him? What was happening to her? Was she losing faith? How could she live without faith...and hope?

Leaving the mill, walking home on the railroad track, she was hypnotized by her steps on the cross-ties, one after another. Suddenly the earth beneath her rumbled and shook, a shrieking whistle pierced her ears. She leaped off the track just as the 4:30 P.M. freight train sped by, its suction almost drawing her beneath the wheels. Instantly jolted back to reality, she raised her head and caught the look of panic in the eyes of the engineer as the train roared past. When the rumbling ceased and the cinders stopped flying, Norma realized her feeling of doom was gone, the weight lifted. Feeling lightheaded and giddy, she began to laugh. The warning had been for herself, not for Harry. *He* was all right; she knew it! And now, so was she.

Over the past two weeks, she hadn't gone to wait by the mailbox. Its emptiness had been unbearable. But Saturday, she stood beside it, waiting. Mr. Lowrance sounded his car horn right up to their mailbox as he skidded to a stop, waving an airmail letter, his face radiant. The old mailman knew far more than he was ever told and at that moment, Norma loved him. As he drove away, her face was radiant too and *she* was waving the letter. In her room she pressed it to her heart, not wanting to read it, only to hold it, and give thanks to God for keeping Harry safe. Leaving the house, she climbed to the top of her hill, dropped to the pine-needled earth and leaned against her tree, breathing in great gulps of air. Shuddering, she opened the envelope flap and her eyes raced over his words.

21 April, 1945

My Beautiful Darling!

Turn your back to the mirror and look over your shoulder. Do you see wings? You must, because you are an angel. Today I received nineteen heavenly letters from you. Norma Mine, I hope I shall be deserving of your wonderful devotion. You've done so much to make me happy, and I love you more and more as time goes on and our wedding day draws nearer. I can't possibly answer all of your questions or reply to your suggestions in this one letter, but I'll try to catch up, sweets, in the near future. I'll write a few lines every time I have a moment to spare and perhaps I shall be able to send a letter at least once or twice a week. I think that from now on our mail deliveries will be quite frequent and regular.

I found something the other day that I think you will like. It is a pair of candle holders or small flower vases made of glazed china. They are deep blue with interesting designs in green, orange, and gold, and I think they were handmade. I'll send them to you the moment I reach the States so they will arrive before I do. Is there room in your chest to pack them? They are small--only about eight inches high and three inches wide.

Bewitched

Yes, Honeychild, I did plan carefully to win your love because I fell in love with you instantly and utterly, and I almost desperately wanted you to love me too. And now after you have given me your promise, I love you and want you more than ever, and because of that I know our love is real.

Your description of Gatlinburg and vicinity was as delightful as it was vivid and interesting. Shall we decide now, definitely, to spend our honeymoon there? I'd rather like that. Your reference to your already packed suitcase and your little blue nightie, and the games you play with it, gave me a most pleasant thrill. How I long for the moment when I see you step from the bus with your suitcase and I can come to you and relieve you of it, set it down, and give you a great big bear hug! Then offer you my arm, pick up your suitcase and walk away with you on the very first part of our journey through life together! It won't be so very long until we can do just that, Norma dear. Does it make you happy to think of it?

I'm glad your little music box still gives you such keen pleasure. I also like the "Blue Danube Waltz" and never tire of hearing it. I think that when I hear it played by those tinkling little notes while you are beside me, I'll be transported straight to heaven.

My parents were Lutheran, Norma, and that, naturally, was the religion I was taught, but I don't attach a great deal of importance to the difference in religious denominations, for we all, whatever our religion may be, worship and pray to the one only God. Even though the methods may vary, the goal is the same.

Norma darling, we can have our baby any time you want it. I can think of nothing that I'd rather be tied down to than you and our baby. That is what I want and long for more than anything else in life.

Congratulations on the completion of our quilt. Do you think it surprised me? It didn't, honey, I knew you would finish it.

I don't know why you should feel reluctant to mention to me such things as the subject of Jean's pictures. Don't you believe, dear, that I like you to speak to me frankly about *anything* you want to? I had about forgotten Jean, and her pictures too. You may tell her that her large portraits are in my trunk which was sent back to the States, and her snapshots are with some baggage left at our rear base and I'll return them to her as soon as I can. Does she know about us? I haven't heard from her since...I think it was August and I didn't answer her last letter. I'm sure she didn't expect me to. I'm glad you didn't send her my address.

I'm sorry that your 'certain times' are so painful. Do you think that after we are married the change might give you some relief? I've heard it sometimes does. Why do you wonder if our intimacies might be abhorrent to you? I'm sure it won't be like that because we love each other, and I promise I will never be inconsiderate of your wishes in that respect no matter how eager or impassioned I may be. At first, there may be a strange feeling of bewildered emotions, but soon it will become an act of love and endearment which will give us soul-satisfying and intense ecstasy and will leave us with a feeling of pure tenderness and oneness. Do I seem to know too much? (I've read articles by psycho-medical authorities on the subject) Do you think it indelicate to discuss this? Would you rather wait until after we are married to talk about it? or would you rather not mention it at all? Perhaps I'm wrong, but I think a mutual understanding of desires and reactions helps people to please each other in marriage.

Honeychild, I don't mind the torture some of your pictures cause me. It's a delightful pain and I enjoy it--and I do *not* think you aren't nice for sending them to me. Send me more! The more I see of you the more I want you! Good night, my sweet and lovely.

Harry.

6 June, 1945

Hello Sweetness!

How is my sugar today? Got lots of it for me? Save it, sweets, every bit of it 'cause I'll want it all in just a little while--and you'll have to forget about rationing even though I'll have a ration book the same as anyone, and we will be able to get the things we need without any trouble. I don't know much about the rationing system. It hadn't yet started when I left the States, but Marines with families who have come out here since then say they got along nicely in that respect.

Your idea of our kitchen has all the marks of a cunning plot and I see through it. You want the kitchen to be small so that when we are both in it, I will of necessity have to crowd close to you, and that will be the weakness that you play on when you want me to help wash the dishes!

Surely you shall have a budget to manage the house with and I'll budget my expenses too. Will you want to keep books: a journal and ledgers with columns for such things as light bills, groceries, savings for the children's education, savings for the next vacation trip, laundry, income tax, fur coats--er, no, never mind that last item. Let's make that insurance--and oh! yes, bobby socks? They look so cute on you.

Thank you, sweets, for the pictures. They're swell! I wonder why your little girl pictures made me start humming "You must have been a wonderful baby". If you want to know the truth, I think you are still a wonderful baby. I wish I had just one picture of you that wasn't perfectly lovely, because many times when I sit and gaze at your pictures, every one of them so beautiful, so sweet and lovely, it's hard for me to believe you are actually real. I don't think I'll ever be really sure until I can see you and hear you and feel you moving in my arms.

I do want children, dear. I am as eager as you and if we can't have any of our own, I'd be glad to adopt one and I know we would love it as much. We'll see, Norma, and whatever happens I'm sure we'll have no difference of opinion about it. You will never be really happy without a baby. The mother instinct in you is very strong. It's a wonderful thing, dear, and I love you for it.

It's true, Norma, I know it's true, that you love me more than I dared hope you would. I'm happy now, happier than I have ever been before and darling, you know I'll love you forever. My love for you is my life. It's greater than space, as true as the blue of heaven, and as eternal as time. If only I could hold you close to me and keep you in my arms forever! Oh! Norma mine, I need you so!

16 June, 1945

Hello Sugar!

It's me again. I just keep hanging around, don't I? You may as well become used to that because I've a feeling that hanging around you will be one of my unbreakable habits. You just try and break me of it and see how far you get!

You ask, "What are you trying to do to me? Another letter today." Honeychild, I'm trying to keep you in love with me. How'm I doing? Do you still want to stand beside me before the minister and say, "I take you, for better or for worse, to love and to honor, until death do us part"? Do you still want to make my coffee and toast for breakfast? Wait for me to come home from work? Make me go to church with you on Sunday? Let me take you to a night club to see pretty girls modestly display their charms as they go through the routine of a dance? Rest your head on my shoulder while I hold you close and whisper, "Norma darling, I love you so"? And sometimes draw my head to your breast and say, "Harry, there's a little visitor coming to our house"? Do you, Norma? You do?! Then you love me. All's well with the world. And I'm happy.

Norma, I have a strange feeling about wanting to go to church with you. I don't know why. I've never gone before except occasionally when it was convenient, but now I am conscious of a real desire to go when we are married. Oh! Norma darling, I just want to go there because it seems to me to be the most fitting place to give thanks to God for your love and all the goodness it has brought me.

I'm glad Julia is being so nice to you while I'm gone--bringing you bunches of sweet peas. Wish I could do the same. Does Mary Lee speak plainly now or still use baby talk. Tom's attendance record for the school year was quite an achievement. I could never do it. I'd sometimes get spring fever and leave home in the morning with my pockets full of line and fishhooks, and usually entice my younger brother John to play hooky too. Of course, that was never very difficult. I suppose Joan is looking forward to being a junior next school term as well as playing basketball on the first string. Congratulate her for me, will you?

I wondered how your father planned to build a new house at this time, materials being as scarce as they are. Perhaps it's just as well that we can't have a permanent home during the first few years. That will give us time to get really good things to build into our house and have everything completely finished when I leave the Marine Corps. In our budgets we'll have a house fund too, shall we, to which we will add a certain amount each month? I'm glad I've been saving. We already have a good start. We won't have to borrow to pay for it, and when it's finished it will be our very own. We'll be members of the landed gentry. And we'll furnish it with many new and handy gadgets that our mothers didn't have when they were married. Will you let me come into the kitchen once in a while to play with them or will you be the stern disciplinarian and say, "No! No! Mustn't touch"? I suppose I could get a toy train and amuse myself in the living room. Are you getting tired of so much housekeeping? So am I. Come on, sweets, let's sit before the fireplace and listen to soft music on the radio and watch the flames...and darling! I love you! Harry.

                                                   27 June, 1945

Darling,

This is our day, isn't it? And what a lovely moon --going to waste! Mmm! How I miss my sugar bun tonight! I want some loving so bad. And I'll be missing you when the next full moon comes around too, but the one after that, I'll see reflected in your eyes. I guess you know I'll be very, very happy then.

Oh! darling mine, thank you, thank you for the swell little lighter. It is exactly what I needed. And it *really* works. You know, don't you, that I will use it very gently and make it last for ages? You made a promise to me that I hope you will always keep. Remember? "Long after this flame has died, my love for you will still be burning!" Honeychild, I'll do anything under the sun to keep it burning--forever.

No, darling, love is not blind. It brings to view many lovely things that might otherwise remain forever invisible. If I weren't so deeply in love with you I might never have known how sweet and lovely and wonderful you really are. That's why I am so very glad I love you, and soon you will know it. You won't be able to doubt it even though you should try.

No, dear, you didn't tell me about the liver extract injections before. I'm sorry they make you feel so miserable. Do they help? How many have you had now, and how many more must you take? Won't you tell me about your treatments? Do you still have those pains? Are you gaining weight? Forgive me for asking so many questions but I want to know because I can't help being concerned about your health. I love you and it hurts me that you must suffer.

Why, of course, I'll take you out once in a while to sleep out under the stars and cook our fish and coffee outside over an open fire. I'm glad you like such things because I do too. I know we are going to be happy, Norma, because our likes and dislikes in many important ways, and our ideals, are nearly the same. We'll just naturally stay in love forever.

I'm sorry, sweets, that you were so disappointed at finding only an envelope for Marsha in one of my letters. She is a darling for not letting you know what was in it, don't you think? And you were grand too for not peeking just a little. The temptation must have been awful. I hated to be so mean, but I just couldn't help it. In time, you'll know.
    'Nite, dear. Sweet dreams! Your very own,
                                            Harry.

Norma guessed Harry's motive behind the sealed envelope and Marsha confirmed it, holding his letter behind her back,"Yes, it's a surprise and he's askin' for my help. It won't do any good to beg because I'm not sayin' another word. You're just gonna have to wait until your birthday."

On that day, Norma was awake at dawn, expectant, but it was nearly noon before she heard the crunch of tires outside. It wasn't Marsha who came but a delivery man bringing a long white box to Norma's outstretched arms. A sweet perfume wafted upward and outward as she pushed aside the green tissue paper covering eighteen long stemmed red rosebuds, nine at each end. Eighteen! One for each year of her life. On the stems lay an envelope; inside, a note in familiar handwriting. "They're from Harry," Norma said, her eyes shining, her voice breathless as she read the message aloud: Dearest Norma, My wishes for a very happy birthday. Love, Harry.

Mama's eyebrows arched upward and she looked at her daughter in a new light, "My goodness, he must think a lot of you to send such high-priced roses."

Julia brought a half-gallon milk jar filled with water and Norma arranged the rosebuds. The jar was too large to sit on the ledge of her roll top desk or on the mantel piece, and they had no table except the eating table in the kitchen. From her cedar chest, Norma selected a luncheon cloth embroidered in colorful wreaths and placed it corner-wise on the large square table. It made a perfect frame for the vase of heart shaped rosebuds. The sight was so beautiful and smelled so fragrant that everyone tiptoed around the kitchen speaking in hushed tones. Even Tommy who usually played outdoors all day remained inside to look and smell. Julia, Joan, and Mary Lee took whiffs from up close even though the sweetness had spread to every corner of the room. Mama smoothed the edges of the luncheon cloth and cast curious glances at Norma's glowing face.

Bewitched

30 June, 1945

Greetings!
Congratulations! And my sincere wishes for a very happy birthday. May the years to follow be filled with everything your little heart desires. I have never wished anything more sincerely than that. If only you were here with me tonight! My tent is up high on a windy hill surrounded by cool clean pine trees, with winding valleys and the ocean below, a big round moon among the stars, and my heart is filled with burning, white-hot longing for you. Norma! Norma! Sweet, beautiful, lovely darling mine, I WANT YOU!! NOW!! You asked me what I want besides you. Frankly, honeychild, I've been wanting you so eagerly and constantly that I've never even thought of wanting anything else. I guess what I want most next to you is me. Don't you think that would be nice? I want next to make you my wife at the very first possible moment. And don't you think *that* would be nice?

One of my best friends is going home tomorrow. He is leaving at 5:30 in the morning. We have been together nearly six years and I am going to miss him a lot, but may see him again soon. When you meet him you'll know why I think so much of him.

Yesterday I received a little card from another Marine friend announcing the birth of a seven pound baby boy. He (my friend) left us last August; his Barbara met him at the pier in San Francisco. They were married immediately. Their boy was born on the 27th of May. Ain't that something?! Soon, we too will begin to really live. Gee! honey, I'm so glad it's you who will share everything in life with me.

Norma dear, if I couldn't have you I am sure I would never marry. It was you who awakened in me the desire for a mate to travel the long road of life with me. It is you, and only you, who can keep that desire alive in me.

What did your mother say when you showed her my ring? Was she pleased and enthused about it? Did it make her a little bit sad? Did she become more than unusually affectionate toward you? It must hurt your parents to think of losing you so soon. But they won't be losing you really. You can be their daughter and my wife too, can't you, sweets? We can visit them often and I'll be happy to think of them as my parents too.

> This, your first day of womanhood is nearly ended, dear, and I know you know how reluctant I am to leave you now, but I must. Oh! my darling, how I wish I could have contributed some little thing, however small, toward your happiness on this wonderful day. All I can offer you is my love. I give you that freely, gladly, every last bit of it, and my every thought and consideration is for you.   Forever your adoring Harry.

Naturally he thought she had shared their wedding plans and his ring with Mama, but she hadn't. With them, she simply endured and complied. They spoke no more of her wasted life as a mill hand, still accepting a fifth of her weekly wage. They accepted her compliance as well, but she felt their watchful eyes during her nightly ritual of writing to Harry and they commented on the number of letters now arriving from him. Letters which she kept locked in her desk drawer although his picture sat on the desktop beside her music box. They watched also her fingers busy with needle and thread filling up her "hope chest" with quilts and linens. They must know *something* was in the making. The birthday roses had provided an opportunity to tell them, but she hadn't wanted to risk a blowup so near to Harry's arrival. She had waited this long; she could wait until she and Harry could tell them together. And they *would* be told beforehand. She wouldn't run off and get married as some of her friends had done.

>   27 July, 1945
> My Love,
>   You seem so close to me tonight, just as if you were here. I can almost feel your head on my shoulder, and I'm very happy. I am always happiest when I am reading your letters, looking at your pictures, or writing to you. Tonight that feeling is unusually strong. Perhaps it is because this is the special night of each month that is so peculiarly our very own, perhaps it is because we are in reality coming very near to each other. We need no longer measure our separation in months. We can say 'weeks' now. How many would you guess? Six? Seven? Let's say eight, and then we will surely not be disappointed again. I have a feeling that it will be less, but let's say eight anyway, shall we? Norma dear, just think of it! Only eight more weeks until you will be my wife, until we awaken and can say "Good morning" to each other, until we can argue about who shall have first access to the bathroom, until we have breakfast

at the same little table and we are together all day long, and until our slippers are resting side by side under the same bed each and every blissful night. Thinking of that makes me both miserable and happy at the same time--miserable because I am suffering for you now--happy because I know that soon you will be in my arms.

Eight weeks from today is the 21st of September, isn't it? Will that be a good time for us to be married? I'm afraid (I hope) that I won't receive the letter in which you can answer that because I may be gone from here before it arrives, but I'll try to phone you the day I reach San Francisco. You can tell me then and perhaps I can arrange to have my leave begin at such a time that we can have our entire honeymoon without any days of unpleasantness for you. Would you like me to do that or shall I take my leave at the earliest possible moment? But, Norma, do continue to write, won't you, until I tell you definitely that I'm leaving.

Yesterday I crossed swords with a *habu*, the fightingest and most venomous snake in this neck of the woods. As I was sleepily arising from my cot, I saw him curled up on a large cardboard box, and since I live in a one-man tent, we promptly engaged in mortal combat for possession of it. He put up a gallant fight but couldn't quite overcome my advantage of weight and superior footwork, so, like many other creatures of Japanese ancestry, he died in glorious defeat and lies buried in an unmarked grave. He was four feet and five inches long!

Guess what I'm reading? *Forever Amber*. What a book! I met Kathleen Winsor's husband some months ago at Guadalcanal. He was tossing notes of U.S. currency all over the landscape like a flower girl at a May party because his wife had just sold the story for some fabulous amount of money. Her characters are certainly free of the most common inhibitions. Becoming acquainted with them made me appreciate *you* more than ever. The people in her story belong to an era of the distant past but I guess that many of their counterparts still live and flourish today.

I still have the little lock of hair you sent me long ago. Often I hold it in my fingers, gaze at it, kiss it, and press it to my cheek How I long to bury my face in the lovely tresses it came from and breathe in the intoxicating woman smell of you! Oh, my dearest one, I need you and I want you so! I've got to have you--I can't live without you! And I won't!   Forever your Harry.

29 July, 1945

My Darling,

This is Sunday again, the lonesomest day of the long lonesome week for me. There is nothing to do, and all day long I think of you, miss you, and yearn for your kisses. It's a miserable feeling--like a gnawing painful illness for which there is no cure, and I'll never be free of it until you are in my arms. Oh, darling mine, *when, When, WHEN* will this agony of longing for you end? The days seem like years and the weeks are endless. I think I'd be happy if I could only leave here and be moving toward you, knowing that with each step, with each turn of the propeller and each revolution of a wheel I were drawing nearer to you, but just sitting here waiting and squirming is almost unbearable. I just think and dream, and think and dream some more but when I awake you are still ten thousand miles away from me.

Norma darling, I still want you to be my wife. More than ever, and I'm still coming back for you as soon as I possibly can. Do you know that when I asked you to marry me, I was afraid you'd say, "What? You want me to be your wife! Poor fellow! Where does it hurt you most?" It was like clutching at a straw but I wanted you so. I knew you were the one girl I really loved, and the only one I wanted to be my wife. And you said, "Yes". What a lucky guy I am!

No, sweets, I don't know where I'll be stationed when my leave is over, but I'll try to get a small station away from the crowded cities so we can get a house to live in by ourselves. California is so crowded now that it would be difficult to get even an apartment. As for visiting my aunt and uncle, I'd sort of like to see them, if you don't mind going to New York, but we can decide that later. Let's save our honeymoon for ourselves without any prearranged plans and then we can do exactly as we please, shall we? But we'll probably do what we like anyway, plans or no plans. Right now I like the idea of a cottage in Gatlinburg best of all. What would you like best?

I'm sorry you had to work so hard at canning peaches, but never mind, honey, we'll make your mother give us some of them when we go back for a visit at Christmas time. Peaches are my favorite fruit, and that isn't all--you know how I feel about a certain little 'Georgia Peach'. There just isn't anything sweeter.

Are you sure that nice dream you had was a dream? I often steal into your room at night and sit on your bed and kiss you awake. Sometimes I stay until the sky grows red in the East. Being alone with you in the still of the night, whispering to you, caressing you and holding you close to me is the only heaven I know. How I ever leave you is more than I can understand, but each morning I find myself back here again, alone and lonesome, but trembling with the delightful sensation of having been with you.

Norma darling, I know now for sure that I'm coming home and in a week or so, I'll know when. I'll tell you just as soon as I can, Be patient, dear. Soon we'll be together forever. Harry.

On August 6, the world was paralyzed by the news of the atomic bombing of Hiroshima, Japan. Three days later another bomb was dropped on the city of Nagasaki. Along with millions, Norma fled to church to pray--filled with terror for the world--God help us! But maybe now, the war would end and all the men could come home.

18 August, 1945

My Wonderful Sweetheart,

I got two precious letters from you today and a *beautiful* kiss. You really know how to keep me happy, honey, and you're doing a swell job. Don't you think it's a sin to have lips as exciting as yours? How will I ever be able to stop kissing you?

Congratulations, darling. Another quilt. I knew you would finish it, but I didn't expect it to be so soon. You must have worked at it steadily for many long hours. I'm sorry the border color didn't turn out to be the shade you wanted when you dyed it, but I'll bet it's much nicer than you admit. As for its shade of yellow setting one on fire--what's the difference? When it covers you and me there will always be a little fire under it anyway. You won't be afraid of *that* fire, will you, sweets? It will be a gently glowing fire to warm your heart and keep you comfortable and contented. The flames will be wild and hot only when we want them to be that way. I'll bet we'll be the two best firemen in the world!

Tomato juice is one food item we are definitely agreed on. It's my favorite beverage and with coffee it's usually all I want for breakfast. It isn't much help though to people who are underweight. I wonder how I'll ever manage to make you plump and chubby on the foods you like. Guess I'll have to make my own breakfasts and let you sleep late. But that wouldn't be so good either. Maybe you can learn to like steak and potatoes and lots of bread and butter. Would you try? Those things won't always be scarce you know.

How much do you weigh now, sweets? You haven't been reporting your progress very regularly. Surely you must know that I am very much concerned about the health and personal well-being of my own wife. Gee! honey, I said that unconsciously as if you were truly my wife. I often feel that way about you, and I always wish it were so in fact. I've been wishing that for about nineteen months, and wishing harder and harder each day. If wishing could make it so, you'd be in my arms this instant and oh, baby, what a lovin' you'd be gettin'!

Norma darling, you needn't read my letters backward or skip from paragraph to paragraph looking for news of my homecoming, 'cause when I get my orders I'll tell you in the very first sentence. That will be too good to keep to myself for a single instant. It will be the beginning of our life together, darling. It is the one thing that is always in my thoughts along with you.

'Nite, honey. Close your eyes and dream I am with you.

Harry.

27 August, 1945

Darling,

It is nearly midnight and I still have work to finish, but I've got to visit my wife before this day ends. Move over just a little, dear, and let me sit on the edge of your bed. Yes, you may leave the light on. I do like to look at you in the light even though I can always see your loveliness whether it be in the brightness of the noonday sun or in the blackness of darkest midnight. My heart is never blind to you.

I'm sorry, hon, that the visiting preacher was so inconsiderate. He can't be a very tolerant man at heart, and even though he is a preacher, he seems to be very much lacking in the true Christian spirit. You've gotten over his grandmotherish tirade by now, haven't you? Never mind him, sweets, we can't let people like him take the joy out of our life. I wear only shorts without even a midriff blouse during hot weather and I find it mighty comfortable, and I don't feel that it is at all sinful.

Norma darling, I've got to leave you now even though I want so very much to lie down and rest with you in my arms. I'm very tired and sleepy, but there is work that must be done. I'll come back to you, sweet. Go to sleep my lovely one, and dream of me a little. I love you, Norma. Good night. God bless you and keep you for me. Your lonesome husband is missing you. Harry.

4

4 September, 1945

Darling!
If this note is unintelligible, forgive me. I'm a bit excited and happier than I've been since the first time you said,"Yes, I'll be your wife." I'm coming home to you, sweetheart, to make you my wife and to love you forever. I'm leaving tomorrow. Perhaps you won't hear from me until I reach California, but I'll write as soon as I possibly can. Norma darling, if I should arrive in time, will you marry me on the 27th? It will then have been exactly one year and one month since you gave me your promise. I'll have your rings, sweets, both of them. Good-by, Honeychild, for just a little while and for the last time. I'll be seeing you soon and--Oh, Darling! How I love you!   Harry.

MOANA HOTEL
Honolulu, Hawaii
11 September, 1945

My Darling Norma,
I hope you received my last letter from Okinawa so that this won't be too great a shock to you. My orders came in suddenly and I flew directly to Pearl Harbor. We stopped at Guam, Kwajalein, and Johnston Island just long enough to change crews and service

the plane. The trip took thirty-six hours and I was half dead upon arriving here so I slept from six o'clock of the first morning until after seven of the next. Then I met some old friends whom I hadn't seen since a long time ago and we spent the next two days visiting old familiar scenes and places.

Gee! honey, I wish you could be here with me now. Everything is so beautiful. But I am already anxious to leave. My heart is aching for you, darling, and the thrill of your embrace. Oh! my lovely, wonderful, sweetheart, it will really be soon now! I tremble with happiness each time I think of holding you in my arms and loving you as I have so long dreamed of doing. Perhaps by the end of the month we can be married. Norma darling, think of it! Our life is about to begin!

I'll have to go by ship from here and as yet I don't know when there will be room on one for me. There are so many ahead of me waiting to go back. Some have already been waiting ten days so unless I am very lucky, it will be two weeks from now before I reach California. I'll send you a telegram when I arrive to let you know when to be at Mrs. Patterson's. Will you be as excited as I? I just can't wait to hear your voice. I love you so!

Harry.

VGF 18 NL   PD=F   SANFRANCISCO CALIF SEP21
MISS NORMA CLINTON =LA FAYETTE GA =
ARRIVED TODAY WILL PHONE HERE BETWEEN EIGHT AND TEN SUNDAY PM IF POSSIBLE. EXPECT TO REACH CHATTANOOGA ON THIRTIETH. WILL PHONE AT EIGHT PM SAME DAY. WILL THAT TIME BE ALL RIGHT. WIRE REPLY TO ME AT HOTEL WHITCOMB
SAN FRANCISCO. REVERSE CHARGES HURRY LOVE
HARRY E. KIPP SEP22 8:37 AM

FN 15= LA FAYETTE GA 22   1138 P
HARRY E. KIPP
HOTEL WHITCOMB=SFRAN=   SEP 22 AM 1039
=PHONE AT EIGHT PM ON THIRTIETH
AWAITING CALL ON SUNDAY EVENING WITH WILD ANTICIPATION LOVE NORMA CLINTON

She was bursting to tell her parents that Harry was coming home to marry her. Instead, trying with all her might to be matter-of-fact, she told them that he was coming to La Fayette to meet her in person. Could she invite him to their house? Would he be welcome?

"Yes," they said, "Invite him, he'll be welcome."

23 September, 1945
8:30 Sunday evening

Darling,

I don't remember a word you said, but I still hear the sound of your sweet voice echoing in my heart. How can I wait seven whole days to hear you talk to me again? But this is the end of our long time of waiting. Will you marry me soon? Monday? Tuesday? I've never loved you more than at this very moment.

We didn't say much in our conversation, did we, honey? You were simply breathless and I was nearly the same, and we could hear each other so very faintly, but I wouldn't have missed it for worlds. The sound of your voice went straight to my heart.

If my present plans carry through I will leave here Tuesday evening and should reach Chattanooga sometime Sunday, and unless I let you know otherwise, I'll call you at eight that evening. Do you suppose we'll be as excited then as we were tonight? Well, why shouldn't we be excited? Nothing as important as this has ever happened to us before. I can hardly realize that so very soon the dearest, sweetest, loveliest little darling in all the world will be my wife. We've waited nearly two years now, and if we do find ourselves a bit embarrassed when we meet, it will be no more than it is natural to expect and the awkwardness will disappear in a moment, because deep in our hearts we understand each other, and we know that our two individual lives are bound to each other inseparably and nothing under the sun can ever change that.

Oh, Honeychild! Monday! Monday! Monday! I'm so happy I could turn handsprings in the middle of Market Street. And Monday morning I am going to give you the greatest, biggest hug you have ever heard about 'cause I love you, I love you, Norma, I love you and that's for sure!!

Harry.

Norma, her mother, and sisters set out to make the house ready for Harry's arrival. Pots and pans were scrubbed, windows washed. Curtains and bedspreads were laundered, ironed, and put back in place. Not a cupboard nor floor escaped a scrubbing, not even the front siding of the house where months of dust from the unpaved road had settled. Norma and Joan attacked it with scrub brushes and soap suds while Julia, too small to scrub, squirted hose water against the wall, soaking her sisters.They slid and skidded about on the slippery concrete surface of the porch, giggling until they were breathless, losing their balance. Sprawled across each other, they were slightly hysterical. Suddenly, Norma realized that this was her farewell to childishness; within a week she would be a married woman, if she could hold herself together until then. Looking up at the new screen door she had talked her father into buying, she became solemn knowing the rest of the house would show their poverty. But Harry might as well know from the start that they are poor. Poor, but clean. Mama always said, "We may not have much, but what we've got is clean. And cleanliness is next to Godliness."

On Sunday afternoon, the house was ready and Norma was waiting for Harry's call from Chattanooga. Like the call from San Francisco, she would take it on Mrs. Patterson's telephone. Marsha's mother lived across town and Norma practically floated to her house to hear Harry's voice again and tell him her surprise: a meeting was possible *tonight*! Inez, her friend from the hosiery mill, would drive her to Chattanooga.

It was Inez who suggested the Smoky Mountains for a honeymoon when Norma confided her fear of embarrassing Harry if they went to any of the cities he had mentioned. She also lent Norma her copy of Emily Post's book on proper etiquette.

At Mrs. Patterson's, dressed in her brown and white houndstooth suit, Norma waited, as jumpy as a cat on hot coals. She sat, she paced, she sat. Eight o'clock came, ten after, fifteen after. She paced some more. Suppose he hadn't got to Chattanooga! Then Mrs. Gilbreath, from next door, came running up the front porch steps calling,"Yoo Hoo! Naomi! Come quick! There's a long distance call for you comin' in on my phone. Hurry. The operator's waitin'."

At the sound of 'long distance', Norma sprang through the door, passing the startled neighbor like a bullet, explaining, "The call's for me." And to the operator,"No, I'm not Mrs. Patterson, but the call's for me." Harry's voice broke in,"Yes,operator.The call is intended for Miss Clinton," and to Norma, "Miss Clinton! How are you?"

Bewitched 43

"I'm out of breath. I had to run from next door."

"I'm breathless too! and sorry for the delay and mix-up, but never mind that now, darling, we've made contact, and tomorrow is only a few hours away and we..."

"Harry!" She interrupted, "We don't have to wait until tomorrow. If you want, I can leave now...as soon as we finish talkin'...and be there in less than an hour. Inez and her husband will bring me."

"If I *want?* How can you ask *if I want?* Hang up and leave. I'm at the Read House on Broad Street, 827. How 'bout that?? *Eight twenty-seven!* I'll wait for you in the lobby. No, make that outside. Good-by for a little while, and for the last time, my darling."

Half the people on Magnolia Street were listening from the Gilbreath's front porch and Norma suspected the other half had been listening on their party lines. Too happy to reproach them, she made a call to Inez,"Harry's waitin' for me, and I'm ready to go."

The drive from La Fayette seemed to last forever. Would they ever get out of the city limits, through Chickamauga National Park and its thirty mile speed limit, strictly enforced, past Fort Oglethorpe--another restricted speed zone--and into Tennessee? Finally, they reached Rossville, the border town. They were so near! She moved forward on the back seat. In just a few more minutes she would see him. Her heart pounded in her ears and her knees seemed to have disappeared. A glimpse of herself in the rear view mirror showed her looking as calm as a cucumber except for a flush of her natural cheek color, blue eyes wide but steady, shiny brown hair cascading over her shoulders with every strand in place. Well, she might *look* calm, but she felt wild. Would she be able to put two sensible words together when she finally came face to face with him? What should she say? Would he speak first? Would he expect her to be ladylike and wait for him to open the car door? Of course, he would. And would her legs hold her up if she was able to move?

Tyre turned the car onto Broad Street and drew near the curb in front of the Read House. When Norma saw the Marine in uniform standing beneath the marquee, she flung open the car door and with a few running steps found herself stopped against his hard, broad chest. She couldn't believe a chest could be so hard, nor lips so hot and wonderful on her lips, her eyes, neck and throat. Spasms of pleasure coursed from her breasts to her knees and back to the pit of her stomach. She would surely fall if he weren't holding her so tightly against that great chest and the hard pressure of his thighs.He was whispering huskily,"You *are* real! Oh, my

Honeychild! You're real and moving. I feel you moving in my arms. But, let me look at you."

He held her head between his hands, and they stood, seeing deep into each other's hearts--time and place counting for nothing--touching at last. They never knew how long they stood like that before returning to the world of Broad Street. When awareness returned, Norma was the first to move. Taking Harry's arm she turned him toward the car as Tyre and Inez got out to meet him. With sparkling eyes fixed on Harry she said,"This is my fiancé!" How wonderful those words felt on her tongue and how wonderful they sounded to her ears. She wanted to shout them to every passing person.

Trye and Harry exchanged handshakes as Inez beamed,"Welcome home, Harry. It's a real pleasure to meet you, but I feel I know you already."

"Thank you, Inez, and please accept my gratitude for bringing Norma tonight as well as for your other kindness to her. She's written me of it." His voice was deep and friendly in short, clipped Yankee speech.

"It was nothin'," Inez's laugh was bubbly,"We're happy to do it for Norma and you too. And may we offer our guest room while you're in La Fayette. We'd be pleased if you'd use it tonight."

Harry's eyes went quickly to Norma, then returned to Inez."My thanks again, but..." He looked at Norma, questioning.

"You don't have to decide right this minute," Inez said, "Tell us when we come back from our walk. Don't worry if we're gone a while.We're going to the coffee shop down the street."

Inside the car, in the back seat, Harry's face was illuminated by the street lamp shining through the rear window. Norma gazed in fascination at his eyes: deep, brilliant, vibrant blue; teeth, white and even; ears that lay close to a perfectly shaped head, and a slightly bent but otherwise fine nose. Several horizontal lines crossed a broad forehead above blemish free deeply tanned skin. She sensed the tremendous energy, held just beneath the surface of an outward calm, a power held in leash at this moment, though she had felt it unleashed in his kiss and embrace a few minutes ago. He submitted to her visual onslaught until her gaze dropped to his service ribbons: three rows, four battle stars and the combat "V". Then,"Your verdict, Miss Clinton?" An intense light burned in his eyes, a half smile lifted the corner of his mouth.

"You are mistaken, Captain," she proclaimed with a tilt of her head, "You are handsome, but even if you weren't I still love you!"

"Oh, Honeychild!..." His arms surrounded her slender body, pressing it to him with such force that she gasped for breath. He released his hold to take her hands in his, "Now, what is this about your not staying with me tonight?"

Her gaze was steady, imploring, but her voice was halting, "Harry,...before we stay together....will you do something for me...please?"

"Of course, my darling.You have but to ask," his expression expectant.

"Will you ask Daddy for me, for my hand in marriage?" Her chin lifted resolutely, "But don't worry, no matter what he says, I *will* marry you."

He stared, his face expressionless, surprised eyes searching hers. Half a minute passed before he smiled, "Of course, Norma. I should have anticipated that you would want that. But after I speak with your father, how long do you think it can be until you marry me?"

"Would Tuesday evenin' be all right? I couldn't arrange it before then. Marsha and Houston will drive us to the preacher who married them; he has a darlin' little chapel in Rossville and his name just happens to be *Hart!* Isn't that a perfect name for a man who joins two hearts in marriage?"

"Perfect, yes, and so are you, Norma darling! You've planned everything perfectly, but how can I let you go back tonight?" His fingers tightened on her shoulders.

"You're not comin' with us?" She cried in dismay.

"Unfortunately, I've got damp laundry drying all over my room," he grinned, "and then there's another detail. A trip to the jewelers. I had planned for us to choose your rings together. Since you're not staying, I'll get them tomorrow, both of them, and then come straight to La Fayette. Now, tell me how to get to your house."

"We live out of town several miles, but the taxi driver will know where Clarence Clinton lives."

And so Harry came to her house on Monday afternoon, to the poor house that sparkled in its cleanliness, and met her parents, sisters, and brother. After supper, through which Norma's father explained the virtue of corn fed beef as opposed to grass fed, Harry asked for Norma's hand in marriage. It was granted and on Tuesday's early evening, Norma dressed herself in the gray suit bought for her wedding a year ago. When Marsha and Houston came at six, her family watched her ride away with a bouquet of pink carnations in her right hand and a one carat diamond on her left, both from Harry. They stopped on Highway 27 near the Army Post to get the marriage license from a Justice of the Peace called "Frenchy", known for issuing licenses to under-aged couples. They went to him because he was open after hours. Norma wrote her age as eighteen, which she was, but in answer to his question, "What year were you born?" she blurted *1929*, to her horror--Joan's year of birth--then quickly corrected herself. Mr. French looked at her over his spectacles for what seemed forever, but he took the money Harry offered. Norma noticed that Harry gave his age as 34; he had never been definite about it, saying only, "--about twice your age--" when she had been 16 at the beginning of their correspondence.

"Would you like me to marry you?" Mr. French asked.

"No, sir." Norma answered quickly, seeing the license in Harry's grip. "We want to be married by a preacher." And they were. The ceremony was performed by the Reverend Hart as planned.

For their wedding night Harry took his bride to La Fayette's only hotel, the Foster House with the bathroom down the hall. Norma used it first and then while Harry was gone, she lay in bed in her little blue nightie thinking about her wedding, the long awaited wedding. She was shaking still, the shaking that began September 23 when she first heard Harry's voice on the telephone and knew for sure this day was finally going to arrive. And it had; she was now Mrs. Harry Ernest Kipp! And any minute her husband would walk through that door and she would become his wife--not just in name and on paper--but in flesh. 'What God hath joined together'. Now she was shaking on the outside as well as the inside.

Before Sunday night she had never been in a man's embrace, nor been kissed. She had wondered where the noses went, but that hadn't been a problem. Probably because Harry knew what to do. She had never seen a man's body unclothed, nor shown hers to any man. She was giving him an unseen, unused one and what he would do with it she wasn't exactly sure. She knew that somehow he would put a part of himself inside her to reach that part of her that called for him, but how? and how long would it take, and what was she supposed to do? Would this be the time for talking about what would please each other as he had once suggested they do? She had heard that men got hard...and he was. His chest, his thighs; he'd been hard all over. Around other people he didn't touch her except after the ceremony, then he had stood for a full minute after he kissed her before he moved away. On the ride back with Marsha and Houston, he had only held her hand. Now that they were alone, would he kiss her again as he had in front of the Read House in Chattanooga? Would he unleash his power that had made her go limp and dizzy?

Bewitched 47

She heard him at the door and watched him enter in robe and pajamas. Walking toward her, his robe came off and then the pajama top. His upper body, bare and bronze with high pectoral mounds and muscled biceps, delighted her eyes. The pajama bottom fell and for just an instant, before he slipped beneath the bed covers, the sight of an enormous pulsing thing, as big as her forearm, standing up against his flat belly, turned her delight to concern. Could that possibly be normal, she wondered in panic, or was he deformed? The drawing in the Red Cross Home Nursing book showed it hanging down. He was under the sheets with her, reaching, his arms pulling her to him and that hot, throbbing hardness was between them and his trembling shook the bed. "Honeychild, my sweet, lovely honeychild." His words were muffled against her breasts. Then he raised himself to look down on her, "You're so tiny, I'm afraid you'll break. I love you so, and want you so! Tell me you want me as much as I want you!"

"I do, Harry. I want you...but tell me what should I do?"

"Help me...not to hurt you." He pleaded as his hand stroked her back, her hips and legs and finally found a place to rest while he kissed her throat, eyes, and mouth, making her go limp. Then his lips were on her breasts and she couldn't be still. Flames of wanting him leapt through her. She thought she might fly apart or go wild. Her hands were on his head, fingers intertwined in his hair. Her body arched toward him in pleasure and with a cry of joy he pushed where his hand had been and a giant shudder shook them both. Somehow he had gotten that hard part of him inside her, or at least a bit of it. She didn't know how all of it could ever go inside her; it was too big or she was too small. Oh, what was he thinking?

For a long while he said nothing, just holding her, trembling still. Then his lips were at her breasts, thrilling her as before, and once again he was entering her, not so big now, pushing a bit at a time, gently, deeper, deeper. She felt a piercing pain and gasped, waiting for more. There was none, and she relaxed. He began to grow within her, moving his strong body and groaning in pleasure as she joined his rhythm until finally in a spasm, his movement ceased. He held her tightly, silently, and she felt his tears fall on her face. In the dim light, she saw his contorted face and cried in alarm, "My darlin', are you all right?"

"Am I all right? Honeychild, do you know what you just did? You sent me straight to paradise!" He took her face between his hands, "Sweetheart, are *you* all right? There is only one first time and I wanted it to be perfect for you. I hope you're not disappointed."

"No, no, Harry. I'm not, if you're not. I'm just so very happy that we're together, truly together, at last. No more waitin', not another day, not another hour. There was so much waitin', I thought it would never end." She burst into uncontrollable sobs, covering her face with her hands. He drew in his breath and took her hands away to kiss her tear-drenched face. "Norma darling, I am here. Hush, please, hush. You're breaking my heart. Please, stop crying." He folded her in his arms, pressing her face into his shoulder. "Please, stop, darling. If someone should hear you, they'll think I'm hurting you." He stroked her head and shoulders, whispering softly,"I know how awful the waiting was, but Norma, it's over. We are together, and we're going to be together for always." He rocked her in his arms, "Believe that, Norma, my sweet Norma."

When she woke it was early morning and he was holding her still. Releasing her, he rose to dress. "Wait here, sweet. I'll be back soon." He returned with warm, moist washcloths wrapped in towels to gently bathe her at the place that had given him so much rapture, then he arranged her blue nightie and smoothed the sheets about her. "Honeychild, I'm going to find somewhere to get breakfast for you."

Norma laughed, "Not in La Fayette, you aren't. There's no place here, not even at the bus station. We can go to Mama's; she'll fix us some breakfast, or I can." She looked to him for agreement.

"Then we'll do that. You need to eat. I've got to fatten you up, little darling. How much do you weigh? You never answered the last time I asked." His eyes surveyed her slight form covered by the sheet.

"Ninety-eight pounds," she told him, then added, "but I lost two pounds this week, waitin' for you."

"Then our goal will be to add at least five to that by the time we leave Gatlinburg. That reminds me, while we're near a telephone, I should call for reservations. Shall I make them for tonight? I'm kind of anxious to get you off to myself on that honeymoon I've been promising you for such a long time." On the taxi ride to Norma's folks, Harry arranged for transportation to the Smoky Mountains that afternoon, a three hour drive. After breakfast, Norma packed her few clothes in the small brown overnight case she had bought so many months ago for just that purpose. All morning while she carried on in a normal way, or so she hoped, she could still feel him inside her, and she smiled a little smile to herself.

Before they left, Norma took Harry to her special place up the long hill behind her house to the tree he recognized at once: the 'victory' tree of her picture. He lifted her and placed her in the 'V', her mouth on a level with his, then hers against his. She slid from her perch down his body, pressing against him. "Honeychild..."incredulous wonder in the word, "what are you doing to me? Let me warn you..." Then he stopped with a look of mock horror, "are you wanting me here...in the bushes?!"

She broke away laughing, "And why not? This is our place. I used to bring your letters up here to read and I dreamed of...but I never dreamed it would be so wonderful."

"And I dreamed too, high on my hill. But, Sweetheart, can't you restrain yourself until we get to our cottage in Gatlinburg?"

They had their cottage, for two weeks, a little stone cottage with its own bathroom, beside a busy little rock-filled stream, reveling in their love for each other, indulging every whim. Harry's adoration allowed Norma to release a self-expression that delighted him and surprised her.They knew each other completely with no disappointments nor feelings of strangeness. Their only regret was in having to leave their paradise after so short a time to rejoin the world. In sixteen days, Harry must report for duty to Camp Pendleton, California, twenty-five hundred miles away.

5

Harry sent another telegram to Marine Corps Headquarters, his fifth. Every time his location changed, he notified them by wire, from San Francisco, Chattanooga, La Fayette, Gatlinburg, and now again in La Fayette."Why?" Norma asked, unpacking their clothes in her parents' house.

"They want to know where I am."

"Just like you're married to them, huh?" She asked, fingering his wedding band playfully.

"They own me, Honeychild," his fingers closed over hers.

"Body and soul?" Her smile teased, but her eyes were pensive.

"Totally...until 2 October. Now they must share me with you." He grinned, drawing her to him. The grin faded as he grew serious. "Norma, you do know that so long as I am in the Corps, it must take priority, don't you? When it calls, I answer. That's what my commission requires."

Norma frowned, pulling back, looking at the captain's bars on his shirt collar points, "Somehow I got that idea all through those long, long months of waitin'."

He touched a finger to her brow as if to erase her frown,"It's peace time now, and I think you'll find the demands not too difficult to live with. Since much of my service has been foreign assignments, I expect to pull stateside duty until I retire in seven or eight years. Perhaps we'll have only two or three duty changes at most. And we'll have thirty days leave every year to use as we please, to go where we please. My darling, we've just started to live! You'll like it, you'll see. Right now, though, there is the small detail of getting transportation to Camp Pendleton, my chore for tomorrow. Do you want to go with me to Chattanooga, or would you rather stay here and save yourself a lot of hassle? I'll be trying the airlines first, then the train, and last of all the bus. If I can't get a flight, we'll have to head West in a few days. My leave expires 2 November, and I would prefer to arrive in California a few days before."

"Then I'll stay here and get things ready in case you can't get a flight."

Harry returned with no travel arrangements by air or rail, but the possibility of travel by car with Harold Martin, the cab driver who drove them to Gatlinburg, "He offered to drive us to San Diego for what I feel is a reasonable fee. His wife has relatives in Santa Monica they'd like to visit. Driving us could make it possible and solve our problem as well. What do you think of his idea?"

"It sounds like a good solution. How long would it take to go by car?"

"I thought of allowing a week which, if all goes well, would give us four days in San Diego to look for our own car before I report in. Don't you think that would be better than trying to buy a car here under pressure of time and the risk of getting one with problems?"

"Then we could stay here until the 24th?" She asked excitedly.

He nodded, "There's no other choice except to go by bus which would be rough on you. By train,I could get reservations for two only to St. Louis. Martin's offer appeals to me. Shall we accept it?"

Five more days here! Time to make a black chiffon blouse to wear with the lime green suit Harry had bought her in Knoxville. Time to introduce him to everybody so they could see what a gentleman he is, holding her chair for her, saying *Thank you, Please,* and *Pardon me,* always knowing what to say, and not hanging his head when he spoke. His dialect would raise eyebrows though, for they would know he was a Yankee as soon as he opened his mouth, although a handsome, polished one. One who had come into town and claimed a local girl to marry and take away, from right under their noses, and nobody had had the least idea it was happenin' except Marsha and Inez, and probably Mama after the arrival of the long stemmed roses. And at last everyone knew why she had given up the Cadet Nurse Corps to work in the hosiery mill: *she had been waitin' for this man!*

Harry wanted to hire a taxi for their jaunts about town, but Norma said, "No, let's walk." She didn't tell him it was because she wanted to show off her handsome husband who looked like a million dollars in his tropical worsted uniform, always wrinkle free except where it should be creased, his shirt with three rows of campaign ribbons, four battle stars and the Combat "V", his cap visor and shoes so highly polished the glare was blindin'. No, she didn't tell him. Her modest husband would have been embarrassed. So in daylight they walked, but after dark they took a taxi.

The five extra days passed too quickly and the final evening in La Fayette was upon them. Norma was deciding what to pack and what to leave behind in her cedar chest. Each of them, the Martins and the Kipps, were limited to two cases and her two were filled with her entire wardrobe, and no room left for the letters from Harry nor the music box. In frustration she turned to him, "What did you do with my letters when you left Okinawa?"

"I had a big bonfire!" He confessed sheepishly.

"You burned them?" She looked at him, aghast. "But why?"

"There was barely room for me on that small plane, and I didn't want to risk their getting into other hands, three hundred or so smoldering letters that hardly required any ignition." His eyes were amused lights in an otherwise serious face.

"You couldn't have burned them!" she cried. "You're teasin' me... aren't you?"

"No, I'm serious. Your letters were downright provocative and had me thrashing about on my cot all night, many nights. I took so many midnight dips in the ocean I feared I'd be wrinkled before my time and you'd change your mind about marrying me! You little vixen, you *are* provocative, your innocence notwithstanding!" He moved against her, "See what just the mere thought of those letters has done to me?" He whispered against her throat, "Oh, darling mine, how I long for us to be alone again."

Her arms encircled his chest, "Tomorrow night, if I can ever get packed so we can leave in the mornin'." After giving him a sizzling kiss, she turned to the cases lying open beside the fat bundle of letters. "Oh, dear, I can't leave them behind, there isn't room to pack them. What shall I do?" She put her hands to her head, thinking. "I know! I'll keep twenty-seven, and burn the rest... and this bonfire we'll have together. Let me see,

I'll keep the first one, the last ones, and the one with your first proposal, those written on the 27th..."

"I know when I've been dismissed," Harry said and left her sorting through the letters to go to the kitchen for a cup of coffee.

By suppertime, the chosen letters were tied with a narrow red ribbon and packed along with the music box. Norma closed the cases, snapped the locks, humming to herself, "California, here I come!"

After supper dishes were done, and with the nearly full moon lighting their path, Norma and Harry climbed her hill again. In a clearing, they brushed the earth free of pine needles, rimmed the spot with stones, and began the burning. "How is it possible to feel so happy and so sad at the same time?" she asked, staring into the fire, watching as the flames curled the pages of his letters. "I think it's because if I didn't have the sadness to mix with the happiness, I'd simply die from it. Oh, Harry, my dearest, dearest love," she took his hand to press her lips into its palm then placed it over her heart, "do you **know** how happy I am to be your wife?"

The leaping flames illuminated his eyes, full of knowing, and he tightened his arm around her. Already she felt safe there. "I wish we didn't have to say good-by. If only I could wake up in the mornin' and be somewhere in Alabama with the good-bys already said. Oh, why am I so sad and yet so happy?"

"I think it's because tomorrow you're leaving the familiar, going into the unknown, feeling both a loss and an exhilaration, but I promise you, if it is in my power to control, you'll never regret going with me into the unknown." His eyes danced in the firelight, "Honeychild, tomorrow! Think of it. Just the two of us, answering to no one..."

"Answerin' to nobody," Norma reminded him with a roll of her eyes, "except the Marine Corps."

Norma woke before dawn on October 24 and rose from the warmth of Harry's arms, leaving him sleeping, taking her clothes to the bathroom to dress. The house was quiet as she slipped out to climb to the top of Reservoir Hill. She cleared a place to sit beside the residue of ashes from the burned letters of the night before, lifting a few in her fingers and watching them drift back to the earth. She dreaded the leave-taking and needed time to herself, to get control of her emotions, and if it was possible, this was the place to do it. Her hill... which always gave her what she needed.

Bewitched

Looking down on the house and grounds around it, she thought of that first Spring when they had moved here from the boarding house in town. Joan had been half way to four, and she had been almost six. In town, they'd had two rooms, upstairs, with no place to play except on the upper veranda, and quietly at that, since most of the other boarders worked at night and slept in the daytime. How many times she had run along side its rail with her arms spread wide, looking out over the main street below, pretending to be the swallows that Mama sang about! But here, there was lots of room for playing, and a set of tire swings that Daddy hung from the limbs of two pine trees growing in the side yard. She could soar through the air, singing to the top of her voice, truly becoming a swallow flying back to Capistrano, wherever that was.

The six room house seemed like a whole boarding house all their own and stood close to an unpaved road which curved out of sight at each end like a long ribbon. She liked to sit on the porch steps and watch up and down the road for something exciting to come along. One day a pair of peddlers came walking by, pulling a wagon load of home grown fruits and vegetables. The lady smiled at her. She smiled back and as they passed, she had the urge to go with them. With a shout to Mama, who was stirring clothes in the wash pot in the back yard, she went off to learn the peddling trade: knocking on doors, exchanging food for money, carrying the money bag, and by noon, knowing pennies from nickels and dimes. The shadows were long on the ground when she returned home, happy and pleased, only to be met by a slap on the fanny and whisked into the house where the bedpost was set on her dress tail. To add to her shock and indignation Mama shouted, "This should clip your wings, you little swallow!"

It subdued her for a while, until the last day of June when she had her sixth birthday and began thinking of adventure again. Being six meant she could go to school and that meant learning to read. When she lived at the boarding house, she went to Sunday School up the street all by herself. The teacher read wondrous stories from little Bible books with shiny colored pictures and she got to take hers home. The two stories she liked best were about baby Moses hidden in a little basket in the bulrushes at the river's edge and found by the Pharaoh's daughter and Joseph with his coat of many colors who was sold by his brothers for twenty pieces of silver, later to become ruler over the land of Egypt.

When they moved away from town, Mama read the stories to her on wintry nights, after the supper dishes were done, and the family was settled around the hearth and a warm, glowing fire. The flames lit up the room near the fireplace and cast giant shadows on the far wall. She sat on the floor and looked up at Mama's eyes gliding back and forth across the lines of print like two swans on a mill pond. Between the covers of books there were lives as real as hers and she wanted to know about all of them.

"Tell *me* how to read!" she implored.

"Just wait, you'll learn when you start to school," Mama promised.

"I don't want to wait. I want to read *now!* Tell me how."

"Well, first, you've got to know the words."

"Then tell 'em to me."

So, Mama told her the words. Night after night they worked on them until finally she cried in frustration, rubbing her eyes,"There's too many and they're too little. Just read them to me and I'll remember."

Mama read the Ten Commandments over and over until Norma knew them by heart, pretending to be reading as she held the booklet before her eyes. When Uncle Pete saw this performance, he winked at Daddy and said, "Clarence, you've got a real smart young'n here, readin' already. Ain't no need to send her to school."

Afraid Daddy would believe him, Norma told the truth; she had been pretending and really needed to go to school. Through July and August Mama took pretty dresses from the big, gray trunk, put them on, looked at herself in the chifferobe mirror then made them into school dresses for Norma. The first was a lavender flowered dress with a white organdy pinafore, then a pink and white striped jumper with a pink blouse. The third was a yellow dress with appliqued pockets that looked like big, red apples. For all these dresses, Mama made bloomers to match. Then Uncle Pete brought over a white sailor suit and Mama made it into a sailor dress with navy blue binding and a navy blue tie. Uncle Pete liked to tell about his time in the Navy on a ship in a place called 'Frisco. It was in California, far away. Norma asked him if he had seen the swallows.

"No, I didn't see no swallows," he laughed, "but I could tell you plenty about seagulls." Uncle Pete was always laughing, but she couldn't remember the last time she'd seen Daddy laugh.

As each dress was finished, Norma decided, at least for a little while, that she would wear that one on the first day of school. And when the day came, she chose, as usual, the last one made: a red and white gingham with butterfly sleeves piped in red binding. Up and dressed at dawn, she put on red stockings and the pair of black patent leather Roman sandals that had been a birthday present from Aunt Ruby and saved for this special day. Aunt Ruby, Mama's older sister, lived far away in Alabama and Norma wished she could see her wearing the shoes. Like Mama, she looked at herself in the chifferobe mirror, walking before it so many times that Daddy took notice. "You don't like that dress very much, do you?" he asked with a wink at Mama.

"Yes, sir, I do." Norma twirled around, flaring the skirt.

"No, you don't. And you don't like them red stockings either."

"Yes, sir, I do!" Her voice grew louder.

"And I know for sure you don't like them patent leather shoes."

"Yes, sir, I do! I do!" Her voice becoming shrill as she jumped up and down.

"Well, aw right, I guess you do," Daddy agreed and Norma noticed he was almost smiling.

"Stop that, Clarence. You get her all worked up and then you leave," Mama called after him, half mad.

Norma had expected him to take her to school on the first day. She turned to Mama anxiously, "How'm I goin' to find the school?"

"The Wallin boys will be goin'; just follow them," Mama said.

She looked at Mama, then at the bedpost, and finally at the skirt of her new dress. "No more bedposts," Mama laughed. "You're a school girl now. You just make sure you find your way home, little swallow."

"I will," Norma promised and taking up her new book satchel, she set out on her first day of school feeling the happiest she had ever felt in her whole life. She waved good-by to Joan and then walked down the road and off into the world. On other days, together, they had watched Daddy walk down that road and wondered what it was like around the bend. She had gotten a glimpse of the world on her peddling trip, and now she was doing it again, and she could barely keep from running ahead of the boys she was supposed to be following.

Returning home at the end of the school day, she saw Mama, Joan, and Dorothy from next door waiting for her on the front porch. She ran the last few yards and bounded up the steps reviewing her day in a burst of words, "The schoolhouse is so-o-o far and so-o-o big! There's stairs goin' up and stairs goin' down. There's hun'erts of kids and I didn't know none of 'em 'cept the Wallin boys. My teacher's a pretty lady and her name is Mrs. Deariso." Stopping to catch her breath, she flipped the satchel strap over her head. Opening the flap, she began pulling papers out and giving them to Mama, "Here, look at what I colored, and I found a whole bunch more in the trash can and my teacher said I could have 'em. Here, Joan, this is for you and this is for Dorothy, and I'll be the teacher. You have to do what

I tell you, and you can't speak unless you raise your hand and I call your name."

Norma felt she had a new calling in life. School was better than she expected. Not only could she learn herself, she could pass it on to Joan, Dorothy, and the neighborhood kids...and where had they been today? She hadn't seen a single colored kid at her school! She'd have to find out about that. The next day, she asked her classmates, "Where's the colored kids?"

"You mean the niggers?" one of them snickered.

"No, I mean the colored kids," Norma repeated.

"Well, we call 'em niggers," another said."They can't come here. They've got their own school."

"Why?" Norma wondered.

" 'Cause they live on Nigger Hill and that's where their school is."

"No, they don't. They live on Reservoir Hill just like me, and I come here."

"That's 'cause you're white, silly." A third one said.

"You live with niggers!" All three chorused. "You'd better be careful or you'll turn black."

"You're wrong," Norma cried, turning in a circle to face them,"all wrong...all of you. And you're mean. I like them better than you."

She asked Mama why the kids had been so mean."Some folks are nice and some are not," Mama explained. "That's just the way they are."

"Maybe keepin' the colored kids out of school stops people from seein' that they're nice," Norma decided. "I'm goin' to tell my teacher. She's a real nice lady. She'll believe me."

"She might," Mama said, "but it won't change a thing. Things has been this way for a long, long time."

"My Sunday School teacher said Jesus loves all the children," Norma said. A moment later she asked, "Does Jesus love grown up people too?"

"What did your Sunday School teacher say 'bout that?" Mama asked.

"She didn't say nothing about grown up people, just children...all the children of the world. Do you think Jesus loves mean kids?"

"Probably," Mama conceded.

Norma learned a lot at school. Colored kids had their own school, some kids brought sandwiches of sliced bread and flat circles of pulpy sweetness with holes in the middle, called pineapple. Sometimes they swapped them for her biscuit with salt pork inside. She learned about toilets in the basement of the school, one end of the building for girls and the other for boys. She learned about that from Dewey Wallin. When she asked him where the bathroom was, he took her and showed her. Only he showed her the boys' bathroom, and laughed at her confusion and anger when she went inside and then ran out. She learned not to trust just anybody, not even a neighbor.

"What do toilets look like?" Joan asked, squinting with curiosity.

"Well, they're little rooms with doors on 'em, that is in the girls' part, and there's a place to sit with a tank of water behind. You push a little handle on the tank," Norma explained, "and a lot of water swirls round in a big bowl-- what you sit on--and then ever'thing in the bowl gets sucked down and goes away through the floor. Then the bowl gets full of water again for the next time." Norma leaned close and confided, "It's fun to make the water and stuff go away. A lot of times, I raise my hand to go to the basement even when I don't really have to go. And the teacher lets me." She felt big and important, telling Joan and Dorothy all the things that happened at school. Every morning they watched her leave, waving until she was out of sight, and every afternoon they were waiting for her.

"Tell us what you did!" they squealed in one voice, and she did. "Read to us," they begged, and she did. "Teach us to read!" and she tried.

Time flew by past Halloween, Thanksgiving, and into December. At midmonth school let out for winter vacation and the rain began. On Christmas Eve, it had lightened to a fine mist. After breakfast, Daddy climbed onto a chair to reach the rifle he kept above the kitchen door. "I guess you're goin' huntin', " Norma said.

"And you guessed right, 'cept *we're* goin' huntin'. *I'm* goin' for rabbits. I figure this is a good day for it. They'll be flooded out of their burrows just sittin' there waitin' for me and my rifle. And *you're* goin' huntin' for us a Christmas tree. I'll even let you carry the hatchet."

Daddy's hunting trips got them rabbits and squirrels for their dinner table when he was lucky; this day he was. He shot two rabbits and she found a perfect tree. With a few swift strokes, he chopped it down and dragged it home. He shook the water off and made a stand for it. Mama went to her big trunk and took out thick red ropes and hung them on the tree. She put a silver star on top and a white sheet around the bottom. On the sheet she placed a package, wrapped in green tissue paper, addressed to *Norma* and *Joan*. And on Christmas morning they had a beautiful little tea set from Aunt Ruby. Santa Claus left them two rag dolls, one with black yarn hair, the other with brown. Joan chose the brown-haired doll wearing a blue dress. The black-haired doll wore pink and Norma liked it best. "How did Santa Claus know we liked pink and blue?" she asked.

"Because he's a very smart man," Mama answered.

All day long the rain drizzled on and the girls wandered from window to window looking out at the puddles forming where they played when it was sunny. Soon tiring of that, Norma sat at the kitchen table and traced the outline of the floral pattern on the oilcloth covering. Then with her chin in her hands, she watched Mama dip rabbit pieces in flour and heard the hot grease pop in the skillet as the meat fried. "That sure smell good, Mama. What are we eatin' with it?"

"Your favorite...okra, that is if you'll get it from the pantry."

Norma ran to get the flour sack of dried okra she'd helped with last summer. She liked okra, fresh from the summer garden, battered in corn meal and fried to delicious crispness, but in winter they ate dried okra. She loved to see the hard, dry pieces plump up and get soft when they were soaked in water, and she remembered that was the way okra was in the summer, freshly sliced, crosswise, before it was put inside the sack. "You're too young to do the slicin'," Mama had told her,"but you can climb up the ladder to the back porch roof and I'll hand up the sack and the rocks to hold it down." On the roof she spread the sack on the hot shingles and let the sun start to dry out the water.

During the day, she climbed up to shake the sack to let the okra dry evenly. By sundown the sack, full of okra at the start, would be only half full and have a rattlely sound when she brought it down from the roof. It never lasted until they had fresh okra again, but there was always plenty of onions hanging in big bunches from hooks on the pantry wall. She'd heard Daddy say, many a time, "I'll tell you right off, I couldn't eat black-eyed peas ever' day of my life if we didn't have onions." He would chew a few mouthfuls, then say, "I'm not complainin', mind you. I'm still grateful to Mr. Mahan for lettin' me and your mother pick his pea crop on halves. It's these here peas that's keepin' the wolf from our door."

She was thankful too because even though she'd never seen a wolf, she didn't want one comin' to their door. She could tell by the way Mama blinked her eyes and bit her lower lip that the wolf was something to fear. Today, Christmas dinner was not only black-eyed peas and onions but rabbit and fried okra. And she and Joan had a little tea set! "Mama, can we make a little table to eat on, me and Joan?"

Mama spread a towel on an orange crate then washed the tiny tin ware cups, saucers, and plates painted pink and decorated with blue flowers. Placing them on the makeshift table Norma asked, "How did Aunt Ruby know we'd like this tea set?"

"Because she was a little girl herself some years back."
"Like me and Joan?"
"Your Aunt Ruby and me, we're sisters just like you and Joan."
"I wish she'd come and see us sometime. Can't you ask her to come?"
"She lives a long way from here, in Alabama, and she has to work."
"To buy us things?"
"Not just us, the whole family. She's the only one that's got a job...a government job, in a post office. Hardly anybody nowadays has a job. But she came to be with me when it was time for you to be born, Joan. That's how you got your first name *Ruby*."
"I'm Ruby Joan Clinton," Joan pranced around the room.
"I like Aunt Ruby," Norma said, "Does she know we like her?"
"She knows."
"When I learn to write, I'm goin' to write Santa Claus and Aunt Ruby."
"You do that, " Mama said, "Now let's eat."

6

The last school day in March ended with rain pouring in gray sheets from a black sky split by jagged streaks of lightning. Wide-eyed with fright, Norma stared out the school house door and thought of Joan and Dorothy warm and dry and safe at home. At that moment she didn't feel so big and important as she tried to get up enough courage to start on the long walk home. Just then Virginia Chapman called out, "My daddy's here with our car, he'll give you a ride home." Children were packed and squeezed inside so tightly that Norma could only see out the top of the small high windows, but she didn't mind. She was very happy with her good fortune and settled down for the ride.

Driving a circuitous route to deliver the various children, Mr. Chapman stopped the car, in turn, only long enough for each child to disembark, and then went on his way. When Virginia said, "It's your turn," Norma got out quickly. The car sped away. Too late Norma shouted, "Come back, come back! It's not my house," her voice growing fainter with each word until the last one came out in a whimper. She looked around in every direction, recognizing nothing. "Where am I?" she asked, turning in circles, appealing to the the wind and rain.

She didn't know which way to go, and like a lost rider whose horse knew the way, she let her feet choose the way, and they took her along a row of mill houses lining both sides of the road. Closing her coat over her schoolbooks and tucking her chin into her upturned collar, she protected her face from the pelting rain and her eyes against the sight of the jagged lightning, but the sharp cracks of thunder frightened her most. Too scared to cry, she just kept walking, walking until finally there were no houses and the road narrowed then stopped at the edge of a plowed field. Her mind still yielded to her feet and they took her across the field, upward toward a stand of trees. Reaching the top, she looked down on a swollen creek whose water was now a swift moving current fed by the day long rain and final cloudburst. But on the other side, up another rise smoke billowed from the chimney of a small house. Daylight was fading and at last her mind took hold. *"Go to the house. It means crossing the creek, but you can't get any wetter."*

Searching for the safest place to cross, she saw where a tree had fallen, too small for a walking bridge but perfect for grasping. She stepped into the foaming torrent, colored red by the Georgia clay. It dragged at her legs. She hugged the tree trunk, knowing if she turned loose, she'd go under. Inch by inch she crossed, and nearing the far bank she held on to the tree top with one hand while an outstretched foot felt for solid ground. Lunging forward, she fell face down on the bank, trembling. Her clothes, stained and heavy, gripped her body, weighing her down. Lifting her sodden shoes, putting them down step by step, she labored up the hill, waiting to rest until she reached the house. In answer to her knocks on the door, a gruff voice from inside called out, "What d'you want?"

Trying to sound grown up, Norma asked, "Sir, can you tell me where Clarence Clinton lives?"

"Clarence Clinton? Yeh, he lives right next door to Archie Wallin."

I already know that. She knocked on the door again and heard a groan, and then a thumping noise coming toward the door. It opened and a man on crutches stared down on her. "Please, sir," Norma looked up into his tired, old face,"I'm sorry to bother you again, but where does Archie Wallin live?"

The old man squinted at her for a moment, "Go down the hill to that road yonder. When it forks, you go that'a way," pointing to the left with his crutch.

"Thank you, kindly, sir." Norma turned to leave the porch.

"Little girl..."
"Yes, sir?" Norma stopped on the bottom step.
"Are you lost?"
"No, sir," Norma smiled, "not any more."

Taking the fork to the left, she saw a house she'd seen before, one her daddy had painted. She'd carried his lunch to him there last summer just before school started. Mama had poured vegetable soup into a lard bucket and laid a half-pone of cornbread on the lid, and she took it to him the mile or so, three days in a row. On the last day, when the painting was finished, she'd waited to walk home with him, running to keep up with his fast pace. Just when she thought she could run no more, Daddy had stopped at a cedar thicket growing close to the road and asked her, "Do you see a tree that looks good enough to hang decorations on?"

Puzzled, she thought a minute before she understood his question. Then she jumped into action, running around through the trees until she spotted just the right one for a Christmas tree. It was the one they returned to when she and Daddy went out huntin', him for rabbits and her for a tree.

Now, at the cedar thicket, she knew home was very close and even though it was dark, she wasn't afraid. At the bend of the road, lamplight in the windows of her house drew her like a moth. The last few yards, she ran, squishing up the beloved front porch steps. She knocked at the door, then stooping, took off her muddy shoes. Mama came, with the week-old baby brother in her arms, to stare at a drenched and red-stained figure, as if she were a stranger and then cried, "Where in the world have you been?"

"I been losted!" Norma wailed.

"Don't just stand there, come on in where it's warm and dry." Mama put the baby in the bed, hustled her to the kitchen, stripped her of the soggy clothes and wrapped her in a quilt. Norma heard the front door open and close, and Daddy came into the kitchen, soaking wet himself. Seeing Norma and the pile of dripping clothes on the floor he snapped, "I guess you know you've worried your mother half to death."

"Yes, Sir, Mr. Chapman gave me a ride in his car, only he let me out at the wrong house," Norma answered in a quivering voice.

"Didn't he *ask* you where 'bout you lived?" Daddy shouted.

"No, Sir, he didn't. He just asked me my name."

Daddy was speechless for a minute,"Then he must'a thought you belonged to that set of Clintons over in West La Fayette, down on Broomtown Road." He thought for another minute "You mean you walked home from there?"

"Yes, sir."

"Then you must be a homin' pigeon, that's all I can say."

Norma thought that meant something good and later, warm and cozy in her bed with a stomach full of warm soup and Joan looking on in wonder she felt it was somehow worth it all, now that it was over. Besides, she'd got to ride in a car! She couldn't wait to tell Dorothy.

The next day, the day before Easter, when the rain stopped, Norma saw her daddy climb onto the chair for his rifle. "Are you goin' huntin', again, Daddy?"

"That's right. Last night I went huntin' for you. Today, I'm going huntin' for rabbits."

Norma's worried eyes followed him out of sight. Turning from the door she asked Mama, "Do you think he might shoot the Easter Bunny?"

"No," Mama sighed, "The Easter Bunny don't live in these parts."

"Where does it live?"

"Somewhere, far away."

Norma pondered this for a time then asked, "Will it know we moved?"

Mama looked at her quickly, "Probably not, and I don't think you better count on it payin' you and Joan a visit this year."

"Can we put out Easter baskets, anyway...just in case?"

Mama's lips tightened, but she began searching in the cupboard drawers and found two brown paper bags. With them looking on, she folded the tops into stiff cuffs until the bags were the height of Easter baskets. Norma printed her name on one, Mama printed JOAN on the other. They skipped to their room to put the baskets at the foot of their bed, talking of the egg hunt they would have in the morning.

Daddy returned, not with rabbits but something better in his hunting bag. "Why it's a hen!" Mama exclaimed.

"Not just any old hen," Daddy said proudly, "She's a settin' hen."

Mama's eyebrows raised and she looked quickly at Daddy.

"What's a settin' hen?" Joan asked.

"A mighty tough bird," Daddy said. "Heat up some water, Annie, and I'll get rid of these feathers." Soon the hen, minus feathers, feet, and head, was simmering on the stove and the girls went to sleep smelling the good smell that would be their Easter dinner tomorrow.

Norma woke to the sound of pelting rain against the clapboard siding, hoping the Bunny hadn't drowned in so much rain if it had tried to find them. She dreaded to look in the baskets at the foot of the bed. Would Joan cry if they were empty? Yes, she would cry. Then I will have to be brave, she resolved, creeping out of the bed covers daring to look. "Wake up, Joan, wake up! It found us!" She shrieked, looking at the eight hard boiled hen eggs left by the Easter Bunny.

Norma hid the eggs first. In the empty milk churn, on the sewing machine treadle, behind the mantel clock, in the coal bucket, in the globe of the kerosene lamp, in each of her shoes, and the last one in the dishpan. "You can open your eyes now and hunt!" Joan started her search with Norma giving clues. "You're warm, gettin' warmer, you're hot!" or "You're cold, gettin' colder, you're colder than ice!" Joan darted about the room giggling and enjoying the hunt as much as her finds.

When it was her turn to hide the eggs, Joan put four under each of their pillows. Finding the eggs in a bunch reminded Norma of her egg hunt at Sunday School last year. She had run this way and that way spotting 'almost hidden' eggs in bushes, flower pots, behind rocks, or under benches. But someone always got to them first. Oh, how she wanted to find the Prize Egg, wrapped in golden foil, its hollow holding a dollar bill--or even the Silver Egg with a quarter inside. But the hunt was ending and she didn't have a single egg, not even a candy one.

Suddenly two hands had encircled her waist and lifted her high above the tall, wide, flat-topped hedge where five candy eggs lay in a cluster. The hands held her high until she had gathered all of them, two in her left hand and three in her right hand. With her feet on the ground again, she looked up at the tallest man she had ever seen. He smiled at her, bowed at the waist, and walked away. She had looked after him, beaming in gratitude and clutching the treasured eggs against her chest. Mama wanted to know if she had thanked him. She'd answered, "I kinda said it with my eyes 'cause my mouth was busy smilin'."

Now, sitting at the table, munching on her hard boiled egg, she thought she should say thank you again, "Mama, did you ever talk to the Easter Bunny?"

"No," Mama answered, "Nobody ever sees it."
"How do you know?"
"My mother told me."
"Did it bring eggs way back then?"
"It sure did, and even to my mother when she was a little girl."
"Then it must be really old."
"I don't think it gets old. It stays young, making children happy."
"Do you think it can read?"
"I wouldn't be at all surprised."

"Then when I learn to write, I'm goin' to write it a letter and say thank you for bringin' the eggs to me and Joan."

"You do that," Mama said with a funny look at Daddy.

After Easter the rain stopped and the weather turned warm. Spring plowing was started, for people with a horse and plow. Daddy used a hoe. Mama took seeds from the Mason jars, sorted, shared, and traded them with neighbors. Rocking chairs were put out on front porches and left out, just like last year. Soon, in the evenings, after supper, the grown folks gathered to rock back and forth in the rockers and talk about the way things used to be, back in the Twenties, and the way they were now.

When the chairs stopped rocking that meant the men were talking about the DEPRESSION. She didn't know for sure what the DEPRESSION was, but she noticed Daddy always tightened his lips when anyone mentioned it, and she knew that because they didn't have any money her school dresses had been made from Mama's clothes. Mama had said she didn't need them anymore and started wearing those funny dresses until Tommy was born, and afterwards she still wore them, only now with a belt. Norma thought also that the DEPRESSION was why Daddy didn't go off to work anymore.

Some evenings the grown folks gathered on the Clinton porch. They came bringing their own chairs. Archie and Eula Lee Wallin lived on the town side of the Clintons and had three of the meanest boys she'd ever known about, always punching each other and their cows. Mr. Wallin worked in the cotton mill, but it ran only three days a week now, and only the first shift. That put lots of people out of work. He said it was because of tariff and cotton from Egypt and India, and that the government and Mr. Hoover had forgotten about American people. She knew about Egypt, that's where Joseph got to be ruler of a long time ago.

Dorothy's folks lived on the other side. Mr. Swift was a preacher on Sundays and a feed store clerk during the week. He had his ideas about the cause of the DEPRESSION. It was because of the sinful city folk who rode around in the chariot of Satan--he meant a car, she told Dorothy--and drank bootleg whiskey. The DEPRESSION was God's punishment. Daddy agreed with the part about Mr. Hoover forgetting about the working people, but sometimes he drank bootleg whiskey with Uncle Pete and Granddaddy Clinton so he didn't say anything about that. Daddy had his own idea for the cause of the bad times. It was because the working man didn't have any say about anything--his hours, his wages, and she'd heard him say that

Bewitched

if the big boss didn't like the way a man parted his hair, he'd fire him. Archie Wallin didn't have enough hair to part, and Preacher Swift's hair was too curly to part. Only Daddy's hair had a part, and he was out of work. Probably the big man hadn't liked Daddy's part on the left. She wondered why he didn't change it so he'd get some work.

The evening talks went on every time there was a gathering on the porches. The women just listened and picked beans to soak for tomorrow's meal, letting the men do the talking. The talk was not as loud this spring (1934) as it had been last spring. Maybe it was because different people was talking. Last spring in the boarding house, just before they moved, all the boarders had sat in the dining room one night and listened to the new president talk on the radio. She'd heard him too and saw the men sit a little straighter as the talk went on. The president talked about a New Deal and some of the men shouted and stomped their feet and slapped each other on the back, bragging 'cause they'd voted for him. Norma watched Daddy. He didn't shout or stomp his feet, but he looked kind of happy as they went up the stairs to their rooms.

When she and Joan got into bed and the lamp was out, Daddy started talking, low, but she could hear. "I think this feller will turn things around. I honestly believe he cares about the common man. Did you hear him say he's gonna put us back to work?...over twelve million men like me with no regular jobs...jus' doin' whatever we can find to do, pickin' cotton in the fall and plantin' seeds in the spring...not workin' at our trade. I thought I'd better myself when I learned the brick layin' trade and got outa that sweat box of a mill." He sighed loudly, "It's been so long since I had a trowel in my hand I reckon I wouldn't know which end to put the mortar on. I tell ya, I'd give most anythin' jus' to get a chance to lay a thousand bricks."

Norma curled up into a ball under the covers, wondering what Mama was doing. She never said much when she was worried, just rubbed her hands together and blinked her eyes. But it was dark and Norma couldn't see across the room. Then Daddy started talking again, "I saw Ben Loughridge down at his grocery store last week and he told me he's got this six-room house standin' empty out on the edge of town. He said some drifters has been stayin' in it off and on and the neighbors are startin' to complain...said he'd rent it cheap and part of the rent could be for fixin' it up. It's run down some, and it's got damaged, needs paintin' bad, he said."

"What d'you tell him?" Mama asked.

"I told him,'Why Ben, you know I ain't got no steady job. I can't guarantee to pay you rent, even if it is cheap.' But he said he'd be much obliged if I'd move in. Said it would be worth somethin' just to have somebody livin' there, and of course he knows me."

"Are we goin' to?" Mama's voice sounded happy.

"I had decided against it, but tonight, after hearing that fella Roosevelt on the radio, I think I might chance it. There's a good-sized garden plot we could work. Might as well work our own garden and keep it all than work somebody else's on halves. And there's fruit trees, peach and cherry, and maybe in time, if things pick up, and I'm hopin' they will, we could get a cow and some pigs. There's a shed for a cow. I could build a pen behind it for a sow. I think I'll go out there and take a look anyhow."

And that's how they got to move into the house next door to Dorothy, But that was a year ago and things had not picked up. And now they had another mouth to feed Daddy said. But Mama fed the baby, and cried while it was happening. She never *heard* Mama cry, she just saw her. And then Daddy would walk out of the house and go to town. She hated the DEPRESSION! It made Mama cry and Daddy sit and look at the floor and sometimes hit the table with his fist or slam the door when he went out.

When her feet got too big for her patent leather shoes, Daddy said she'd have to wear them anyway. It was warm enough 'cept her teacher didn't like it when she came to school with bare feet. So she wore them there with her toes scrunched up, but the rest of the time she carried them. And Mama cried when she had to say "No" to the hungry men Daddy called hoboes when they came to the back door for handouts. "Why are they called hoboes?" she asked Mama.

"Because they don't have no money, no home, nothin' to eat and go around from place to place lookin' for work, sometimes riding on freight trains, sneakin' free rides, hidin' underneath or on top or inside empty cars." Mama looked at Daddy with a hopeless look, "Why do they do it?"

"Because they're fools, poor desperate fools. I ought to know," he sighed, "I did it too. I thought lookin' for work that way, in far off places, was the answer. I found out it wasn't, but at least it kep' me from losin' my mind. I felt like I was doin' *somethin'*...I must of been crazy to let Pete talk me into it, him footloose and fancy free and me with a wife and two kids."

"But you did," Mama said with her eyes lowered, "you listened to Pete and him little more than a kid. You sent me and the kids to stay with Ruby. Joan just a baby in my arms and Norma a three-year old into ever'thin'. At least I could do the cookin' while Ruby worked at the post office, and we had something in our bellies. But I'll never forget them three months. Not a word from you the whole time, me not knowin' your whereabouts or even if you was dead or alive. I'd look at the kids and wonder if they had a daddy or not. Then one October day you jus' came a-walkin' in, skin and bones. I hardly knew you, and Joan was so scared when you picked her up, she started cryin'."

Norma wondered if she had cried, but when her parents were talking she knew better than to butt in. Like the women on the porches, she just listened. Later, alone with Mama, she asked, "Did I cry when Daddy came back?"

"No, you never cried. You jus' ran up to him and said, "I be'd good, Daddy, and I tooked good care of Mama and Joan. Aunt Ruby said so!"

"Mama, when Daddy was a hobo, did he go to back doors and beg for bread like the men that come to ours?"

"I 'spect he did."

"Get Daddy to tell us about when he was a hobo, please?"

"He loves to tell about that trip. Don't get him started now; wait 'till after supper," Mama cautioned.

As usual after supper, the family went to sit on the front porch. There, sitting in the late afternoon twilight, Mama said,"Clarence, Norma's been askin' about hoboes. I told her you was the one to ask."

"And you're right," Daddy said. "I could tell you things that would curl your hair and they happened to me and your Uncle Pete. It's not a made-up story. Like I said, we lived it." He stared past her for so long she began to think he had forgotten she was there. This was one evening she hoped the neighbors wouldn't come because Daddy might not tell his story if they did. She looked toward the Wallin house, not a soul in sight. At Dorothy's house, Mr. Swift was washing up at the back door washstand which meant they hadn't eaten yet. Daddy was still staring like he was seeing something far off. She wanted him to hurry before the neighbors came. She looked to Mama for help, but she just sat waiting. When Daddy didn't want to talk, no one could make him, he just acted like you weren't there.

In the quietness, she heard the whistle of the evening freight train. Daddy must have heard it too; he sort of shook himself. Then he clasped his hands behind his head, leaned back in his chair, and started. "In 1920 I was sixteen years old. That's the year I moved out of my dad's house to go live with his older brother. I couldn't stand my step-maw no more. My dad married her not even a year after my mother died birthin' my brother Pete. There was Pete, my sister Lousie, and me...all seven years and under. Well, me and her, Miss Hattie she was called, we never got along. So at sixteen, I left before I did somethin' I'd be sorry for. My uncle said I could come to Sylacauga, Alabama and live with him and Aunt Esther."

"Alabama! That's where Aunt Ruby lives."

"And that's where I met your mother. Her folks ran a boardin' house and I lived there for a while. But before that, as I was sayin', I went to live with my uncle and his wife. He was a bricklayer and taught me the brick layin' trade.Work was fairly good through the Twenties, then jobs got scarcer and scarcer. My dad was doin' pretty good as a house painter in Aragon, Georgia and said I could help him as long as work held out. By that time I had married your mother and we had you and Joan. Work held a little over a year--until July of 1930--and then I was out of work again. Even when I worked, I hadn't made enough money to keep the grocery bill paid, and I couldn't see no chance of gettin' work in the near future. I decided to let your mother and you kids go for a visit with her sister Ruby.

"Pete--the year before--at eighteen had went to New York City on a freight train. And he had itchy feet again. He suggested that him and me hop a train and go up north again, sayin' we could probably find work there." Daddy got up and walked back and forth across the porch. The lights went on in Dorothy's house. Crickets started chirping and fireflies darted about. Everybody waited until Daddy sat down again, "It was some twenty-five miles from where we lived in La Fayette to the freight yards in Chattanooga, Tennessee. We had no way to get there 'cept by foot, and we spent a day coverin' that distance. While we was waitin' for the train to pull out of the yards, I sold a hand gun, a 38 Police Special Smith and Wesson. With some of the ten dollars I got for it, we bought some baloney sausage and bread. We was layin' on the grass jus' outside the place to board the train, eatin', when some four or five young colored men saw us from a distance and called out.They wanted a cigarette, they said. They was some hundred feet from where we was. We didn't pay them no heed, not havin' any cigarettes, but they kep' on walkin' to within reachin' distance of us. One of 'em pointed a hand gun at us and two others searched us, lookin' for a gun. We was clearly outnumbered and I still had the most part of the money I got for the gun and I figured they'd find it and take it. About that time the train crew had finished makin' up the train and blew two short toots from the engine whistle, that was the pullout call. Pete and me, we jumped at the sound of it and the colored men laughed. Then we all ran for the train and was on our way."

Daddy crouched forward, clasping his hands together between his knees, squeezing his fingers so tight his knuckles turned white. "It was some four hundred miles from Chattanooga to Cincinnati, Ohio and there was thirteen tunnels in between. Pete knowed about them and he got inside a box car right away, but I didn't quite make it and had to ride the top. Just before a train entered a tunnel some ropes or cords hanging down from a gallows warned anybody that might be standing erect. When the cords hit you it meant to lay down right then or be knocked off and killed. It just so happened that I was lookin' straight ahead, and it was still light enough for me to see the tunnel comin' up or I'd have been knocked right off that train. By the time the train had got through all the tunnels, I was covered in soot and ashes from head to toe and my eyes stung from the wind and cinder dust."

Daddy squeezed his eyes shut and then rubbed them and she wanted to sit in his lap the way she did with Uncle Pete, but Daddy never let her or Joan sit on his lap. So she moved closer to his chair. He crossed his knees and went on with his story, "When we'd pull into the division where the trains got broke up and rearranged for the next pull out, we'd leave the train and go to what the 'boes called a jungle. It would be situated away from the freight yards, usually in a grove of trees. You could spot it from the tracks by the smoke comin' off the camp fires. There was always some 'boes at the jungle and somethin' cookin' even if it was only watery soup. Ever'body that came was expected to bring somethin' for the pot which was always kep' boilin' on the fire. The 'boes would go into the towns or cities close by and ask for food and they was scarcely ever turned away empty handed. Whatever they got was brought back and shared with the pack. That's what we was, a pack of hungry, homeless men tied together in that time and place. But there we was all equal so we helped each other any way we could, maybe it was jus' with talk--we had plenty of that and it was free--swappin' tales and advice. But some 'boes, they wouldn't talk at all to nobody; they'd jus' set on the edge of the circle starin' out. If it hadn't of been for the jungles, we'd of been worse off than we was. Still, sometimes we went for one or two days without eatin' because a train didn't stop for nothin' but to let off cargo.

"Most 'boes traveled light, their baggage was what was on their backs. I spent the whole trip up without takin' off my clothes or sleepin' in a bed. Course, takin' a bath was out of the question, but gettin' water to drink was the worst problem of all. One time, I recollect, the train was almost to a stop goin' up a steep grade and I saw a barn about twenty-five feet off the track. A big white horse was drinkin' from a waterin' trough so I stepped off of the train and ran right up beside it and drank all I could hold and then splashed water all over me. I finished jus' in time to climb on the last freight car. I had to laugh to myself wonderin' what that horse thought." Daddy dropped his jaw and opened his eyes wide trying to look like a puzzled horse, and then he doubled over laughing. "I can still see that horse lookin' at me," he said between bursts of laughter.

She had seldom seen her daddy laugh at all, that she could remember, and this outburst sent her into a giggling fit. She couldn't stop, no more than Daddy, until she caught Mama's look which said, "That's enough." She thought Mama wasn't enjoying the hobo story.

"Another problem for us," Daddy said when his laughing stopped, "was the railroad detectives. They tried to keep 'boes off of the trains. Pete and me, we got to be pretty sneaky characters, course we was lucky in some ways, one was that we was small men and could hide easier than bigger men. Well, finally after two weeks we got to Jersey City, New Jersey. We boarded a ferry boat to cross the Hudson River. Then we took the subway to get to the 3rd Street YMCA. It was on the East Side waterfront, sometimes called the Bowery. Pete, he knowed about this place and how to get there, being as how he had been there the year before. We was took in as residents. It was a place to get one meal a day and have a bed for twenty-five cents a night. Ever' mornin' we would report to the so-called Employment Office until they found us a job. The only one we ever got was in a cold storage place. On the outside it was stifling' hot being in late August and early September. We'd come out of that plant blue from the cold and hit the streets in the high eighties, and it jus' nearly 'bout did me in. After a while I did get sick and had to quit the job. It paid twenty-five cents a hour and helped us keep body and soul together for as long as we had it." He turned to Mama, "Annie, get me something to drink."

Mama shifted the baby, starting to rise, but Norma jumped up, "I'll get it," she said, darting inside, returning with a large glass of water. Daddy drank it in one long swallow then held the glass, looking at it. "This trip to New York City was during national prohibition time. So we had a chance to visit what they called a 'Speakeasy' or saloon. For whiskey, wine, or beer, or any kind of alcohol drink the price was ten cents a glass. There was men of all ages beggin' for a dime to get what they called their eye-opener. For the most part they were pitiful excuses for human beings wallowin' in filth and misery wantin' nothin' more. That's the way they lived and died. Well, I had spent some three months myself livin' like a rat. My situation seemed as bleak and hopeless as ever so I made plans to hit the tracks back home and try to figure out how it all happened to me. So me and Pete, we checked out and I headed home. Pete, he joined the Navy."

Daddy looked sad, and his voice sounded different from before, "I was twenty-six at the time...that was four years back... and it's as clear to me now as it was then. In fact, I don't think I'll ever be able to forget it. Sometimes I wish I could. I could of lost my life many times over. I covered about two thousand miles to New York City and back home, and I was no better off than when I left. I was worse off really for I'd had to do some things I never thought I've have to do. One was to beg for food to keep myself alive, but I don't recollect ever bein' turned down. I never did steal though, so at least my conscience is clear. And now the shoe is on the other foot and men are comin' here askin' for food...and we're havin' to turn them away...empty handed."

Mama was biting her lip and blinking her eyes. Tommy was asleep at her breast and Joan was asleep on the floor. Norma was glad Daddy wasn't a hobo anymore. He went into the dark house and when the lamp was lit, she woke Joan and they all went inside. In her bed, she made a promise to herself: the next time a hobo comes to their back door and said he was hungry, she'd find somethin' herself to give him.

7

Daddy raised the French harp to his mouth like a man in slow motion. He was standin' on top of a train headin' toward a tunnel. Then the train and Daddy got swallowed by the huge round blackness leavin' behind only the train's whistle and the harp's tune blendin' into one long lingerin' scream. Norma sprang up, her throat aching, relieved to see her familiar room and hear Mama's singing floating in from the kitchen. She fell back on her pillow, pulling the bed sheet to her chin, listening to the song above Joan's soft snoring. "I come to the garden alone, while the dew is still on the roses." She knew Mama's moods by the songs she sang. One happy song was about the swallows that flew back to Capistrano bringing so much happiness that the mission bells rang and the chapel choir sang, and she sang too. But the most happy song of all was "Alabama Gal" because sometimes Daddy joined in, playing on his French harp, and at the end jumping up and doing a buck dance, clapping his hands together, then slapping them on his thighs. And the others would laugh and clap their hands together too. But that had been a long time ago.

This morning Mama was singing the garden song and that meant she was sad. "...And the voice I hear falling on my ear, the Son of God discloses. And He walks with me and He talks with me, and He tells me I am His own..."

The garden was clear in Norma's mind; everything about it, every stone on the path, the path bordered by red rose vines climbing on a white lattice arbor leading to the center of it. There the path made a wide circle and branched off in three directions. Once she asked who *He* was. "Why, the Son of God," Mama had told her, "like the song says."

She left the bed and went to the kitchen. At the stove Mama was stirring oak flakes into boiling water. Daddy was in the garden pounding a sawed-off broom handle into the ground, tying a plumb line to it then stretching it tight across the patch to another broom handle. He began to dig a furrow beneath the string. Mama sent her to say the oatmeal was ready to eat, but he kept on digging.

Inside, Mama poured the watery oatmeal into bowls. Norma soaked a biscuit in her broth, ate the sodden bread, then drank the rest of the liquid. She put two dry biscuits inside a paper bag for her school lunch and went to dress for school. The back door slammed shut behind Daddy and she heard him ask, "And jus' what do you call this?"

"Oatmeal." Mama told him like he ought to know.

"Oatmeal?...looks like hog swill." Daddy sounded mad.

"Maybe, but it's better'n nothin' and that's what we'll be havin' in the mornin'. I just don't know what we're gonna do."

"You know there's jus' one thing left to do and I ain't ready to do *that* yet." Daddy must have slammed the table because a spoon fell to the floor.

"Then are we jus' gonna go hungry?" Mama's voice sounded like a woodpecker pecking on a tree. Norma went into the kitchen to have her pinafore sashes tied and Daddy didn't answer; he just glared into his oatmeal bowl. "Go on, now," Mama handed her the lunch bag, "Go on to school or else you'll be tardy," pushing her toward the door. All the way to school she couldn't forget Mama's face, looking part mad and part sad. She wanted to do something to make her happy. When the teacher gave out art paper, she didn't listen for the assignment, instead she began drawing a picture for Mama. Lost in her work, she didn't notice Mrs. Deariso standing beside her desk. "May I take a look," she asked, then smiling said, "What an original wheel!"

Bewitched

Norma looked up in surprise then, picking up a red crayon, made the roses redder, a white crayon made the arbor whiter, and with a brown crayon she darkened the path. She held up the drawing, her face expectant. "You might want to put more than three spokes on the hub and then draw a rim around them all." Mrs. Deariso suggested with a smile and walked away. Norma, puzzled for a moment, looked after her then returned to her work, drawing Mama, short and slim, with straight black hair touching her shoulders, green eyes in a happy face, wearing a flowered dress and standing in the middle of the rose garden. She couldn't imagine how to draw the Son of God, so she left Him out of the picture and added a big yellow sun.

After school she gave the picture to Mama and asked her to sing the garden song. Mama sang it once, but no more, and kept walking back and forth from the kitchen to the front door, looking down the road toward town. Norma went to the swings to play with Dorothy and tell her about the hobo trip. "Was he scared?" Dorothy asked, her eyes big and round.

"No," Norma assured her,"My daddy's not scared of nothin."

The girls swung until suppertime. But Daddy didn't come home for supper. "Where'd he go?" Norma asked between mouthfuls of peas.

"He went to town," Mama said, "On business."

"To work?" Norma looked up from her plate hopefully.

"No....to see some people and he might be in a bad mood when he gets home, so you and Joan be quiet." Mama gave them a warning look. And he was in a bad mood when he returned. He didn't say a word to anybody, just sat and ate the peas Mama put on the table then went to his bedroom. Mama sent her and Joan to bed. Through the curtain that separated the two rooms, she heard Mama ask, "Well, Clarence, did you do it?"

Daddy didn't answer for a long time, then he said, "I tried. It took me awhile jus' to get my nerve up to get in line, and when I did, I heard what Mrs. Inlow was askin' them fellas ahead of me...and, I jus' couldn't hang around no more. She had to know their life history, ever'thin' about 'em, how long since they'd worked, whereabouts they'd looked for work, all who lived with 'em. Did any of 'em work and why not? Did any of 'em have any money and how much? Them fellas jus' stood there with their heads hangin' down...I guess you think that makes me a coward, but I left."

"But, Clarence, we can't afford to be proud no more.We've been proud ever since you got back from that hobo trip to New York ...oh, it's not been so awful, you've had a few jobs, off and on, until here lately...but now, with three kids and nothin' in sight for the table but peas..."

"You don't have to tell me," Daddy shouted,"I know what we ain't got! Why, I can't even go huntin' no more; we ain't got no shells."

"And you ain't got no *choice,* either!" Mama said in her woodpecker voice.

"Awright! Awright!...I'll go back...tomorrow," Daddy's voice got louder, "I'll answer her damn questions, if it'll make you happy. I'll even beg if I have to...on bended knees...even if it kills me!"

Norma wished she hadn't heard. She looked over at Joan already sound asleep and making her funny noises. Turning her sister onto her side to stop the snoring, she wished she was asleep too.

Norma passed the county courthouse twice a day, going and coming from school. The huge building was made of stone blocks as long as she was tall and half as wide. The steps leading up to the door seemed to reach almost to heaven, more than she could count when she started to school eight months ago. The first twelve went up from the ends to a veranda extending across the front of the building. From there, twenty more steps led up to a big door in the center of the upper level. She longed to see that turning door up close, but Mama had warned,"You don't go to the courthouse unless you got business there, and you'd better hope you *don't* have business there!"

Passing it today, she looked up at the magical door. There was Daddy in a line of men! Waiting to go in. Last night he'd said he'd go somewhere tomorrow...well, that's today. If he had business at the courthouse, then she had business there too, waitin' for him! She streaked across the square, keeping Daddy in sight until he went through the turning door. At the top of the twelve steps she stopped on the veranda landing to get her breath before climbing the other twenty up to the glass door. It was like a little room divided into four pie shapes. She pushed and got inside one of them. Pushing again and again, she made the door turn faster and faster while she ran in tiny steps inside. Outside, a man with a broom pushed the other way and stopped the door. "Don't play here, little girl. Go in or out."

She went in. Daddy was not in the long wide hall straight ahead or in the side halls with windows looking down on the town square with its mounted cannons pointing upward at each end of the large grassy lawn. From up here, they looked small, not big as when she rode on them pretending they were horses. But the pyramid of cannon balls in between looked just as shiny as when she stood next to them to rub their smooth black surfaces. The Rexall drugstore was across the street where she liked to spin around on the high stools at the soda fountain and catch blurry images of herself in the mirror, and where the year before she used to be taken for ice cream sodas by the men at the boarding house.The boarding house...Daddy...where was he? Where had all the men gone? She tiptoed from door to door looking through those that were open. Reaching the last open door, she heard a lady's voice and peered inside from around the door frame. Men were sitting in chairs placed around the walls and two men were in line behind Daddy. A smiling lady with silver hair looked up at him from behind her desk. "Didn't I see you in line yesterday, Mr. Clinton?"

"Yes, Ma'am, I was here." Daddy didn't look at her; he was looking at the work hat in his hands.

"But, as I recall, you were next in line. Why on earth did you leave?"

"Mrs. Inlow, Ma'am, the truth is that I heard what you said to them fellas ahead of me and I didn't want to hear you say it to me." Raising his eyes from his hat he looked at the lady; his voice hard and cold, "But that was yesterday." Norma hoped he wouldn't hit her.

"Oh, come now, Mr. Clinton, surely you don't think I'd want to shame you." She clicked her lips."I know you would work, but all the men are not like you." She raised her eyebrows and lowered the corners of her mouth like they were sharing some kind of joke.

Daddy's back stiffened, "But I am ashamed, and I'm not different from them other fellas. We're *all* ashamed we can't feed our families. If it was jus' us, you wouldn't be seein' us here, but there's others that's sufferin'. They look to us to provide for them, and we can't. They *ain't* no work, so how can we work? I hate bein' here askin' for handouts, but I had to come back. I begged once for myself, I reckon I can beg now for my wife and kids. Now, just what is it that you want to know 'bout me?"

Norma didn't know what Daddy was there for, but his voice scared her like he was mad and at the same time about to cry. She ran down the hall to the turning door, not stopping to play, and down all those steps, running until she was on the other side of the square. Safe in the Rexall Drug store, she looked back. Mama was right; the courthouse wasn't a place you'd want to go.

At daybreak the next morning, she and Joan heard a truck stop in front of their house.Through the window curtains, they watched two men walking back and forth from the truck to the porch, then stacking firewood beside the steps. "I'm scared. Get Daddy," Joan cried, then dived under the blankets. Norma ran to tell him then went back to watch out the bedroom window while he talked to the men. When they left, he picked up a big bag and threw it over his shoulder. He called to Mama and both of them began bringing things inside. When she and Joan ventured into the kitchen, the table was covered with things to eat. Mama was touching all the things as she named them, "Ten pounds of flour, five pounds of sugar, a pound of salt, a bag of pinto beans, a gallon of lard, a case of Pet Milk and a slab of side meat" She started to cry, softly, hardly making a sound, the way she always cried.

Daddy turned his head away, but not before Norma saw a strange look in his eyes, like the way his voice had sounded at the courthouse.

"Where'd all this come from?" Norma broke the silence.

"I know!" shouted Joan, "It's from the Easter Bunny."

Daddy turned to look at Joan strangely then doubled up his fist and hit the wall. Everybody jumped at the crack it made.

They had lots to eat now, but Daddy was still in a bad mood. Mama cried a lot and never sang her happy songs. They hardly ever talked to each other, not even at night when they thought she and Joan were asleep. If the good food hadn't made them happy, her news wouldn't make them happy either. The boils she'd been gettin' for months were comin' closer together and gettin' bigger. And now she had another one. Mama always watched them grow and when she thought the boil was 'coming to a head', she would doctor it with potato poultices to pull the poison out.

"How does the poison get in?" Norma asked.

"It's just there, in the blood," Mama explained,"and it's in Springtime that it comes out, one way or another."

"Does ever'body have poison in their blood?" she asked, her eyes wide.

"Probably, some more than others,"Mama decided after some thought. The first few boils hadn't been so bad and Norma was glad to be getting rid of her poison, but this new one was in a place where her bloomers rubbed it every time she moved, and it hurt more than the others. She'd have to tell Mama about it sooner or later, so she went to the darkened room where Mama was putting the baby down to sleep.

"Let me see," Mama sighed.

"It's here," Norma pointed, "where I sit."

"Come over here by the window," Mama pulled the window shade aside, "Pull down your bloomers and bend over." She looked, then pressed. "This'n is a big one. How long you had it?"

"Not long," Norma answered, "But it really hurts."

"Well, I'll keep my eye on it," Mama promised. And she did, giving a daily report, finally concluding, "This'n is gonna be the granddaddy of 'em all. I'd say it's got two, maybe three, heads, and it's takin' its sweet time to ripen." The hard, swollen hump felt hot to Norma's hand and after a few more days it was so painful she couldn't sit, not even sideways. Mama kept her home from school, applying the usual poultices and hinting at the likelihood of Daddy lancing it with his pocket knife if it didn't ripen soon.

"No, don't tell Daddy," Norma pleaded, "I don't want him to look. Please, Mama, don't tell Daddy." The word *lance* made her cringe. Daddy had used his pocket knife to open a stone bruise on her heel the first summer they lived in the new house. He had held her down so she couldn't see and when the blade pierced the skin it had hurt a lot, but it stopped the throbbing. Still, she didn't want the boil lanced; she could stand the pain.

"Alright, for now," Mama said. "We'll give it two or three more days, but after that I ain't promisin'. I don't like the looks of them red streaks."

Norma stayed in bed to let the potato pulp do its work. Joan came to keep her company. They played school for a while with Norma teaching the twos tables, but Joan couldn't get past $2 \times 2 = 4$. Next, she recited and Joan repeated: 1,2 buckle my shoe; 3,4 shut the door; 5,6 pick up sticks; 7,8 lay 'em straight; 9,10 a good fat hen. Then came "The three little kittens have lost their mittens and they began to cry", and Joan cried. Norma switched to Humpty Dumpty and Joan laughed and bounced on the bed. Their inside play was always quiet if Daddy was home because he couldn't stand noise. But today they forgot he was home. Joan bounced higher and higher until she bounced off the bed, landing on the floor with a loud thump and her laughter changed to screams. From the other room came Daddy's shout, "Stop that racket!"

Norma froze in fear, but Joan kept screaming as if she enjoyed it. Daddy yelled again, "I said cut out that racket."

"Hush up, Joan, you're not hurt," Norma pleaded, but Joan screamed even louder. Daddy burst into the room, pulling Joan up from the floor and shouted into her face, "Didn't you hear me?"

Joan stopped screaming at once, shaking in fear. "It's Norma's fault; she pushed me off the bed."

Daddy wheeled toward Norma and jerked her from the bed with one hand and with the other, gave her buttocks three hard smacks. She let out a piercing cry and slumped to the floor, blue in the face. Mama ran into the room from the kitchen with a paring knife in one hand and a half peeled potato in the other. She saw Norma hunched on the floor with her rump in the air, blood staining her nightgown. "You hit her?" Mama questioned, "You hit her on that boil? You must of busted it."

"How was I to know she had a boil? Nobody told me." Daddy picked her up, carried her to a straight chair and bent her, face down, over the seat. Mama pulled up her nightgown and pushed down her bloomers exposing the ruptured carbuncle. Daddy started for the kitchen,"I'll get somethin' to clean it with."

Norma sobbed, "You do it, Mama. I don't want him to. Please, you do it." But Daddy did it, clumsily wiping the area clean while she lay on the chair seat with all eyes on her bottom, sobbing in pain, humiliation, and anger. Joan had lied to save herself, and Daddy had believed her. She didn't want him bein' nice after hittin' her. Lots of times she'd wanted him to be nice, but he never touched her except to whip her. The smashed carbuncle didn't hurt half as much as her insides. She refused to eat the supper Daddy brought and cried herself to sleep.

Thumps on the front porch outside her window woke her and she lay listening to another handout delivery. The first time the men had left a big bag of flour, the second time a bag of corn meal; what was the big thump this time? Maybe it was a case of canned milk they left every time or the slab of side meat Mama salted down and stored in the big ice chest. She always hoped they'd leave at least one can of pineapple, but they hadn't. "Don't expect it," Mama told her. "Canned fruit is for rich people and rich people don't need handouts. Poor people eat fruit when it's in season. And no fruit is in season here in April."

"When is it in season?"

"When it's growin' on trees, and as far as I know there's not a single pineapple tree in all of Walker County--or even in the whole state of Georgia. I think pineapples grow in Hawaii, far across the waters. That's why it costs so much."

Norma's mouth watered remembering last year's peaches growing on the three trees in back of their house--Elbertas, Mama called them. The biggest peaches had grown on the spindliest tree; its branches so low she could pick the fuzzy fruit without climbing. Fifteen perfect peaches and she had eaten them in fifteen days, fuzz and all with bees swarming around her arms where the juice ran down. Daddy said that little tree was dying, and its few perfect peaches was its last hurrah, and then he helped it along by cutting it down when its last peach was gone. It grew in the wrong place anyway, he said, and there were two growing in the right place, and he needed the lower part of the half acre for growing beans and potatoes.

While Daddy brought in the handouts, Norma got Mama to go with her to the outhouse to unwind her bandage. Mama looked at her sore and

Bewitched

said it was draining well. With the cloth in place again, they returned to the house and Norma went back to sleep. She woke to the smell of side meat frying and the weight of Joan's eyes, "Does it still hurt?"

"A little." Norma sat up in bed. "I can sit better, if I don't sit on it all the way. I bet I can go to school on Monday."

"Do you want me to bring your breakfast in here?" Joan asked.

*You're just bein' ni*ce *to make up for causin' the whole thing.* "No, I can go to the kitchen." After breakfast Daddy wanted to inspect the boil and once again she leaned over the chair seat and the others gathered around for a look. Joan whined,"Why don't I get a boil? Ever'thing happens to Norma."

Sunday morning Norma waited for Dorothy to come home from church. Soon the feed store pickup truck stopped in the Swift's front yard, lent to Preacher Swift to take his family to church and now he was returning it. He hollered "Howdy" over the idling engine as Mrs. Swift heaved herself from the cab and Dorothy climbed from the bed.

"Hidy," Norma called to all of them.

"Hidy yourself," Mrs. Swift's jolly face beamed, "And how are you this fine mornin'?"

"I'm all right now, thankee. My carbuncle's nearly 'bout well. Mrs. Swift, I was wonderin' if I can play with Dorothy."

"I don't see why not. It'll be a while 'fore Bill gets back and I get dinner fixed. Run ask your Mama if you can eat with us."

At the dinner table Mrs. Swift said,"You've been havin' a lot of them boils, ain't you?"

"Yes, Ma'am."

"Ummm," Mrs. Swift offered her more dumplings and gravy. "You been takin' any sulphur and molasses?"

"No, Ma'am."

"Drinkin' any sassafras tea?"

"No, Ma'am."

"How's that baby brother?"

"I don't know, Mrs. Swift. He sure cries a lot."

"What's his name again?"

Norma swallowed her mouthful of food and took a deep breath, "Thomas Traggo Clinton."

Preacher Swift laughed right out loud,"That's sure a mouthful. No wonder the little fella cries."

"We don't call him that, sir. We call him Tommy."

"That's good. I thought maybe he cried on account of that big name."

"No, sir. He cries 'cause Mama puts him down."

"He couldn't be a mite spoiled, could he?" Mrs. Swift winked. "I 'spect your Mama's mighty proud of that little boy and jus' likes holdin' him. It don't take long for a baby to figure that out." Mrs. Swift dished out canned peaches on to all the plates. "These here is some of the peaches off'n your Daddy's peach trees. Your Mama gave 'em to me last summer. She said they'd jus' spoil, all gettin' ripe at the same time, and her with no jars to put 'em up in. You be sure and take her a couple jars when you go home and tell her thankee again from me."

"Yes, Ma'am, I will. They sure taste good the way you canned 'em."

When she left for school Monday morning, Daddy was already in his garden weeding in between arrow-straight rows of sprouting vegetables. And when she returned, he was putting down stakes for the tomato plants. Daddy spent all his days in the garden from sunup to sundown. He never sat on the porch anymore; after supper he went to town.

While Daddy worked in the garden and went to town, Mama cleaned house, washed clothes, and cooked meals always holding Tommy in her arms. At night she slept in the kitchen in the rocking chair with Tommy leaning on her shoulder because his crying kept Daddy awake. Sometimes Mama let her hold him. "Why does he cry all the time, Mama?" she asked. "Is he spoiled?"

"Spoiled?" Mama snapped, "No, he's not one bit spoiled. Where'd you get such an idea as that?"

"Mrs. Swift says when babies cry, it's because they want attention."

"Well, you jus' tell Mrs. Swift to come look at his face. She'll see mighty quick he's not cryin' for attention; his ears hurt and they hurt most when he's laying down. That's why I hold him, to keep his head high."

When Norma told Mrs. Swift why Tommy cried, she put down her dishrag, dried her hands, patted her silvery hair into place and crossed the yard to the Clintons. She talked with Mama, took a look at Tommy, then left. She came back with a bottle of warmed camphorated oil and put drops in Tommy's ears. In a little while, he was sound asleep in Mama's bed. Mrs. Swift turned to leave. "Oh, by the way, Mrs. Clinton. That's sassafras bark in the bag. I'll bet you're plumb out of that too. Might not hurt to boil up some tea to give Norma ever' now and then; might help with them boils."

With the oil for Tommy's ears and the tea for Norma's boils, things got a whole lot better around the Clinton house.

8

May was ending, as was Norma's first year of school. A year in which she had found another world under the care of a kind teacher. Mrs. Deariso had presented new ideas and Norma soaked them up as parched earth soaked up rain. And what she learned, she took home. "You're learning for all of us," Mama told her proudly.

Mrs. Deariso was firm but fair, always pleasant, always patient. Her classroom was filled with beautiful things: fresh flowers in pretty vases, pictures on the walls, sea shells and colored rocks on the window ledges, things Norma had never seen before. Just before Christmas, she showed the children how to make a paper Santa Claus. His pink face was topped with a red hat, trimmed with cotton fluff and a ball of cotton at its tip. Cottony eyebrows almost covered his round black eyes, his cotton beard was full and long. His red suit had a big black buckle to match his black boots. All morning the children worked, cutting and smearing the sweet smelling paste, following the guide lines drawn by their teacher. Norma hung her Santa on her bedroom wall, its only adornment. It represented one of the happiest days of her life.

Mrs. Deariso's hair was in finger waves all over her head, and Norma longed to place her fingers, all four at once, in their shallows, and she wore soft, fuzzy sweaters, silky smooth dresses, and high heeled slippers. One dress was the color of ripe peaches with a woven belt of the same color, knotted in front with fat pompoms hanging from its two ends. Whenever Mrs. Deariso leaned over to help her, the pompoms sometimes rested on her desk. Oh, for just one squeeze! And how good she smelled, every time she came near, Norma got a whiff. Never had anyone or anything smelled so good until Mama's sweet peas started blooming. "Just like my teacher!" Norma exclaimed. "What makes 'em smell so good?"

"It's a kind of perfume Mother Nature gives flowers." Mama smiled, "I had a bottle of perfume, myself, once. Your Daddy gave it to me jus' before we married. He liked sweet smellin' things too."

"What d'you do with perfume? Wash with it?"

"No, it's too strong, a little goes a long way. You jus' put a dab here and there, behind your ears, on your neck, or wrists. That's why it lasts so long. My bottle lasted a year. I put on the last few drops right after you was born." Mama's eyes sparkled.

" Tell about when I was born," Norma begged.

"Oh, you've heard it lots of times; you probably know it by heart."

"But I like to hear you tell it." She settled down beside Mama who was mending socks, stretching them over a light bulb she'd brought from the boarding house. She bit off a length of thread, wet her fingers, touched them to it, put the thread through the eye of the needle, knotted it, all in one swift movement."When it was time for you to be born, my oldest sister Thelma came to be with me. It was near the end of June and scorchin' hot. It hadn't rained in weeks and not a breath of air was stirrin'. About noon time Thelma sent your daddy to town for the doctor. They came back about an hour later. Dr. Porch looked at me, said it'd be a long time yet, and left. He kep' comin' and leavin' ever' few hours until the next day. It jus' got hotter and hotter in that bedroom. I thought for sure I'd burn up. Jus' when I thought I couldn't stand it one minute longer, a lightnin' storm came up and thunder was a-crackin' ever' other minute. Dr. Porch got back to the house jus' before the sky opened up and rain poured down in bucketfuls. The wind blew the rain in on me through the window and all of a sudden, there you was, a six pound baby girl. It was 5:15 P.M. on the last day of June. You was Thursday's child. I'll never forget the blessed relief that rain brought. Thelma sponged me off after the doctor left and I put on the last of my perfume. I even put a dab on you."

"And what did Daddy say when I was born?" Norma asked wistfully.

"Not much," Mama's eyes and her needle were on the sock.

"But what'd he say *exactly?*" Norma knew, but she hoped each time the answer would be different.

"He said, 'Maybe next time you'll do me the favor of havin' a boy'. "

"And what did Aunt Thelma say?" Norma leaned forward, eyes sparkling.

Mama's eyes sparkled also like always when she answered that question. "Thelma said, 'Clarence, you ought to be ashamed of yourself. You've got a lot to be thankful for with this fine healthy baby, even if it is a girl, and I might add, the *first* granddaughter out of six grand babies! I know lots of folks that's gonna make this little girl welcome, and I'm one of them.' " Mama smiled behind her hand, "Thelma always did stand up to your Daddy, but she was the only one that did."

"And what did Daddy say?" Norma's eyes danced.

"Well, he didn't say a thing to Thelma, but to me he said, 'She'll be goin' back home in a few days then Bob Bruce can listen to her bossy mouth.' " Mama sighed along with a shrug of her shoulders, "But your daddy had the last say. He didn't name you after Thelma but after his sister Louise and that picture show woman Norma Talmadge. My sister Ruby came when Joan was born so she was named Ruby Joan...after her and another picture show woman Joan Blondell."

"What did Daddy say when Joan was born?" Norma already knew.

"He said, 'Not another heifer!' " Mama blinked then closed her eyes.

Norma said quickly, "Don't tell Joan he said that," then she asked, "Is that why he whips us, 'cause we're girls?"

Mama frowned, "Course not. That's not why...he didn't use to whip you...but *now*, he's got things on his mind." Mama sounded tired. "You're big kids and you're noisy...if you could jus' be quiet 'round him...when things get better...well, then ever'thin' will be better."

"Tommy's a boy. Why can't Daddy be happy?" Norma asked sadly.

"He's got things on his mind I told you! If he could jus' get some work and make some money." Mama jabbed the needle into the sock.

"We don't need money now. We get food on the front porch."

Mama looked at her sharply, "I hope you don't go tellin' that around."

"No, ma'am."

"Good. Your Daddy wouldn't like it if you did." Mama finished the socks, balled them into pairs and put the light bulb into her sewing basket. "Jus' two more days of school, young lady. I tell you what, in the mornin' 'fore you go to school, we'll pick you a bunch of them sweet smellin' flowers to take to your sweet smellin' teacher."

Norma was satisfied with a small bouquet but by the time Mama finished picking, the vines were nearly bare. The blue, pink, and lavender blossoms made a bunch so thick Mama cautioned, "Don't hold 'em so tight, you're gonna squeeze the stems right off. Hold 'em with both hands."

The blossoms reached to her nose and Norma breathed in their sweetness on her way to school, sure of one thing. The two mile walk now seemed a lot shorter than it had last August when she first laid eyes on her school house sittin' up on top of the hill way off from the street.The flagpole was halfway up the hill and surrounded by evergreen shrubs and a concrete sidewalk like the hub of a wheel. Four spokes branched off to the corners of the huge lawn. In winter after a rain, when the temperature was freezing, the hub was like a round skating rink. The bigger kids were able to make it around and off onto one of the spokes. Others went skiddin' on their backsides, the way she had , but even that had been fun.

She always ran up the sidewalk beyond the flagpole to the six steps leading to the arched entrance and the huge glass-paned doors, hinged to open in both directions, in and out. Sometimes they played 'war' with those doors, kids on the inside pushing against kids on the outside, like armies on a battlefield. She had been one of the 'soldiers' though not always in the winning 'army'. Then the doors were locked to the early arriving students, and they could only stand outside and look in on the teachers going up and down the hallway, in and out of the classrooms, everyone waiting for the school bell to ring... The school bell was ringing, the doors were opening, and the students were flooding inside. She came out of her reverie and raced up the sidewalk, semi-circled the flagpole, on to the steps and to the swinging doors just as the last students disappeared inside. One door swung toward her and she thrust her hand forward to stop it, missing the door jamb, striking the pane broad-handed. The glass broke with a sharp crack. She wasn't hurt by the flying glass but stood frozen in fear. *Look what I did! I'll surely get the belt for this.* The second bell brought her to life and she ran to her classroom, pushed the flowers into Mrs. Deariso's hands, and fled to the safety of her seat.

She struggled through the morning in fear, but nobody came for her. No one even mentioned the broken pane. At recess, she was drawn back to the spot. The floor was swept clean and the jagged glass was gone from the door. The day dragged by while she wondered what to do. Should she wait and tell Mama? Yes, she'd do that. But at home, she thought she should tell Mrs. Deariso. Yes, she'd do that.

She spent a miserable night huddled beneath the bed sheets believin' her whole world had changed. This was the worst thing she had ever done, damagin' school property that Daddy would have to pay for, with no money. She knew she wouldn't even be in school except for the first time in Georgia history school books were free. If school had cost even one penny, she couldn't go. Daddy had said so. And now, she had broke the glass. She was afraid for tomorrow to come. But tomorrow came. She went to school with heavy steps, dragging her feet up the sidewalk, around the flagpole, and on to the swinging doors. When she dared to look, through half-closed eyelids, there was a new pane in the empty place!

Just before noon, Mrs. Deariso said, "When I call your name, please come to my desk for your report card." Norma's turn came and the teacher gave her a big envelope explaining that it held another paper for her to take home. She took the envelope and returned to her desk in absolute terror. At dismissal, she lagged behind and barely mumbled her farewell. Mrs. Deariso hugged her saying, "Good-by, Norma, good luck, and thank you for the lovely bouquet."

The distance home also seemed shorter than before even if she walked at a turtle's pace. Mama was waiting. Arriving at her side Norma fumbled in her satchel for the big envelope, handing it over in dread.

"Why so solemn, young lady? And what took you so long gettin' home? Why, it's sealed!" Mama exclaimed. "Did you see it before your teacher sealed it?"

"No, ma'am." She said, staring at the death sentence.

"Well, let's open it," Mama broke the seal and took out the report card, reading it on both sides. "You've been promoted to second grade, but that's no surprise with all those A's. Miss Padgett's your new teacher." Mama looked inside the envelope and pulled out another paper, a big one. "Look, it's got a seal, with a purple ribbon, and it's signed by your teacher and the principal. Well, I'll declare, it's a certificate for gettin' all A's in Deportment. We expected you to behave in school and be a credit to your raisin', and I reckon you are."

Norma stared at Mama, then bolted through the open door, not stopping until she was on her bed, curled into a ball. When the school people came to get money for the glass, they'd take back the certificate. But they could have it. She didn't deserve it. Worst of all, she'd never get to second grade. She'd be dead soon after Daddy found out about the money he'd have to pay because she'd been so careless. Her nights were sleepless; her eyes dark-rimmed and she jumped at the slightest noise. Mama said, "I expected you to miss school, but I didn't think you'd lose sleep over it."

Norma decided it was time to tell and take her punishment, no matter how awful it might be. Taking a deep breath she blurted to Mama, "I did something bad at school. That's why I can't sleep. I didn't mean to do it."

"Don't beat around the bush. *What* did you do?" Mama eyed her anxiously.

"I broke the glass in the schoolhouse door."

"How on earth did you do that?"

"I meant to push on the wood but my hand slipped and hit the glass."

"Let me see your hands!" Mama looked and saw no injury, "You was lucky. Was anybody else hurt?"

"No, ma'am."

"When did it happen? What did your teacher say?" Mama sounded like the woodpecker again.

"It happened before school stopped and I didn't tell nobody, but somebody already put in new glass."

"Well, then, the matter's settled, I guess. They're probably glad nobody was hurt. Broke glass is easier to fix than broke skin." Mama didn't even bat an eye.

Norma's relief couldn't be described. She felt light as a feather and soon was running again, instead of walking, even when she carried water in buckets to the tender green shoots in the garden. There were no weeds because Daddy had taught her how to pull them out without disturbing the growing vegetables. The garden was his pride and joy and everybody that passed would stop and say, "Ain't no need to have arrow straight rows, but they sure are a pretty sight to see. My, my, your Paw must be a mighty particular man, mighty particular." Norma agreed, glowing with pride at their praise of Daddy.

Summertime set in with its attendant heat. Sometimes showers brought relief and settled the dust. And if Mother Nature didn't, county trucks with their water tanks and sprinklers did with Norma and Joan running behind getting wet along with the road. With July, the heat increased. No one could sleep until the late night air cooled things down. Grownups sat on the porches and rocked. Children ran around after dark catching fireflies, storing them in covered jars, watching them blink on and off in their transparent prison cells until bedtime, finally releasing them.

Cove Road had one street light where Reservoir Road joined it at the Clinton property line. Its giant circle of light brought children from a quarter mile away, black and white alike, to play games on the grassy lawn after dark on those hot nights. Games of hide-and-seek, crack the whip, slinging statues, and stiff starch. Norma liked stiff starch most of all and she and Dorothy were the undeniable champions of the game. Joining hands, facing each other and leaning backward as far as their extended arms allowed, they turned in a circle as fast, and for as long, as they were able to stand. Then they fell to the ground and watched the spinning world slowly wind down. Then they got up and did it again. Some nights these games went on as late as ten o'clock until the various signals from parents beckoned their youngsters home.

When August heat bore down, the children escaped it by playing underneath the houses, crouching on the cool, damp earth, shooting marbles, playing jack-stones, mumblety-peg, pick-up-sticks, or tiddlywinks. The big event of those August afternoons came when the iceman delivered the fifty-pound blocks of ice. He'd chip off hand-sized pieces for the children to lick like unflavored popcicles. On one very hot afternoon, Norma and Joan took their ice and climbed to the lower limbs of the cottonwood tree pretending they were looking down on their kingdom. They soon stopped licking the ice and started rubbing it over their arms and faces. "It's coolin' me down," Norma giggled.

"Me, too." Joan agreed, pointing skyward, "Lookit--the sky's yellow!" A sudden wind gust blew the back screen door open, banging it against the house. Wash tubs sailed through the air. Chickens were squawking and flying about. Sheets on the clothes line were flapping. The sky darkened and white streaks of lightning preceded sharp claps of thunder. Mama ran out the back door shouting, "Hurry, hurry, get the sheets off the lines before the rain starts!" The girls jumped from the tree gleefully snatching at the sheets, jerking them from their pins. Dragging them behind, they raced to the house, getting inside just as hail slashed at the door.

The cyclone had hopscotched its way across the football field behind the high school, uprooting the massive oak along side the brick building and slamming it against the northwest corner of the upper story. Part of the wall and roof was torn away. Daddy was hired to repair the wall and wouldn't take pay for his labor since his daughter attended the school. He told them at the supper table. Norma's face was shining as she met Mama's eyes. Neither said a word. Mealtime was for eating, not talking. She could be happy now, thanks to Daddy, she and the school were even.

A week later Norma was a second grader and Dorothy a first grader, escorted around by an experienced guide who pointed out the dangers of the swinging doors, showed off the girls' bathrooms, and the wall Daddy had fixed after the cyclone. And she could walk right up to the glass-paned door without feeling guilty. The year whizzed by, summer vacation came and went, and she was back in school, a third grader showing Joan in first grade around the place.

Joan didn't do well while Norma got her usual straight A's which meant a free ice cream soda at the Walgreen Drug Store at the Square. Each month on report card day, the names of the eligible students were written in white poster paint on the mirror above the soda fountain. Those being rewarded sat inside at little round tables and sucked their sodas through straws while the unfortunates stood outside on the sidewalk looking in. Not Joan. She went inside to share her sister's soda, and with her vigorous pull on the straw often got more of the soda than Norma.

Mama was wearing those funny dresses again like before Tommy was born and her waistline had disappeared. Norma watched more closely. Sure enough Mama got bigger and bigger around the middle. Now, she knew that babies didn't come from stumps as she had been told, but from *stomachs*. She was so proud of this discovery that she told Dorothy who right away told her mother. Mrs. Swift went straight to Mama, and Norma got a spanking for talking dirty. "It may be dirty," she sobbed, "but it's true." Mama didn't deny it. Soon Julia was born and Mama's stomach wasn't big any more.

9

Julia grew so beautiful, with her curly brown hair and huge brown eyes--the rest of the family had blue or green --that Norma lived in fear someone would steal her. When the Lindbergh kidnap trial made headlines, she was certain of it. Mama said nobody kidnapped poor children, but when Aunt Grace sent cousin Beverly's outgrown Shirley Temple dresses to Julia, Norma was sure people would think they were rich. Mama said kidnappers knew when dresses were hand-me-downs, and Norma shouldn't worry. But she worried just the same. Her premonition of loss was valid but it was Dorothy not Julia who was taken away.

For six years Norma and Dorothy had been best friends. In the beginning they played at being cowboys riding around on broomstick horses, their bare feet flying low over the sedge grass hills and valleys. Growing older they organized the neighborhood kids into clubs, taking turns being the leader, jubilant in their reigns of power. In between riding the range and forming clubs, they fashioned a make-believe boarding house in the floor of the pine grove behind their homes, piling fallen needles into room dividers, and taking in 'boarders', and having revival meetings in their make-believe church.

Later, they played at being teachers, herding the younger children into classrooms in the cow shed, passing on what they had learned. From radio programs and an occasional motion picture they learned about acting and gave plays, making up plot and dialogue as they went along. For costumes they raided Mama's big, gray trunk for her clothes from better times--from the Twenties, Mama said-- and found fancy dresses, high-heeled slippers, purses, a string of beads, and a long silk scarf. The scarf was long enough to wrap them both at the same time and sometimes that's what they did, wrapping themselves back to back like Siamese twins, each wanting to go her own way but having to settle for only looking opposite ways. This act pleased the kids most of all and even the grownups howled with laughter or felt sadness depending on the story.

They were explorers, discovering the creek banks where poke salad thrived and pools where crawdads swam. They knew the places along the railroad tracks where the biggest coal lumps fell from swaying freight cars; these they gathered and carried home to the hearth fires and potbellied cook stoves. When each season yielded its particular fruit, they were there for the harvest. In summer they carried home plump blackberries from the most inaccessible briar patches and juicy plums fallen from heavy-laden trees. In autumn, they found hickory nuts with the paper thin shells that could be cracked without smashing the meat inside. At Christmas, they led their daddies to the fullest, most perfectly shaped cedars to be axed and dragged home. In springtime, they filled May baskets with long stemmed violets, purple ones, and the rare whites with purple centers, as big as half dollars, to give to their mothers.

In their third summer together, the girls got brave enough to venture into the depths of the forest a mile from their homes. They followed the narrow, silent creek through the denseness where other children were afraid to go. With good reason. Norma and Dorothy had seen snakes slithering away as they jumped back and forth across shallow water, landing on the spongy moss-covered banks. One day as they rested on the soft, green cushion, looking up through the tall tree tops to the blue sky above, Norma thought of making a magic carpet. Not there, where the moss grew but close to home where at night they could sit on it and look up at the stars and moon. They chose a shady spot in Dorothy's yard and began transplanting the moss, keeping it watered until it took hold. By summer's end they had two spots large enough to sit on; a year later the spots had joined into one large mossy cushion. More transplanting increased the size until they could stretch full length upon their green oasis. Surrounded by barren soil, it was quite a striking sight and became their special place for sharing hurts, joys, and secret dreams. They did more: they traveled in fancy to all the places near and far that they had ever heard about. They sailed the Seven Seas, explored the Poles, rode the Pony Express, swung like Tarzan from jungle trees, swam in tropical lagoons, danced with Salome and her seven veils, and rescued baby Moses from the bulrushes. They were Chinese princesses with bound feet, Indian maidens kidnapped by cattle rustlers, or Florence Nightingale on the battlefield. They arrived at Plymouth Rock with the Pilgrims or went as missionaries to darkest Africa. They were as rich as the Rockefellows or as poor as hoboes who rode the rails. They played with Shirley Temple, danced with Fred Astaire, ice-skated with Sonja Henie, and rode with Roy Rogers and Gene Autry. Their happiness was complete with no idea that it would ever change until, at sunset one day in June, Dorothy called Norma to their meeting place with something to disclose. With bowed head, she fingered the short green tufts of the magic carpet and split their world in two. "Daddy says we're moving to Tennessee. We're goin' as soon as we can get packed."

Through the following days they were like sleepwalkers, meeting at the no longer magic carpet, mostly to stare at the moss, hardly talking. When they did, each word left a dozen unsaid. "I'll write you every day," Norma promised, knowing she had no money for stamps. "I'll come back and visit you," Dorothy promised, knowing she had no way to do it; she didn't have wings like Norma's swallows.

The terrible, final day arrived. The big moving truck parked at Dorothy's house. Norma stared at it for a time, then went to Mama's trunk where they kept their treasures, the things they used when they played 'dress up': a string of glass beads, a deep blue scarf fringed on each end, and an embroidered cloth purse with a brass clasp. Norma held the beads to her throat, then placed them around her neck, smoothing the scarf across her shoulders, carefully straightening the fringe. Then slowly, purposefully, she removed the beads, wrapped them in the scarf, and put them inside the purse and closed the clasp. Going next door, and finding Dorothy, she pressed the gift into her hands. It was all she had to give, except her heart, and she had already given that.

"No, I can't take it!" cried Dorothy.

"You have to," Norma's eyes swam with unchecked tears,"But don't open it until you get to Tennessee," and turning, ran as fast as she could toward home, never looking back. She rushed into her bedroom and covered her ears with a pillow so she couldn't hear the moving truck drive by, carrying Dorothy away.

For awhile, Norma went to the vacant house and carried water to the carpet. When the new neighbors moved in, she asked them to dampen the moss, but they were unfriendly and didn't care at all for the beautiful green spot. And their hungry-looking hounds growled when she went close enough to see the carpet dying in the heat. The sight of the dried brown moss hurt almost as much as the hurt she felt inside. Her family said her

Bewitched

sadness would pass, but it didn't, and a sore erupted just below the hollow of her throat soon to become an inch across and growing. Mama used her poultices but the sore didn't respond. The doctor came but he couldn't help. Neighbors talked about the strange affliction. One day, a colored crone, too old to walk unaided, came with a companion to the back door, saying, "Ole Alma gwine tuh hep Miss Norma."

Ole Alma wore a turban around her head. Some people said it was because she had no hair. They said she was a witch. "Beware her eyes," they warned. But when Norma looked into those deep, serene eyes she felt that Ole Alma could see right inside her, right into the enormous emptiness. And with her fingers, warm and gentle, though old and twisted, Ole Alma rubbed some honey-colored oil, which the younger woman said was healing oil, into Norma's sore. Ole Alma said not a word, and it was just as well because people said she talked a funny talk. She rubbed the oil, talked with her eyes and when she left, she took the oil with her. After seven days the spot began to heal and Ole Alma came no more.

When Norma ventured next door to look at the carpet, there was no sign of it. The ground had returned to its normal state just like the skin on her throat. She went next to the dense forest to walk the length of the silent stream, sit on its mossy bank and look up to the sky through the trees. Before leaving, she lifted a tiny piece of moss and held it to her heart, then let it float downstream. At peace, her vitality soon returned along with the color in her cheeks. Her eyes were luminous pools of blue above a dimpled smile. On the outside, she was herself once more. Inside, in her secret self, she would never be the same. Something had closed around a precious memory, closed like the clasp of an embroidered purse on its contents, never to be opened again.

On November 28, 1940, Norma became a woman according to Mama. It was the punishment of God, visited upon all womankind, because Eve had eaten of the forbidden fruit from the Tree of Knowledge. It was hog killing day when Norma made the discovery. She was sick of the sight of blood, but she was a little bit pleased too that now she was like the other girls, still it would be another year before she had any reason to wear a bra.

'Becoming a woman' elevated Norma to another station. Two days before Christmas, Mama said, "You know about Santa Claus, don't you?" She had a way of talking with her eyes, eyebrows, and a twist of her mouth, and Norma knew what she meant. "Then you'll have to help. Bryan's delivery truck will be bringin' things for Christmas and storin' them in Mrs. Wallin's back room until tomorrow night. You'll have to keep the other kids from seein'."

That Christmas Daddy got her the roll-top desk she wanted more than anything in the entire world. Maybe it was because she had been so sick when Dorothy left. She just couldn't believe he would do that for her. She sat at her desk all during the holidays, writing and rewriting her school assignments until they were absolutely perfect. Then she locked them in the drawer. For the first time in her life, she had a private place all her own.

'Santa' brought Joan a scooter, Tommy a big, red wagon, and Julia a red and white tricycle. It was the best Christmas ever. Norma had the added joy of being Mary, mother of Jesus, in the Drama Club's Christmas play in her first year of high school. She thought it was because of her very long hair which fell almost to her waist. But no more. During winter vacation, she'd cut it to shoulder length and that probably saved her life. On a freezing January morning, while standing too close to the fireplace her flannel nightgown ignited, blazing upward to her hips before she was aware of it. Her attempts to slap out the flames failed and, responding to a voice in her head, she ran to smother them in Mama's bed. Her right thigh and both hands were badly burned as well as Mama's prize-winning appliqued bedspread.

Norma's charred fingers looked as though they would never again hold a pencil and the fear of that was a greater pain than the burned flesh. Writing was a big part of her life, her expression: stories, letters to aunts, cousins, and pen pals promoted by her teachers. One pen pal lived in Oslo, Norway. Egil Ellingson had written only three letters before his country was invaded by the German army, and he never wrote again.

Two weeks of bed rest and good care healed the burns and a week later she regained full use of her fingers. Missing those weeks from school had been a revelation. More than ever she realized the separate worlds she lived in: the one on Reservoir Hill and the one at school. Books, movies, and radio had introduced her to other, far away worlds. And through her letter writing, a loving Providence had allowed her to know Harry and give her the best world yet. And today, yes, this very day, she would leave one world for another, stepping from an often sad and painful world to one of who knows what? Except for one certainty. She was the center of Harry's world and it was a wonderful place to be! She jumped up to go to him, at that moment seeing the back door open with him holding it for Julia and Mary Lee. He waved to her and she started down the hill. They met half way, his eyes examining her curiously, "Are you all right, Honeychild?"

"I'm fine." She smiled, taking his arm. "Now, I'm better than fine."

"Your mother is preparing a tremendous breakfast. We wondered where you were."

"I was saying good-by to my hill." She rose on her toes to brush his lips with hers. "But I'm not hungry--for breakfast."

He winked at her, "You will try to eat, though, won't you? For your sake as well as hers?"

"Of course. I know that's how Mama shows her love...with food. And she's a very good cook to boot."

Eating had always been serious business in their family and today Norma was thankful no small talk was expected. No one spoke except in passing and receiving biscuits, ham and gravy, eggs, or butter and syrup. Harry's enormous appetite pleased Mama and she kept urging him to 'take seconds' three or four times. When all the dishes were empty, Norma rose to clear the table, but Mama said, "No, leave 'em. I'll have all day to do 'em and I'll be needin' somethin' to keep me busy..." her voice trailing off.

Everyone walked to the front room. A car horn signaled the arrival of Harold Martin and his wife. Harry carried their luggage to the car. Norma looked around and saw everybody and everything with a sudden clarity. The plain, nearly bare house that had been her home for almost as long as she could remember had its place in her heart and would always hold good, as well as unpleasant, memories. And her father, remote and dictatorial, stood non-threatening to her now. By changing her name to Harry's, she had become another person and both she and Daddy knew it. They were now on different footing and whatever each of them might be feeling, neither was moved to acknowledge it, except to know that it had happened. Then quite surprisingly, Daddy opened his wallet, removed a ten dollar bill, and with a flourish handed it to her. "This might come in handy," he said, his face aglow with generosity. Norma accepted it remembering when, only a few months ago, she had been sick from working and had to cash the war bond from Harry to pay her doctor bill. How welcome some help would have been then, when she hadn't any money at all. But all she said was, "Thank you, Daddy, I'm sure it will."

Joan, barely sixteen, and Tommy, eleven, waited self-consciously until time for a brief embrace. The greatest wrench of parting came from Julia and Mary Lee, both like her own children.

"I want you to stay," Julia cried. "Please, don't go."

"My little dark-eyed beauty," Norma held her close,"I want to stay, but I want to go. Remember when you sat with me while I wrote to Harry and you asked me why I wrote him every night?"

Julia looked up into Norma's eyes, nodding.

"And what did I tell you?" Norma asked softly.

"That you loved him, and it was our secret."

"That's right, and I love you, and I'll write to you too...will you write to me as he did?"

"I can't write very good," Julia lifted her pinched little face to Norma.

"I'll tell you what. When I get a house in California, I'll write you and I'll expect you to write back. Will you? Promise? Cross your heart?"

Julia crossed her heart and finished the saying, "If I don't, I hope to die."

"Now give me that hug and kiss. Ummm, so nice. I'm going to miss my good helper."

"Come back, Norma, promise me you'll come back, " Julia pleaded.

"I promise," Norma's tears fell on Julia's upturned face. *The memory of another parting, years ago, flooded her mind...Dorothy...*

"Cross your heart?" Julia's face brightened.

Norma crossed her heart. "Now give Harry his big hug and kiss."

Julia had wholeheartedly accepted Harry and hugged him mightily. Mary Lee followed her example and planted a sloppy kiss on his lips.

"Well, Mama," Norma looked at her tight face,"It's time for me to go." Sometimes she felt that she was the mother and Mama was the daughter, a victim of life, Daddy's will, and her own lack of self-confidence even though she was a good homemaker. Mama stood stiffly, always embarrassed by a show of emotion. Norma held her tightly nevertheless.

"You're going so far away, I wonder if I'll ever see you again." Mama put her fingers to her trembling lips.

"I'll bring her back, you can be sure of that," Harry promised. To Norma he whispered,"Don't prolong this, Honeychild. Everyone's suffering." He guided her to Martin's car and in a moment they were riding away with Norma looking out the car window, waving until she lost sight of her family standing in a row on the front porch. The set, hopeless look on Mama's face and her empty eyes hurt Norma most of all. She had seldom seen her parents happy and her own happiness seemed somehow wrong. Struggling with unspeakable sadness, feeling cut in two, she gripped Harry's hand like a vice. He drew her to him and holding her close, they began the long journey west.

WAIT FOR ME
PART TWO

SEMPER FI

In La Fayette, Harry sent his sixth telegram to Marine Corps Headquarters and then the Martins and the Kipps headed for the Georgia state line at Cloudland and crossed into Alabama. The silence was comfortable; each being occupied with his own thoughts, strangers in some ways until eating and searching for motel accommodations forged common bonds. Norma was disappointed at crossing the mighty Mississippi River in darkness. They crossed Louisiana in the same darkness and reached the Lone Star State just before dawn. Finally in Marshall, Texas, they found a motel vacancy.

"Who would ever imagine that everyone in the United States was traveling west?" Harry asked as he and Norma stretched out in bed after eighteen hours of riding, alone at last. She discovered that her monthly cycle had started, right on time and with none of the usual warning cramps.

After twenty hours more of driving, they slept in El Paso, then again in Yuma. On their fifth day of travel, they crossed into California just after noon. At the dunes in Winterhaven, Norma asked Harold to stop the car. She ran up one dune and down the next in absolute abandon, laughing, scattering sand, slipping and sliding, holding a shoe in each hand. The others watched in wonder at the young lady who had begun the journey in sorrow who now was so happy.

"Come join me, Harry," Norma coaxed from the top of her high dune. "You can't imagine the beautiful view from up here!" He climbed up to her and together they stood on the golden sand, her arms tight around him. "I'm so happy. I love the sand dunes, and I love you!"

Three hours later they were registered at Tops Motel on Pacific Highway in San Diego. After a final dinner together, the two couples said farewell, Harry settled the bill, the Martins left for Santa Monica, and the Kipps moved into their cottage behind the restaurant. With four days remaining of his leave, Harry did not send a wire to Marine Corps Headquarters; instead he sent one to Norma's parents.

Monday morning while Norma washed her hair and soiled clothing, Harry went out to buy a car. He returned with a 1942 two-tone green Packard Clipper touring sedan with red and green plaid seat covers.

"It's gorgeous!" Norma exclaimed, examining it from front to back. "And green, my favorite color. Please take me for a ride." Harry drove along the bay then north on Highway 101 at thirty-five miles an hour to 'break in' the brand new engine, he told her. But only for the first five hundred miles.

Tuesday night he took her to the Pacific Ballroom but couldn't persuade her to dance. "I've never danced with a man. Back home people thought it was a sin. I've only danced with girls--and then I led--you'll have to teach me to follow."

"Then will you have a cocktail with me?"

She took one sip, screwed up her face, and pushed her drink over to him,"It tastes awful, like medicine. Besides Daddy says drinkin' is a sin...smokin' too."

"I don't think it objectionable for a woman to smoke, but I'm glad you don't."

"And I don't cuss either,"she laughed,"not a single bad word. My parents never allowed it. It was absolutely taboo. When we got mad enough to cuss, we had to say *Shoot* or *Dad-blame-it*. I doubt that a bad word could pass my lips, especially one that uses God's name. That was the worst sin of all. To even hear it makes me cringe, like a blow to the ears. Daddy said our soul would die little by little if we said God's name in anger, or even heard it. Harry, darlin', I'm so glad you don't cuss."

He stared at her. Almost spoke, but didn't.

"Don't worry," Norma touched his arm, "I'm not as strict as Daddy is, but a lot of his teachings have stuck with me. I hope you won't hold that against me."

Harry covered her hand with his, squeezing it gently, "Norma, don't even entertain such a thought. You are exactly the woman that all my life I've dreamed of," his voice grew husky,"I always knew you were somewhere in this world and some day I'd find you."

On Halloween Eve while Norma dressed for dinner, Harry left to buy an evening paper. He returned with the San Diego *Evening-Sun,* reading the headline MARINE, BRIDE, GEORGIA TAXI ALL MISSING.

"I wondered what was happening in the rest of the world," he chuckled. "Apparently the Marine Corps has a problem. A missing Marine...and bride...sounds a bit like us, doesn't it, Honeychild?"

"Maybe, except for the last part. We're not missin'."

"It seems the Corps thinks we are." Harry stated. "This *is* about us!"

"Oh, Harry, quit teasin' me. Of course it's not about us." Norma dismissed his comments and reached for her purse. Turning, she saw perplexity cross his face and stepped closer. "It can't be true...unless it's a Halloween trick, but who..?" Her eyes looked where he pointed. There on the front page in a two-column spread was the story.

Marine, Bride, Taxi, All Missing

San Diego, Oct. 30-Take two newlyweds, a taxicab, $750, the 3000 miles of distance between La Fayette, Ga. and San Diego, the Marine Corps, and mix them all together. Then lose track of them all, except the Corps, and you have the mystery which is puzzling officers at Camp Pendleton. It all began because Capt. Harry E. Kipp, of Silver Creek, Minn., returned from overseas, was in love and married the girl with whom he had been corresponding for twenty months. Then, the captain and his bride, the former Norma Clinton, of La Fayette, Ga. took a honeymoon trip through the Great Smoky Mountains. His leave ran short and the couple returned to Georgia to leave for Camp Pendleton.

Orders Changed

With things regarding trains and reservations as they are, the couple couldn't get out that way. So, as anyone would do when street cars, buses, trains, and planes are not available, the dauntless captain called a cab. With the stipulation that the meter stop at $750, the newlyweds, taxi and driver, Harold Martin, also of La Fayette, took off for San Diego. Now they all have disappeared. If they get here, the Marines at Camp Pendleton have a distressing surprise awaiting them, because Kipp's orders were changed ordering him to report at midnight tomorrow to Marine Corps Schools, Quantico, Va. which is just two stop lights and three policemen from Georgia.

Telegram Puzzling

Speculation at Pendleton is running high that the captain received word of the change of orders and has turned back. But in a telegram to his brother in La Fayette last Saturday, Martin said that Mrs. Kipp had been ill and their next stop probably would be in Phoenix. State agriculture inspection men on the California border have seen nothing of them, and the public relations officer at Quantico reports that Kipp is expected there tonight. Which he is, as far as the Marine Corps is concerned. But does Kipp know it? Uncle Sam and Cupid could be near the breaking- off- of-relations point.

"My goodness! What if my parents hear about this? They'll be worried sick. This newspaper story says I was ill. Why on earth would they print a lie? Why would they print any of this? Please, Harry, send another telegram and let Mama and Daddy know we're all right."

Harry's concern was with his reported change in orders. His calls to Camp Pendleton for clarification met with consistent busy signals. "I'll have to go there. This can't wait until my leave is up."

"Why didn't the Marine Corps let you know before we left La Fayette? Didn't anybody read the telegrams you sent?"

"Apparently not. I'm at a loss to understand any of it. If there was a change of orders, *who* opened and read them and then notified the press?" Harry snapped his fingers against the newspaper.

"And why do they say you hired a taxi?" Norma asked in disbelief. "What a silly idea...all the way across the country... it makes you sound goofy. And when do you suppose Harold sent a telegram to his brother? and why?This is so crazy. I hope you get some answers at Camp Pendleton tomorrow."

Harry returned with two pieces of news. "It's true; my orders were changed to Quantico. But they have been rescinded and for the time being, I'll remain at Pendleton. And there are no quarters for us, however a major in Personnel is vacating his rental place in Oceanside for ten days and offered it to me. We can move in after five today."

The upstairs apartment over a garage was on the Strand, near the municipal pier, and completely furnished. All they needed was food and ice for the ice box. From the living room, through the large window, they looked down upon the wide beach and out to the dazzling sun, setting on the blue Pacific, and listened to the unceasing roar of the surf. "This is paradise!" Norma exclaimed, popping a grape into her mouth. Grapes in November! And fruitcake and cheese, foods she never ate in La Fayette in any season.

When darkness hid all outside except the lights on the pier, Norma closed the blinds and Harry dealt a hand of cards. She was learning poker-- another sin, she informed him--with beginner's luck. A few hands later, he was shivering in his skivvies, grinning in surprise, telling her that if he caught pneumonia from losing at strip poker, he'd never live it down.

"You're lettin' me win," she accused.

"Why would I? Don't you think I'd rather see you than show myself?"

"Then instead of takin' off, you can start puttin' on. We'll call it dress poker." But her luck changed and soon she sat shivering.

"Let's call it a draw, Honeychild, and try out the shower, then hit the sack. Your old man joins the working force tomorrow. No more burning the midnight oil for us."

He rose at seven the following morning and left Norma sleeping. At ten he was back and found her sunning on the beach. She sat up when his shadow fell across her face. "Harry, darlin'! What a nice surprise. You're back so soon."

"The CO gave me the rest of the day off. Come inside and I'll explain." Upstairs he spread three different newspapers, each with stories of the missing Marine and his bride. "Look at this file the first sergeant made from clippings since this whole thing started a week ago. It's because of this that I'm back and we're having visitors in an hour."

"Who's comin'? We don't know anybody here."

"No, but they know us...or want to...a reporter and a photographer from the *San Diego Union*. We're giving an interview--by orders of the Commanding General of Camp Pendleton. I'm sorry, Honeychild. I've no choice. I was ordered to put an end to the story; he thinks the only way is to grant an interview and allow photographs."

Norma's stare shifted from the newspaper clippings to Harry's exasperated expression as he explained, "All lines into the base are jammed with journalists trying to get tips on my whereabouts; little military business can be conducted. After proof that we're no longer missing, perhaps the story will be laid to rest. The sooner we do that, the better. By the way, they wanted to come here for the interview and pictures." Harry jabbed a cigarette into his mouth, lit it, and after a pull, let out a stream of smoke. His eyes were narrow glints of blue steel under the severe line of his brows.

She didn't blame him for being mad; she was furious herself, getting more so as she scanned the clippings from the *Tribune-Sun, Los Angeles Times, Herald-Examiner,* and the Oceanside *Blade Tribune,* all from the Associated or United Press dating as far back as October 26--two days after they had left La Fayette. Each caption was more repugnant and baffling than the last: "Where's Kipp? New Game in the Marine Corps"; "2,500 Miles Off Course After $700 Taxi Trip"; "Is They Is, or Is They Ain't?" Over a high school picture of Norma was printed "Taxied--And How!"

"Where'd they get this picture?" she cried. "Why I was just sixteen! Only Mama has a copy of it. And here's Harold Martin propped on his "Coast to Coast Taxi" covered with dirt and back home in La Fayette from his 6,000 mile trip. Famous taxi, indeed! And it wasn't 6000 miles. It was 4400 miles." She pushed the folder toward Harry, her eyes flashing. "They don't have your age right either, or your middle initial, and look at this ridiculous cartoon of you with your captain's bars like wings handin' a grizzly cabby a stack of bills about a foot high, sayin' 'Keep the change'! And this one, "Honeymoon Taxi, About Face! Surprise (Not on meter) Awaits Couple", and "Captain, Bride, Cab Reported Bound for San Diego Still Missing." Norma's voice had almost reached screaming level. "This is so humiliatin'. I wanted to announce our marriage when we got settled here. After this, what would be the point? They've robbed us of that." Her voice trembled in rage.

Harry snuffed out his cigarette. "Goddammit to Hell! If I could get my hands on who's responsible for this..." He saw Norma flinch at his obscenity, cupping her hands over her ears. "Forgive me, Honeychild. I won't say that again ...in your presence." Taking the folder, he tossed it across the room, "Come here, little sweetheart. Let's try to calm ourselves. They'll be here soon. You should get dressed. Just think what they'd do with a picture of you in that fetching bathing suit."

At precisely eleven o'clock, Harry opened their apartment door to the two newsmen. Upon seeing Norma dressed in a tailored suit and high necked blouse, the photographer chuckled, "I had something frilly in mind with you two in bed."

"You are insultin'," Norma gave him a chilling stare. "I'll have you know this is not our idea or I would refuse to let you take our picture after that remark." She turned to the reporter with a challenge in her voice, "We are decent people and this sensational story is full of untruths. Now that you are finally talkin' to the people involved, maybe you can get the facts straight and print *them*." She whirled to the photographer, "Put down your camera. I won't let you take a picture in our home."

"How about in a car?" he asked, slightly more respectful.

Downstairs Norma was told to sit in the passenger seat with Harry standing at the open door ready to help her from the 'taxi' they were supposed to have hired. "This is as false as most of the story," she glared.

"You're too sensitive, Mrs. Kipp," the reporter replied. "This is a delightful story; the public's eating it up."

"At *our* expense. And *story* is a good word for it!" she snapped. "Where I come from *story* means lie. I'll never again believe what I read in a newspaper, at least not all of it. I used to think the printed word was the gospel; you've ruined somethin' precious for me," she said, close to tears. "Good afternoon, gentlemen. I'll leave you with my husband so you can get on with the interview."

After the newspaper men left, Harry joined Norma upstairs, "I'm delivering some records to the Artillery Range. Ride along with me." He drove through the main gate onto Camp Pendleton and along Vandergrift Boulevard for miles before they turned off to the boondocks as Harry called this stretch of desolate terrain. No life was in sight until they came to a settlement of long, low, prefabricated buildings situated on a rise of land. "Wait in the car, Honeychild. I'll try not to be long."

There was nothing to do, nothing to see but the dry, barren landscape and far off in the distance a series of red banners. Numerous rumblings reminded her that he had called it the artillery range. She noticed a manila packet on the front seat. Had he meant to take it with him? No, she guessed not. It was his medical records. The cover bore his name, rank, and serial number. She loved his name: Harry E. Kipp, Captain, 09066. Nice numbers. She pulled out the contents and began to read. Date of birth: 3 June, 1899. She blinked. What? *1899!* It should be 1911. That's quite a mistake. Surely he had noticed it.

Harry returned and climbed in beside her, looking at the pages in her hand and the question in her eyes. His were alert, searching...and fearful?

"So you read it. Good. I hoped you would. Now comes the moment of truth." His expression was guarded.

"1899?" Her tone incredulous.

"Add three years to that. I lied to enlist at fourteen."

She mentally added, then subtracted, "But that still means you're 43, like the newspaper says!"

"True."

"But you wrote 34 on the marriage license!"

"I lied again, clever fellow that I am!" His eyes a bit more daring.

She thought for a minute, then smiled. "Not really, you just reversed the numbers. Why didn't you tell me before?"

"Before what?"

"Before we married."

"I didn't think you'd marry me, and I wanted to prove to you that we could be happy, that we were right for each other."

They studied each other's eyes.

"Wasn't I right, Honeychild? Tell me I was right."

"Yes," she agreed. "You're right, my darlin'. *Your* age doesn't matter to me anymore than *mine* matters to you. We are what we are, I think, regardless of our age. And I am so very happy...except for this business in the newspaper. Maybe today you got it all straightened out."

The final edition of the *Tribune-Sun* carried the interview, with accurate quotes from Harry, and a two column photograph of the couple on page one.

Marine, Bride Arrive, Doubt 'Missing' Tale
Failure to Find Couple Laid to Cab's Paint Job

"I began to wonder if I was really missing," Marine Capt. Harry E. Kipp, 43, said today after a 2200-mile trip by taxi which brought him from La Fayette, Ga. to San Diego where he found his orders had been changed to Quantico, Va. Kipp, who married Norma Clinton two days after they met after twenty months of correspondence, took the taxi after train and plane reservations were unavailable. The couple, Harold Martin, driver, and his wife, left La Fayette Oct. 24 and arrived here Sunday. When they could not be contacted on their cross-country trek, they were reported as "missing". While everyone was looking for a taxicab with the usual gaudy paint, Martin's cab was a plain two-door Chevrolet with an ordinary paint job, which is probably the reason it wasn't spotted. "I wish they had seen us and told me about the change of orders," Kipp said. "I'd rather be in Quantico since it is only a few hours from my wife's parents."

The trip, Kipp said, cost only a little more than $500 which is close to the regular pullman fare. On the way across, they drove from La Fayette to Marshall, Tex., a twenty hour hop, because no rooms were available. The fast time was made by Kipp and the driver changing off at the wheel. The next leg of the trip ended at El Paso where they stayed overnight. Their next stop was at Yuma.

The couple had been staying at Top's Motel but now are temporarily living in a beach cottage in Oceanside. Kipp and his bride checked in at Top's Motel, 2137 Pacific Highway, on Sunday. Mrs. Bessie Kenyon, one of the operators, said they moved from the motel yesterday. "They certainly acted like honeymooners," Mary Robertson, a maid at the motel, said. "But the girl was terribly homesick."

Kipp has been assigned to the boat basin at Oceanside as a gunnery instructor until the Marine Corps can get a clarification of his orders. He has been in the Marine Corps 22 years and served with the 3rd Amphibious Corps Artillery.

The Oceanside *Blade* ran the article on page two. "I think they listened to you, Honeychild," Harry sighed gratefully. "Although I felt a bit sorry for them. You were mighty fierce."

"It paid off, though, didn't it?" Norma laughed gleefully.

TAXI RIDERS HUNT HOME
* * * * *
Captain Kipp and Bride Tell of Long Trek

OCEANSIDE, Nov. 3, (Special)--Marine Capt. and Mrs. Harry E. Kipp, the "galloping ghosts from coast to coast", reported wearily here today that their 2200-mile post-honeymoon dash by taxicab from La Fayette, Ga. was a breeze compared with fighting the Battle of Oceanside. The captain and his bride are hunting a place to set up housekeeping while Kipp is on duty at Camp Pendleton. Kipp, who won the Bronze Star while overseas with the Third Amphibious Corps, admitted that the search had him "about whipped." But Mrs. Kipp said she still had hope.

The couple became a center of national interest last week when it was disclosed that they had left Georgia by taxi in a race against time to arrive at Camp Pendleton before Kipp's leave expired. Newsmen throughout the southwest intensified a watch for the travelers after it was learned that Kipp under a last-minute change of orders was expected to report at Quantico, Va., instead.

The captain explained today that it was a "small town" taxicab--an ordinary sedan bearing no distinctive markings- and the driver, Harold Martin, was accompanied by his wife. This, he said, apparently accounted for the fact that they arrived in San Diego this week without having been spotted. Actual cost of the journey, made by taxi because no train nor plane reservations could be obtained, was about $500, Kipp said. Until the mix-up in his orders is cleared up, the captain will be on duty as gunnery instructor at the Camp Pendleton boat basin.

The San Diego *Union* morning paper carried the same article, but the three column photograph had been altered. From the hem of Norma's skirt, a large pie-shaped slit exposed a portion of her leg above the knee. Her fury spilled over, "That photographer intended to cheapen our image no matter how he did it. We ought to sue him!" She stamped around the room kicking at the newspaper.

"Leave it alone, Honeychild. You can't win against the press. They always have the last word. It all will die down soon; they'll find another story to exploit and forget about us...and we can forget it too." But the story was repugnant to them; they felt violated, their marriage tarnished by sensationalism. Yet the Sunday paper spread was worse still. Apparently Norma's parents had been interviewed and the story of the courtship by mail, Aunt Jean's part in it, and private talks with her mother after the honeymoon had been misquoted and spread over an entire page of the magazine supplement with a picture of her that only her mother could have provided. A letter from Mama confirmed that the reporter had been Luke Martin, from the Chattanooga *Free Press,* and a brother of Harold Martin.

"That explains a lot," Harry said. "Still nobody wants to admit to opening my orders," he scowled until he read Julia's letter.

> Dear Norma,
> I read about you and Harry in the paper and I saw your pichurs to. My techur said you put La Fayette, Georgia on the map. Do you have the map? I'd like to see it. Write me back. I love you cross my heart. xxx Your sister Julia.
> ps My techur said hi.

Norma remembered that sweet letter whenever they were stared at or accosted by people who recognized them wherever they went, and she longed to be 'unrecognizable' again.

11

As Harry predicted, the story died down. And about that time they moved from the beach apartment into temporary housing in a Quonset hut on base. These huts were made of curved sheets of corrugated steel which formed the sides and roof in a half-circle over a composition wooden floor. Acres of huts squatted side by side in rows so close together and with walls so thin that conversations within could be heard by those passing in the narrow alleys separating them. Two families to a hut, one in each end, were wrapped inside the rounded roof like larvae in a cocoon.

Camp Pendleton was teeming with Marines returning from the war, uniting with their families or creating new ones, like Norma and Harry, and thousands of single men attempting to adjust to stateside duty and life again among females--reckless, careless, loud young men not always honoring military decorum. Norma knew little about military decorum, but she did know about and expect common courtesy.

Public transportation was strained to the limit and the roads were lined with hitch hiking service men. Whenever she and Harry went to Oceanside or San Diego from the base, he never drove past Marines thumbing for a ride. Four could crowd into the rear seat of their sedan and he always filled it time after time, even though some seemed unappreciative and even rude, getting out without a thank-you, or making crude remarks about the speed Harry chose to drive, or using profanity in front of her. She saw Harry's jaw tighten but he said nothing and signaled her to silence. Later he would tell her, "Try to understand their situation, Honeychild. They're just youths suffering from battle fatigue and deprivations, thrust back from war into a world they've forgotten how to live in. Give them time; they'll adjust." He was forced to remember his own advice when often in restaurants these 'deprived youths' stopped at their table and invited her to leave with them. Any rejoinder only served to lengthen the contact, so they pretended not to notice and continued eating and drinking or talking to each other until the offender went on his way.

Harry told her that the best way to gain control over a situation was to first gain control over oneself. "Why is it," she asked, "that the burden always falls on the responsible people?"

"Because they are the ones who really run the world, and the others...well," he sighed, "we just have to bear with them."

Some evenings, after they ate in Oceanside at the White Front Cafe, the two strolled up and down Hill Street window shopping. Norma looked but showed little interest in anything until she saw the music box that played "Tales of the Vienna Woods". She listened several times through then returned the box to its place. The next time they were on Hill Street, she asked to see it. Jane, the sales lady and their neighbor in the hut across the alley, said it had been sold and there wasn't another.

"Why didn't you buy it the night you saw it?" Harry raised her downcast face with gentle fingers.

"It cost too much, I thought," Norma answered, "and I have one already, remember? One is enough, but it would be nice to have another Straus waltz."

"Honeychild, when you see something you like, tell me. Don't you know that I like to get you things to make you happy? You never ask for anything, so how can I know what you like if you don't tell me?"

Norma shook her head, "It's all right; I'm satisfied with the one I have, really I am."

He had observed her nightly bedtime ritual with her music box, playing it just before she went to sleep. This night he said almost to himself, "You must indeed love that little box; many times you mentioned playing it while you wrote to me, and you wouldn't leave it behind in La Fayette. Tell me, is it the tune that pleases you so?"

"No, even though I like the tune, that's not the reason." She smiled suggestively. "It's because of who gave it to me."

"Tell me, then, who it was," his voice tightened.

She looked at him strangely. "Please, tell me." His voice was choked and the light had left his eyes. "I want to know."

Kneeling on the bed before him, she exclaimed incredulously, "I can't believe you don't know!"

" Believe me. I don't," he murmured so softly she could barely hear.

"Why, darlin', *you* did!" She took his somber face into her hands. His eyes searched hers in bewilderment. She dropped her hands to his, grasping them tightly. "Remember the Christmas gift money you sent and asked me to buy something for myself and pretend it was from you? Something to remind me of you once in a while until you could come and take me in your arms? Those were your very words. Well, the music box was what I bought. I wrote you about it."

She watched his face as comprehension took hold, saw its expression change from gloom to joy and sparkle return to his eyes. "I swear to you, I never received that letter. How I wish I had! Darling, I hope you'll forgive me, but I have almost been jealous of your little music box."

"Forgive you? Why, of course, except for not askin' sooner. To think that you have suffered with this and I had no idea. Oh, Harry, my sweet darlin', forgive me. If you weren't so upset, it would be funny." She picked up the box and began to laugh a little. "It *is* funny!" Her laughter increased. She wound the key and let the tune begin, holding the box out to him, "Your rival!" and she fell over onto the bed, doubled up in laughter. And with the mystery solved, he began to laugh too. For a while the bed shook with it, and then they were quiet, clasped in a tight embrace. She whispered in his ear, "Don't ever doubt that there isn't, and never will be, anything for you to be jealous of. I give you my word on that."

The music box mystery was solved for Harry, but the mystery of her speech remained for Norma. Everywhere she went, she was asked to repeat herself, sometimes twice. Often people gathered just to listen to her talk. She thought she spoke plain English; they acted as if she spoke a foreign language. She wasn't so sure she was going to like these California people. She knew for sure she didn't like the flat, brown and barren landscape, so unlike the green mountains of north Georgia. No wonder everything looked dead; it hadn't rained one time since they'd been here.

Well, no matter what the surroundings were, she had Harry! Life with him was just one day of joy after another. He made her happy with his kisses and caresses, his kindness and calmness. He was never cross or critical no matter how badly she cooked or if she slept until he left for work. That happened often because they were always up late playing cards, or talking, or making love, usually all three. Each morning they'd vow to go to bed earlier, but when night came and Norma came into her own--his moonchild, he called her--they would stay up until midnight again.

They'd been unable to buy an alarm clock, just one of the many things unavailable in postwar times, until a shipment came to the Post Exchange Annex in the Quonset housing area. Norma and twenty other hopefuls waited outside for the doors to open, telling of their desperate need for a clock. Unfortunately there were only six for sale, so names were drawn. She wasn't one of the lucky six, but a Marine winner offered his to her. Thanking him gratefully, she wouldn't accept it. He persisted; she refused still, saying, "You need it as much as we do."

At suppertime, Harry answered a knock at the door and Norma heard a familiar voice, "Good evening, sir. Please accept this with my compliments." Harry returned with a small square package.

"It's the clock!" She cried, clapping her hands in joy.

"Perhaps you want to tell me about it, Honeychild," he grinned.

"I was goin' to surprise you with a clock, but I didn't get one today at the PX. A Marine who did offered his to me. It had to be him at the door! Isn't this wonderful? Now you won't have to depend on the light shinin' through the high window to wake you."

"It seems he had no difficulty understanding your charming drawl," Harry mused.

"Yes, as a matter of fact, he did. I had to tell him everything twice," she sighed, "but he was a gentleman, like you. He didn't laugh at me." They finished eating, cleaned up the kitchen, played a game of gin rummy, then prepared for bed. After Harry set the alarm in their new clock, Norma lay in his arms silently--unusual for her. At last, he asked, "What's troubling you, Honeychild?"

"Nothin', " she answered. Then turning and propping on her elbows she repeated, "Nothing," emphasizing the end of the word. "I'm going to change my way of talkin'...I mean talking." She laughed. "I'm going to talk faster, like you, make my *r's* harder, and put the ending...see, I did it...on the *ing* words. If I forget, will you remind me?"

"If that's what you want, but remember--it's your idea, not mine. I love you just the way you are. But promise me something?"

"I promise. What is it?"

"Change the way you say loving, if you wish, but please don't change the way you do it."

Early in December Norma went Christmas shopping in Oceanside with a group of Marine wives. Harry wanted a studio picture of his bride, the bride who had missed her November period and who sometimes was nauseated in the mornings. On this day she hoped it held off until she sat for proofs. A week later when she viewed them, she was happy that she didn't look sick but not one showed the dimpled smile Harry loved, and there wasn't time for a retake if a portrait was to be ready for Christmas giving. She chose the least somber one and ordered an enlargement for Harry and small ones for her family.

When the order was ready, Harry drove her to Hill Street and parked near the Service Studio. "Wait in the car,"she commanded. "I don't want you to see the portrait until Christmas morning." Harry waited and watched as crowds of Marines gathered before the studio showcase window, entered, came out, and left. This scene repeated itself several times until Norma exited the studio and started toward the car. A throng of excited, shouting Marines, jostling each other in eagerness, immediately encircled her. The exuberant herd advanced with her in the middle pleading for them to let her pass. Seeing this, Harry leapt from the car, forcing his way into the center. At sight of him, the Marines broke into salutes and scattered in all directions leaving Norma alone on the sidewalk, close to tears. Harry pulled her to him, "Honeychild, are you all right? What was going on?"

"I don't know," she cried, huddling against him. "Those Marines wanted a picture of me...or a date...they wouldn't take no for an answer."

"I don't understand," Harry said. "What caused that stampede?"

"There! There in the window," she pointed toward the showcase display. Harry stared in amazement for a moment then said, "Wait in the car...No, stay with me." He walked closer where, in a sort of shrine, he saw, hanging by itself, a large portrait of Norma delicately tinted, matted, and framed. Her slightly tilted face, surrounded by a cloud of hair, was filled with innocence yet a mysterious promise in the full, closed lips. The pleading eyes held both a question and its answer. The total countenance exuded a yearning, irresistible appeal. Harry stood immobilized, his eyes riveted to the portrait until like an arrow long held in the bow then released, he shot into the studio aiming for the man behind the counter. "That portrait, the one in the window. I want it."

"Sorry, Captain, not for sale. And you're not the first to ask. It's brought all kinds of offers since I put it there a few days ago. We've had hordes of Marines in here wanting the name and address of the mystery lady..."

Norma moved from behind Harry and took his arm. The salesman gaped, "I get the 'picture', Sir," he blurted. "You bet! I'll sell it to you, and I congratulate you, Sir." He moved at once toward the display window.

"The negatives, too!" Harry commanded.

"Sure thing, Captain."

On the drive home she sat silently, holding the two portraits, the eight by ten unframed one she had ordered and the twenty by twenty-six framed one he had bought. She stole a look at Harry's unreadable face, looking straight ahead attending to his driving. Timidly she asked, "What are you thinking? Please, tell me what you're thinking."

He turned, a half smile softening his face, "I'm thinking what a lucky man I am," and delight filled his eyes. "I've got the portrait *and* the lady! And I'm feeling sympathy for those hapless Marines; how can I blame them? I fell in love with your picture, too, remember? Also, I'm thinking of asking you to refrain from having pictures made, unless I take them."

"But do you really like it? I look so sad, not smiling the way you wanted. You didn't buy it just to get it out of the window?"

"Like it? You ask if I like it? How can I answer? Let me try." He pursed his lips and rubbed his forehead with his fingertips, then he rolled his eyes and winked. "Mystery lady, you'll just have to wait and find out!"

Christmas Eve came with two surprises. First, a steady drizzle at dawn increased to a steady rainfall by evening. Second, Harry was assigned to officers' quarters at Sterling Housing in Oceanside. Theirs was a downstairs unit in a building of eight apartments in a row of many rows on Bougainville Street. They moved into 926 Apartment B in the rain after dark. Their perfect little Christmas tree with its homemade yarn pompoms was carried inside under an umbrella. It was December 24, exactly two months since they left La Fayette and already they had lived in four different places. But this was a permanent home, a perfect Christmas gift. They set up the tree, put their gifts beneath it, and went to bed to the sound of rainfall patter on the window panes. *Another gift. Oh, how much she had missed the rain!* She stretched her arms upward, "Look, I can't touch the ceiling."

He snuggled close, "You're not missing the low curve of the Quonset hut, are you?"

"Did you know that I could practically feel it pressing down on me in the dark?" she asked him. "No, I'm not missing it one bit."

On Christmas morning she found, tucked away beneath the lowest branch of the four foot blue spruce, a small package wrapped in a most masculine manner. Its size and shape, and Harry's twinkling eyes, signaled its contents. "How on earth did you find it?" she squealed, tearing away the wrapping.

"I didn't find it; I bought it that first night you played it. I asked Jane to put it away for me. I drove over to Oceanside for it one day at noon."

"It's been in the house all this time? How could you keep it a secret?"

He laughed, "It wasn't easy, but I salved my conscience by giving you an allowance to use whenever you saw something you wanted--and Honeychild, it was worth the restraint just to see your eyes at finding my Christmas surprise for you."

December 24 held another surprise. By then Norma had missed two periods and believed she was pregnant. In January doctors at the Santa Margarita Naval Hospital confirmed it, and her morning sickness extended into an all day ordeal. She controlled it by lying flat in bed day after long day. To help her pass the time, Harry brought home a photograph album, mounting corners, white ink and a pen for labeling. She propped the album on her raised knees and spread the photographs about her on the bed: baby, school, and family snapshots, those she had sent him in letters and those taken on their honeymoon. One photograph she didn't want to include was of a high school pen pal from Oslo, Norway. She put it aside to throw away later. When the album was completed, she shared it with Harry, telling about each picture, and letting her fingers linger on those of Julia and Mary Lee. "You miss them, don't you?" Harry asked.

"Yes," she answered, "I've lots of time to think."

"How long do you suppose this nausea will last?"

"Not too much longer, I hope. Sometimes I feel better at night, Maybe it's because you're here."

"Do you feel up to a drive? We could stop for a seafood dinner at the Captain's Mast. They have the best seafood around."

She savored the salad and consommè but the sight of the whole trout--with its glazed eye staring up at her--brought on an attack of nausea that sent her to the restroom. By the time she rejoined Harry, his plate was empty. She walked out without another look at her plate, and at home, lay in bed still and silent until she fell asleep. She woke the following morning alone except for a note from Harry propped against the lamp base.

He returned from work, unusually quiet, warmed a can of beef and vegetable soup and took two bowls to the bedroom. They ate it with buttered bread and no conversation. Harry read the newspaper, listened to the radio for a time, and then came to bed, turning away from her. She felt miserable, believing he was upset over what happened the night before. Suddenly the soup was on its way up; bent double, she rushed from bed to the bathroom to let it come up violently into the wash basin. Harry came to hold her up, wash her face and neck, and carry her back to bed.

"Don't be mad at me," she sobbed into his shoulder. "I hate being sick, but it's because of our little baby."

"Is it?" He placed her in bed and sat with his back toward her on his side of the bed. "Or is it because you wish you hadn't married me?"

"Oh, Harry," she moaned. "How can you ask me such a question? Of course I don't wish that. I love you. I'm happy to be your wife and to be having your baby even with this horrible sickness. I know it will stop soon...it just has to." She reached to surround him from behind, resting her head on his back. "Please, don't be mad at me," she entreated. "What can I do to stop you from being mad at me?"

"Answer this question," He turned to face her, causing her arms to fall from him. "Why did you marry me if you wanted someone else?"

"I don't!" she cried. "I don't. There has never been anyone else. How can you think there was?"

"Because of this." From beneath the lamp base he took a photograph of smiling Egil Ellingson standing beside a snow-banked house.

One glance at it and Norma fell back on her pillow. "Oh," she said. "Where did you get that?"

"I found it, under your pillow, two nights ago."

"It must have slipped there when I was working on the photo album.

It was with the pictures I brought from La Fayette and I didn't want to put it in our album. I meant to throw it away--but I lost it, and then forgot about it--now you can throw it away!"

Harry looked at Egil, shook his head, and started for the waste-paper basket. He stopped and turned to her,"You're sure?" A slow smile forming, "Absolutely sure?"

"I'm sure, positively one hundred percent sure! If only I could get rid of this queasy feeling as easily."

But the queasiness did not get better. It worsened. Norma couldn't retain food long enough to be nourished, Harry feared. He searched markets and restaurants for foods she liked, hoping that some or one would stay down. Often he had to hold her over the basin when vomiting attacks overcame her strength. Then the worst possible thing happened. On Friday, black Friday, Harry got orders to the U.S. Naval School of Justice at Port Hueneme, California for a two week course beginning Monday. As far as Norma was concerned, Port Hueneme, one hundred sixty miles north of Oceanside, might as well be to China. And two weeks might as well be forever.To her it was doomsday. Harry frantically arranged with Jane, their neighbor from Quonset days, to stay with her and then stocked the house with food. He left late Sunday afternoon. Norma waited and waited but Jane never came. Feeling sick and abandoned, she cried herself to sleep. The delivery of Harry's telegram woke her early Monday morning.

SA 11 NL PD=PORT HUENEME NAVAL BASE CALIF JAN20
MRS. H E KIPP
926 B BOUGAINVILLE ST OD=
ARRIVED FIVE O'CLOCK WILL WRITE LATER TAKE CARE OF YOURSELF LOVE HARRY

Norma dressed in a robe and sat on the step of their front stoop just to have some contact with the world she felt was slipping away. The early morning sun was warm and soothing. Neighbors discovered her, surprised that she lived there, since from her arrival she had remained inside in bed. They brought broth, crackers, and jello to her for every meal. And between meals she lay in the healing California sun.

Harry's letter arrived Tuesday. The first letter addressed to Mrs. H.E. Kipp, that beautiful name, the dear handwriting. And once again she was looking at the Marine Corps emblem on his stationery: the Globe, Anchor, and Eagle, fighting men on land, at sea, and in the air.

8 P.M. Sunday

My Little Honeychild,

    I am already in bed and have a terrific headache, but I couldn't sleep if I didn't wish you a good night and tell you "I love you."

    I hope you and Jane are finding a lot of things to 'gossip' about so the time will pass quickly for you. If only I could know that you are well and being cared for, I wouldn't mind anything else in the world, but Norma darling, I'm worried about you. You were so upset about my having to leave you! Don't let it get you down, sweets, I'll be back soon. Did you get my telegram?

    From the very little I've seen of this place so far, it doesn't look very promising for you to come up here with me. It is really tucked away in the back country. I got lost a couple of times and I think I could have taken a shorter route. Had to drive into the sun during the last hour or more and that put my headache into high gear. It will be all right by morning, though.

    We had butter-beans for supper but I could hardly eat them knowing how very much you'd like some. Oh! my darling! My heart is crying to be with you now. You were so sweet and lovely when I left you. Did you know that I nearly cried before I could leave? Good night, little sweetheart. I love you! I love you more than ever before! Harry.

    Wednesday night at nine o'clock, Harry walked through the front door, having left Hueneme when his class finished at six. He found Norma in bed, flushed from her days in the sun, writing a letter to him. "Honeychild, You look fabulous! What happened? Where's Jane?" Hearing that Jane never came, he swore under his breath, then dropped to his knees, "My darling, I'd *never* have left you behind if I'd thought for one minute you'd have been alone. I swear it! You believe me, don't you?" He held her at arms length to look into her face, then sighed in relief, "But I see that you managed to help yourself; tell me, what happened?"

    She told him of their caring neighbors and the friends she had made. "God bless them," he said, "but I promise I will find a place near Hueneme and take you back with me this weekend." Their days at Ventura, near Hueneme, were like another honeymoon except on this one, they went shopping for maternity clothes. And a week later on Sunday, they left Port Hueneme with Norma reading Harry's reward for two weeks of school:

U.S. NAVAL SCHOOL
NAVAL JUSTICE

This certifies that

CAPTAIN HARRY ERNEST KIPP, USMC

Having successfully completed the studies required and passed the examinations prescribed in Naval law, the Naval Judiciary System and Procedures, Charges and Specifications, Naval Discipline, Evidence, and the Fact Finding Bodies

is Awarded This Certificate
This 2nd Day of February A.D. 1946

(Seal)　　　　　　　　　Chalmers E. Jones, Jr.
　　　　　　　　　　　　　　Lieut. Comdr., S (L)
USNR
　　　　　　　　　　　　　　Officer in Charge

12

Norma had never imagined that cooking could be such a challenge. Growing up, her duties had been caring for the younger children, not helping to cook. And Mama had made it look so easy. Besides, their meals had been very different from what Harry liked to eat. Steak, to her, meant tough beef pounded tender, with the edge of a saucer, battered in flour, and fried in grease. The steaks he ordered in restaurants were thick slabs surrounded by fat, grilled on the outside and juicy on the inside, and covered a large platter. His other food preferences were as foreign to her as the steak. Most she'd never heard of and had no idea how to prepare. She asked for help from other Marine wives, bought The Good Housekeeping Cook Book, and applied herself diligently. Harry didn't complain while she was learning. He ate whatever was placed before him, so long as it wasn't lamb, saying that to know she was doing her best was nourishment enough for him. By the time he invited Colonel Nickerson for dinner, she was confident her skill was sufficient not to disgrace either herself or Harry. While sunbathing on the afternoon of the appointed day, she told the other wives of her dinner plans.

They all shouted in chorus, "You're having Harry's colonel for dinner and you're lying here so calmly?!"

"I've got plenty of time," she assured them, "It takes only two hours to cook a meal and he's not coming until six."

"How can we help? Maybe lend you serving dishes?" Bonnie asked.

"No, he'll just have to take us as we are. He must know things are hard to get."

"But aren't you nervous?" Leona leaned toward her, "A colonel?"

"Should I be?" Norma asked. "Harry thinks we'd be doing him a favor by having him for a home-cooked meal."

"Is that what he said?" Wilma asked.

"He said Colonel Nickerson liked to eat and I should fix a lot of food."

And she did. The oven and all four burners were necessary to cook it. The meal began with Harry's favorite tomato juice cocktail, then a lettuce and pear salad, followed by oyster stew. Meatloaf, green beans and new potatoes simmered in bacon grease, creamed corn, and cornbread followed. Mince pies, Harry's request for dessert, were put into the oven when the meatloaf and cornbread came out. They ate and ate and ate. Norma took the pies out just in time for serving. The colonel took his first big bite while the steam was still rising. His eyes popped open wide and tears ran down his crimson face. He spat the pie into his hand a split second before Harry emptied his mouth. "I was afraid you weren't going to do that, Sir!" he exclaimed, reaching for a glass of water.

"I couldn't stop myself, Harry. I know I'm called Iron Mouth when it comes to hot coffee, but I couldn't handle that pie; it set my mouth on fire."

When the evening ended and Colonel Nickerson took her hand at leaving, he said, "Thank you, Mrs. Kipp, I've seldom been so completely satisfied with a meal. I hope to have the pleasure of coming again."

At sunbathing time the following afternoon, Norma's friends clamored to know the outcome of her dinner for the colonel. All she told them was the truth, "Harry was proud of me."

He was also proud of the clothes she was stitching by hand for herself and the baby which required many hours. He wanted to buy her a sewing machine. Since none could be found in stores, they turned to newspaper ads and bulletin boards. In all of Oceanside there was only one sewing machine for sale: a cabinet model converted to a portable and fitted with an electric motor. It vibrated across the dining room table, but stitched well. It was overpriced, but Harry bought it.

Late in February Norma felt the first flutter of life within her. She expected their child, due August first, to be born in California where it was conceived, but unknown to her, Harry had requested a two-month leave and a duty station closer to Georgia. Both were approved with the leave effective 29 March and orders to report to Parris Island, South Carolina on 29 May. They didn't have much to pack for the move and the Marine Corps would have to ship only two barrels and a bookcase. The sewing machine would go with them. She looked around the empty apartment, seeing it as it had been on that rainy night three months ago when they moved in. But that was with her eyes; seeing it with her heart was different. How many others, like them, had moved in and out of these four rooms? and left good friends behind? She pressed her head into Harry's chest and shut her eyes tightly against the tears. Words couldn't pass the constriction in her throat.

"Remember how you jumped up and down like a jack-in-the-box when I came home with our orders?" he asked. "Now, you're so sad."

"The going I like; it's the leaving that makes me sad. If we were leaving the Quonset hut, I wouldn't feel so heavy-hearted, but from here--Oh, Harry, I know I'm going to cry when we say good-by to everybody." She cried and so did they, wishing them a safe and pleasant journey.

One last time they drove down to the beach, past the pier and their first home in Oceanside, then to US 101 through the little beach towns and on to San Diego to take 80 East, the route that had brought them West five months ago. She had left Georgia on this very highway that had crossed the Mississippi River and the Rio Grande. She had stood beside a giant saguaro in the Arizona desert, run barefoot over the ivory colored dunes near the southeastern border of California, waded in the blue Pacific and conceived a child in rhythm with its pounding surf. She had seen the palm trees of Ventura, driven through the Hollywood Hills, and visited the mission where the swallows returned on St. Joseph's Day. She had made friends from many states of the union, and she was a member of a very large family known as the United States Marine Corps. Best of all, she loved and was loved by an extraordinary man, the man of her dreams, one who she had been scoffed at in her youth for believing would come her way; the kind of man she vowed to wait for until she found him or he found her, and Harry was that man. Norma reflected on this and the changing landscape, from her pillowed back seat, riding eastward the two hundred or so miles that Harry drove each day in the springtime of 1946. The trip was uneventful until they reached Alabama on their tenth day. The noontime heat and high humidity were oppressive, and judging from the bumpy streets, there must be nothing but railroad tracks through Birmingham. Her back was hurting terribly and she remembered the doctor's warning of a risk of miscarriage if she took the trip by car. She had promised to be very careful because they wanted this baby. "Please, Harry, stop the car. Now, right here! I have to get out and walk!" And she walked, back and forth, back and forth, beside the car with Harry beside her, white-faced with concern. Then, back in the car she curled up in the back seat, tense and frightened, hugging her stomach.

"Hang on, Honeychild, I'll find a place to stop for the night," Harry reassured her, but not himself, seeing only a few farmhouses along the rural highway. Suddenly, he swerved off the highway, up to a group of small, shabby cabins almost hidden behind tall flowery hedges. Norma raised up to look out the window, "Where are we?"

"At a motel," he answered, "not much of one, not what I'd like us to have, but perhaps you can get a cool shower and rest. Honeychild, I think we shouldn't continue driving." An old colored man ambled toward them and Harry asked, "Do you have a room?"

"Sho 'nuff, Cap'n."

Harry lifted Norma from the back seat and carried her inside; the man went ahead, pulling down window shades. Harry paid him and he left.

"Wasn't he helpful?" she asked, looking around, "You're right, this isn't much of a place, but we've never had such service before."

A shower gave her immediate relief and Harry rubbed her with lanolin until her skin tingled. Patting her rounding midsection, he said, "Rest, you two, and I'll drive down the road for something cold to drink. I'll lock the door behind me; just say you're fine if anyone should knock."

Soon after Harry drove away, Norma heard a key in the lock and the door opened. The man from before shuffled in and began raising the window shades. From beneath the sheets she shouted, "What are you doing in here?"

The man jumped and whirled around, "I'ze sorry, Miss. I seed the car go and I thought you'll wuz gone."

"Gone? Why should we go? We paid to stay. You'd better go before my husband comes back. And lock the door behind you!"

The man bowed, backing out the door. Norma got up, dressed and waited. When Harry returned she met him at the door, anxiety in her voice, "That man came back. He simply unlocked the door and walked right in. Let's not stay here."

"We're not; he didn't expect us to stay for more than a short while. I went looking for another place. At the gas station down the road, a man said there's a proper motel about forty-five miles north of here. Do you think you could ride that far?" Without answering, she went to the car. They found the motel and after registering went to a nearby restaurant for supper. The air had been heavy and suffocating. Now the temperature was dropping and a sudden wind billowed her skirt. A few huge rain drops spotted the ground. Norma looked skyward and shivered,"Greenish yellow, tornado weather." She took Harry's arm, "Hurry."

Inside, they were seated at a window booth overlooking a bed of bright red and purple tulips. Norma loosened the string tie of her maternity skirt as the waitress left with their order. At that moment lightning streaked the sky, the lights went out, and a gale force wind blew the entrance door open. A large vase shot from a foyer table scattering daffodils in all directions. Glass cracked as hail struck the window. Harry sprang to his feet pulling Norma from the booth. Her skirt fell to the floor and he held her, shaking in her smock and petticoat, until the commotion ended. Then he stooped to lift her skirt back into place. She tied the belt and looked up, feeling everyone's eyes upon her.To their relief she laughed. Then everyone sat at the counter drinking milk and eating crackers.

The tornado had swept through the town with no more damage than broken windows and a power outage. In their proper motel room, they showered in the dark, happy that mother and baby were still one, and that they were only a hundred miles from their destination.

The next afternoon Harry parked the car with the California tags in front of the Clinton house. Julia ran to throw herself into Norma's arms, screaming, "You did come back!"

"Didn't I tell you I would?" The two danced in circles.

Tommy was reticent in his greeting, but enthusiastic in his gratitude for the fishing gear he had received for his birthday in March. Mary Lee climbed into Harry's arms. Joan eyed Norma's thickening waist line and in private, Mama predicted the baby would be a boy.

A visit to the family doctor confirmed that all was as it should be with the pregnancy and within a week Harry left to visit his uncle and aunt in New York. Norma remained behind, not because she didn't want to go, but because it was best for her and the baby. She had never expected a mere pregnancy to control her life as it was doing. And she felt that Harry and her mother were too protective of her, now suggesting that she stay in La Fayette for the birth of the baby. Also everyone thought it would be nice if the first grandchild was born in the new clinic Daddy had helped to build. As it turned out, when Harry reported for duty in South Carolina, there were no quarters available on the base nor any civilian housing in nearby Beaufort or Port Royal. Norma had no choice but to stay with her parents. Thus began another separation, and their letter writing began once again.

Parris Island
28 May

Darling,
I arrived safely and am already missing you. I'm assigned to the Recruit Depot which is primarily concerned with the training of recruits. What my job will be I won't know until tomorrow. From what information I have gathered so far, houses are not easy to get and everyone arriving here has to wait two or three months for one. The situation may change though before long. Anyway you can rest assured that we'll have a place to live in by the first of August. At present, I am in a room in the BOQ (or should I say Bachelor Officers Quarters?) It's for free and I'm still being paid our quarters allowance. Well, it's almost free since it costs only two dollars per month.

Had a very busy day and accomplished practically nothing, but I'm tired anyway. It seems that most of my days here will be busy ones. There is an acute shortage of officers and everyone has two or three jobs to handle. I won't mind that though for it will make time pass quickly while we have to be apart. Norma darling, I am already lonesome for you and miss you even more than I thought I would. I hope this is the last time we shall ever have to be apart. It seems as though only part of me is here and I'm not even half complete. I wouldn't mind that--I wouldn't mind anything, if I were only sure that you are well and not too unhappy. Honeychild, please, take good care of yourself and don't worry about anything. We'll be together again in a few weeks--all three of us!

I'll write again tomorrow. I love you, my sweet, and I am praying that you are well and happy. Forever your Harry.

Thursday night, 13 June

You Angel!

Two lovely letters and the cutest Father's Day card from you today! And you don't know how happy I am to know you are gaining weight again and your blood pressure is improving. Perhaps we owe it to the liver injections. Have you completed the series yet? I was much more worried about you than I could let you know, but now I feel so relieved because I'm sure you will be all right, so all's well in my world.

I'm sorry you couldn't get an electric fan. If you don't get one by the time this letter reaches you let me know before Saturday and I'll bring this one up with me when I come.

Norma, your mother and dad have been so very good to us that I wish we could repay them in some way. Won't you try again to pay them? They have kept us and taken care of us for months and I know that you, as well as I, feel very much indebted to them. If they won't accept remuneration, then I don't know how we can repay them. Can you think of someway? Isn't there something we could get them as a present?

Guess what I did today. Okay, you give up. Well, I had my name put on the waiting list for a new car. Didn't make any deposit or in anyway obligate myself to buy it, but when my turn comes (months from now) we can take it if we want it.

Gee! I'm sloppy. Just now filled my pen and spilled ink all over my desk. But it's cleaned up again and no sign of spilled ink remains so there is no need to cry. Anyway, it's spilled milk that people usually cry over, isn't it?

Norma, you may give Joan and Max my congratulations and best wishes, but please don't tell them I can't help smiling a little when I think of them seriously contemplating marriage. If Max were six or seven years older their plans might materialize, but a boy of 15 doesn't stay in love with the same girl more than a year or so. There may be an exceptional case, but I don't know of any.

So, you got a rolling pin! So the honeymoon is over! Now look, little lady, just what do you have in mind? Mince pie--or shall I start running? Right now I'd better start running to bed. It's nearly ten and I have to be at the rifle range very early in the morning. 'Nite, my sweet and lovely, Your adoring husband,

Harry.

Thursday night, 27 June

My Dearest,

Another heavenly letter came today; it was so very sweet, but Honeychild, I'm sorry about those technicolor nightmares. Your red blouse must be beautiful, but do you think you ought to sew so much?

Yes, I do like Anne for a girl's name. Norma Anne would be a beautiful name and it is my choice, but you can give it the name *you* like best and not have to feel that you have done something contrary to my wishes because I do want you to be pleased. What do you think of Thomas Charles or Thomas Joseph for a boy? Those are merely suggestions, dear, to use if you like, but please, darling, *don't*, if it is a boy, name it Harry. Somehow I just don't like that name and perhaps our boy wouldn't either.

Do you find this more difficult to decipher than my usual scrawl? I am lying on my bed in the full blast of the fan and it's a bit awkward, but I'm feeling too lazy to sit up. It has been hot and sultry all day. We had a few short showers, but that didn't cool things off at all, just made it more sultry. The breeze from the fan really feels swell. Is it getting hotter in La Fayette?

I got the straight scoop on my retirement today. On the first of May, 1952, I can retire at $210.94 per month and for each year I stay in after that, I'll get an additional $8.45 per month until May, 1957, when I could retire at $253.13 per month. I can retire in 1952 or anytime after that, but the longer I stay in the more pay I'll get, so that gives us somewhat of a choice. If the contemplated pay raise becomes law, and if it should be applicable to our retirement benefits, it would boost us to $242.55 in 1952 and to $291.09 in 1957. Anyway, whatever happens we will have at least something to fall back on, even if I don't find much of a job on the outside after I retire. I'd like to start some kind of a little business or shop that you could take over in the event something, like landing on my head while pole-vaulting, should happen to me forty or fifty years from now.

Yes, Norma darling, I know you love me, and knowing that is the most wonderful thing in my life. Your love is the only thing in this world that I couldn't live without. Good night, dear wife. I adore you and long for your sweet presence. Your devoted

Harry.

Sunday night, 30 June

Dearest,

I was Officer of the Day (OD) last night and had a rough night. Have been sleeping since 3:30 this afternoon. It's nearly nine now and I'm all confused. But I did want to wish my Honeychild a Happy Birthday before the day ends. Hope my package and card arrived in time for your celebration today. I sent them with all my love. I'll be seeing you on the 6th, and I can hardly wait.

I always used to wonder why *fathers* got so excited when a baby is about to be born. Even now I couldn't explain exactly why they do, but I know that they do get excited. It seems as if the whole world and the scheme of life is about to be changed, and in addition to being excited I am very, very happy. And Norma darling, I think of you every minute of the day and want so very much to be with you. And if you sent your clock to me, I am going to bring it back. You will need it while you are in bed and I can get along without one until you come back with me. Oh, Norma, you are so generous and good to me, but I just can't let you deprive yourself of the things you need just to make it more convenient for me.

Jesse Griffin is still here. His wife is in Monroe, Georgia--too far to go on the weekend without a car and there is no place for her to stay here, and he is very much in love too, so you can imagine his frame of mind. Several times I have given him a ride on my way up to see you. He is becoming pretty well acquainted with you by listening to me talk when we are together.

Haven't wrapped that can of pineapple yet. Guess I'll bring it with me Saturday because it wouldn't reach you much sooner anyway. I'll be seeing you soon after you read this. I love you, Norma Mine, I love you so very much! Take good care of yourself. Always your Harry.

Monday night, 15 July

Hello Darling,

Gee! Hon, I was so very happy being with you yesterday and Saturday night. If only that boy would hurry and come so I could take you back with me and be with you every day! There I go, after telling *you* to be patient. I guess I am more impatient to be with you than I am to have a son. Is that wrong? I can't help it, honeychild, it's you that I love. I'd rather have just you alone than a hundred children. And I could even wait for you with a certain degree of philosophical calm if I didn't know how you have to suffer now. Just knowing that you were well and that you love me would make it all seem so much easier to bear, but honeychild, I know what a difficult and painful burden you have to carry and my mind won't rest until I know that you are well again and not suffering anymore. Oh! days roll by and bring in August and our little boy-or-girl so my lovely Norma can be well and happy again.

There are sixteen more days at the very most. That isn't many, is it? When you stop to think that once upon a time, years ago, there were 270 days. And a lot of them were really bad ones, remember? Those maddening days and nights when I was at Hueneme, that horribly long trip across Texas, the frightening time and heat in Birmingham and the hail storm? All that covered a long, long time and you suffered a lot through it all. Now it's nearly over, darling. Keep your chin up a few more days and soon you'll be bouncing around like Mary Lee with her cat and happy as can be. I'll be bouncing right with you and before long we'll be a bouncing threesome. Say! What are we going to get the baby for Christmas? Guess I had better go to sleep and rest my brain. It seems to be getting weaker by the minute. Always your Harry.

Saturday night, 20 July

Hello Darling,

The letter you mailed Thursday came today. I'm sorry, honeychild, but I'll have to disagree with one statement you made. I am not the one who has done the most suffering of the two of us. There have been times when I felt hurt because I thought you were unhappy or dissatisfied, and I was unhappy when you were sick and I could do so very little to help you, but I have never suffered in the way that you have. I knew how lonesome you were in California and how at times you worried, even though you never mentioned it to me nor complained about it. At those times, and especially when you were so sick, I was unhappy but Norma darling, you have never caused me to suffer, and you could have if you had been mean or thoughtless. You have been a wonderful and precious wife to me and honeychild, I adore you for that. If I suffer at all it is because I can't be with you to do the things for you that I would like to do, and for that I can only blame myself. It isn't your fault that I chose to be a Marine. But I am glad that you too realize that the present hardships and difficulties we are experiencing because I *am* in the Marine Corps will, in a very few years, pay us good dividends. We'll have security for life, and more freedom with it than most people ever dream of having.

  I had O.D. duty last night and decided not to drive up today. I hope you understand that I do want to see you as often as I can, but I'm afraid to make the trip after having been up most of the night. Up and back is as far as it is across the state of Texas and it's very hard to stay awake during the last few hours on the way back, even when I have Friday night to sleep. But, honeychild, I'll come the minute I can get away when you tell me the baby is coming, or if you become seriously ill. Oh! Norma, it's only a matter of days now! Soon I'll be, not walking, but running back and forth in this room at night. If only I could be with you! If we do a little plotting and get some cooperation from the Red Cross maybe we can arrange it. There is a chapter in La Fayette, isn't there?

  Good night, dear Norma. I love you so very much and I miss you so! Always your very own,

            Harry.

            Monday night, 22 July

"Sweet and Lovely",

  I've been singing, whistling, and humming that to you all evening. Surely you must have heard me, for the song came right from the center of my heart and went straight out to you.

  This last weekend was a nightmare. I'm just no good without you, honeychild. The most pleasant times I have when I'm away from you are the times I sleep, because then I sometimes dream you are with me. I never knew eight weeks could be as long as these last ones have been. I guess you know much better than I how long a week can be, but keep up your courage, darling, the week after you get this letter will surely be the last one before a new and happier life will begin for you, and you won't ever be lonesome then with our little baby near you all the time. You may not even care whether you come to Parris Island or not. Believe me, I'll care! And I'll be begging you to come long before you are ready.

Had a terribly poor supper tonight. The waitress who served my table had just been bawled out by the head steward and was so upset she didn't know whether she was serving food or carrying in coal--and neither did I. That school for waitresses is still going on and it's getting mighty tiresome. And our breakfasts are getting tiresome too. We have eggs, toast, coffee, and fruit juice every morning without fail. Never any hotcakes, French toast, cereals or fresh fruits. They never have to ask us what we want for breakfast; all they ask is "How do you want your eggs?" Awful, isn't it, what we have to contend with down here?

"Nite, little darling. Stay sweet for me, and always remember: I love you. Harry.

Thursday night, 8 August

Darling,

Our little daughter is just one week old today. And such a short while ago you were hoping she would be born. In just a little while you will be making school dresses for her, and then gowns for graduation and formal dances. Whoa! I'd better stop before she marries and makes you a grandmother. Before all that comes to pass, let's get you two to Parris Island and start living these last five or six years we have to be knocked around by the Marine Corps before we can settle down in our real home. That time will pass too, and if we can be together through it all, it will pass all too quickly, but how happy we will be through it all. Even Oceanside, with all its difficulties, lies pleasantly in my memory now because we were together there. Gosh! what a garbled line of thought in this paragraph! But that's the way my mind operates these days. It may be caused by the heat or too much work, but I think it is because I am missing you so much.

I'm sorry to hear that they neglect you so in the clinic. I don't suppose they can help it since they are so busy, but still that doesn't make it any easier for you. Cheer up, sugar, in a few days you will be up and about, a little weak and wobbly maybe, but it will be better than lying helpless in bed, and you will be growing stronger each day.

Honeychild, why did you write, "I'll bet you're missing that big girl of yours, aren't you--and me, too--do you still remember me?"

Yes, I am anxious to see that big girl, but it's *you* that I miss and it's you, my beloved darling, whom I will think of and love until the last breath of life leaves my body. I know I can never love anyone, not even our own children, the way I love you. I do love our little daughter, Norma, and I am thankful to God for entrusting her to our care, but you, my beloved wife, I love and will always love most of all. Your devoted husband,
                                Harry.

   Anne Amelia, named for both grandmothers, weighed at birth eight pounds thirteen ounces, seemingly born hungry. Norma thought she should feed on demand; the nurses thought every four hours. By the time Anne was at her mother's breast, she was enraged from hunger and any milk she was able to draw out was promptly expelled. Both mother and child were in tears after every feeding. Soon Anne was screaming constantly. To spare her, the nurses told Norma, they kept Anne in the nursery until feeding time. And Norma wasn't allowed out of bed even though she felt well enough to get up. Her delivery had been short and easy, but the Captain had said to take good care of his wife, and to the staff that meant complete bed rest for ten days. It also meant an unnecessary hospital bill, Norma thought. The clinic provided no food, there was no restaurant in town, so Mama was preparing her food and Julia was delivering it. She had no say at the clinic over the baby or her own life. On the eighth day she checked herself out, called a taxi, and took Anne to her parents' home. There she kept the baby with her constantly, patiently encouraging her to breast feed at the least sign of hunger.
   This paid off. After a week, Anne was sleeping between feedings and Norma was waking every morning refreshed and encouraged. At last, she was free to be of help with household chores and summer canning. On August 16, with Anne asleep after a cooling bath and warm feeding, Norma took a tray of iced tea and glasses to the front porch where Mama was snapping freshly picked pole beans. Julia and Mary Lee were playing in the tire swings. Joan was at work in the 5&10 cent store in town. Tom was disappearing around the bend of the road on his way to the Mahan farm to play with their ten year old son before bringing home a gallon of fresh milk. Two hours later, with Anne still asleep, the snapped beans were ready to be packed into sterilized Mason jars. Leaving the porch, Norma and her mother paused momentarily at the door to notice Dr. Kitchens

speeding by in his gray Ford coupe, leaving behind a cloud of choking dust. He didn't wave. Following close was an ambulance with its siren piercing the afternoon stillness.

"Somethin's happened," Mama concluded, peering after the vehicles with a frown. "Well, we've got to get these beans to cookin'. It's about time for Tom Boy to be gettin' back with the milk, and he'll know; he knows all the neighborhood goings on." In the kitchen she filled eight quart jars with beans, sealed them, and started the burner under the water in the pressure cooker. Norma carried Anne to the front porch for another feeding. This was getting to be enjoyable. Anne rooted around, her lips finding the ample artificial nipple of the breast shield, soon pulling Norma's nipple out enough to permit a good grip and settled in to drawing milk out. Mama came to watch, her work finished. The two mothers sat and rocked in the summer heat, listening to Anne's contented little swallowing noises and the periodic hissing of the pressure cooker valve releasing excess steam. Suddenly the siren of the returning ambulance pierced the afternoon calm as it raced past. The familiar gray coupe followed, but it stopped in front of their house.

"Would you look at that?" Mama brightened. "Dr. Kitchens gave Tom a ride home. Now, that's mighty nice of him." Her pleasure quickly became alarm as the doctor and Tom, both solemn and white-faced, left the car and walked up the steps.

Dr. Kitchens touched Mama's shoulder and said, "Take him inside. He's not well." When they were gone he explained, "There's been an accident. Tommy's rifle discharged and the bullet struck Mack Mahan. I'm sorry to have to tell you that he died, instantly."

"Sir, you must be mistaken," Norma said with conviction, "I saw Tommy leave; he didn't have the rifle. It's hanging above the kitchen door where Daddy keeps it. Tommy isn't allowed to use it unless he's with Daddy. Come in, I'll show you." She started toward the front door.

"Tommy told me he took the rifle without permission, carrying it in front of him as he left so his mother wouldn't know." Dr. Kitchens looked apologetic, sighing heavily, "I'm sorry, really sorry--for all of you--for everybody. Will you tell your parents that?" He started down the steps, "Now, I've got to get on to town to take care of all of this. Can you take care of things here?"

Mama had returned to hear the doctor's words and stood staring at him, her face blank. Norma took her by the shoulders, turned her around and led her inside. In the bedroom, she removed Mama's shoes and helped her into bed. When Daddy came home, Norma told him what she knew through chattering teeth. He looked at her as if she had gone mad, his face losing color, his eyes glazed, staring at her for a long time before he walked into the bedroom like a mechanical man.

Norma's legs couldn't support her, and even when she sat her heels tapped the floor like a drum. Her breast milk dried up overnight, and she gave up the idea of nursing Anne. She prepared a formula which miraculously the baby accepted. Mama stayed in bed for two days, Daddy sat in the front room with the Bible in his lap. They paid one visit to the Mahans before the funeral which was held the day after Julia's tenth birthday. The suffering in the Clinton home was indescribable. Bitterness, blame, shame, and guilt came to dwell there. Four days later, Daddy had his birthday; he was forty-two.

> Monday night, 26 August
>
> My Dearest One,
>
> I don't know what to say or do. Your letter today was so very sad. It was like a knife in my heart. I am so worried about you that I can't think of anything else, and there is nothing I can do to improve conditions for you. There is still no place for you and the baby to live in near here. There will be sometime, but right now I can't get a place for love or money. You can't live out under the open sky. Norma darling, there is no house. I can't build one. Even people who have more than enough money plus the legal right to build one can't get what it takes to make a house. What shall I do? What can I do? I want a house. I have done everything I possibly can to get one. My name is on four waiting lists. Right here in this little swamp settlement there are hundreds of men looking for a house so they can bring their families here to live with them. All they can do is wait and hope, and that is what they are doing. My chances to get a house are far better than ninety per cent of the others, but still we have to wait.
>
> Norma darling, if we aren't patient, and if we don't make the best of what we can get and when we can get it, then we'll be lost, our happiness will be destroyed and all of our dreams will vanish into thin air. These are hard times for many people besides ourselves. Let's not give up, darling. Let's be strong enough to survive these dark days. We have our wonderful love and faith in each other. Let's cling to it--hang on to it tooth and nail. Before long

we'll see it was worth fighting for and we will come into our rightful happiness. Look up on the hill, darling. Can't you see our own little home up there. The path between it and us is dark and rough but I can see lights shining through the windows. Help me, Norma darling. Be patient and forbearing with me. I am doing the best I can. I know it is hard now, and may be again, but before long our reward will come to us. Shall we work for it, Norma? Shall we hang on until we have won our fight, until we can enjoy the happiness we have so rightfully earned? Honeychild, we'll be so proud, so close, so content, and rich in mind and heart for having stuck it out together through all the difficulties that lay in our path on the way to our *home!* I want it that way. Dearest Norma, please help me! I love you, darling, I always will. Harry.

Tuesday night, 27 August

Dearest,

This has been the usual silent Tuesday. As always, I missed your sweet letter very much, but for some reason I feel much better than I did last night. After I finished writing to you, a few minutes before ten, I went to bed but couldn't sleep. I lay there thinking until early in the morning. Norma, do you know what I believe is happening to us. We worry too much. And what on earth do we have to worry about? You have Anne to take care of and she doesn't give you much rest, but honeychild, every mother in the world who ever cared for her child had that to go through. It's tiring and it's work, but it's natural, and as she grows older her needs will become less exacting.

We are not together and we worry about that, but aren't we proving ourselves to be just plain d--- fools to worry for that reason? Didn't we decide before the baby was born that six weeks would be the very earliest that we could hope for you to come here? Anne is three weeks and six days old today. We still lack more than two weeks before the minimum time expires. Honestly now, aren't we a pair of fools to be worrying because we are not already together? If we went about it properly we could be very happy in the knowledge that soon we *will* be together in our own little home again--with our own little baby.

Of course, Tommy's accident upset you and your family, but it happened, it's over, and couldn't be helped. Even though it may not soon be forgotten, the shock and its sharp pangs of pain will gradually wear away. Please, darling, don't let that keep you upset. And honeychild, Saturday I am going to see you! Oh! how heavenly it will be to hold you in my arms again! I can't worry about anything, or be unhappy, when I think of that. I can't wait to see that big smile on your dear face when I walk through the door.

I can't tell at what time I will arrive. It may be 8:30 or it may be after ten, so just go on with your regular routine and let me surprise you when I come in, won't you?

Norma, please tell Tommy not to feel that I think less of him because of the unfortunate thing that happened. I have seen such things many times and they just can't be helped. I certainly don't blame Tommy the least bit and I think he would make a great mistake if he blamed himself. He has no reason to. He has got to carry on and everybody will be right along with him. He is a fine young man and I know he can do it.

I will say good night to you now, my dear sweet little wife. If you get this Saturday, I'll be pushing on the steering wheel as you read this, and I'll be getting nearer to your every second. Mmmm! I love you so. Are you gonna squeeze me hard tonight? Gee! I wish I were there now! I want to make love to my honeychild!

Always,
Harry.

13

**VG 104 9=PARRIS ISLAND SOCAR AUG29 6:30P
MRS H E KIPP=
CARE CLARENCE CLINTON LA FAYETTE GA=
PLAN TO RETURN WITH ME SUNDAY HAVE A
COTTAGE FOR US= LOVE= HARRY**

Ten seconds after reading the wire, Norma went into action. By the time Harry surprised her Saturday evening, she had arranged and organized everything for her departure from La Fayette--and she wanted the car loaded before they went to bed, everything but the baby's bassinet. Harry's hot kisses were everywhere and she welcomed them completely. Never had she been so happy! Never had she felt so alive!

Leaving La Fayette, Harry drove, Norma talked, and the baby slept, seeming to enjoy the movement of her bassinet in the back seat. Norma didn't mind how long the drive might take; they were together on the road to their own home. After a long, comfortable silence she asked, "How did you happen to find the house?"

"Don't call it a house, Honeychild. It's a cottage, and that name fits exactly. How it happened is that I had the car in for servicing and mentioned my many trips up to see you while we waited for quarters. The owner overheard and said he had a cottage on his property that his children used when they came visiting. It was furnished and vacant at the moment. He offered it to me, and well, you know the rest. I took it sight unseen and wired you immediately. Friday night I drove out to take a look. It's small, with barely enough room for the bassinet at the foot of the bed and I think you'll have to be on the bed in order to make it up. The kitchen table is a shelf that hinges to the wall when not in use; there's not enough room to cook at the stove with it down. Corner windows have padded seats; that's the living room couch. The head has no shower, no tub, only a seat and a basin. That's it, but it's ours. We'll bump into each other when we move around in it, but I'll be gone during the day, so there'll only be you and Anne, and both of you are pretty small. In the evenings when I'm home, we can always go to bed...or a movie!" The gleam in his eyes made it plain which he preferred.

The cottage was located in a grove of huge old oaks draped in low swags of Spanish moss some three hundred feet from the inland waters of Port Royal Sound. It was in McDaniel's cottage, as they called it, that their family life began and flourished. Norma passed the days caring for Anne and preparing for Harry's daily home-coming, and they spent the nights in each other's arms. As glorious as the nights were, the mornings arrived and with them another pail of dirty diapers to be hand washed in the toilet bowl. Norma said it was time to go into Beaufort and put their name on the waiting list for a washing machine.

In Ramsey's Appliance on Bay Street, a slender, attractive young woman with an upswept hairdo took the name. "Captain H. E. Kipp," she repeated, smiling broadly, "My husband Staff Sergeant Smith thinks you hung the moon, Captain. I'm happy to meet you, and you too, Mrs. Kipp.

And this must be the reason you need a washing machine." She reached for the baby who settled happily into her arms.

Norma liked her immediately, and Terrance Smith from Abilene, Texas said on their next encounter, "My friends call me Terry. I wish you would also." That was the day a washing machine came in and Terry as manager passed it on to the Kipps. It arrived in time for their first anniversary. A week later, they moved into MOQ 56 on Parris Island.

It wasn't an island, Norma discovered. It had been, in 1927, when Harry took basic training there--the year she was born--but since then a causeway had joined it to the mainland. That one-mile connection, lined with pink and white oleander bushes became her own personal yellow brick road, taking her to the land of Oz.

She was all eyes as they drove that first time through the main gate, with the sentry saluting Harry, then across that magic highway past Horse Island and on to Boulevard de France.Everything, everywhere looked clean and orderly, and at sunset so peaceful. The vast parade field was off to the left and Harry pointed out the white building of the First Recruit Battalion where he worked. They were passing a huge brick building bearing a fluttering red flag with two gold stars."General Hart is aboard," he told her in the Marine Corps lingo she would be hearing often. He drove on along streets named for battles she had heard about.When they came to Guadalcanal, there was their bungalow--the second house away from the water's edge and surrounded by tall oleander bushes.

In the middle of the living room sat their two barrels and bookshelf shipped from Pendleton; beside them were Harry's two footlockers, finally having caught up with him. He gestured toward the shipped things, "Along with that, what's in our car, and the washing machine, you see before you the sum total of our worldly possessions. We can now settle down to living a long and fruitful--dare I say *fruitful?*--life."

"No! Don't say it, don't even think it! Here, hold tooty-fruity while I look the place over." She ran from room to room."One, two, three bedrooms. One for us, one for our love child, and the one at the end of the hall for my sewing room. And there's a great, big bathtub in the back bathroom." She whirled back into the living room. "A lovely fireplace, big dining room"--through swinging doors to a pantry and an enormous kitchen. "Why, McDaniel's cottage could fit in here with room to spare. I simply can't believe it! *This is our house?* It's the biggest one I've ever lived in, filled with furniture, everything we need. What on earth will it cost?"

Semper Fi

"It's part of my pay. We have this in exchange for quarters allowance like at Sterling Housing and the Quonset hut. Now that we have it, don't you think it was worth the wait?"

"Now that we have it, yes. But it was quite a wait, just as it was quite a wait for you. I'm beginning to think that "wait" is the Marine Corps' middle name. But I'll have to agree, it and you were worth waiting for."

That night, Norma lay pensive in Harry's arms.

"Something wrong, Honeychild?"

"No, the opposite; everything's perfect, and I want it to stay that way."

"And why shouldn't it stay that way?"

Norma gave a deep sigh, "'s what you said earlier about being fruitful."

"Oh, that. Just my clever attempt at humor," he paused, "but I sense it wasn't funny to you. Right?"

"And neither was my reply." She sat up, looking down on him, "*I* was serious. I hope you don't mind but I don't want to have another baby."

He was silent, looking up at her.

"I know I said I wanted children, *plural,* but that was before," she grimaced, "before I knew what being pregnant meant.That awful, never ending nausea. What would I do if I had to take care of Anne along with that?" she asked plaintively.

"Honeychild, if you don't want another baby, that's fine with me. I won't hold you to what you said before, but I will remind you of what I said, and still feel: you are the baby I want."

"Do you think we had Anne so quickly because I wanted a baby? And now that I don't, we won't have another one? Is that the way it works?"

"No, my little ignoramus, that's not the way it works. We didn't concern ourselves with contraception, and for that I must take responsibility. Aboard ship coming from Pearl Harbor, I had a sperm count taken. It came out very low since I've taken Atabrine continually as treatment and prevention of malaria since 1940. I was actually afraid I'd never be able to make you a mother and knowing how very much you wanted to be one, I suggested that we adopt a baby if we couldn't have one of our own, remember?"

"Yes, and I wondered about that since I got pregnant so soon."

"It surprised me as well. I believed the doctor when he told me it would take months for my count to return to normal, if indeed it ever did. I don't know what happened. You must have stimulated those little guys so much that--Oh, my darling, you can't imagine how much you do stimulate me, all of me, and how I love it! But we'll have to do something now, won't we? Have you talked with your mother about birth control?"

"Heavens, no. She'd never talk about *that*. She didn't even tell me about menstruation. I knew she bled every month, and when it happened to me, all she did was give me a stack of cloths and two safety pins. I never knew what caused it. She said it was a curse and everyone else called it that too. And if it didn't happen, it meant you were going to have a baby. According to her, men had the fun and women had the labor."

"Is that the reason you asked me once in a letter if our intimacies might be repugnant?"

"Well, I wondered if all women felt that way. I never got the idea from any women I knew that they had any use for that part of marriage. Mind you, it wasn't talked about--what actually happened--but whenever any girl got married, the women in our neighborhood raised their eyebrows and turned down their mouths and said, 'The poor thing, she's in for it now'." Norma laughed suddenly, "Remember at Sterling Housing when everyone was so happy that I was pregnant? And how hard Fred and Leona were trying? Every time they made love upstairs above us and we heard it, we hoped that would be the time. It was different when we returned to La Fayette. The women all sighed in sympathy for me. The only one who made me feel good was that precious little Julia bringing me hot chocolate every morning before I got out of bed. She had no idea why I was sick in the mornings and Mama didn't want the kids to know, not even Joan, as if my protruding stomach wasn't there. Joan knew all right; she asked me to keep out of sight when Max came around.

"Mama asked me once if you ever 'bothered' me now that I was 'in the family way'. I told her you didn't, and she looked happy. When I added that you had never 'bothered me', she looked strange. How could I talk about that with her when she thinks it's foolishness or something to be endured? Marsha feels the same way, I think."

"Then you spoke with Marsha about this?"

"No, not really. All she ever said was that she had to give Houston what he wanted and sometime she just pulled her hair while it was happening. Once she was ironing a whole stack of handkerchiefs and I asked who had a terrible cold. She said, 'Nobody, silly, these go under the pillow.' I didn't know what she meant, but she laughed, so I did too." Norma shrugged, "I still don't know what she meant. Do you?"

"It's a method of contraception I don't think we want to use. There are better ways. Do you want me to deal with it or should we get an

appointment at the dispensary and find the best way to go about it? But, Honeychild, please don't even consider abstinence," he implored.
"You and your big words. Abstinence.I can hardly say it.What on earth is it?"
He touched her cheek playfully, "It means having no intimate contact."
"In other words, no lovemaking."
"In other words, Yes."
"Then, no, I won't consider it!"

Next morning, before leaving for work, Harry moved the barrels into the kitchen. Norma had a breakfast of juice and rolls, then unpacked and put away the dishes, glasses, and cookware. She placed Harry's ashtrays on the rattan tables in the living room. The bookcase, used as a pantry at Sterling Housing, was there already waiting to hold their nucleus of a library, begun in La Fayette from a mail order book club, and bearing their personalized bookplates. She read each title, thinking of its characters and plot, as she placed it in the case, finishing with *Ramona* her favorite of the lot. Ramona, the half-white, half-Indian girl, who left the luxurious home of her childhood to marry the sheepherder Alessandro. Their love for each other had been absolute as they endured extreme hardship ending in his death. Ramona, with an infant daughter, was forced to return to the rich and powerful Spanish family that had raised her, to be taken in marriage by the heir Felipe who had loved her from childhood. Alessandro had called Ramona *majella,* little wood-dove in the Luiseno tongue, and he had told her that the wood-dove was true to one mate always. And in her heart, Ramona was forever true to Alessandro, the Indian, and for all her days whenever she heard the song of the wood-doves, calling to each other, she heard also Alessandro's call to her, "Majella! Majella!"

Harry had told her that in Spanish the dove is called *paloma*, and that his favorite song was *La Paloma*. Someday she must read *Ramona* to him. There were so many things they could do now that they had a house. She rose to walk through the rooms she would make into a home, comfortable and beautiful. Their refuge from the world; that was what Harry said he wanted. She felt a new surge of commitment as a wife and to prove it she asked at bedtime, just before they drifted off to sleep, "Wake me in the morning if I don't hear the alarm."

"I'll wake you if you're sure that's what you want," he said, "but with getting up every four hours to feed Anne, perhaps you should sleep when she sleeps." He didn't need to wake her. At the first ping of the alarm, she was out of bed and into the kitchen to cook a hearty breakfast even though he was satisfied with juice, toast, and coffee which he usually prepared himself. Afterwards, they sat on the back steps to watch the rising sun dissipate the mist over the tideland.

With each successive day of early rising, Norma's vitality waned. Wednesday night, she went to bed as soon as Anne. By Thursday evening, fatigue caused her to fall asleep at the dinner table. Harry put mother and daughter to bed, gave Anne her midnight feeding and left Norma sleeping Friday morning to wake of her own accord. At half past nine, she jumped awake to find herself alone. His note was propped against the clock.

> Honeychild,
> I hope you are feeling better.
> Take good care of yourself for me.
> *I love you!* and I'll see you
> this noon. Harry.
> P.S. I fed the little chow hound
> before I went to work.

At noon he greeted a rested and bright-eyed wife. "Welcome back to the land of the living, and never mind seeing the sunrises with me. I'll settle for seeing sunsets with my honeychild, when she's wide awake." So it became the evenings when they watched the events of nature--the tides in their comings and goings, the sunsets casting shimmering paths on Beaufort River, and the moon in its climb above the palmettos lining Guadalcanal Street.

As autumn waned the evening sea breezes strengthened and brought relief from the heat as well as a most unpleasant stench that often drove Norma and Harry indoors. There was no escape; the disagreeable odor permeated every nook and cranny. She didn't know about the paper mills in Savannah and no one bothered to tell her even when she accused the beautiful oleanders growing outside their windows as being the source of the smell-- that distinctive smell of dirty diapers she had to contend with every morning. Surely she didn't have to endure it in the evenings. Please, she begged Harry, ask someone to cut down the bushes. Even though there was a paucity of shade, she would sacrifice that little bit to be rid of the awful smell. Finally, a man from Maintenance came and cut down the oleanders. Then the aroma from the paper mills had no barrier at all and she felt like a perfect fool.

14

"Hurry," Norma urged, "I can't wait another minute to find out what's inside this big green thing!" She sat on the floor beside Harry's footlocker as he inserted the key into the lock.

"It could be dangerous," he warned with his sideways grin."You've heard, no doubt, of Pandora's Box?" Norma loved his craggy face, inscrutable until a grin transformed it into openness, lips curving into a crooked smile, eyes sparkling with an inner mirth.

"Yes, I have, but this is Harry's box, and I'm not afraid."

"I wonder, Honeychild, when I'll get to delve into your past. Must I wait until your cedar chest gets shipped from La Fayette? Mmmm, what deep, dark secrets does it harbor?"

"My past, my lurid past! All sixteen years that you don't know about. Well, I'll tell you, some time--when my imagination improves. Right now, its *your* past we're dealing with, so quit stalling."

"There's not that much to tell. You'll soon be bored, that's for sure." The lock sprang open and Harry raised the lid, looking inside a moment before removing the two porcelain vases he had found on Okinawa. The brilliance of gold leaf contrasted with the depth of the cobalt glaze and stark white of lotus blossoms with jade colored leaves. "They might be a pair, though they're not identical," Harry noted. "That's why I believe they're handmade. They were at the crest of a high mountain, partially buried in mud. I stepped on one, pushing it deeper. Bending to rescue it, I saw its mate. I think they may be valuable by reason of their distance from a village. The islanders, fleeing ahead of the invasion, took with them only what they were able to carry on their backs. Climbing up the steep terrain, they must have discarded those things they valued least. I found these at the entrance to a cave. Someone had carried them all the way to the top." Harry held one in each hand. "I thought of you, Honeychild, and of the little music box you often wrote about. Somehow the thought gave me a connection with the owner of these vases. Now they belong to you." He put them into her hands then reached for two ebony letter openers.

"These I carved with only a sharp knife and two files on Guadalcanal. I felled the tree and stripped it down to the core for this black one. The other was carved from the edge of the core and the sapwood. It's a bit lighter in weight as well as color. Ebony is very hard wood. Neither of these will float. And ebony warps until properly seasoned and must be worked on at night." He rubbed the black opener absently. "One night in a bombing raid, I left a black cribbage board uncovered, finished except for polishing. Five months of work warped by the morning light an hour after dawn. I was quite proud of that board. You can be sure I was more careful with these. Balance them here, like this," Harry showed her where to place her finger, "just past where the blade joins the handle. Both are balanced the same."

"They're works of art, Harry. So smooth and graceful. I wish we had a desk to put them on. Until we do, I'll put them on the mantel with the vases." She returned to find him holding a large, white pillow sham with openwork butterflies embroidered in each corner, and four yellow cornucopias in its center with orange and lavender flowers spilling out. "This was made by an old woman in Nicaragua, one of the Central American countries. Her grandson was in my garrison. I sometimes ate in their thatched roof shelter. Their *comida*, food, was unbelievably tasty even though it was prepared in a most primitive way by our standards. It was in Nicaragua that I learned to live on rice, beans, and tropical fruits. Did you know that they never ate the first inch of the ends of bananas? They thought the little insects that live there cause disease. Shortly before I left, months after I had admired some of her needlework, she gave this pillow cover to me saying, '*Es para su novia cuando usted la tenga*'. At last I have a bride to give it to and I hope she likes it."

"Oh, Harry, I do! This is better than Christmas. Such wonderful, beautiful things, all made by hand. I love them! This really is a treasure chest...What's in that little bag?"

"Open it and see."

She untied the drawstring and emptied the contents into her hand: bronze and silver athletic medals, nine in all. Basketball and 220 and 440 yard dash competitions from Carleton College in Minnesota; relay races from Hamline University in St. Paul; and running broad jump from the University of Minnesota interscholastic competition. The medals were for the years 1921-23. "These say you were quite an athlete, Harry, and help explain your fantastic body. Remember the tiny picture you sent me? You were sitting on a stool before a bucket of some kind. Your shoulders, chest and arms were bare. I used to get uncontrollable quivering inside when I looked at it."

"So now you tell me the awful truth: you married me for my muscles. All this time I thought you married me for my wit," he feigned dismay.

"I did--but what a bonus I got in your flat belly, rounded behind, and muscular arms. Make your biceps stand up for me. No, don't! It'll only distract me and I'm anxious to see what else is in here," she bent over the footlocker as he withdrew a long scabbard, holding it in both hands before unsheathing the sword. Norma caught her breath, "Oh, a souvenir!"

"You might say that," he replied dryly.

"What kind is it?" She asked, her eyes on the corded hilt.

"The traditional sword of the Japanese foot soldier, a Samurai, a professional warrior, such as I, who had the right of committing suicide by hara-kiri rather than living to face dishonor." A fleeting grimness crossed his face, belying the drollery in his eyes.

"How did you get it?" She was almost afraid to ask.

"I was on foot patrol in tall brush--higher than my head--when suddenly we were face to face, and I relieved him of his weapon," Harry stared at the sword, his fingers stroking the length of the nicked blade, "and here it is."

"You took it from him?" She asked in wonder.

"Let's say he wasn't as polite as Japanese are purported to be; he didn't just hand it over. And he didn't have time for *hara-kiri.*" He sheathed the blade and laid it aside, reaching for a white silk banner with its bright orange-red sun in the center.

Norma shivered, "You didn't write me about the sword."

"No."

She shuddered at these reminders of the war, knowing that if they weren't here, he wouldn't be. Turning her back on them, she lifted from the second footlocker a very large envelope. Opening the flap she withdrew the contents and stared into the smiling face of a glamorous, auburn haired woman with arched eyebrows and very red lips. Years ago she had had her own smaller version of Aunt Jean's portraits. Harry's eyes met hers,"I'm sorry you had to see these. I had forgotten they were there. I'll mail them to her if you'll get her address. And after they're gone, we won't have to think of Jean or her pictures ever again. Please don't let this upset you. Those were put there years ago and have been in storage ever since."

"I'm not upset, really. I'm grateful. For those years that Aunt Jean and I wrote, she was good to me. She must be unbelievably sad to know you've married someone else--me--especially since she introduced us to each other." She looked for something in Harry's face, some reaction of what he was thinking, but found nothing. "I wonder how my life would be if I had never written to her or to you. Have you ever thought of that?"

"No, because it had to happen; we were destined to meet." Now his face was filled with emotion. "I know that as surely as I stayed alive all those years simply going through the motions of living until the time came that we should meet. And as you pointed out, Jean was instrumental in that. I often wondered why I met her, perhaps that was the reason." His hand touched her face, lifting it so their eyes could meet, " Jean loved you; she wrote me that she did. And my darling, with each passing day, I love you more. Sometimes I think I will explode with the force of it. You do know that, don't you, Norma Mine?"

"Yes, you make it clear to me in so many ways, and I believe that nothing in this world will ever change the way we love each other."

He sat on the floor beside her, his eyes traveling over her face and his fingers touching where his eyes feasted. He touched his lips to hers softly, tenderly, in little short kisses, over and over, then let them cling, not in passion, but in reverence. Norma opened her eyes and saw his, expanded and mysterious, deep pools of raw emotion, and their souls connected. The kiss ended, but he continued to stare, whispering, "I'm still half afraid you will evaporate, disappear, right before my eyes as you did so many times long ago when I could only dream of you."

"Is that why your eyes were open?" She whispered the question shyly.

"Yes, my lovely, beautiful Norma. They can't get enough of you."

"Do you know what Mama said when we came back from our honeymoon?"

"No, tell me."

"She said it was downright embarrassing the way you stared at me, like a love sick school boy who didn't know there was anyone else in the world. She said she hoped people wouldn't think you were daft."

"She said that?" he laughed. "And what did you think?"

"It made me nervous, at first. Now that I'm used to it, I like it."

"That's good, since your daft husband is never going to stop looking at you."

On Saturday mornings, Harry washed the car, and as she did every day, Norma washed diapers. This Saturday while waiting for the wash cycle to end, she was at the footlockers again, looking at hundreds of photographs: Harry's duty stations in the United States, Hawaii, China, and Nicaragua. Big seacoast guns in bunkers, and field headquarters in Pacific Island jungles. There were pictures of high school athletic teams with Harry as captain of the Buffalo High School basketball team, of him in his wrestling tights, of his graduation, family, and friends. She made a mental note to put them all in albums for him.

Beneath Marine enlisted uniforms were envelopes of official papers. The first held a letter of commendation from the Secretary of the Navy dated 22 August, 1930, citing Harry for courage and extreme coolness in rescue efforts while his own life was in danger in the collision of the *USS Fairfax* with the tanker *Pinthus* near Boston on 10 June. There was a newspaper account of the disaster and rescue. An envelope labeled Nicaragua held a notice of his service on the National Board of Elections of the Republic of Nicaragua as president of the Canton of Waspook, Department of Bluefields in November, 1928. A citation for *La Cruz de Valor* from the Republic of Nicaragua, and its translation into English, The Cross of Valor, still another citation from the Secretary of the Navy regarding that award; a Christmas card from President Juan B. Sacasa dated 25 de diciembre de 1932, Managua. She was examining the Nicaraguan passport of a yellow haired Harry when he came to stand behind her. She looked up, laughing, "*Pelo, amarillo!* Was your hair really this yellow?"

"Yes, and while you're finding out about your old man, the washer's beating hell out of the diapers."

Norma ran to the washer, putting the diapers through the wringer and changing the wash water to rinse water. That done, she returned to the dining room, "Is there a picture of the lady who made my pillow cover?"

Harry spread the photographs over the table top, searching. Norma saw village houses, some thatch-roofed and built on stilts, others with tiled clay roofs; cows lying in front yards; horse drawn carts; bandstands, parks, a cemetery, and street market of Managua, the capital city; jungle scenes, banana groves, monkeys, and iguanas; wide, muddy rivers and waterways; United States Marines and native troops with and without rifles, standing in formation or mounted on horseback, in or beside long, narrow dugout canoes; Marine Corps barracks and headquarters, and caissons bearing flag draped coffins. A photograph of Harry on a big white horse caught her eye. "That's Fifty-seven," he told her.

"You mean the number? That's its name?"

"He was Government Issue, like me."

"You were a GI cowboy!" she exclaimed.

"Cowboy, indeed!" Harry scoffed. "We were Horse Marines, and that's a campaign, not a cowboy, cover.Ah, here is *La Señora Reynosa de Vega*."

Harry pointed to a family gathering, three women in front and four men behind.

"They dress just like us," Norma noticed, "But they look so solemn, even unfriendly."

"They're not unfriendly; they just never smile for photographs."

"We're the opposite, always smiling in pictures. Do they have curly hair?"

"Some do, those Misquitos who intermarry with Negroes of the West Indies. This is the Caribbean side. The rainy side, at Bluefields."

"Bluefields? That can't be Spanish."

"No, it's a corruption of Blewfeldt, a Dutch pirate. For some two hundred years the eastern strip of Nicaragua was under a certain amount of British control. Blewfeldt made raids on it and the place was named for him. The British supported a Nicaraguan chief as a nominal ruler there and it wasn't until around 1900 that it became part of Nicaragua."

Her attention was back on the *Señora*. "If I could talk with her, how would I say, "I like the pillow cover very, very much"?

"*Me gusta muchisima la funda de almohada.*"

"*Gracias,*" she said proudly and laying aside the picture she picked up two letters, "These are almost as old as I am. They're addressed to Mrs. Amelia Stimson."

"Yes--to my mother. They never got mailed."

"Stimson--I read that name in the article about the ship collision. It said she was your mother but I thought it was a mistake, you know how newspapers get things mixed up."

"No mistake; she remarried after my stepfather died."

"Your stepfather?" Norma's head raised in surprise.

"Kipp was my stepfather, and some years after my mother married him, I assumed his name.

"Then Kipp wasn't your father's name?" Confusion settled on her face.

"No, his name was Sorenson."

Norma's brow furrowed, "Then Stimson was your mother's *third* husband?" Her voice rose on the word.

"True." He raised his eyebrows, but his eyes were steady looking into hers.

"My goodness," Norma looked dazed, "I can't get this straight. You do have some things to tell me, and I don't think I'll be bored at all." Motioning to the letters, "I would like to read them. May I? After I hang the clothes?"

Puerto Cabezas, Nic.
7 July, 1928

Dear Mother,

Hello, how are you, and how are the rest of the folks? I suppose you are just getting over the big celebration. The Fourth passed very quietly down here, in fact, I didn't realize that it had passed until this morning. However, the last sixteen weeks have been so filled with interesting events that the loss of one holiday doesn't matter.

When we left Parris Island our career in the Marine Corps just began, it seems, for since then we've been in Guantanamo Bay, Cuba, gone through the Panama Canal to Corinto on the west coast of Nicaragua, then inland to Leon, back to Corinto, through the canal again and to Puerto Cabezas on the east coast. We arrived here on the 24th of April and on the 26th we started on a hike into the "Hills". That hike lasted 59 days and those 59 days were one long nightmare. Our course lay through jungles so thick we couldn't see the sky for days at a time, and we had to cut our way through the vines and undergrowth with long knives, called *machetes.* These jungles are infested with poisonous snakes and insects, and ants! ants! good God! you'd think the ground was moving under your feet every time you looked down.

Then after about two weeks we reached the "Hills", where with the aid of vines and small trees we'd climb up one slippery side from two or three miles and down the other. One day I'll never forget: we arrived at a place where we couldn't possibly continue in any direction except up or down the river that rushed along between two mountains that were steep as walls, and we had no boats. The captain said we'd go down the river, so down we went, about twenty miles, always in water varying in depth from two to five feet, dirty water, rocky slippery bottom, coarse gravel in our shoes grinding our feet which were already covered with open sores, rain all day long, the beginning of the rainy season.

Finally we found a place to leave the river. It was nearly eight o'clock so we camped. No dry matches, no dry clothes, no fire, no supper, everywhere yellow stinking mud over our ankles, and a million mosquitoes, and rain, the night so dark you could move your hand back and forth two inches in front of your eyes without being able to see it. We lived through the night somehow although we all hoped we wouldn't. In the morning we managed to start a fire and had coffee, beans, and hard tack which we carried in waterproof bags. Then for nine more days we waded and crawled through stinking mud, our shoes were just shreds of leather dangling from our feet. No one had socks and our clothing was torn and covered with mud. We arrived at an Indian village called Bocay where a large river flowed by. We stayed there a few days to rest and get cleaned up. There we bought two large boats from the Indians and started down the river. These boats, cut out of solid mahogany by the Indians, were long and narrow and terribly clumsy and heavy. They called them *cuyukas*.

Well, by following this river we reached the coast at a point called Cape Gratias, about 100 miles north of here. There we hired a motor boat to carry us over to Puerto Cabezas and here we are, twenty-six men out of thirty-three in the hospital with malaria, typhoid, and other kinds of fever. I was blessed with malaria, but expect to be out of the hospital within ten days.

We started with thirty-six men but one got lost in the jungle and I guess the leopards have gotten him by this time, another man drowned in the river on the way back when our boat upset in the rapids, and another had the fever so badly that the doctors sent him back to the States--to die, I guess.

Oh! yes. I nearly forget to mention one very important phase of our hike, namely, the company cuisine. For breakfast we had rice, hard tack, and unsweetened black coffee and for supper we had beans, hard tack, and unsweetened black coffee. No dinner. That's what we had to hike on for 59 days from four in the morning until dark at night, with a rifle and ninety pounds of equipment, ammunition, grenades, etc., on our backs. Three hours guard duty every night, and four hours to try to sleep.

I've forgotten Charley's address so send it to me when you write. And please answer right away for I'll be going back to the Hills again in about a month. My address is: CPL. Harry E. Kipp, 60th Co. 3rd Bat. 11 Reg. Puerto Cabezas, Nic. % Postmaster, New Orleans.

25 July

I haven't had a chance to mail this letter. Am out of the hospital now and feeling fine. Tomorrow thirteen of us are being sent to a school at Bluefields where they will teach us Nicaraguan politics and Spanish and then we will be sent to various places to supervise the elections and to see that the voting is done as it should be.

I wish you could see how it rains here now, all day long, and so heavy that when the wind blows it looks exactly like a Minnesota snow storm. Write soon; my address will be the same.

Waspook, Nicaragua
26 September, 1928

Dear Mother,

It will probably be several days before I have a chance to mail this letter, but when the chance does come, I'll have it ready, that is if I can find an envelope to send it in. This place is 230 miles from the nearest railroad and 170 miles from the nearest steamship port. Our food is brought to us in small boats from the coast by way of the Coco River. We have a small radio set which sometimes enables us to communicate with Puerto Cabezas, and about once a week the planes come up from "Port" to see that we are getting along all right.

I am chairman of the election board for this district and will have to stay here until the elections are over on Nov. 5th. Then I'll go back to Puerto Cabezas and <u>maybe</u> back to the States shortly after.

I'm so shaky that I can hardly write. Still have a touch of malaria. Yesterday I lay on my cot all afternoon and shivered while I had two woolen blankets over me and the mercury was playing around 90 degrees in the shade. One of the other fellows has it too, but we have a good supply of quinine so I guess we'll manage to fight it off till we get back to Puerto Cabezas where they have a hospital and three doctors.

Last Monday we had an unpleasant little experience. One of the fellows happened to be looking over the river and saw a body floating down stream. We went out in a boat to get it and found it was a white man. He was stark naked and the only means of identification we could find on him were a green gold ring set with a large sapphire and a vaccination mark on his left arm. There were three bullet holes through his head. We wrapped him in burlap sacks and buried him.

3 October, 1928

Will try and finish this letter today. Nothing much has happened during the last week, except that the Indians around here claim that Sandino is going to attack Waspook some time in the near future. I don't believe that he really will attack us, but if he does we are well prepared for him. There are sixteen of us Marines here, and we have two machine guns, an automatic rifle, and pistols, besides the regular Springfield rifles, of which we have sixteen, one for each Marine. And we have plenty ammunition and grenades.

Am just about over my fever now and am feeling fine again. Am sending you a sample ballot for the election down here which will take place on Nov. 4th. Next Sunday, October 7, is the last day of registration and after that I won't have a thing to do until election day. Have learned a little Spanish, just enough to make my wants known, and to understand what is said in Spanish. What! You don't believe it? Well, listen to this: *Adiós, Madre mia, de su hijo mayor*, Harry.

My address is the same. Tell Grandmother I'll be home soon to see her in a few months, for Easter maybe.

Norma folded the letters and returned them to their envelopes. "I'm sorry your mother never got to read these. I hope you did manage to mail others. When did she die? You never did tell me."

"Honeychild, how about stowing this stuff and going into Beaufort for dinner?" They liked the food and the warm welcome they always received at the Ocean View Cafe on Bay Street. Since Anne was five weeks old, she had gone with them, lying on a pillow placed in the booth seat while they dined, and afterwards, they pushed her carriage along Bay Street and window shopped. Norma had learned not to linger too long before a store window display or something would appear gift wrapped on one of their special days. Harry was the inveterate gift-giver, and had infinite patience in buying and hiding presents for her until the day arrived that he wanted to celebrate, such as his latest gift, an AIR PAC travel case given to her on September 30th, the anniversary of their first meeting just over a year ago. "How did you guess I wanted it?" She had asked in surprise.

"From observing you when you saw it, and I know you think you should do something extra nice for me, such as washing and ironing my uniform before you ask for anything. But please don't wash them anymore, even with a washing machine. I can send them to the post laundry as I did before you came to Parris Island. Honeychild, I didn't marry you to be my servant."

Today they did more than window shop. They selected china and flatware patterns and bought a place setting of each. For china, Norma chose Havilland's Rosalinde with its tiny pink flowers in a spray of green leaves on milk white ground. For flatware, Harry selected Gorham sterling with simple classic lines. "We'll buy a place setting of each, every month," she said happily, "and by January we can invite two guests for dinner and by Easter, four. And next week I'm starting to make curtains and slipcovers."

"Why don't we buy service for six today?" he suggested.

"No, that would be extravagant. It's better to do it my way and look forward to it month by month. Just like I'm looking forward to hearing about your fathers, one by one!"

"Can it wait until we get home?" Harry asked. "I think the occasion calls for a drink." They left Beaufort, driving out Ribault Road, across Battery Creek to the sentry gate where Harry slowed the car for entry, then across the two lane causeway. Norma watched the late afternoon shadows flit in and out between the oleanders. At Headquarters Building the color guard lowered the flag as the bugle sounded. Harry stopped the car, got out, stood at attention, saluting. When the ceremony was completed, he got into the car and drove home. Her heart expanded with happiness at living on a military base, being married to a Marine.

15

Norma put Anne to bed and Harry took his Jack Daniel's over ice to the living room, got an ashtray and settled himself on the couch. "Sure you don't want one?"

She shook her head no and sat beside him. He drew her against his chest, his left arm around her waist. "Mmm, this is my version of heaven: twilight time, comfortable in our own little home, my woman in my arms. What more could a man want?"

Norma curled her legs on the couch, luxuriating in the pleasure of his body close to hers. Harry took a sip from his glass, lit a cigarette and began, "My mother was sixteen years old and already separated from my father when I was born on a small backwoods farm in Minnesota. My maternal grandmother, a widow about forty-five years old, was the head of the family which consisted of my mother, two uncles and an aunt, all under twenty. The family abode was an unfinished clapboard house, hurriedly built by my grandfather before he died. There was a damp cellar, one room at ground level, and a small attic accessible by way of a ladder, down which, as a child, I had many painful falls.

"Soon after I first heard the wolves howl in the nearby tamarack swamps, my mother left me with the family to accept gainful employment as a housemaid in Minneapolis to a Lutheran minister. It must have been within the next year that she was married to her employer's son. I was two years and eight months old when my half brother was born.

"A year or two later, my stepfather acquired a farm some fifteen miles from my birthplace, and thereafter my place of residence alternated between my grandmother's house and my mother's in cycles of approximately three months duration until I reached school age. My formal education began at the usual age of six and my home from then on was with my grandmother. The one-room school house, in which eight grades were taught by one teacher, was two and one fourth miles from home. The first mile was a footpath most of which passed through a tamarack swamp inhabited by wolves that were wont to begin their calls at early twilight. Many times, when I played too long after school was dismissed, I would fly through that swamp, literally crying with fright. Upon reaching home, I would congratulate myself for outrunning the wolves. I recall now though, that rabbits and other lesser game were then plentiful.

"The summer after I had successfully completed two grades in school we saw the Halley Comet and with it, my grandmother was certain, came a complete crop failure on the farm. A payment was due on the mortgage. The tax collector was to be reckoned with. Coffee, salt, sugar, kerosene, and clothing for the winter were still to be gotten. I remember that my grandmother cried a lot.

"At that time my aunt used to read Horatio Alger stories to me. When one of my uncles, somehow, got a job as manager of a large wheat farm in the western part of the state, I thought Alger should write another story. We now had a big three-room house to live in, a big barn, five horses, a cow, all kinds of machinery, and soon there would be more money than we had ever had before. But most of all, at that time, was the wonderful day long train ride. I never knew anything could go so fast. The telephone poles, far apart, went by so quickly. But the memory of that ride faded quickly. There were so many other things to be marveled at. Jack rabbits, badgers, prairie chickens, gray gophers bigger than squirrels, dozens of grain elevators on the horizon, some of them twenty miles away but clearly visible across the flat oceans of wheat, the long freight trains that passed within a half mile of our house, and the school house only a mile away. From our porch I could count the windows. In the plowed fields there was white stuff that looked like patches of snow. I was to learn more about alkali soon, but now everything was wonderfully fine. Especially after my uncle got a pony for me to ride when I carried his lunch to him in the field.

"Life was pleasant there. The school was big and modern, two rooms and two teachers, only four grades in each room, and so near home. The neighbors were friendly. The nearest were only a half mile away, and we visited often. There were only three in the family now. My aunt and uncle had gotten employment somewhere. I missed my aunt, but didn't think about her too often. We were always busy. I had chickens, ducks, and turkeys to care for and a cow to milk.

"The first year passed pleasantly. Late one evening during the second harvest time I saw a peculiar black cloud, shaped like an hourglass, moving toward us across the prairie. Wind began to blow harder than usual. My uncle seemed quite excited and hurriedly put all the animals into the pasture. It grew dark suddenly and we ran to the house. My grandmother and uncle didn't speak but they acted strangely, closing all the doors and windows. Rain, heavier than I had ever seen, pounded on the windows and seeped through the frames. It was dark as midnight, the house trembled under the wind's impact, and my grandmother prayed, in German. She didn't speak English very well. My eyes must have been two round balls set in chalk as I sat still listening to my heart beat above the roar of the storm. If that lump would only be still so I could talk!

"The next morning our floors were still wet but the weather was clear, sunny and still. One of the neighbor's big barns was completely demolished and scattered about the vicinity; another was still standing, but at right angles to its foundation. It was all very interesting but soon put out of mind. The harvest wasn't damaged.

"One day, a few weeks later, during plowing time, my uncle came in early from the field and put up the horses. He coughed and spat up blood. He went inside and got into bed. The next morning he didn't get up. There were nearly three hundred acres of wheat field to be plowed and frost would come soon. My grandmother said I would have to stay home from school. She and I, standing on boxes and milk cans, harnessed the four-horse team, drove it to the field, hitched it to gang plow, and I was in business at the age of ten. She walked to town and returned with the doctor. After ten days my uncle again was able to plow. But before the field was plowed, he suffered another attack. The doctor came again and I learned that the alkali in the drinking water didn't agree with my uncle's constitution. Within a few days we were on a train again. Going East.

"My uncle recovered and found work in Canada. My grandmother and I remained in Minnesota with various near and distant relatives, living with different ones for various periods. I attended at least two different schools each year until the eighth grade.

"The Lusitania had been torpedoed by the Germans. War tension was mounting. One evening in February, 1917, the sun at setting was ruby red. My grandmother said, 'That is a sure sign of war.' Some Marines had passed through town in their blue uniforms with red and gold stripes and shiny brass buttons. I read their recruiting literature and was convinced that if it were possible to make the world safe for democracy, the Marines would do it.

"A few days later I earned a quarter by helping the depot agent move several tons of freight in the warehouse. As he was paying me, the four-fifteen local whistled its arrival at the outskirts of town. I waited to see it. The engine stopped right in front of me. A few seconds later it whistled again and began to move. I watched it for a moment, then ran toward the tender and climbed to a place in front of the baggage car. At five-thirty the train reached Minneapolis and stopped at the station. I jumped from my hiding place and fell down. My legs were numb with cold. I was bewildered, hungry, and covered with soot and coal dust. A policeman came toward me and, after asking a few questions, took me to a Salvation Army home. There I was told to wash up, was given some delicious hot soup and a bunk in a large room with many strange men, different from any I had ever seen before.

"Early next morning we were roused and put to work at mopping floors, making up bunks, polishing cuspidors, and cleaning the wash room. Already somewhat disillusioned and lonesome for my close friends, I left there and began my trip to the Marine recruiting office thinking perhaps a bit hopefully, 'They won't take me, I'm only fourteen; they'll know I'm underage.' But recruiting offices had to meet their quotas. There was a sinking feeling in the pit of my stomach as my train began to move out of the station that night. I was on my way to California.

"Time passed at a gallop. Everything was new to me, exciting, and not unpleasant. I completed training with flying colors. Then came my assignment to guard duty at the Mare Island Navy Yard. War had been declared. There was hard work during the day and little rest at night. The ammunition depot exploded with a blast that shook the island. I was transferred there to help guard the remaining powder magazines. After having been a Marine four months I wrote my first letter home, to my grandmother. In it, I described in vivid detail the difficult and dangerous times I had experienced. One month later I was back in Minneapolis living in a small rented house with my grandmother and my uncle who had returned from Canada.

"At the beginning of the next school term, I re-entered the eighth grade but did not complete the term. The war songs and recruiting posters were more than I could resist. In March, 1919, I enlisted in the Navy under the name of my stepfather to conceal my previous underage service in the Marine Corps. On arrival at the training camp near Cape May, New Jersey, I promptly wrote my grandmother and begged her to let me stay this time. She gave me her blessing, and I completed training, was immediately promoted to petty officer rank, and then hospitalized with scarlet fever and placed in an overcrowded ward with patients suffering from influenza, spinal meningitis, and venereal diseases. Before I had recovered from scarlet fever, my right eye became infected with gonococcus, and during the next ten days a nurse was stationed at my bed twenty-four hours a day to prevent the infection from reaching the other eye. Not until after my eye became normal again was the nature of that ailment explained to me. From the hospital I was transferred to New York for duty on the coal-burning cruiser *Montana*. My arrival aboard was timed to coincide with the beginning of an operation called 'coaling ship'. After shoveling dusty coal almost ceaselessly for two days, I thought I would die, but was afraid I wouldn't. Before we had scrubbed and washed the coal dust off the ship, we sailed past the Statue of Liberty, and at sea we rendezvoused with a number of transports which we escorted to Brest in France.

"Being on watch two hours of every six, working between watches, and sleeping only three or four hours a night, in a hammock, soon reduced the fire of my patriotism to a dull red glow. But I managed to survive the war without having heard a shot fired in anger. After a few trips to Bordeaux on a transport returning troops to the United States, I was discharged in July, 1919.

"Then I worked at a wagon factory in Minneapolis painting wagon frames until the end of September when I returned to my grandmother's small home town and started my first year in high school. I completed four years of high school by working in foundries, with construction crews, and railroad steel-laying gangs during the summer months, usually into October. My scholastic work was slightly below average, but I starred in basketball, track, wrestling, and baseball and was graduated in 1923 on my twenty-first birthday.

"During my junior year I fell in love and it was then that I began to feel my lack of family and social background. It was then too that I first harbored a desire to achieve a definite goal. My objective was to somehow provide a home for a family of my own. I was offered an athletic scholarship at St. Thomas College and I attended one year. My scholarship was renewed. Over the summer vacation I earned one hundred dollars. Everything was going wonderfully well until I got talked into joining a poker game. I was just a pawn and when the game was over, I had been separated from my earnings. The blow to my self-respect was greater than to my pocketbook, which was bad enough. I didn't return to St. Thomas and I have never gambled again.

"I accepted a civil service appointment to a clerical job in Washington, D.C. My salary was ninety-five dollars a month. During the next two years that was increased to one hundred fifteen, but my savings amounted to less than I deemed necessary to establish a home. Feeling discouraged and beaten, I gave up the idea of marriage and quit my job to drift aimlessly for several months. While working at a temporary job in a Chicago post office, I again enlisted in the Marine Corps and had my 1926 Christmas dinner here at PI. Following the completion of yet another recruit training course came an assignment to the island boat crew where I operated a fifty-foot motor launch transporting workers, mail, and cargo to and from the mainland. That was before the causeway was built.

"After a few months, I was made coxswain of the general's barge. When he was assigned another command, I was sent to Nicaragua, arriving there in April, 1928. That tour of duty was culminated by an eleven month patrol in the jungle where we chased the elusive Sandino like a St. Bernard trying to corner a fox. Of that forty- man patrol, one died with black-water fever and another disappeared while on sentry duty one night, never to be heard of again. Of the thirty-eight gaunt and haggard survivors, thirty-six were hospitalized with malaria and dysentery when we returned to our east coast base.

"In January, 1930, I arrived at the Charleston Navy Yard in Boston for five months of pleasant duty as sergeant of the guard. With June came orders to Nicaragua again, for duty in connection with the national election there, which was to be supervised by Navy and Marine personnel. At five one afternoon, I boarded the coastwise steamer *Fairfax* bound for Norfolk for further transportation. Three hours later in a pea-soup fog, we collided with the loaded tanker *Pinthus* off Cape Cod. The tanker and her crew perished in a mountain of fire. The *Fairfax,* surrounded by mast high flames, somehow backed out of that inferno, but with a loss of forty lives. Some weeks later, I received a letter of commendation from the Secretary of the Navy for my part in bringing the fire under control and for my assistance in the restoration of order on the ship--it said.

"Although detained two weeks to testify at the investigation of the collision, I eventually arrived in Bluefields, Nicaragua to attend a six-week course in Spanish and electoral law. From there I was sent to a settlement near the Honduran border, via dugout canoe, about two hundred miles up the Wanks River as it flows, to organize election procedure and to assure those natives who wished to vote that they could do so freely, secretly, and without fear of reprisal regardless of the election results. A squad of Marines constituted my authority, and it was respected. Slightly more than a hundred ballots were cast, ninety-five percent of them signed with an **X**, which I officially witnessed.

"With the election duty completed, I was farmed out to the Nicaraguan government to serve as an officer in the recently organized native army. My first assignment was that of district commander of an isolated area in the mountainous northwest province of Segovia, where the bandit rebel leader, Sandino, and his followers were operating most vigorously to challenge the authority of the legitimate government. My garrison consisted of twenty-eight semi-literate natives, none of whom could speak or understand English. My only means of communication with the area headquarters, thirty-two miles away, was a battery powered telegraph system which the rebels kept inoperative by cutting the wire.

"On my eighth day there we were attacked at midnight by a howling, screaming mob armed with rifles, shotguns, handmade bombs, and a few automatic weapons. At the sound of the first shot, I literally jumped out of my native cot, but before my feet touched the dirt floor my men were already firing the machine guns and grenade dischargers. How they got out there so quickly, I never knew. Perhaps I was even more paralyzed with fright than I realized and was temporarily immobilized. As daylight drew near, the attackers withdrew carrying their dead and wounded with them. One of our men was wounded, his stomach torn open from side to side by a bomb fragment. We poured a mild solution of potassium permanganate over the wound and then carried him twelve miles on an improvised stretcher to the main trail. From there he was taken to area headquarters in an ox cart escorted by a squad of our men. He survived.

"That experience filled me with a deep sense of respect and admiration for my little brown brothers, which they sensed and returned generously. Although some of my acquaintances, in other districts, were killed in mutinies, I always felt secure in the loyalty of my men, even though they were highly emotional and subject to violent passions.

"Of the many strange events I witnessed, or participated in, during my five years in Nicaragua, one relatively minor incident returns to my recollections more often than any other. Early one night during a torrential rain which had begun several hours before, one of our rebel prisoners, a giant of a man with the docile disposition of a kitten, approached me and said, 'On a night such as this, Cupertino will be in his hut. I know where it is and can guide you to it.' Cupertino was a rebel official who acted as Sandino's postmaster general, and it was known that he was somewhere in our district. The night was foreboding, mountain streams would be high and fast, trails would be knee-deep in mud, but Cupertino was a big fish and his capture would add glory to our ambitious little garrison. We decided to try for him. I and five of my craftiest jungle men sat out behind our rebel guide. Before we arrived there, I wondered if he was leading us into a trap, but finally he stopped short and whispered, 'There it is!' In the darkness it took several seconds before we could discern the dim outline of the little hut in the vines and bushes a few yards ahead of us.

"We spread out along two sides of the hut. I turned on my flashlight and my sergeant called out, 'Whoever is in there, come out.' We were answered with the flash and crack of a rifle. Instantly we returned that fire with a dozen or more volleys and then called out again. There was no reply, but we could hear a small whimpering sound in the hut. I again turned on my flashlight. Nothing happened. In a cold sweat I walked the few steps to the door, pushed aside the wet, ragged cloth covering, and looked in. Cupertino, his woman, and another man were lying, bullet riddled, on the muddy floor. On a native cot, half nude, lay a baby boy, softly crying but unharmed. We couldn't take him with us over the arduous route we had to travel in the rain and darkness. We couldn't stay in that rebel stronghold until daylight and get out alive. We left him, and hoped that others of his kind would rescue him before the mountain lions, drawn by the smell of blood, arrived. Even to this day, I think of him often. He should be about fourteen now. I wonder if he ever knew the love of a kind, sympathetic grandmother and uncle.

"After American intervention in Nicaragua ended, I was returned to San Diego and admitted to the hospital with scurvy which lasted about three weeks. In March, 1933, I was transferred to Shanghai, China. American dollars were big money there. Leisure time in abundance. To Marines, recreation was synonymous with Russian princesses, cabarets, and vodka. I partook to excess. After a few months, disgusted with myself, I requested to be discharged. My request was granted.

"Early in 1934, I visited my remaining relatives in Minnesota. My grandmother was still alive and in good health. My mother was married to her third husband. My half brother, who had completed his college courses and was commissioned in the Marine Corps aviation reserve, was superintendent of schools in a small town. No jobs were to be had there during the depression. I finally found work at Hoover Dam. My foreman had attended a school of mines. He knew of the gold in Nicaragua and suggested we go there. We did, and found a good pocket from which we panned three or four ounces a day. Things looked promising until a group of armed bandits chased us out one day and destroyed our equipment. It took us twelve days to get back to Puerto Cabeza where we had deposited money in a bank to pay passage back to the States in the event of an emergency. I was disembarked on a stretcher in New Orleans and taken to Charity Hospital with dengue fever.

"Discharged from the hospital, penniless, and no jobs available, I went to a relief station for aid. Then I hitchhiked from one relief station to another and eventually enlisted in the Civilian Conservation Corps at a camp near Springfield, Missouri. In November, 1935, I re-enlisted in the Marine Corps. At Quantico, Virginia I became interested in artillery and completed a correspondence course in mapping and artillery mathematics. During the following four years, I performed various artillery duties in Puerto Rico, the Virgin Islands, and Panama. After fifteen months on Midway Island, where we established a defense system and moved heavy seacoast guns to the tops of sand dunes, by the same method which I believe the Egyptians used in building the pyramids, I was sent to Pearl Harbor for a rest period. I was still resting when the Japanese bombed our fleet and other facilities there on 7 December, 1941. On Christmas day I boarded a seagoing tug bound for Johnston Island. There I was commissioned to second lieutenant. Returned to the States a year later, I spent Christmas 1942 in San Diego. After the holidays I was again sent to Pearl Harbor and from there to Australia, New Guinea, Woodlark Island, New Britain, Guadalcanal, Peleliu, and Okinawa.

"At the end of the war, I was returned by air to Pearl Harbor, by ship to San Francisco and given a forty-day leave. With the first available transportation, I was on my way to Georgia to meet a girl with whom, for more than twenty months, I had maintained a correspondence initiated by a mutual friend. Two days following our meeting we were married and spent a delightful honeymoon, of two weeks duration, in a one room stone cottage in the Smoky Mountains of Tennessee where we lived primarily on love. We had to. We seemed unable to leave for food; our 'just one more kiss before we go' begun at the door always catapulted us back under the covers. Right, Honeychild?" He squeezed her gently and asked softly, "Mmmm, I wonder if that still holds true. Shall we test it?" He turned her towards him, thinking her shaking shoulders were from laughter, but her tears caused his smile to fade. "Norma, why, you're crying! What's wrong, little darling?"

She pressed into his shoulder, her arms tight around him. She had listened, almost without breathing, to the casual description of a life of parental rejection, hardship, isolation, danger, and disappointment, ending with humor and possibly a little bit of fear. In the telling his voice had not matched the tension of his body. And his eyes held the same apprehension as on that day at the artillery range when he had 'casually' left his official health record, showing his true age, on the car seat for her to find. How should she respond? He was not asking for sympathy, only giving her the facts as if they had happened to someone else. But it had happened to him, and he knew it, because in letters he had revealed to her, *I've never known real happiness* and *You've made me want a home, Norma. It has been so long since I lived in one.* Words that, at the time, had chilled her heart. But now she remembered other words: *This is my version of heaven, twilight time, comfortable in our own little home, my woman in my arms. What more could a man want?*

Her tears had been for many reasons, but they were unnecessary; he was happy. She took his face in her hands, "Nothing's wrong, my darling, everything's as it should be! And now, would you like to make the test you mentioned, or would you rather have a ham sandwich?"

"You know the answer to that!" and he held her so tightly that there wasn't breath enough in her to say," HARRY, don't ...please, don't...please!"

16

There were twenty-two windows in their bungalow and except for the three in the living room, Norma covered them with Priscilla style curtains. She sewed together yards and yards of six-inch strips, hemmed one side, ruffled the other, and stitched them to the curved side of wide panels, two to a window. For two weeks she sewed to cover nineteen windows. She made drapes for the living room in one day, hemming the sides and ends of three fifteen-foot lengths, then swaging the middle of each over a curtain rod to form a valence; the rest hung as side panels to frame the windows. These panels could be used in future quarters, no matter the size of the windows, an idea she had borrowed from a seasoned Marine wife at Sterling Housing.

Another week at the sewing machine and new slip covers were on the couch and chairs. By the end of one month, MOQ 56 had become a cozy home, cheerful with red-rosed, green-leafed tieback curtains, peaceful with jade colored drapes, and restful with off-white slip covers. Pastel green scatter rugs hugged the polished wooden floors and the framed black and white scenes of the Smoky Mountains decorated the walls. Harry bought a portable record player from the Post Exchange along with a few recordings and from then on there was music of their choosing in the Kipp quarters.

In Charleston, looking for table linen and crystal stemware, they also searched for "Mood Indigo" by Duke Ellington. They were successful only in linen and stemware; Harry would settle for no rendition of the song save the Duke's.

As last year at Pendleton, Harry was OD on Thanksgiving Day. This year, even with the duty, he planned to eat at home. Norma was cooking her first turkey dinner. She asked him to enter by the kitchen, which he did anyway since he parked the car at the back of the house, because she didn't want him to see the dining room table until time to eat. Tonight was the debut of their new dinner service.

"I left the carving for you," she greeted him at the door, "I can't quite see how to do it. This is the skinniest bird even if it does weigh fourteen pounds, the same as Anne. It looked fatter though before I cooked it. See, it's lying lopsided in the pan."

Harry, sharpening the carving knife, looked down on the roasted turkey. He gave it a deft turn with the knife and fork and flipped it breast side up. She stared in amazement, "Now it looks how it's supposed to look, like in the cookbook. I'll declare, I do believe I cooked it upside down!"

Harry bit his lip to keep from laughing, "My little gourmet cook."

"No," she corrected him, "your little country bumpkin," and they both burst out laughing.

The meal was a tribute to her culinary skill and Harry proved it by eating from dish after dish of delicious food gracing the table. Norma's cheeks were flushed with pleasure, and in the kitchen every pot and pan they owned were stacked for washing, along with six plates, two cups and saucers, two water goblets, and twelve pieces of flatware. "You know," she confided after the meal, "I don't think I'll ever get used to a separate plate for bread and butter and a separate butter knife. I'm not sure I want to be all that socially proper."

Harry helped her clear the table, "You're telling me we could have gotten along just as well with only a dinner plate, water glass, one knife, fork, and spoon?"

"Yes, just as we do at every meal."

Pretending shock he admonished, "Think of all the money we could have saved!"

"And for that, Smarty, you'll have to help with the dishes."

Harry finished his OD duties, slept four hours, then they left for a weekend in La Fayette. There, Norma discovered that Mary Lee had become a four-year old terror, undisciplined and rude, talking back to her parents, doing and eating as she pleased. Mama, looking tired, was clearly resigned to Mary Lee's tyranny. Daddy thought it was hopeless. "Let me have her for a while," Norma offered, "She has both of you wrapped around her little finger and it's not good for any of you. I promise you she'll be a changed child when we bring her back."

"You got that backward," Daddy said, "You'll be the changed one. You don't know how stubborn she is, just like a Georgia mule."

Norma knew because she had heard Mary Lee say, "If I cry long enough, I get my way." And she knew she could hold out against the child unlike her parents who must have grown tired from raising the rest of them with harsh discipline. Discipline that had paid off. Mary Lee was being raised differently and nobody was happy with the results. Before leaving, Norma took Julia aside, the sister she had loved from the moment of her birth, the one with the great brown eyes and gentle ways. "Wait until summer and school is out," she whispered, "then we'll come for you."

Three weeks later, on another whirlwind weekend trip, a transformed Mary Lee was returned home. She was saying "please" and "thank you", taking afternoon naps, smiling and laughing instead of scowling, eating properly and her chronic constipation was corrected. "Why, it's a miracle," her parents marveled. "How on earth did you do it?"

"With a lot of patience," Norma sighed, "and a set of rules we both followed. I gave her choices and held her to them and didn't give in to her whims and demands."

"And I'll bet a lot of spankings," Tommy said.

"No, never." Mary Lee in Norma's lap pulled her head down, to whisper, "Tell 'em 'bout when you made me stay in my room."

"Are you sure you want me to?" Norma whispered back. Mary Lee agreed, then hid her face behind her hands. "All right, but remember it was your idea." And to the family, "I was wrapping your Christmas presents with Mary Lee watching. When I was finished, she came over to the packages and began kicking them, splitting the paper. All my work for nothing. I asked her why she did it and she pouted, 'because I wanted you to play with me and you wouldn't.' I told her she had just lost more play time with me and sent her to her room until Harry came home. When he came through the door, she ran to tell him of the surprise record I had for him, but she talked so fast he couldn't understand." Looking down at Mary Lee's upturned face, Norma added, "Good thing he didn't, Miss Priss, or you might have gotten that long deserved spanking." Mary Lee buried her face in Norma's chest, then stole a look at her parents. Everyone laughed except Mary Lee; she cried, wanting to go back to Parris Island with them.

* * *

The folding crib, ordered to replace Anne's bassinet, had finally arrived at the PX. Its white wooden frame, totally enclosed with screen wire for protection against the prevalent flying insects, was a popular style for Parris Island babies. Norma moved the bassinet out of Anne's room and the crib in. She put on pink sheets and the new quilt she had just completed with the appliqued pink and white gingham animals. She hung gingham curtains over the double windows and rearranged the dressing table, chest of drawers, and rocking chair, then hung the cross-stitched prayer Harry had framed. On a sheet of white cardboard, divided into sections by days and hours, she wrote Anne's daily activities: Eat, Bathe, Play, Nap, Carriage Ride, Time with Daddy, and Bedtime. Across the top in one-inch letters she printed: S C H E L U D E

Standing back to look at her handiwork, she could hardly wait for Harry to come home to see it. Hearing him arrive, she rushed to lead him with a grand flourish down the hallway to Anne's room, "Your daughter's nursery awaits your inspection, Sir."

He surveyed the pleasant room in a sweeping look, "It's a swell little nursery, Honeychild."

"Do you think she likes it?" Norma asked excitedly.

"That's difficult to judge from a five month infant, but see, she's drooling over the quilt you sewed for her."

"Oh, Harry, be serious," she chided gently.

"Want to know what I like best?" He almost suppressed a smile.

"Yes, tell me!" Her face glowed with expectancy.

"It's your sche-lude."

"My what?" Norma threw him a puzzled glance.

"Your *sche-lude*," and grinning, he nodded toward the schedule posted by the door. Norma stared hard at the chart, saw its misspelled title, and instantly her joy was gone. Lowering her face to conceal spilling tears, she ran from the nursery. Harry, close behind, quickly caught and held her to him. "Let me go," she moaned into his chest. "Let me go."

But he held her until she ceased to struggle, "Norma darling, that was so thoughtless and mean of me. Forgive me--surely you know I would rather die than deliberately hurt you." He cupped her face in his hands, "Forgive me, please, and open your eyes to look at me. Please."

Opening her eyes narrowly, she saw the contrition on his face. Suddenly the humor in her officious and proud attitude, along with her overreaction, struck her as very funny, and she began to laugh, her body shaking from it, "Spelling was always my downfall," she gasped when she could speak, "but I wanted so much to impress you."

"And you do impress me, Honeychild, in so many wonderful ways, but in spelling, well--but I married you anyway, didn't I?"

"Oh, my," she sighed. "Then I've done it a lot?"

"A few times--certain words-- and I always had to smile when you wrote anniversary, spelling it *anniversity*. It made me wonder if it was deliberate or a Freudian slip." Now he laughed, but carefully.

Disengaging herself from his arms, Norma assumed a stately stance and broke into verse: *Sweet are the uses of adversity; which, like the toad, ugly and venomous, wears yet a precious jewel in his head and this our life exempt from public haunt, find tongues in trees, books in running brooks, sermons in stones, and good in everything...*

Harry bowed, "Perhaps you're not a champion speller, but who else quotes Shakespeare to me?"

"I could quote more, but first tell me about a Freudian slip."

Harry winked, "A Freudian slip is an unconscious word choice to express a real intent. You always spelled anniversary as anniversity."

"It wasn't that; it was just poor spelling."

"I accept that," he took her in his arms again, "How about a recess from education? Let's play a game of acey-deucy. Is there time before dinner?"

"If you settle for a sandwich and a bowl of soup. But I should tell you that if I win the next two games, I'll win the tournament and you'll have to give me a prize."

"And you know what it will be, don't you?" His amusement evident once more.

"No, tell me!" She was joyful once more.

"*Webster's Dictionary!*"

"Oh, sweet are the uses of adversity--" and laughing she set up the game, threw the dice: an ace and a deuce. "See, I told you! I'm going to win."

* * *

On Christmas Eve, Norma made a nest of pillows on the rug before the blazing fire, the first Harry had made in their fireplace. They were waiting for midnight.

One day we'll be sitting hand in hand before our fireplace, silently dreaming as we gaze into the dancing flames while some little body near us in a little white crib stares in uncomprehending wonder at the new toe he has just discovered. Believe in that, Norma, and it will come true.

"Come back to me, Honeychild; you were so far away."

"Not really. I was with you, but back in time with you." Her eyes found his and she asked, "Harry, do you think 'wishing makes it so'?"

"I think 'believing' makes it so. Isn't that what we did, for all those months we waited? To me, belief was as tangible as your letters. I sent it out to you, intending to keep it before us both, until as time moved forward and the miles separating us grew fewer, we would finally be side by side. And here we are, and look, it's midnight!"

Norma jumped up to gather their presents from beneath the tree, handing him first, obviously, a record, but not just any record.

"*Mood Indigo!* By the Duke! You angel, tell me, how do you always find the things that are so hard to find?"

"This, I found in the Sears and Roebuck catalogue."

"If I play it softly, do you think it will wake the baby?" They listened and the baby slept on. "Do you like it, too?" he asked.

"It's dreamy," she answered, swaying with the music.

"Dreamy, yes, and so are you," he kissed her ear lobe. "Here, this is for my dream girl."

She unstoppered a bottle of Prince Matchabelli's Beloved and whiffed its sensual fragrance, "Oh, Harry, I could never live up to this."

His eyes danced, "I think you'll find a way."

She moistened her finger with a drop and touched it to his nose. He sniffed, appraisingly, "It's perfect. Wear it for me tonight," he invited. She touched it to all the places he loved to kiss while he thumbed through the fat photograph album which now held all his pictures from the footlockers, except those of Jean. "Gee! Honeychild, these pictures never had it so good. And neither have I. Here, allow me to show my appreciation." From the pocket of his robe he withdrew an envelope. Across its face he had written: **This is a cocktail dress.** As she continued to stare at it, he commanded, "Go on, open it."

"Oh-h-h-h," Norma drew in her breath, looking at Benjamin Franklin's face. "I've never seen this before."

"Old Ben Franklin?"

"No, a hundred dollar bill. My goodness, Harry..."

"I want you to buy the nicest dress you can find to wear to the Officers Club when I finally persuade you to go with me, and rest assured that day is drawing close." His firmness made it clear that it was futile to argue.

"But, Harry, with a hundred dollars, I could buy *five* nice dresses."

"Don't!" he said emphatically, "for once, please don't economize."

"All right, I'll think about it," she yielded. "Now, you open this." His package was wrapped in royal blue corduroy; inside more was made into a robe. "Try it on," she urged, standing to hold it ready. He rose, dropping the robe he wore and slipping his arms into the new one. She moved closer, smoothing the shoulders, adjusting the collar, tying the belt, inspecting for fit. Satisfied, she deftly untied the belt, opened the robe and slipped her hands inside to slide over his bare, muscled body. As she knew it would, his desire rose between them, he held her tighter, whispering in astonishment, "Honeychild!" and kissing her with a fierceness that sent her near to swooning. She clung to him, trembling in expectation as he lowered her slowly to their bed before the fire. And later they lay in a heap, covered by his new blue robe and when their breathing quieted, she listened to the low flames fluttering about the burning logs. And then his exclamation, "My God, I didn't give a thought to that damn diaphragm!"

"Shhh," she soothed him, "I did."

"Mmmm, it seems you thought of everything."

"I was only following orders. Didn't you tell me to 'find a way'? Well, how'd I do?"

"Oh, Honeychild, what a stroke of genius on my part when I bought that perfume."

17

Norma's cedar chest arrived three days after Christmas and Harry placed it at the foot of their bed. Together they removed the things she had put into it so many months ago: towel sets, matching sheets and pillow cases with elaborate hand-embroidered borders; dish towels hemstitched and labeled by the days of the week; tea cloths with napkins, two embroidered with floral designs and one appliqued with colorful fruit in each corner; and two full sized quilts, one with the linked wedding ring pattern, the other a sunburst. Harry examined each and every thing in detail, smiling in appreciation, "Norma, I had no idea the things you wrote of making were so fine, and so many, there must be a million stitches here!"

"And everyone a stitch of love; all I could bring to the marriage."

"Not all, " he corrected her, "you brought the most important thing of all: yourself."

"Yes, myself--and these few things, my only possessions as Norma Louise Clinton. I don't have such fine medals as yours but I do have one for perfect attendance in Sunday School four years in a row. And this. She opened a small leather bound Bible to its first page.

Presented to Norma Clinton
for perfect attendance at Sunday School
by her teacher Mrs. W.D. Dunwoody
December 1937

"During those four years I practically memorized this Bible and when you were on Okinawa, I read it every night."

"Maybe that's why I was allowed to come home, Honeychild. I always sensed a great protection during that time." He took the Bible to hold while she showed him a copy of *The Rambler*, her high school newspaper, final edition of 1943-44 whose cover featured the "Senior Class History" by Norma Louise Clinton; her high school diploma; and school letter, an orange L bordered in black. Alone in the bottom of the chest lay a lavender crocheted sweater. Norma reached for it to hold against herself, "Aunt Ruby made this for me when I was ten years old."

"So tiny. Please, tell me about the little girl who once wore this."

"From the beginning?" She asked, smiling. Seeing his nod she began, "Do you remember where we stopped for an hour at the motel of 'ill repute' just north of Birmingham? That was near my birthplace, my parents too. They moved from Alabama when I was a baby, going to Aragon, Georgia where Joan was born in 1929, and then a year or so later they moved to La Fayette. We lived in various boarding houses until I was five, then Daddy rented a house and later bought it, the one where they live now. A year later, I started to school. Things were great there, not so great at home. We were three years into the depression and the lean years were getting leaner. Daddy couldn't find work in his trade. I guess we were close to starving. Tommy was born that spring of 1934 and Daddy was forced to ask for food, diapers, and firewood at the relief office. Mama said that changed him, that he was never the same afterward. She was probably right. Before, he used to play his French harp or sing. Sometimes he'd put on his minstrel suit, a wiry black wig, black his face, and buck dance on the stage at the movie theater with three other men. He was light on his feet; a boxer, too--a light weight--small but strong, and handsome with his jet black hair and deep blue eyes. Every Wednesday night there were boxing matches on the stage of the movie theater. Sometimes, we got to go when Daddy was boxing. The winner got part of the admission money; Daddy won once. The last time he boxed he broke his hand. He gave up boxing to save his hand for brick laying. He had high hopes of finding work after Franklin Delano Roosevelt became president.

"Daddy along with all our neighbors pinned hope on him and they were rewarded. Daddy practically worshipped that man. After President Roosevelt got the WPA projects going and Daddy was able to get bricklaying jobs, be became obsessed with work and the garden he planted every year. He worked every daylight hour, well or sick. He didn't trust banks, kept his savings in a sock in his underwear drawer. Sometimes Mama would take it out and we'd all count it. We felt rich, knowing we had some money, even if our clothes were too small or patched. Daddy wouldn't spend a penny that he didn't have to, and he wouldn't buy a thing on time. Never has, even now. Mama was great on pinching pennies and we never threw a thing away, always finding some way to use everything once, twice, or even three times. To this day, I can't be wasteful."

"So that's where your frugality came from," Harry frowned. "Sometimes, I wish you would be frivolous, Honeychild."

"I couldn't be, I'd feel guilty remembering how hard Mama had it, working in the garden, canning all summer long, washing clothes in a wash pot, making our clothes from hand-me-downs, doing without. She never left the house. I was her errand girl, going to town with money tied in a handkerchief and a list of things to buy. That's how I learned to shop and I wouldn't take a million dollars for what it taught me. I used to feel so sad hearing Mama tell of their hopes in the Twenties when they were first married before the crash of the stock market. By then they had two babies. And it didn't stop with two. Tommy was born in 1934 and Julia in 1936. That summer Tommy nearly died from colitis. Joan had it too. She got well; Tommy get sicker. His hair came out; he forgot how to walk and talk. The doctors said they couldn't do any more for him; he was in God's hands. When he got cold up to his knees, and his lips turned blue, Mama asked our neighbor, a preacher, to call a prayer meeting. A lot of people came, mostly people we didn't know, and prayed around Tommy's bed. Almost at once he began to get well.

"For some time Mama had been unhappy with Daddy's drinking. He, his daddy, and uncle would have drinking binges and when he came home drunk or sick, we were terrified. He'd get mad if we made the least bit of noise or walked across the floor and made it shake. But after Tommy got well, Daddy stopped drinking and joined the whole family to the Methodist Church, not the church of the people who prayed over Tommy, but the one in town where the doctor went, the one who couldn't help Tommy.

"That Sunday was the first and last time we all went to church together as a family. We lived two miles out of town and someone from the church came in a car to drive us. I don't know why, but I felt sick and didn't want to go, but Daddy said I had to. I can still see the six of us going down the aisle, Julia in Mama's arms and Tommy in Daddy's, Joan and I walking down to the curved banister of the pulpit where the minister waited for us. It was steamy hot that August day, the church was full of staring faces, and

I had on a scratchy pink dress with white dots. I felt so sick all I could do was lean on the banister and rest my head on my arms and wonder whether or not my panties were showing.

"Then began Daddy's Bible reading, every day and twice on Sunday, and hour long prayers before meals while food got either hot or cold. He stopped drinking but was still distant and cross, still said we were millstones around his neck. He laid down the laws for us to follow: no work or play on the Sabbath, it was for worship--except for Mama. She could cook on Sunday. No swearing, absolutely none, no matter how angry we got. Worst of all was using God's name in vain. That would bring a fate worse than death, Daddy said. There was just never any thought of disobeying him. Since I was a girl with an oversized sense of duty and commitment, I began a four year stint of perfect attendance at Sunday School. No matter where I was or how bad the weather, even if no one else in the family went, Sunday morning found me at Sunday School at some church. I was honor bound to go and the people where I was were honor bound to see that I went. I showed up on wintry Sundays with ice frozen in my hair and blue from ankles to thighs from freezing rain. I had no knee socks, nor gloves, and my coat was too short. Mama said it looked tacky for a dress to show below a coat and Daddy said my coat still fit. It did, except that my legs had grown so long the coat was much too short. The boys called me Splinter Legs. I steeled myself against the weather, but the teasing really hurt. To keep anyone from knowing just how much it hurt, I put up a front of toughness. At school I used to play outside without my coat just to prove that cold didn't bother me. I think I fooled even myself. If I couldn't have something, I wouldn't let myself want it."

Harry pulled her to him, "My little toughie! Is that how you got that defiant lift to your chin? When Jesse Griffin saw your portrait in my BOQ, he said he could see right away who was boss in the family."

"Do you think that? that I'm bossy?"

"No, but you do know your own mind. Tell me, how is it that you stopped at four years with your perfect attendance?"

"Oh, I got careless and caught my clothes on fire one cold winter January day and had to miss two Sundays. Deep down I was glad to be free of that obligation, but it didn't end there. I had Sunday School at home. Daddy's version. I had reached the age of accountability, according to him, and I had to take responsibility for my soul and his job was to show me how. He made me sit in a chair in the middle of the room while he paced in circles around me, preaching, and reading from the Bible, and praying.

Well, I could read the Bible and I had my own ideas about God, sin, and my soul. I had questions too, but Daddy said my questioning would bring the wrath of God down upon the house. Even so, I felt a direct line to God, that He was kind, not wrathful, and that I could go directly to Him and by-pass Daddy. After a while I stopped voicing my beliefs and questions, but I still had them. After the new grammar school, the Post Office, and the Coca-Cola plant were built, Daddy had to go out of town for work. So I was spared his Sunday afternoon sermons. We all felt a great freedom and life became almost joyful. Mama had taught us to keep our problems to ourselves and she did whatever it took to keep peace. But when Daddy was away, Mama could be a lot of fun, and we could have our friends stay over night as often as we wished.

"That summer, Joan and I spent a month in Leeds with Mama's parents, our aunts and cousins. We were there on my thirteenth birthday. That was the first time Joan was able to stay away from home without getting homesick and having to be taken home. Granddaddy Butts ran a grocery store and every day we'd go there and he'd give us a treat. He was a very tall man with white hair and baby blue eyes and he talked funny; Mama said it was because he was Welsh. He had the nicest smile; it went right up to his eyes just like yours." Norma smiled as Harry wrinkled his eyebrows and made the furrows stand out on his forehead.

"Mama had warned us before we left not to eat up Granddaddy's profits. She had to explain that meant to share a candy bar or a Ne-Hi soda, and at the table never to take seconds. We did as she said, even while our cousins took a whole candy bar and soda. Joan and I didn't mind though. At home, we didn't have even half a bar or soda, and we felt proud when everyone said that Ann's girls were the most polite and considerate girls they knew. We wanted to make Mama proud of us.

"That summer Aunt Jean was visiting in Leeds also; she had come to see her little boy. He was the same age as Tommy and had always lived with Grandmother. Everyone in Leeds called her Genie, short for Eugenia; Mama still does. In Savannah she called herself Jean, and when I started writing to her I called her Aunt Jean and she called me Norma Jean. That summer in 1940 was the only time I ever saw her." Norma looked at Harry, "That's about the time you knew her, wasn't it?"

"For a few months, yes. I left Parris Island in September for Midway. Our relationship had already broken down and I didn't hear from her again until nearly four years later, surprised to learn she had married soon after I left. I shouldn't have been; she had been very anxious to marry--someone."

"Oh, Harry, to think that when you knew her I was just a kid whose main goal in life was trying to get enough money to go to 4-H Camp. I did all sorts of odd jobs, picking cotton, tufting bedspreads, picking and selling blackberries, baby sitting our neighbor's three boys, but I never was able to get two dollars to pay for camp.

"I started high school that fall and took classes to prepare me for college in case I could get scholarships to Martha Berry College and become a teacher. I took two years of Latin and gloried in conjugating verbs, declining nouns, and translating the 'dead' language. My favorite Christmas carol became *Adeste Fidelis*. I felt special being one of only thirty people in town to know a bit of Latin. It paid off a few years later when I started getting letters from a Marine whose stationery had *Semper Fidelis* across the top! Because of the war with Germany, my second language was changed to Spanish. After one year of Spanish, the teacher moved. I took two years of Algebra and one year of Geometry before Mr. Holt was drafted. All of his math students knew he was a drill instructor before the Army made him one, but he was an excellent teacher.

"On December 7, 1941 when the Japanese bombed Pearl Harbor, Daddy was away from home. He had been traveling around the South looking for and usually finding work. That day, we didn't know where he was; we were so scared. There was talk of drafting every able-bodied man and we wondered if Daddy would be drafted before he could come home. Mama said they wouldn't draft him because he was married and had four kids even if he was only 37. When he returned we were very glad to see him, but he wasn't home long. He went to work lining coke ovens in Rome, Georgia; then he came home on weekends.

"With the war came other changes besides our teachers being drafted and courses canceled. Rationing started and I worked as a junior volunteer at the ration board, folded bandages and passed the collection plate at the movies to raise money for the Red Cross. We streaked coloring into our margerine--butter was sent to the front--sliced our bread, saved grease, aluminum foil and tin cans for the war effort. We waved and threw kisses to the soldiers who passed through town in convoy trucks. They threw out addresses, but Mama wouldn't let me write to any soldier-boy. She let me write to you only because of Aunt Jean.

"In the summer of 1942, Daddy had work in town again. He had paid off a ten year mortgage in eight years by working night and day to do it; then he started improving the house. His first project was to build a concrete front porch enclosed by the low brick wall, four brick columns, and wide steps down to a sidewalk that led to the road. As he was planning it, we thought it would make our house look mighty fine, the nicest house on Reservoir Hill. We all did our part in making it happen. Joan and I dug dirt from beneath the house for fill, crawling to where the dirt almost touched the floor, scraping and pushing it out to where Tommy and Julia could load it into his little wagon and haul it to where Daddy wanted it. When the fill dirt was packed, Daddy started his part. Julia was the lookout and signaled from the bend in the road when she saw him coming home from work. I measured sand, lime, and cement and mixed it with water in the mortar box. Mama put supper on the table. By the time Daddy finished eating, the mixture was ready for pouring. While he got it settled in and got rid of the air bubbles, I mixed more concrete. He was a fast worker and I tried to keep up with him. I did, for several evenings until my period started and then Mama told him not to work me so hard. It took two weeks to do the porch working in the late afternoons until dark. And it was a sight to see when it was finished.

"The next summer we built a concrete back porch, this one flat to the ground so it took less work and time. Then Daddy dug ditches and a hole for a septic tank, and at last, we had an inside toilet and a bathtub. Daddy even bought a washing machine. We thought we were rich having an inside toilet and no more stirring clothes in an iron pot over an open fire. We also had water in the house and a hot water heater.

"I got a Saturday job at the 5&10cent store which paid two dollars less two cents for Social Security tax. Now I had money to go to 4-H camp, but no time! In my junior year I took a home nursing course. The textbook said that babies grow in the body of the mother, as I had already figured out. And I noticed that Mama's stomach was getting bigger again and soon she told me she was going to have another baby. I was thrilled, but she wasn't. She cried when she told me that Daddy had neglected the kids he already had and now another was coming, but he could always find money to give to the church.

"We had very little furniture. Daddy said we had all we needed: beds, eating table and chairs. We didn't have proper clothing and what we did have, Mama got for us by taking in sewing and washing, but Daddy had a suit for every season of the year to wear to church. We had no recreation, but Daddy went to the movies every night, alternating between the two theaters in town. Mama said that was all right: he worked hard. She never went anywhere, not even to the doctor. I took her urine samples to him on my way to school. All she had was her flower garden.

"I don't believe Daddy had any idea of what other fathers provided for their families, but he glowed with fatherly pride when he was complimented on what fine children he had. He didn't mention then that we were nothing but millstones around his neck. I never asked what a millstone was, but I figured it was a burden of some kind.

"Late on March 26, 1943, Mama went into labor and Daddy went for the doctor. As the labor pains got closer together, Mama told me I'd have to help with the delivery. I was scared, but willing. Then Daddy returned with the doctor and I was sent to bed. In about ten minutes, 12:40 A.M., I heard the lusty cry of a new baby sister: she was a big one, ten pounds one ounce. That was Mary Lee, the only one of us that Mama named.

"Three months later, I was sixteen and finally able to answer Daddy's repeated question, 'When are you going to go to work and help out with the family?' I applied at the hosiery mill on my birthday and went to work on the second shift. On pay day, I was expected to give a fifth of my wages for room and board and from then on, I was also responsible for my clothes and school expenses. Two months later school started and I went to work straight from school working from four in the afternoon until midnight and then I walked three miles home.

"I was senior class historian and in the drama club acting in almost every play we gave. I studied on weekends and holidays. All my classes, except Chemistry, were easy, but if I failed that, I couldn't graduate. I planned to get caught up over Christmas vacation. Aunt Jean was hounding me to write to some Marine in the Pacific, and to please her I did, then forgot about it until late in February when your answer arrived." Norma looked at Harry with stars in her eyes, "Your letter seemed to come from another world and another time, as if we were characters in a book or movie, and I was not Norma Clinton at all. I suppose I was a silly girl, but it was like nothing else that had ever touched my life. I literally walked on air for days. And as you know, I made time to answer it.

"Soon I was behind in Chemistry homework again and three-month exams were due. I dropped out of the drama club, put aside research on the class history, and spent every spare minute on study, even through my supper hour at the mill. One night in April, I began crying and couldn't stop. My boss told me to go home and not come back until school ended, that my job would be waiting for me then. I loved him for that. But it was too late, I needed liver shots and to pay for them, I had to cash in some of the war bonds I had bought. The doctor scolded me for risking my health by working and going to school. I didn't tell him it was expected of me; I was too ashamed. But Daddy wasn't ashamed; he never even asked me about my doctor bills, only if I had enough money for the collection plate at church. Oh, I had that; ten per cent of nothing was nothing. And he wouldn't let me file an income tax return to claim the refund I was due because he was claiming me as a dependent.

"The liver shots, and rest, and your letters--by then I had five--were what I needed. I took final exams and passed all my classes with honors! Third in line for a scholarship, but third was not good enough.

"On graduation day, Daddy's ankle was sprained and he said he couldn't attend the ceremony. I couldn't bear the humiliation if he didn't go. My girl friends had already noticed that he didn't speak to me when we passed on the street in town. I told them it was because he didn't see me, or had things on his mind. When I asked him why he ignored me in town, he said, 'I see enough of you at home.' I had no answer for that, but if he didn't go to my graduation, I didn't know how I could explain it to my friends. It would be clear that I didn't matter to him. I knew I didn't, but I didn't want the world to know. So I got up enough courage to tell him that if he stayed away, I would never forgive him. I guess I mattered some because he went. And do you remember what he said when you asked for permission to marry me?"

"Yes," Harry answered softly,"I was impressed, and I agreed with him. He said I'd never find a better girl to marry."

Norma's eyes filled with tears at the memory, "That was the first time he had said a nice thing about me. I was stunned." She struggled with her emotions for a moment as Harry looked on with a mixture of sympathy and perplexity. "Well," she drew in a deep breath, shook her shoulders, "I was finished with school and returned to the mill, this time on the first shift and that's when I met Inez Nash. Our looping machines were side by side. She became my confidante as I waited for September 4th to come when I would be leaving for the nurse's training program in Chattanooga. A month later, I had something else to think about. Your first proposal, then your second, then your third! I struggled with my feelings and my reason, and they came together with the same answer on August 27th and I agreed to marry you. Those months from August through March were the happiest of my life, then came your "good-by for a little while". Your letters were my very life and to have them stop was like having my breath cut off. April was horrible until the 30th when your first letter came from Okinawa.

"Then came another problem. The mill got a contract for Army socks so heavy and coarse they were very hard to loop, sewing the toe ends together on a rotating machine. I was looping fifty dozen mercerized cotton socks a day for ten cents a dozen. But with Army socks, I was lucky to loop half that many and by the end of eight hours of stretching those burlap-like socks over twelve needles to an inch, my arms were ready to fall off. Yet I was paid the same: ten cents a dozen. The Army paid six times what the mill sold mercerized socks for, but they refused to pay us a penny more than ten cents a dozen. The mill was making a huge profit off the labor of the workers. Some of us protested, even tried to organize to get more pay, but we got no where. People were too afraid of losing their jobs to support a union. They just buckled under. I did too, but by late July, I wasn't able to work any more. I was bone tired. I had already bought your ring, my overnight case to take on our honeymoon, and wedding clothes. My cedar chest was paid for and it was filled with things for our home. I saved enough money for stamps and stationery to write you through September, then I quit.

"It was too late; I needed liver shots again and there went the rest of my war bonds. Even the one from you. I used my very last pennies to send you the telegram in San Francisco; I was penniless. Now do you understand why I cried so much on our wedding night?"

Harry sat speechless, his face like white stone. He reached for a cigarette, tapped it on his thumbnail before lighting it, inhaled deeply, then slowly exhaled the smoke. His eyes were hard and piercing. At length he spoke, "I don't know what to say, Honeychild. It appears I was blind or stupid, or both. You wrote about the liver injections, but I must have been too thickheaded to understand what that meant, or perhaps I didn't receive some of your letters. Did you write me exactly what was happening with you at work and at home?"

"No, in the beginning I thought you'd be coming soon, we'd be married, and I'd leave. So why mention any of it? Then, as time went on, I didn't know how to tell you, where to begin. I thought it would sound like complaining. And I didn't expect to get sick, either. We were brought up not to tell family problems, and besides, I didn't want you to know." Her fingers were pleating the fabric of her skirt and he took them to hold, looking at them intently for a time. "I'm not scolding you, darling, but I want to remind you of something. Remember when I wrote from Okinawa that I was on standby to return to the States on the first available space?"

"Yes, but it was two more weeks before you left."

"That's because one of my men got an urgent message from home and I let him take my place. I thought a week more or perhaps less wouldn't make that much difference with us, but leaving immediately made a great difference to him. Had I known you were suffering so much--Honeychild, don't you think I had the right to know?" His eyes, burning like hot coals, bored into hers. "And now I have to wonder why you wanted your father's permission for us to marry."

Norma returned his probing stare unflinchingly, "I did it because I thought too much of our love and marriage to just go off and get married as many of my friends did. And I think it's the same as your giving that man your turn at going home; it simply was the right thing to do."

"Oh, my dear, sweet wife," Harry drew her to him, "of course, you're right, and I knew at the time you wanted to give our marriage the dignity it deserved. It's for such reasons that I love you so very much. But if I had known about the things you've told me, I would never have left you in La Fayette to have the baby. And even though I did, you kept from me how unhappy you were, until at the very end. Honeychild, why didn't you tell me before?"

"I thought things would be different after we married. They were the only family we had, and I thought it could be a new start for all of us, and a better life for my mother and sisters with you in it. You were the best man any of us had ever known. And, I think, my parents wanted to make up for some of the things of the past. And it was better until the shooting, so soon after Anne was born. Everyone was so upset--the horror of it all--the funeral--and later, the gossip. I just blurted out all my frustration to you in that horrible letter, the worst possible way to tell you, and I'm so ashamed. You were just as miserable as I was with our separation." She touched her fingertips to his furrowed brow.

"It's true, your letter upset me, more than I care to remember. To read that you thought you were dying scared me more than bombs or bayonets ever had. But it jolted me into doing something I might never than done otherwise. I confided in a stranger of our predicament, and it got us our little cottage. And Norma, I want you to promise me, if in the future I'm too thick-skulled to see the obvious, then *tell* me." He placed his hands on her shoulders, "And now I understand why you disapprove of drinking, but Honeychild, you have my word, I'll never abuse it. I admit that I enjoy a cocktail when I get home from work and perhaps another after dinner when we play cards or talk, and I like to offer drinks to our friends when they expect it. But you will never suffer, or lack for a single thing, because of it. Now I also understand those prayer sessions your father subjects us to when we leave. I still won't participate, but I'll endure them, as I have in the past, for your sake." He lit another cigarette, took a draw, exhaling the smoke into the air, "I had expected to learn from your father how to be a father, especially to a daughter, but I think that won't be the case. My experience with girls, little girls, is to say the least, limited. Anne is a baby still, but as she grows--"

"Harry, my darling, you don't have to worry. You feed, diaper, and bathe Anne as well as I do, and surely you know that Julia dotes on you. Because of you she thinks "Jeepers, Creepers" was written just for her big brown eyes. And Mary Lee loved being here, despite my discipline. Little girls are not different from little boys when it comes to wanting attention. And I love you for offering to have Tommy live with us while the town gossip over the shooting was so strong. I only wish Daddy had allowed it, but he thought Tommy should stay there and face the music. He really believes he does everything exactly right." She collected her treasures from the cedar chest and stored them in the linen closet. Returning to the bedroom, she put her arms around him and rested her head on his shoulder, "You know, it would be an education for Daddy to meet our Marine friends. They help their wives instead of expecting to be waited on, and they take part in caring for the children and not just in the getting of them. Whatever they might have done in combat, at home they're gentlemen, and gentle men. All that goes double for you. I feel like a queen with you. There is no one in this world that I would rather be than who I am: your wife!"

"Gee! Honeychild! Still? After fifteen months?"

"Still! and forever." Her voice emphatic.

"And my woman? Still want to be my woman?"

"Well, right now, your woman is just a little bit jealous."

"How so?"

"Your wife has been around all evening; your woman is wondering when she'll get to come on stage."

"Oh, is she?" He raised his eyebrows. "Then summon her. She can write the script."

18

"Terry, help me!" Norma pleaded into the telephone. "Harry wants me to buy a cocktail dress and I don't even know what one looks like, much less where to buy it."

"I can take you to the perfect place! How soon do you want it? Is Saturday too far away? Can Captain Kipp bring you to Beaufort?"

Norma relaxed, knowing she could count on Terry, a business woman who looked and dressed like a model or a movie star. It was easy to see why Tuck called her his pinup girl. She had a curvaceous figure, a lovely smile, perfect teeth, sparkling eyes, and a charming disposition. And Tuck was just as handsome as Terry was glamorous. He was an athlete too, Golden Gloves champion in the lightweight division of West Texas. They had met in college which for Tuck had been interrupted on December 7, 1941. The next day he had enlisted in the Marine Corps.

Terry, nine years older than she, was nine times more experienced in life, Norma felt, able to do many things she couldn't, like type, drive a car, dress in high style and arrange her hair in the latest fashion. She'd taken care of herself while Tuck had been overseas in the war. Norma felt very lucky to have such a lady as her friend, her very first one at Parris Island. And she had one thing that Terry didn't...a child, and Terry lavished on Anne her feelings of maternal love, willing to sit with her more often than Norma allowed at her tender age. She preferred to take Anne with her or stay at home. Usually Terry's contacts with Anne were in visits back and forth between their homes. So, of course she was along on Saturday when Harry drove Norma to Beaufort to buy her cocktail dress.

Terry took them to Carteret Street to a large, old white-columned house surrounded by moss-hung oaks so typical of Beaufort. Harry sat in the car with Anne while Terry and Norma entered the enclosed side veranda which had been turned into a salesroom for designer dresses. So many choices made Norma's head spin; never had she seen so many lovely clothes. She decided finally on a royal blue velveteen dress with cap sleeves and a rounded neckline. The bodice fit close and the circular skirt clung to her hips before flaring to mid-calf. Skirt lengths had dropped ten inches almost overnight. Most women said they would never wear them.

"How do you like this one?" Norma emerged from the dressing room, turned in a circle, making the skirt swing gracefully.

"It's beautiful--tasteful, and ordinary!" Terry said appraisingly.

"You think Harry will like it?" Norma wondered aloud.

"He'd like anything you put on, so why not buy something you like? Look at this one. Have you ever worn black?"

"Black?" Norma looked surprised. "Black's for funerals."

"And cocktail dresses! This one is pure glamour. Try it on!"

Norma shook her head, "No, I'm not the glamorous type. I wouldn't know how to act in a dress like that."

"You don't have to act, you just be."

"No, I couldn't," Norma blushed. "I'd make a fool of myself."

"Norma, you don't see yourself the way you are--or could be. There's a mystery about you, maybe it's your reserve mixed with an inviting manner, an innocence yet a knowing. It's no wonder Captain Kipp is the envy of all the Marines in the Battalion."

"I know he's envied, but for himself, not because of me," Norma asserted.

"It's for you! Tuck tells me that when you come on your afternoon walk, pushing Anne in her carriage to ride home with the Captain, all the office guys knock themselves out trying to be the first out the door to fold and put the carriage in the car for you."

"No, he's mistaken. They're just being gentlemen."

"Oh, yeah, they're 'just being gentlemen'. You can't believe that. Don't forget, they're *men*. And you *are* glamorous; you'll be more so in this dress. Come on, try it on. Just for fun?"

The Emily Wilkins original was made of soft faille with three-quarter sleeves, smooth bodice fastened from hip to throat with tiny self-covered buttons and loops. The skirt's tucked section spread from the center front across the hips, finishing in a bustle. From beneath the tucking, a flared skirt fell to a few inches above the ankles. "You look stunning!" Terry sighed. "Oh, do buy it, Norma. Captain Kipp will love it."

At home, Norma modeled first the royal blue dress, asking Harry, "Did I make a good choice?"

"It's elegant, Honeychild, and perfect for you."

"What do you think of the skirt length?"

"I suppose there's no need for austerity since the war is over."

"But do you like it, the length I mean, or should I hem it up?"

"I like everything about it, but most of all what's inside it."

"I don't know if I like the length; it's such a drastic change. And the other dress is even longer."

He smiled, wagging his head, "So you bought more than one after all?"

"They were on sale, after the holidays. Wait until you see it." She left to change into the black dress, buttoning it to the throat then turning to see the bustle in the mirror and how the skirt fabric molded to her small waist and narrow hips which had not been changed by her pregnancy. Facing the mirror again, she unfastened a few buttons, then a few more which allowed the collar to stand out a bit and the deep 'V' opening made her face seem less round. She hated her round face and decided from now on to wear only V necklines. She removed the pearls, leaving her throat bare, put on the gold bracelet Aunt Ruby gave for her graduation, her only piece of jewelry when she married, and walked into the living room to show Harry.

At the sound of her heels on the hardwood floor, he turned to look, rising suddenly to his feet, drawing in his breath. His eyed widened, then flamed. As she came near, he reached for her waist with both hands and bent to kiss where the bodice parted, his lips moving up to her throat, behind her ears, back to the opening, his breath warming her skin. She pulled away, to turn slowly, "You haven't seen the bustle!"

"It's a bombshell of a dress, Honeychild, except for one small problem. But that can be remedied." With quick movements he began to fasten the buttons. "This is how I'd like you to wear it for other eyes to see. Remember, Honeychild, men can look down into that inviting little hollow, and I wouldn't want my wife causing a stampede in the Officers Club--and do you think it's fair, my darling, to advertise what is already claimed by someone else?" He chided her softly.

Norma looked downcast, "I told Terry it was too glamorous for me."

"No, for *me*. I'd prefer that you not display your charms, they're obvious enough already," his tone was serious. "I don't want other men looking upon you with desire, although I don't see how it can be helped, but to tempt them by dressing seductively seems improper to me."

"Then you don't want me to wear it?" Her tone indicating acceptance.

"I wouldn't, if you wore it the way you did for me. But this way, buttoned to here, I don't mind. Actually for me, you could unbutton it completely," which he did and his mouth once more warmed her skin.

*   *   *   *

The weather was mild for the middle of January. Norma was pushing the carriage back and forth the length of the veranda when Harry came home for lunch. "Going somewhere?" he asked.

"No, just keeping your daughter quiet. Hear the silence? The only time I've heard it has been when these wheels are turning. We haven't had a good morning. Anne's been very fretful, wouldn't eat her cereal or take her bottle, fussed all through her bath, and hasn't slept a wink until I got the bright idea of putting her in the carriage. She's quiet now, but your lunch isn't ready." Norma looked apologetic.

"Don't let it worry you. Take care of Anne; I'll take care of lunch. I picked up the mail at the post office. Two letters for you."

Norma stopped the carriage, "I think Miss Anne has finally gone to sleep. Poor little thing, she's teething. Her gums are red and swollen, and she's drooling. Let's hurry. Maybe we can eat before she wakes."

She made beef sandwiches and Harry opened a can of tomato soup, put it in a sauce pan and stirred it while she read her letters. "Marsha's mad at me. She thinks I should've visited her when we took Mary Lee home; I wrote her in the Christmas card of our rushed weekend trip. She also thinks I should write more often since I don't work and she does. She thinks I don't work. Ha! If she ever has a baby, she'll sing a different tune.

"Mama says they had a nice Christmas but wishes we'd been there. They all like their gifts, especially the wool blankets and she's thrilled with her electric sewing machine. Maybe now her leg will stop hurting since she won't have to pedal that treadle machine anymore. She wants us to leave Anne with her when we visit Juliette and Charley."

Harry poured the soup and they ate lunch. Over a cup of coffee, he said, "I think it would please your mother to have more than a weekend visit with Anne, which is all she's had so far since you two moved here, and don't you think it would be nice for us to be alone again? If she really wants to keep Anne, I say let her."

"I'll think about it, but it won't be an issue unless we get the new car."

"We know it will come in sooner or later. Do give it serious thought, won't you, Honeychild?" Moving close, he took the side combs from her hair, letting it fall around her face. Running his fingers through to fluff it out, he buried his face in the waves.

"Keep that up and you'll be late for work," she warned.

"Speaking of work, Colonel McCormick told me this morning that his wife will be calling you; they're hosting a Battalion party Saturday night in their quarters."

"Oh, I forgot to tell you, a lady did call this morning. Let me think, I guess it was Mrs. McCormick. She called right in the middle of Anne's fight with the oatmeal. I told her that if we could find a sitter, we'd come."

Harry's hand stopped in the middle of a stroke. "You told her *what?*"

"I told her we'd be happy to attend her party if I could find a sitter for our baby."

"Honeychild, don't you know that when the commanding officer extends an invitation, it is accepted on the spot?"

"No, I don't know that. Anne was screaming and slippery from the oatmeal, and how could I accept? I wasn't certain we could count on Terry on a Saturday night. Anyway, she said she has a nanny for her children and we could bring Anne."

"Our first cocktail party and you suggest we take our baby with us!" He exclaimed in amazement.

"No, she suggested it. But I'll call Terry anyway."

"She can't keep Anne. Tuck says they're going fishing all weekend."

"Then we don't have a choice, do we? I only hope Anne doesn't drool on my new dress."

"Wear the blue one," he grinned, "Save the black one for when we go alone!"

There were two other babies and two young girls in the McCormick nursery with Anne while their parents partied in the living room. Norma met the wives and officers of the First Recruit Battalion, some of whom she already knew from Harry's bowling team. New to her were Major and Mrs. Draper. She was the niece of Lady Astor and seemed to enjoy shocking people with her strong opinions about every subject brought up; the major offered no opinion on anything. Captain Darner was a perfect likeness of the Marine Corps' fierce looking mascot and his wife Buddy wore a constant look of happiness. Lt. and Mrs. Walden brought their baby. Helen wore an enormous braid wound around her head like a corona and spoke at length of how easy it was to care for very long hair worn that way. Warrant Officer Bishop and Lt. Byrum were unmarried and both on the bowling team as was 2nd Lt. Jim Moore who brought his fiancée Betsy, a Port Royal beauty, shy and delicate and the same age as Norma.

Warrant Officer and Mrs. Godwin were newlyweds, an older version. Toby, a handsome woman towered over Bill and was a matron in Florida State Prison in Raiford before the marriage. Bill took the teasing like a good Marine. Ist Lt. and Mrs. John Campbell and their two young girls were the Kipp's neighbors. Norma thought Lt. and Mrs. Tom Ellis was the most handsome couple there. He was tall and blond and Betty Glee was simply the most beautiful woman she had ever seen with her glowing face, eyes as green as Scarlett O'Hara's and hair as black as Snow White's. She was vivacious, friendly, and as natural as a sunrise. Their little girl was the third baby brought to the party.

The wonderful evening of good fellowship, conversation, and the feeling of a family beginning to take shape completely dispelled Norma's fear of cocktail parties. And at home Harry said, "Tonight I was very proud of my lady in blue with her hair piled on top of her pretty head, but I like this better for bed." He spread her hair across the pillow, "On our honeymoon when I shampooed it and toweled it dry, I had never before seen such a mass of hair." He lifted it forward and arranged it over her breasts, lowering his mouth to touch where the skin showed through.

Norma lay in his arms happy that the cocktail party marked another milestone for her. She, the girl from the wrong side of the tracks, so ignorant of 'society' ways. Her thoughts traveled back to Gatlinburg where she'd been so fearful of eating in the hotel dining room and had managed to steer their steps into quaint home-style cafes with checkered tablecloths when they had eaten out. She'd been happiest with the sandwiches and fruit they had eaten in their cottage. On their final night, Harry had made the choice, telling her, "I want to take you to one fine restaurant before we leave here. I've made dinner reservation in the dining room at the Gatlinburg Inn. It's the nicest in town."

She had been frozen with the fear of not knowing what to do. Why hadn't she simply told him? No, she had suffered through the meal in near paralysis which barely permitted her to chew, much less swallow. He had asked if she wasn't hungry; that was what she let him think.

"That's unfortunate," he said, eating with gusto, "the food is exceptionally good. At least try some dessert--to keep up your strength." he winked, amused with some secret thought, adding, "There's something I want to show you, Sugar, when we return to our cottage."

If he shows me an etiquette book, I will simply die right on the spot.

"Remind me, won't you, if I forget? I'm apt to, you know, once we get back and I hold you again after being deprived for--" he glanced at his watch, "nearly two hours. Every thought except loving you will probably leave my head."

But he hadn't forgotten. Back in their cottage, he had taken a manila folder from the pocket of his suitcase. Then, propping the pillows against the headboard, removing his uniform and shoes, he had stretched out in the middle of the bed. She had sat on the edge of the bed--and tears--until he had invited her to him with an outstretched arm, "Take off your slippers and come closer, Little Angel, nestle here in the crook of my arm and listen to this 'piece of literature'. Unfolding two long pages, he began reading aloud:

SHORT COURSE TO ROTATION

You can still be a gentleman, even if you were in the South Seas.
This Course has been written by leading authorities on etiquette and will prove invaluable to you.

NAME   SERIAL NUMBER
MONTHS OVERSEAS   SCORE on USMC IQ. test
GOOD CONDUCT MEDAL (YES) (NO) Delete one

This application must be accompanied by your 201 file and your procard. Reports drifting back from men who have left to return to the States tell that they are required to attend a school for two weeks. The purpose of which is to teach the men culture and refinement so that they may re-adapt to the far gentler life in the States. The men are anxious to return home and the two weeks delay is hard to take. To remedy this we have compiled this pertinent data. After taking this short course, it will not be necessary for you to attend any school. You may go directly home confident that you are able to mix with any group, be it salon or saloon. Our course carries the Good Tentmaking Seal of Approval.

Harry's bemused expression had made her doubtful enough to ask, "Did the Marine Corps really put this out?"

"Shhhh and listen," he had answered, drawing her head back to his shoulder.

THE SHORT COURSE TO CULTURE

1. Upon arriving in the United States you will be amazed by the large number of beautiful girls you will see. Remember boys, 'Frisco is not the South Seas. Many of these girls have occupations, such as stenographers, sales girls, or beauty operators. Therefore, do NOT approach them with "How much?" The proper approach is "Isn't this a beautiful day?" or "Were you ever in Scranton?" Then ask, "How much?"

2. If you are invited to someone's home, and upon arrival you find that all the chairs are occupied, do NOT squat in the corner in the manner of an Indian and say that you are comfortable. Have patience. Your hostess will soon provide a chair for you.

> 3. Do NOT go about hitting everyone of draft age in civilian clothes. They might have been released on a medical discharge. Ask for their credentials and if they can show none, then go ahead and hit them.
> 4. If you are an overnight guest and find your bedroom uncomfortably cool, ask your hostess for an extra quilt. Do NOT start a fire in the corner of the room.

"WHO wrote this? Tell me, did you have a hand in it?"

He pretended to be wounded, "Why, Honeychild, how can you ask such a question?"

"Here, give that to me," she had commanded and began reading, doubling up in laughter, until Harry had reclaimed the pages to continue reading aloud.

> 21. If by some chance you hear an airplane overhead, do not dive for the nearest manhole. It will not strafe you. It is probably a mail plane or is carrying USO entertainers to some Army camp.
> 22. As a guest at a party you will see numerous couples seated at individual tables. It is not considered good manners to wink at an escorted lady and motion your head toward the door, even though she may nod in agreement. Her escort will immediately develop a strange dislike for you which might lead to bloodshed. He could be a deferred athlete.
> 23. In conversing with natives, you will find them to be very gullible. Don't take too much advantage of them. Someone may conclude that you have misrepresented the truth. Then, if you should ever run for sheriff, you would need his vote. If you must snow them, tell them about the wonders of the Red Cross in combat.
> 24. After reading and digesting this carefully, you should be able to stay at any given place at least an hour before being thrown out for conduct unbecoming a human being.

At the end they had laughed themselves out, and lay back on the pillows, soon to become silent. She had seen, after his mirth, a remoteness enter his eyes and settle on his face. Had he been thinking of Marines still on Okinawa or some other island, and did such thoughts sometimes explain his shivering, moaning, and sweating while he slept? Did Marines ever allow themselves to cry, or did they just joke about things that broke their hearts? Or did they simply refuse to think about them? She had wondered, and lain quietly, waiting, until his attention had returned and his eyes once more focused on her, and he had whispered, "My sweet darling, sometimes in the night I expect to wake and find myself alone again in my tent, and then I feel you move beside me, and my heart is filled to overflowing." He had crushed her to him, his voice breaking, "Norma Mine, tell me you will be here in the morning, if I go to sleep now."

That had been sixteen months ago. His nightmares had stopped; he didn't have the recurring malarial attacks anymore. She had met many, many Marines since then, but still she did not know the answers to her questions. Those Marines she had come to know were as polite, gentle, calm, helpful, orderly as Harry. All family and home-loving men. But this was Parris Island in peace time, a world of order and routine. It was the best of all worlds: life with her Marine. She gloried in him physically, his strong, muscular body, so smart looking in his uniform. She loved the ease with which he stood, the way he walked as if suspended just above the ground, the economy of all his movements, nothing wasted, a purpose executed with grace. She loved to watch the pleasure he took in whatever he did whether it was drying dishes at her side after supper; driving the car--his hands so relaxed on the wheel--or washing it and rubbing it dry; polishing his shoes--the easy way he held them with one hand inside and the other going back and forth with the brush. She could watch his face forever, the stage on which his emotions played their roles, depending on his inner direction.

And now she could feel the evidence of his ever-present appetite for physical love, hot and hard against the small of her back, waiting for a sign of willingness. Her willingness! It gave him so much pleasure even though he seemed defenseless or sort of helpless, yet in charge. And it gave her so much pleasure to thrill him in such a special way. She loved the weight and warmth of him, and he way he held her before and after. And now, if she turned to face him, he would act on his desire. How could she not respond, if not for herself then for him? And so she turned.

19

Life on Parris Island, Marine Corps Recruit Depot, moved in a series of small circles within the larger circle of insular military events. The common purpose and isolation fostered a cohesive relationship among its members. The Colonel's cocktail party had accomplished its goal. The officers of his Battalion had become socially acquainted and the interaction was forging them and their wives into a compatible group. Norma enjoyed the company of all the wives, especially one who called soon after the party. "Mrs. Kipp? B.G. Ellis. May I call you Norma? I dislike my name and my friends call me by the initials. I wish you would too. Would you care to join me and my little girl Sheree in a walk to the PX? Good. We'll be at your quarters, 56, isn't it? in about fifteen minutes." B.G., five years older than Norma, had taught school for two years while Tom was overseas and had a nine month old daughter. From that day their friendship grew on their walks together, pushing their daughters in buggies, and through the exchange of dinners and baby sitting.

Another blossoming friendship was with Betsy Spenser who came to the bowling games with her fiancé. Jim was exact and precise in everything he did and it was an experience to watch him bowl. He had studied it from a scientific point of view, he said. And when his turn came, everyone simply sat down to watch. He would posture and measure, eye the ball and pins, and then the lane from many different perspectives, and at length send the ball on its mission. Sometimes he bowled a brilliant game; other times his score was an embarrassment. Harry recovered the time Jim lost. He took the ball in his powerful hands, stood motionless for a second or two, then with quick, smooth steps and a forceful arm sent the ball speeding to its mark so fast it was a blur. And he was consistent, scoring at least two hundred every game.

Jim was as assertive as Betsy was passive, the perfect example of opposites attracting. Norma suspected that Betsy was troubled even before she spoke of Jim's pressure for premarital sexual relations. "And you're planning a June wedding?" Norma asked. "That's months away. Whose idea? You want to be a June bride that badly?"

"No, it's not that at all. He's Catholic and I'm taking instruction. He wants everything exactly right and it will take until June, but I don't know if we can hold off until then," Betsy laughed nervously.

"If Jim wants to do *exactly right*, doesn't he understand that respecting your feelings is one thing he should do?"

"Yes, he knows. He doesn't want to be inconsiderate; it's just that he's so driven." Concern lined her face.

"You love him very much, don't you, Betsy?"

"Yes," she said softly, blushing, "and I want to make him happy in every way."

"And you will. It's your gentleness he loves, but be strong, too, and true to yourself. In the end Jim will respect you for it."

Norma was soon to have another friend. Jesse Griffin was finally assigned quarters and bringing his wife to Parris Island. He had been a dinner guest quite often and Norma was eager to meet Hilda. "You can show her the ropes when she gets here," Harry told her, "and I know Jesse wants you two to be friends."

On their first meeting Hilda told Norma that she and Jesse had met in Pearl Harbor. She had been with the Red Cross when he came through on his way home after the war ended. They fell in love and married within a month and she was now four months pregnant. Every Marine wife Norma knew was either pregnant, trying to be, or already had a young one. It was no wonder. The men had come home from the war and wanted to start living again. She ought to know.

*   *   *

Their new car was in! The call came February first and Harry drove to Charleston to trade in their old, but beloved, 1942 model. Norma didn't want to see it left on the used car lot, so she waited at the Griffin's until Harry returned driving a brand new 1947 black four door Packard. He couldn't be indifferent about it; he couldn't even be modest about it. Clearly he was thrilled to death with it. On Monday, the black and chrome wonder was the talk of not only the First Battalion but the entire base; in those days any new car caused a sensation.

Sgt. Maj. Railing looked it over and then asked, "What happened to the '42 issue, Skipper?"

"I left it on the lot."

"In Savannah or Charleston, Sir?"

Harry told him without a second thought. When work finished, the sergeant major was on the highway to Charleston to buy the Captain's car. When Norma heard about it she was sick. Harry was sicker. "No matter how little he paid for it, it wasn't worth it," he lamented. "That car had outlived its time, should have been surveyed long ago. I held my breath driving it up there. Frankly, I'm surprised it made the trip back." But Sgt. Maj. Railing was in seventh heaven; he had the captain's Packard Clipper. Within two months the Railings were transferred and Norma didn't have to see their old faithful being driven around the base by someone else. The last anyone knew of the car, it was still running fine.

* * *

Whenever Harry called Norma from work, it was to tell her something important. Today his jubilance alerted her of something unusual, "I've wonderful news. My friend Butch Condo called from Camp Lejeune. They just bought a car and want to come for a weekend visit. I hope you don't mind that I finalized it with him.You'll know when you meet him why I like him so much. We were together overseas for six years. He left Okinawa a month ahead of me and I was certain he was on his way to marry Dolly, but didn't know for sure until today that it worked out. They're both anxious to meet you." And Norma was anxious to meet C.W.O. Charles Condo and his new wife.

Butch and Dolly, Pennsylvania born, had a way of speaking that she found delightful; it was mutual, her southern dialect delighted them. Butch was tall and Dolly was diminutive, like her name, and looked like a gentle brown-eyed fawn. Because of her short stature, she disliked intensely the new dropped hem line, needing as much leg showing as possible, she said, and had hemmed up her new blue raincoat bought to match the light blue Buick, which wasn't new, except to them. Butch said it was the other way around; they had bought the car to match Dolly's raincoat.

Butch kept Norma off balance with his serious attitude and outrageous words or his comic expression and serious words. She could never decide when he meant what he said and when he was joking. And she had a tendency to take everything literally, anyway. Taking coffee and dessert, his countenance wore mock gravity as he slowly stirred sugar into the steaming brew, "I've known this old athlete here for a long time--" his skeptical eyes appraising Norma. "---and I never expected the day to come when he'd throw in the towel and tie the knot." He sipped his coffee, shaking his head in confusion. "Then when those mail bags of letters started coming from some young chick in that rebel state of Georgia, nineteen in one delivery, the skipper got crazier and crazier. The rest of us mail-starved Marines just sat while the mail clerk emptied the whole bag at Harry's feet. I don't know what was in those letters, but I could see that there was just no hope for him." Another sip of coffee and a bite of pie.

"I had to come and see for myself how much damage has been done. It's like this, Norma, according to my way of thinking, nothing short of the best is good enough for this old knuckle-head here," he nodded in Harry's direction, pausing to light a cigarette, "and from the looks of things that's just what he thinks he's got." Butch puffed on his cigarette, blew out the smoke, stroked his short mustache. "But I've got all the faith in the world in the Skipper's judgment, so I have to accept his evaluation of the lady in question." He leaned toward Norma, his dark eyes gleaming with approval. Throughout Butch's monologue, her expression had changed from surprise, to doubt, to defensiveness, and finally relief, and observing this, at the end, the other three burst out in explosive laughter.

Little by little, Norma grew accustomed to Butch's focus on and exaggeration of the lovable flaws in each of them. And an immediate liking developed between her and Dolly irrespective of their desire to form a friendship for the sake of these two comrades whose mutual love and respect were worn as easily as their uniforms. When the four parted early Monday morning, Butch and Dolly extracted a promise that either en route to or returning from New York in April, the Kipps would stop in Jacksonville for a few days.

After work, Harry entered the house as usual by the kitchen door to find Norma busy at the stove. "I thought I'd find you resting up from a weekend of preparing great meals, Honeychild. What a great little cook you've become and I'm not the only one to think so. And you made a hit in other ways too." After a greeting kiss, he poured a cup of coffee and sat to drink it. "I'm beat, aren't you?"

"I can't afford to be, you either. Hurry and drink that. You've just got time to pick out the music. We're having supper guests in a half hour: Terry and Tuck. I invited them before I knew the Condos were coming and in the excitement of their visit I forgot to tell you. I didn't remember myself until I woke from my nap, and I've been in a rush ever since."

At six their guests hadn't arrived and Norma had time to look over the recordings Harry had chosen for dinner listening, his contribution and one he took great pleasure in making. At seven, an hour late, the Smiths arrived with Terry, at least, looking apologetic. She was breathless and her hairdo, usually chic and smooth, was a bit untidy. "I'm sorry we're late," she said glancing excitedly at Tuck who stood robust and relaxed.

"Well, now that you're here, come on in!" Norma said in welcome. "We might as well go straight to the table. Supper's ready and waiting."

Seated, Terry unfolded her personalized napkin, her blue eyes sparkling, "You make me feel so special, everytime we eat with you, seeing my name satin-stitched in red across one corner."

"Yes, in red," Norma said, "for dashing and lively--YOU!"

"And black for Tuck, the big bad guy!" Terry grimaced.

"Hopalong Cassidy wasn't bad," Norma said, and Tuck howled.

"Lavender suits you, Norma, soft and serene," Terry nodded, "but I can't imagine why you used bright blue for Captain Kipp!" She rolled her eyes heavenward.

"It figures," Tuck explained. "The Skipper's true blue. True Blue and Black Bart!"

"No, it's for his eyes," Norma protested, "and black's for yours, Tuck."

"Ah, shucks, I thought it was for my heart," he clutched his chest.

Terry brushed his face with her napkin, then turned to Norma, "How many of these have you made?"

Norma counted on her fingers the couples they'd had for guests, "Fourteen, counting yours and ours."

"It's a novel idea, and so's your potato salad, something's different."

"I used vinegar, bacon, and hot potatoes," Norma cast a look toward Harry, "the way he prefers, especially with roast pork and apple sauce."

"Because he's a Damn Yankee," Tuck, from Kentucky, explained.

"And an outnumbered Yankee," Harry sighed in resignation, taking a third helping of 'his' potato salad.

When the meal ended, the men left the dining room. Terry and Norma cleared the table, gliding back and forth to "Smoke Gets in Your Eyes". In the kitchen Norma said, "I'll do the dishes tomorrow."

"Let's do them now. I'll wash; you dry and put away," Terry's gay composure had vanished and her shoulders shook with suppressed sobs.

"What's wrong, Terry?" Norma asked in alarm.

"It's nothing," she sounded muffled, "I'm fine--just something in my eyes--like the song says--smoke--"

"Nobody's smoking in here," Norma responded, watching tears stream down her friend's face.

"Oh, hell, I can't hide it!" Terry cried, wiping her eyes on her dress sleeve, "I should've gone into the shower at home and got my crying over with as soon as Tuck told me. He was so dad-gummed happy, I pretended I was too. But I'm not!"

"For goodness sake, Terry, tell me what's the matter."

"Tuck's got orders to Ordnance School in Quantico and then to Guam," Terry wailed, "and we just got moved into a house after two years in a one-room apartment."

"Oh, no," Norma groaned. "But can't you go with him?"

"To Quantico, but not to Guam. He'd have to go, put in for quarters, wait probably two years. By then, his tour would be up. That's why he wants to make the most of the week we have left. He--well, he just--if you haven't guessed, that's why we were late tonight. I'll be fine in a moment. I can't let him know." Terry finished with the dish washing, dried her hands, touched up her make-up, and left to join the men.

Norma dried the dishes alone, thinking of how she'd feel if Harry came home with orders, the dreaded fear of all Marine wives. Turning out the kitchen lights, she stood in the edge of darkness to observe the others. Terry, head cocked and smiling once more, sat on the arm of Tuck's chair, his arm draped casually around her waist. Harry, seeing Norma, patted the cushion beside him, "Now that our fourth is here," he said, "how about a game of Rummy?"

"Yes, indeed, Captain, after you tell us your reaction to Norma's new black knockout dress!" Terry said archly.

Norma blushed, looking at Harry's face wreathed in a smile as he answered, "It made quite a hit with me, but she hasn't made a public appearance in it yet." He raised his eyebrows, "I'm not sure I want her to."

"Promise me I can sit with Anne when you decide to risk it," Terry urged, winking at Norma.

"I've been trying to talk her into going with me to the Valentine Day's bash at the O Club, so far unsuccessfully." Surprisingly, Norma nodded her willingness.

"Oh, good! Just tell me the time to be here," Terry chirped. "Honestly, I feel like a fairy godmother."

After the Smiths departed, Norma said, "We're planning for a happy time and Terry's facing Tuck's transfer. He's been back eighteen months, the same as you. Do you think you might get orders too?"

"Our situations are different. Tuck requested the school and I recommended him for it. He's at the start of his career, doing what is necessary to advance in it; I'm near the end of mine. I'm not requesting anything now, but in about five years, I'll be requesting retirement and then you'll never get rid of me. Does that allay your fears, Mrs. Worrywart? Four late nights in a row. What you need is a good night's sleep."

Terry came Friday, the fourteenth, in the late afternoon, looking her customary polished self even after a day of work. "How do you manage to always look so dashing?" Norma asked.

"Do I? I don't feel so dashing. A cup of coffee would surely be welcome." They took their coffee to the nursery where Anne was staring at her hand, a recent discovery. At the sound of Terry's voice, she shifted her attention. Terry picked her up and raised her high in the air. Anne chuckled and drooled.

"Careful," Norma cautioned, "she's teething. Here's a towel for your dress."

"Don't you worry, Mommy. She's a precious baby, and I'd like one just like her, drools and all." Terry raised Anne high again, kissing her laughing face, then cuddling her close. "If you could be anyone in the world, any woman I mean, who would you be?"

"I don't even have to think, Terry. I'd be me."

"I knew you'd say that and I wouldn't want to be anyone but me, but I'm so dad-gummed lonely, it's killing me. Lord, I miss my Tuck, and he's missing me; I've had five letters and a phone call the first week he's gone."

Harry came home, greeted the two women, gave Anne a pat on the fanny, and went straight for the shower. Terry took Anne to the kitchen, "I'll feed her while you put on your glad rags. Don't you dare leave without letting me see you!"

Norma appeared a half hour later, frowning, "I don't think I can live up to this dress."

"My-oh-my!" Terry whistled, "I think I know whose idea it was to keep so many buttons fastened." Harry appeared in his dress blues, winked and nodded with a grin.

The no-host Valentine party was already in progress when Norma and Harry entered the club. Happy talk and laughter filled the big room along with a thin haze of smoke and the aroma of mixed drinks. Beautifully clad women stood in clusters with uniformed officers, striking in their dress blues. Harry guided her through the maze, stopping to make introductions, proceeding to the edge of the crowd almost to the wall of windows. She noticed there were no chairs for sitting, but small tables placed about the room offered ash trays although many smokers held theirs along with drinks; drinking and smoking seemed more important than eating. Hardly anyone served themselves from the deliciously smelling food so attractively arranged around heart shaped floral centerpieces on snow white tabletops.

Harry asked her, bending to her ear so she could hear above the chatter, "What would you like to drink, Honeychild?"

"To drink?" she asked in near panic, "Do I have to drink?"

"How about ginger ale?"

"Oh, yes, ginger ale!" she agreed in relief.

"Wait here. I shouldn't be long."

Her eyes followed as he crossed the room and stood at the bar, looking magnificent in dress blues, the smartest looking of all uniforms. The collar band, edged in red, looked so military, even if she had almost choked him getting it fastened! The red stripe down the trousers glowed next to the royal blue, and the brass buttons were like golden lights up and down his chest. What a sight he was! Better not get too excited; he might not want to leave just yet. She pulled her gaze away to look around the big room, crowded, and noisy. Where were the chairs? Wouldn't they get tired from standing all evening? She hadn't counted on that and wished she hadn't worked so hard cleaning house today. At least she didn't have to prepare supper and the food here looked so tempting.

She walked toward the windows to look out on the terrace and beyond to the water, black and still in the faint light of a three-quarter moon. A movement caught her eye, a reflection in the window. Harry was approaching. She spun around with an eager smile and saw that it was instead a stranger, a fit and handsome silver haired man. She hadn't learned to identify naval officer ranks, and this uniform carried many gold stripes. "My word, what a greeting!" His gray eyes sparkled.

Norma's smile disappeared instantly. "Oh, it wasn't for you; it was for my husband--the reflection," she gestured to the window, "I thought you were my husband, " she murmured in embarrassment.

"Unfortunately, no." He smiled at her confusion. "But allow me to introduce myself. Commander Wright, Bruce Wright."

"Good evening, Sir, I'm Mrs. Kipp." She extended her hand which he took warmly and held, enveloping it in both of his. They stood connected far too long. She was uncertain of what to do as he held on, very much at ease, his eyes alive with interest, his thumb moving across the top of her hand. She attempted to free it, he strengthened his hold, saying, "So, then, you're married. Just my luck!" He looked at her with frank admiration. "I shouldn't leave you alone for a minute if you were my wife."

She tried to free her hand. *This isn't social, it's personal--man to woman. What is he thinking to be so forward with me?* Stiffening her back, she responded, "My husband knows he has no need for worry, Sir."

"Dear lady, it's not necessary to address me as *sir.*"

"I always use *sir* to older men, even if they are not in uniform, the same as with my father," she said, a little edgy.

His jaw tightened for a moment as did the pressure on her hand. "Am I to assume, then, by your upbringing and your speech, that you are one of those legendary Southern Belles?"

"Southern, at least. Yes, sir."

"You are still saying it," he reminded her.

"And you are still holding my hand, " she reminded him.

"Ah, yes. So I am."

"And what might your wife say if she saw?" Norma stepped away.

"If I had a wife, she would have reason to be jealous." He followed.

"I don't think so!" Norma replied lifting her chin.

Leaving the bar, Harry saw the Commander and Norma joined by hands and her effort to free herself. As she stepped backward, widening the distance between them, the Commander closed it. With her back against the window, Harry saw Norma's face flush, chin rise, and eyes flash. Quickly and silently he reached them, a drink in each hand.

"Good evening, Commander. I see you have already had the pleasure of meeting my wife."

Commander Wright turned, "Good evening, Captain. So you're the fortunate husband of this charming lady. Permit me to congratulate you. I'm quite taken with her beauty, and her manners. She tells me it's her southern heritage. I wonder, does she also address you as 'sir'?"

"Thank you, Commander. I, also, am taken with her beauty and manners," Harry's tone was light and even, "and if bourbon is your drink, take this one, and I'll get another for myself. Your ginger ale, Honeychild."

Commander Wright released Norma's hand to take the proffered drink, "Honeychild, is it? I knew your wife was one of those charming Southern Belles. I even told her so." He smiled with satisfaction.

"She's Honeychild to me, Commander. To you, she's Mrs. Kipp or Norma. If you will excuse me," he nodded to each, "I'll return to the bar."

They sipped their drinks in silence. The Commander spoke first. "He is a fortunate man, and a confident one as well. With good reason." And after a studied pause, "Are you as young as you appear, Mrs. Kipp?"

"And how young is that?"

"At last you've dropped the title." Over the brim of his drink his eyes appraised her face, "Like a young maiden, and the rest--" they lowered to take

her in from head to feet, "a very desirable young woman."
"I'm nearly twenty, and a mother."
"Mmm. The Captain doesn't waste time! Do you think there might be another young lady like yourself somewhere who likes older men?"
"If they were like my husband, I'm sure there is."
"I wonder, do you think there might be hope for me?"
"In what way, Sir?"
"Please, call me Bruce... hope in finding the happiness I imagine the Captain has found with you." He looked a little sad.
"You must know that I am as happy as he is."
"Yes, I can see that, and I'll tell you something. I'm as envious as hell." He took her hand again and bent to kiss it. Releasing it at once he straightened and said, "Good evening, Lovely Lady."

He was gone when Harry returned. Soon they were joined by B.G. and Tom and others from the First Battalion. During the evening Norma had more encounters with hand holding officers until instead of offering her hand, she offered a smile.

During the evening she made the rounds of the tables sampling the food, enjoying it even if she didn't recognize some by taste and sight. "I'm having my meal," she whispered to Harry. "I hope you don't leave hungry." But he did. Later, much later, he admitted to being hungry, for food. "Next time we're at a party, you should eat more and drink less," she advised. "And this time, and only this time, I'll fix you something to eat."

"So there's going to be a next time?" he asked. "For a while there tonight, I thought not."

"Do you think it was the dress?" Norma asked.

"No, it wasn't the dress, Honeychild. It's what was in the dress."

*   *   *   *

Jim and Betsy Moore came to the bowling game on March 4 wearing matching wedding rings, having been married in a civil ceremony two days before. Jim made his highest score of the season and the team captured the first half honors in the Intra-Post Officers Bowling League. Afterwards everyone went to the Club to toast the bride and groom and assure Jim that his marriage had been a good thing for the team.

*   *   *   *

The Kipp's neighbors in MOQ 57 were a redheaded, fair skinned, green eyed Irish beauty and her dark, handsome husband. Norma was certain that 1st. Lt. and Mrs. Richard Granger had more friends than anyone on the base. People were always coming or going from their quarters, eating from the table always spread with baked ham and beans, potato salad, pickles, rye bread, and mustard, like a constant picnic.

Marilyn and Dick were Catholic, and it was in their home that Norma met a priest for the first time. Marilyn introduced Father Floyd, then left the room. Tongue-tied and uncomfortable, alone with a stranger in his black suit and white collar, she expected that he would be like her father and try to convert her to his belief. But he didn't even look at her after Marilyn left; he stood staring out the window while she fidgeted one long minute after another. She had come to borrow a cup of sugar, but with the cup still empty she said, "Tell Marilyn I went home." Father Floyd looked at her as if her presence surprised him, then nodded as she left the room.

Father Floyd visited Marilyn often during the following weeks, yet Norma saw her only on those days she came to use the washing machine. She seemed troubled and more intent than ever on complaining about the 'women Marines invading Parris Island'. Her usual good humor had turned to biting sarcasm at Norma's lack of concern. "Don't you worry that they are right there in the office with Harry?"

"No, I can't be worried that the world is half filled with women. Harry sees them everywhere he goes. Besides, I trust him."

"But can you trust the women Marines?"

"They're just doing their jobs, not there to steal our husbands," Norma laughed.

"*You* can laugh! Harry stays in the office all day while Dick drives all over the base with those women in uniforms."

"Harry does not stay in his office all day, but if he did, so what? We're married to Harry and Dick and they come home to us every night."

"What does that mean?" Marilyn snorted, "Norma, you're so simple minded! Besides you and Harry are practically newlyweds. Wait until you've been married ten years," she shook her finger in warning.

"That's proof you don't need to worry," Norma reassured her.

Marilyn wasn't to be reassured, her pretty face was lined with concern, "In ten years a man can get tired of his wife or she can lose her looks."

"It could work the other way. You could get more in love."

"You're so very young, Norma. How I envy you that and your faith in love and marriage. In your case, perhaps you're justified, but in mine..."

Semper Fi

On a chilly, windy morning a week later, Marilyn came again to use the washing machine, using it all day washing load after load of clothes, carrying the heavy damp sheets, blankets, curtains, throw rugs in five-gallon cans from Norma's kitchen to their joint clothesline. "I'd help," Norma said, "But I can't lift those heavy buckets, and you're going to hurt yourself. If you wait until lunch time, Harry will carry them out for you."

"No, I can't wait. I want these things to get dry. My mother's coming and I want the house to be clean from one end to the other." Between hanging loads of clothes, Marilyn washed windows and scrubbed floors in her quarters. Her house would be clean all right, Norma thought, but next morning the last load of clothes still hung on the line and next door the shades were still drawn at lunch time. Harry and Dick drove into the driveway behind their quarters within minutes of each other; Norma met Harry at the car and waved to Dick. He looked wretched, bleary-eyed, and needed a shave. He glanced at the clothesline, "I'll get the clothes off later. Right now, they're the least of my concern...unless you need the lines...Marilyn's in the hospital; she's miscarried."

Stunned, Norma could only stammer, "I'm really sorry, Dick. I wish I had known she was pregnant." In the kitchen, flushed with guilt, Norma stabbed absently at her lunch, asking Harry, "Is it my fault? If I had known...could I have stopped her?"

"No, honeychild; you warned her. She knew, and she didn't listen."

Norma looked at the washing machine. "I'll never feel the same about that machine again."

"Don't blame it," Harry said. "It did only what it was asked to do."

After lunch, Norma took down the clothes, folded, and carried them next door to find Dick sitting at the kitchen table with an open bottle of Scotch, bracing his head in his hands. "Can I fix you something to eat?"

"Thanks, Norma, but I can't eat. I'm going back to Marilyn soon." He took a long swallow from the bottle and set it down with a shaking hand. His eyes were full of sorrow, "This is the third time...the *third* time...she's done this!" and then the sorrow turned to anger, "Damn the clothes! Damn the house! And damn her mother!" His head went back into his hands.

Marilyn came home from the hospital and acted as if nothing had happened, nothing at all. Father Floyd came every day until Marilyn's mother arrived. Norma was grateful until she met Mrs. Hardy, a widow of many years who half the time forgot that her husband was dead. From day to day, she forgot who Norma was, or even Dick. Sometimes she mistook him for her late husband. Soon, Mrs. Hardy began taking her morning toilet outside in the corner where the pantry met the dining room and visible from the Kipp's bedroom window. Dick discovered her there, then locked the house from the outside when he left for work. There seemed to be no activity next door, the shades were always kept drawn and Marilyn didn't come to use the washing machine any more.

One morning after Dick left with Marilyn in the car, Norma saw Mrs. Hardy leaving the house in her nightgown. She ran after her, coaxing her to come inside. "Who are you?" Mrs. Hardy stared blankly at her. Then recognition returned, "Oh, yes, you have that darling little baby. I can't go with you. I've got to mail this letter. My husband will come for me when he knows where I am. They're trying to keep me from him, you know. They lock me in the house, but I know how to get out. You won't tell them, will you?" She asked anxiously, looking toward their house.

"It's too far for you to walk to the post office, Mrs. Hardy. Let me mail the letter for you," Norma took the empty envelope and led the woman inside. She wandered around, her tormented eyes searching in every corner until she came to the nursery. Norma spoke softly to Anne as the frail woman struggled to lift her from the crib. Afraid to oppose her, she said, "You may hold Anne if you sit in the rocking chair. She's quite heavy, you know."

"I like you and your baby," Mrs. Hardy said, and an almost contented look settled into her eyes. She closed them and cooed and rocked, cooed and rocked as Norma stood nearby, anxious until she heard the screech of tires in the drive way outside Anne's window and saw Dick's car rock to a stop. When he and Marilyn were inside their quarters, she called to say Mrs. Hardy was with her.

Dick swore, "Goddammit, I thought I had her locked in; how'd she get out? Thank God you stopped her, Norma. The damn woman's crazy, crazy as hell. Keep her there, I'll be right over."

When he arrived, Mrs. Hardy rushed to him in agitation, grasping his arm, "You got my letter! I knew you'd come!" She raised on her toes to reach his ear, "I don't want to stay with them anymore, please take me home." She clung to him with both arms.

Dick edged her toward the door, turning to Norma, "I don't have to ask you not to mention this, do I?" he asked in desperation. "I don't know what we're going to do; we can't watch her day and night. Marilyn knows that now. Thanks again, Norma. You're a good neighbor." The next morning, Dick drove away with Marilyn's mother. He returned alone at the end of the day and neither he nor Marilyn ever spoke of Mrs. Hardy again.

20

Harry's request for a three week leave had been approved effective 14 April. They would be making the long anticipated visit to his relatives on Long Island. Norma packed baby food, formula, toys, and clothing for Anne's stay with her grandmother. Her crib folded to fit between the front and back seats of the car and made a play area on the drive, and in La Fayette she would have her own familiar bed. Anne was a chubby eight month old blond and blue eyed darling, the very image of her father. So cheerful and good that people often asked if she knew how to cry. She had no eating problem, no sleeping problem, no problem of any kind, and would adjust easily to the separation from her parents when she was left with a doting grandmother and loving aunts. But would her mother?

On the drive to La Fayette Norma had time to think of it. Two weeks away from Anne! No, she couldn't drive away to have a great adventure and leave her baby behind! Why did she have to? They could take her; everything she needed was in the car.

Harry read her mind, "I know exactly what you're thinking and the answer is NO. We are not changing our plans. Look at it this way: we have someone responsible to take care of our little daughter, a new car, and more than two weeks to do with as we please. For the first time in over a year, we can be totally carefree. I am very happy at the prospect of this perfect vacation. Just the two of us and it begins tomorrow. Be happy with me, Honeychild."

Norma cried halfway to Chattanooga, but the worst was over--waving good-by to Anne cuddled happily in her grandmother's arms. Soon they were on the Blue Ridge Parkway which Harry followed to Roanoke, Virginia where they stopped for the night. "The first thing I want," he whispered, holding her close in their motel room, "will have to wait until after a long, hot shower." He looked into the bathroom. "Make that a long, hot bath. You first, or do you suppose we could both fit into the tub?"

She went to look. "Let's try," and smiling, she turned on the taps. The tub filled as they undressed. She slipped in, sighing, "Oh, it's delicious," stretching full length on her side and turning off the water. Harry's weight raised the water level until they were submerged to their chins. Then he sat up and reached for soap to make a handful of lather for her throat and small breasts, his thumbs encircling until they raised her nipples; he rinsed the lather away and took each in turn between his lips until they were cherry pink. Then, on his knees facing her, he presented himself for soaping. Norma lathered his pubic hair until it was foamy white, then daubed a blob of suds on the tip of his dancing penis, then moved upward to smooth lather over his perfectly shaped navel, upward still to the high mound of his pectoral muscles.

"You're misnamed," she said laughingly, "but I love your name and your bare chest." She lathered the light, fine hair of his armpits and along his arms where he had faded tattoos. "My Harry," she murmured, "My Sweet Harry, I love you so much, exactly the way you are, especially the way you are!" She lifted her face from his soapy chest, lather on her nose. He bent to remove it with his tongue as her arms encircled him.

"Honeychild," he whispered, his arms lifting her upward until their bodies were pressed together. "Oh, heaven, what heaven!" he breathed into her hair. They clung together until Norma began to shiver, then Harry quickly rinsed them both, lifting her and wrapping them together in a large towel, patting them dry. "Wait for me in bed," she told him.

He lay on his back, waiting, his arms at right angles and hands clasped behind his head, his eagerness evident. She sat beside him. "That night in Chattanooga--"

"Yes?"

"You expected me to stay, didn't you?"

"Yes, I expected that."

"Should I have stayed?" she asked earnestly. "Please tell me the truth."

"No, you instinctively knew what was best. I never questioned that."

"But you questioned me when I wanted to bring Anne with us."

"Yes, and I was correct in that decision, don't you think? But why this philosophical discussion, Sweets? Can't you see that I have something more pressing on my mind?"

"On your mind? Are you thinking with that now?" She looked at his upright eagerness.

"I was thinking that we can pretend this is that first night in Chattanooga--and see--what develops."

He stood upright, and she ran into his arms just as she had that night in front of the Read House eighteen months ago, but this time there was no audience, no restraints. His arms were like steel, binding her to him, his voice insistent, "I want to make love with my Honeychild! Now! Now!" Her mind flashed back to the time he had shown his Samurai sword, pulling it from its scabbard, his face strange and silent, his fingers on the blade, his fingers slow and gentle. The sword was touching places unexplored until now, searching, probing, discovering. Sheathed, unsheathed, sheathed, unsheathed, then poised in quivering stillness--all time and motion ceased--until she, the scabbard, closed upon and held the quivering blade. They were one: the scabbard and the blade, still and peaceful.

At breakfast, Harry outlined his proposed route, "About fifty miles north of here is a natural bridge and that's its name. Natural Bridge, a limestone arch some two hundred feet high, one hundred feet long, and about that wide. We'll drive over it, then park to see it on foot. Look for George Washington's initials which he carved in stone. The Monocan Indians called it the Bridge of God and the King of England, your King George 111, sold it to Thomas Jefferson for twenty shillings."

You're my King, and do you remember last night?

"Beyond the bridge," Harry continued, pointing to the map spread out on the table, "the Parkway winds its way through the Blue Ridge Mountains. You're going to enjoy that drive, Honeychild! After that, our next sightseeing will be the Luray Caverns. I saw them in 1935 and think they're worth another look. You won't believe the beautiful formations in natural colors in its underground rooms. Tell me, do you know the difference between stalagmite and stalactite?"

"Indeed, I do. Do you?"

"Stalagmite is a calcium carbonate deposit formed on the floor..."

"And stalactite hangs from the roof!" Norma finished.

"I forgot about your proficiency in chemistry, or is it geology?"

"I read your tour book!" she confessed. "One place I really want to see is Mount Vernon. Can we see it? And Monticello too?"

"Let's look at the map." He studied it for a moment. "It's south of Luray, not far off our highway, but it'll add another hour. Think you can handle an eleven hour day and still have something left for me?" He winked at her.

Norma flushed. *He does remember!* And she heard herself asking, "Harry, what do you think of when we're making love?"

"A surprising question--and in broad daylight.You usually reserve such topics for late at night when I want to go to sleep." He shook his head, "But to answer, I don't think, I go blank, completely blank." Grinning, he folded the map. "Let's explore that later because I'd like to know what you think about as you thrash about beneath me."

"I'm not always beneath you!"

"True," he grinned, taking her arm, "Come on, let's hit the road."

Days sped by, miles sped by. They saw their choice sights and Saturday found them having breakfast in Baltimore, lunch in Philadelphia, and supper near their destination. Tomorrow they would take the Holland Tunnel to Manhattan, the Brooklyn Bridge to Long Island, to find Jamaica and the Mistelskis.

"There it is: 90-10 170th Street!" Norma pointed. Harry parked in the street and they walked up the steps to the porch of a small brick house with shrubs bordering a tidy lawn. Juliette answered the ringing doorbell, " 'ello. 'arry." And holding the door open she motioned, "Come in." She waited quietly for Harry to introduce Norma then indicated chairs for them to sit and excused herself to bring a tray of cookies and a pot of hot tea. Not their choice of beverage, but they each took a cup and began to sip. Juliette looked at Norma with small brown eyes, unemotional but not unfriendly, comfortable with the silence, unlike Norma who was uneasy and grateful for the tea which kept her hands occupied.

Harry and Juliette talked for a time between themselves. That suited Norma fine, giving her the opportunity to study this French woman she had heard about and who somehow looked familiar. The imperious lift of chin and regal way of looking down her nose, black wavy hair immaculately groomed around her face and caught in a roll behind. Everything about her was immaculate. Of course! She reminded Norma of the Duchess of Windsor, at least from pictures she had seen.

Charley and Juliette had met in France in 1917 while he was in the Navy. She had immigrated to Minnesota to marry him, encountering immediate opposition from his family. Charley left the farm for the city to become a longshoreman. Juliette had remained a housewife and her contact with English had been limited. Norma could hardly understand her at all, having to watch and listen with such concentration that at the end of several hours, she was exhausted from strain and embarrassment. She discovered that smiling, nodding, and shrugging satisfied Juliette who continued talking as if Norma understood her completely.

In Charley, Norma met a taller, lankier version of Harry, older by twelve years. His blue eyes had the same merry twinkle and he wore his blond hair as Harry had worn his before he got the flat top at Parris Island. Charley's voice and manner exuded the same easy going confidence as Harry's. She sensed the deep and mutual devotion between the two.

Norma openly expressed admiration of Juliette's skill in needlework. Her exquisite embroidery was on armchair covers, chest runners, bedspreads, and tablecloths. Even guest and dish towels had elaborately cut out designs. Juliette made her own clothes by hand: dresses, lined across the shoulders had matching shoulder pads and hung on matching covered hangers. Everything about Juliette, her clothes, and her house was exact, perfect, and orderly. Doorstops at every door were padded and covered in lovely fabric. Every appliance wore a cover when not in use. Norma had never seen such attention to detail, and her close examination pleased Juliette, as well as her comments on the objects of art covering every flat surface, the many photographs of Juliette in fur coats and hats sitting on dresser tops, and the huge lithograph of La Rochelle, Juliette's home town, hanging over the mantel.

During their stay, the four were constantly sight seeing, yet Juliette served elaborate and delicious meals. "She amazes me," Norma told Harry. "Just how old is she?"

"She really was born in 1899," Harry laughed.

"That makes her forty-seven," Norma figured. "Nine years older than Mama. She looks so much younger, but then she hasn't had five children."

No matter how they tried, Juliette and Harry couldn't persuade Norma to shop for the wardrobe he wanted her to buy in New York. What she saw in the store windows didn't appeal to her. But to please him, she bought two dresses of his choosing: an abstract silk print with an elegant side drape and a dusty pink patterned silk suit. She bought two dresses for Anne, and for their kitchen an elaborate stainless steel vegetable slicer. Everywhere they went she looked for a gift for Juliette who seemed to have everything and no place to put anything new. At last, she found something that pleased her, and alone in their room she showed it to Harry.

"Isn't this the cutest thing?" She wound the key to a white enameled alarm clock and the little drum played "The Last Time I Saw Paris".

"You can't resist music boxes, can you, Honeychild?"

"No," she admitted, "Do you think she'll like it?"

"She'd like it for no other reason than it's a gift from you. I'm glad you've solved that problem since we're leaving Thursday. Shall I send a wire to the Condos that we'll arrive at their place late Friday?" He walked closer, "You've enjoyed it here, haven't you? Are you glad we came?"

"Very glad. I was scared at first, wondering if they'd like me. Charley's a dear man and Juliette's been nice to me. I really like them."

"And they like you, Honeychild. It's been pure heaven for me, and you want to know something else? Our 'spiritual communion' here has been as satisfying to me as what we had on those nights when we were alone."

"I'm happy we have both," Norma sighed happily.

They had finished lunch, Juliette and Norma, when the mail carrier rang the bell. "Go ahead and read your mail, Juliette. While Harry's away getting the car serviced, I need to do some ironing." Setting up the ironing board, she started on one of Harry's shirts.

Juliette returned, saying, "I 'ave a letter from Minnie. I wrote her you were coming."

"Minnie?" She was surprised to have actually understood Juliette's words.

"The mother of 'arry. Minnie Lueck. That's her new name. She just married again, for the fort time."

Did I understand her? Did she say 'the mother of Harry'? Are my ears playing tricks on me? Is she saying that Harry's mother is alive? She stared down at the half-ironed shirt trying to remember exactly what he had written about his parents. *Not much really, only that they were both dead. What could this mean?* Juliette continued to read Minnie's letter aloud, her voice coming from far, far away reverberating in Norma's ears.

During dinner, Juliette asked, " 'arry, do you want to read Minnie's letter?"

Harry shook his head and continued eating. Norma watched the others occupied in easy conversation while her mind was in a whirl thinking of Harry's mother, alive, married to her fourth husband. Charley bid them good-by at bedtime since he would be going to work at daybreak. His words were few, but his eyes spoke well and Norma felt she had his approval. Still his unexpected words thrilled her, "Harry is a happy man and the credit goes to you, Norma. Welcome to the family."

Next morning there were handshakes from Juliette, an invitation to return and waves from the doorway as they drove away. Norma leaned back against the car seat, eyes closed. "A big part of my life seems to be saying good-by. I would die if I had to say good-by to you. I know I would." Harry squeezed her hand, "You don't have to, Honeychild. Your old man is going to be around for a long, long time." Then he turned to his driving in the heavy traffic and she turned her thoughts to the question uppermost in his mind. She would have to ask him for an explanation soon.

The warmth of the Condo hospitality made Norma very comfortable and she talked enthusiastically of their visit to New York. The more excited she became the stronger her southern dialect became. She didn't mind that the others laughed; it was loving laughter and she was completely happy seeing Harry so content. And she was only seventeen hours driving time from her baby. She hadn't trusted herself to speak of Anne, and when she showed Dolly the little dresses and hairbrush set she had bought, tears spilled over. "She's finally getting enough hair to brush and it's as yellow as corn silk, just like her daddy's when he was young, according to Charley."

"Go ahead and cry," Dolly patted her shoulder. "I have to have a good cry myself every once in a while. I know how you feel. Chick and I have a little girl too. She's seven and a half, living with his Aunt Kate and has for all her life." Dolly's voice shook. "It's hard to talk without crying, but I'd like you to know."

Norma braced herself. Once again she was hearing unsettling news.

"I want us to be friends and this is a sad fact in our lives, Chick's and mine. It will explain things about us you may wonder about."

She already wondered why Dolly called him 'Chick' instead of Butch. Probably Marine friends had given him that name. But that was nothing compared to what she was hearing.

"We were married before, Chick and I, in 1938. He was a Marine corporal home on leave. We didn't have much going for us except love. I was underage, and in those days--peace time--Marines lower than staff sergeant weren't allowed to marry. We had to keep it secret. He was sent overseas and I was expecting. He sent me what he could, but it wasn't enough. So I lived with his Aunt Kate. When the baby was born, she told lies on me; he believed them and got a divorce. Mom told the judge she'd take me and the baby, but he decided the baby should stay where she was, with Kate. That's what happened. When Chick came home in 1945, he learned the truth and we remarried, but our girl wanted to stay with Kate and the school she knew. Chick thought it best not to uproot her, that sooner or later, she'd want to come live with us. But so far it hasn't happened."

What could Norma say to such monumental injustice? All she could do was let her sympathy flow out to Dolly and Butch. And dear, generous Dolly, let her happiness for them flow out. "I'm so happy for you and Harry. You have your family together, and Chick says Harry absolutely worships you, and you deserve it. There's no taint to you. I wasn't lily white, but I wasn't as bad as Kate painted me. I hope you won't think the worst of us for all this because we want to be a part of your life. We'd like for Anne to think of us as her aunt and uncle, if that's all right with you."

"That would make us very happy, Dolly. I wish we lived on the same base so you could see Anne often. She's so cute and precious and looks so much like Harry that sometimes I wish I had named her Harriet instead of after her two grandmothers."

The visit accomplished a lot. The deep bond that already joined Harry and Butch broadened to include their wives and Anne. Leaving the Condos, Norma settled into reflection. At sunset, Harry stopped for the night. After an early dinner and showers, he turned down the bed covers and Norma dutifully crawled between them. "Just hold me," she said, pressing close to him, he on his back, she on her side, her body against his body, her head on his shoulder, her arm across his chest and her fist in the pocket of his armpit. That was the safest place she knew in all the world. Soon her breathing was soft and regular as she slept. Harry slept until early dawn when Norma's leaving the bed roused him. When she crept back into her safe position, he rolled her onto her back and rested his cheek on the hollow of her belly. "Do you feel rested, Honeychild? And are you just a little bit sad that our vacation is ending?"

"Maybe it's sadness over that, maybe it's something else." She stared at the ceiling. "Dolly told me about their little girl."

"Butch thought she might; he wanted her to tell you. That's a tribute to you, Norma."

"It's because I'm married to you."

"Not altogether," he turned onto his back and then he stared at the ceiling. "Is there something more you want to talk about?"

"Yes, I want to know about your mother."

"After Juliette's disclosure, I wondered when you'd ask. And Honeychild, I would tell you if there was anything to tell."

"But there must be. You wrote me that your parents were dead. Your mother can't be, if she's writing to Juliette!"

"Let's just say that she's dead to me," Harry said with utter calm.

"I can't believe I'm hearing that! What on earth happened--or didn't happen-- to cause you to feel that way?" She asked in bewilderment.

"I don't want to talk about what happened; talking changes nothing. Let's say simply that I don't know her as a mother and leave it at that."

"Those letters you wrote her--the ones you didn't mail--"

"Honeychild, I've said all I'm going to say." His tone was final.

She would have to accept his decree, like it or not, understand it or not. The strange thing is that she wasn't surprised. Many times she had noticed older women and wondered if Harry's mother looked like this one or that one. But she had never allowed those thoughts to take hold. Now she thought of her own parents, and of Butch and Dolly as absent parents. Parenthood seemed to be full of darkness and heartache, making hers and Harry's more of a miracle. Suddenly she took hold of him with all her strength, crying, "I love you, Harry, I love you with all my heart and soul," spreading kisses all over his face.

He held her hands in his to slow her frenzied display, "Angel Mine! It's good to have my happy Norma back. The rest seems to have worked wonders! Then shall we get started on those last miles we have to travel?"
"You mean right now?" She looked at the clock hands pointing to six.
"It's too early to get up. I was wondering if--that sleeping tiger---?"
"What sleeping tiger? Look. Have you forgotten? He's an early riser."

At four in the afternoon they drove into the Clinton yard, and before Harry stopped the engine, Norma leaped from the car, ran up the steps into the house looking for her baby. She found Anne in her crib, swept her into the air, then held her close. The laughing baby grabbed handfuls of her mother's hair, babbling, "Ma Ma, Ma Ma."

"She remembers me," Norma shouted to everyone, "she remembers her Mommy." It was an hour before she parted with Anne and helped with supper. All through the meal, she gave highlights of meeting Harry's folks and the sights of New York and all the places they had seen. No one tried to get a word in edgewise.

Next day came the shopping trip to Chattanooga, the way Norma liked to shop: walking the length of Market Street, both sides, taking mental inventory, then buying in a whirlwind of organization, knowing what she wanted and where to find it. Chattanooga was her town, where she felt at home. New York was just too big.

*   *   *   *   *

At the end of school, Joan's graduating class traveled to Savannah for a three-day senior class trip. Instead of returning on the school bus with her classmates, she came to Parris Island for a week. Running through Quarters 56, inspecting everything, she squealed, "I'll declare, Norma, I had no idea, no idea at all. Why, it's a mansion! Just the three of you with all these rooms. If only Max could see it."

She talked continually of Max, of how when he finished school in one more year, they would be married. He was her dream boy. The captain of the high school football team and the handsomest boy in school with his blond curly hair, blue eyes, and winning smile. Norma conceded that Max deserved Joan's adoration. He was a nice, polite boy, but that's what he was--a boy--younger than Joan by nearly two years, and still in school.

Harry shook his head at the idea of two kids getting married. Norma reminded him that she had been Joan's age when they got married. "Yes, I know," he tousled her hair, "and some say I robbed the cradle. I've overheard talk in the barracks that I married a San Quentin quail."

"I'll have them know I was of legal age when we married!" Norma bristled.

"I overheard something else," he teased. "The young DI's wonder if the Skipper is able to handle his young wife--in every way."

"Oh, really? Well, you can tell them the Skipper's handling her just fine--in every way."

"Yes, Ma'am, I'll do that. Tomorrow, in an office memo."

At week's end they returned Joan to the arms of her 'Maxie Boy' and brought Julia back with them. And their wonderful days together began. Every week day morning, they watched the Marine band march by on its way to morning colors. Dodging children and dogs, the uniformed men with instruments and eyes straight ahead never missed a step nor beat. The sight and sound of it always thrilled Norma and she understood why Anne and Julia couldn't sit still there on the front porch nor at the Friday parade when platoons of graduating Marines passed by in smooth waves of khaki. And when Harry led the parade, floating along with the music, Norma expected her heart to burst with happiness.

In the evenings, Harry showed card tricks or told tales of life in the Paul Bunyan country of Minnesota, of his summer jobs as roustabout and strong man in a traveling circus. The story Julia liked most was how he had flown across the Pacific Ocean to Hawaii, took a ship to San Francisco, a train to Chattanooga, and a bus to La Fayette to marry her big sister.

Some nights they went to the drive-in movie or played records and danced. No matter how they spent the evenings, there was always the bedtime snack of cantaloupe, cut in thirds, and heaped with vanilla ice cream, Norma's choice; or corn flakes with milk, Harry's favorite; or strawberry short cake, Julia's choice. Weekends were spent on Hunting Island playing in the surf and building sand castles in the sand. It wasn't all playing. Julia had chores to do: washing dishes and hanging clothes, sweeping floors and dusting table tops, pouring bacon drippings in grease cans Norma had sunk into the lawn to attract ants away from the house, and making beds military style as Harry had taught her.

On June 28th Hilda had her baby, a son, who was named Linn, and the Kipps were on the road again, taking Julia home. In Augusta, stopped for lunch, Norma proclaimed it to be Julia's city since her birthday was in August. "Anne's, too," Julia said. "We can both claim it." And with a sad smile she added, "I wish I was your little girl like Anne is."

"I can make another proclamation," Norma said, waving an imaginary wand in the air, "I proclaim you to be my big girl. How about that?"

Julia leaned close, and whispered, "Let's let it be our secret, Okay? Just you, me, and Harry."

On Sunday morning, preparing to return to Parris Island, Harry placed Anne in her cubby hole in the back of the car. At that moment, Daddy called for the usual word of prayer at departure time. Harry sent Norma a message of defeat as the family gathered beside the car and with Anne inside, peering out, Daddy began his supplication for everyone to prepare for eternity with God, especially Norma and Harry who were going out on the highway this Sabbath. Thirty minutes later along with his Amen, Julia pressed a small, flat package into Norma's hand, "It's for your birthday." She looked down upon a card of bobby pins and a handmade book of colored drawings. Tears formed but she managed a bright smile. "Thank you, my big girl," she mouthed as Harry drove away with Julia waving them out of sight. Clutching the gift to her breast, Norma sobbed, "This breaks my heart. She used the money you gave her to buy this for me."

"She loves you very much, Honeychild. Accept what she can give you. It would make her sad to know she'd made you cry. Please, no more tears," he gripped her hand. "Tomorrow is your birthday. Do you want your face to be all red and puffy for your birthday dinner? The one I've planned for you at the Club," then laughingly added, "And since Commander Wright takes his meals there, perhaps you'll run into him."

"Now you're talking like Butch. Are you serious or teasing me?"

"I'm seriously teasing you," he answered, " and I hope it works."

"There's something else," Norma sighed. "Do you remember, before we married, I wrote about a preacher coming to our house and scolding me for wearing shorts and a halter top? Well, now, he has his own church and Mama says that Daddy has joined it--as a lay preacher. They think any kind of entertainment is sinful. Julia won't be allowed to listen to music on the radio, go to movies, skate, or swim-- all the things she did with us are forbidden. What kind of life will she have now? Just going to school and to church? I wish she could live with us."

"She'd be welcome to live with us if your parents will permit it, but-- don't get your hopes up, Honeychild."

"I can ask them though," she said hopefully.

21

July! Shimmering heat and humidity, sand fleas, and water bugs in this 'swamp settlement' as Harry called it drove most wives away from Parris Island. Not Norma. Nothing could drive her away from Harry even though they slept under the blasts of two electric fans each and every night, which straightened her hair, and she took numerous daily showers, which dried her skin. Still, she realized, she had it good compared to the Marines who worked and trained under the relentless heat and stifling humidity. Friday afternoon parades were switched to early morning. Even so, some men passed out during the ceremony to be carried away in waiting ambulances. Those who remained standing did so pockmarked with blood from insect bites. Spectators could at least swat the gnats and fleas. It was, Norma thought, a mark of phenomenal self-discipline that Marines did not strike at the insects which plagued any human remaining still for more than two seconds. But of course, self discipline was their middle names.

Because of the heat, the July attendance of the Officers Wives luncheon was the lowest of the three Norma had attended. She was surprised to see the wife of the commanding general there. They were seated at one long table and Norma, finding her place card across from Mrs. Hart, would at last see this legendary lady up close. People almost quaked at the sound of her name not to mention being in her presence. Her stature and bearing were enough to frighten, even if being the general's wife didn't. She always wore gloves and a broad-brimmed hat to shield her milk-white complexion from the intense summer sun. With good results, Norma noticed, seeing her unlined and beautiful skin.

Just as she took a bite of bread, Mrs. Hart asked, "Mrs. Kipp, how do you like living at Parris Island?"

Norma quickly swallowed to answer "I like it fine, thank you, Ma'am."

"You like the heat?" Mrs. Hart asked in surprise.

"No, Ma'am. I'm really suffering from it."

"Indeed? Then will you be leaving us soon for a cooler climate?"

"Oh, no, Ma'am. I'll stay here with Harry no matter how hot it gets."

"You needn't call me 'Ma'am.' I have a name; it's Katherine Hart."

"Oh, I couldn't call you by your first name. Even if you weren't the general's wife, I'd have to call you Ma'am. My mother taught me to be respectful of older women."

Mrs. Hart's face turned red, then white, and her look of disdain would have withered Norma had she seen it, but her eyes were on her food. She heard of it later, however, from Lt. Parker's wife, a self-appointed authority on Navy wives etiquette, who suggested she get a copy of the *Navy Wives Handbook* and educate herself. Once before, Helen had rebuked her for removing her gloves in a receiving line. Norma had defended herself by saying it was friendlier to have flesh touch flesh; Helen had said that was vulgar and 'friendliness' was not proper protocol.

Telling Harry of the luncheon incident, Norma groaned, "Helen's right, of course. I don't know how to act." She reminded him of the time she had stood on the wrong side of him in a receiving line and caused considerable confusion as to which officer she belonged to. Harry laughed. But she said, "It wasn't funny to me. Suppose I do something awful and get you demoted."

"I doubt that will happen, Honeychild, and if I can't hold my rank by my own ability, I don't deserve it. Right now, I have more than I ever expected. Years ago when I was promoted to gunnery sergeant, I thought that was the top of the ladder for me. And when the war ended, most who held temporary promotions, such as mine, were reverted to their permanent rating. It hasn't happened to me yet, but it could, anytime. And if it should, it won't be because of you."

"I wish I'd known about that book so I could be a better Marine wife."

"Has this Marine complained?"

"No, but maybe you should tell me when I do wrong."

"You don't do wrong. Please don't let Lt. Parker's wife upset you."

Still, Norma bought the handbook and took it to study with B.G. who said, "I got along without it, Norma. Now, I won't be needing it. Tom just got termination papers. He'll be a civilian by the first of the month."

The book slipped from Norma's hand and landed on the floor with a thump. "How can that be?" she cried, disappointed at the thought of losing this new friend. "Harry says the Corps needs good officers like Tom."

"Thank Harry for the compliment, Norma, but Tom's out. He hoped they'd keep him. He really wanted to make the Marine Corps his career. But it's not going to happen. Sheree and I are going on ahead. Tom can check us out of quarters. There's no need for us to stay on in this heat."

A week later, Harry brought home two letters for Norma, one from B.G. in Ohio, the other from Enid, Oklahoma. "Who do you know in Oklahoma, Honeychild?"

"Remember the letter from the grandmother whose grandson wasn't writing home? and you said to throw it away? Well, I wrote her to explain why he didn't have time to write; she lives in Oklahoma."

Harry's forehead wrinkled, he bit his lower lip, and fixed astonished eyes on Norma as she read the letter.

July 25, 1947

My dear Mrs. Kipp,

You must be a very nice lady to take the time to write me. I did get the letter you told me about from your husband's clerk and please thank him for me. But it was your letter that set my mind to rest and now I won't worry no more. They sure do keep them boys busy, don't they? But I guess that's what it takes. I'm just a doting grandmother, but Gerald, he is all I got and I miss him a lot. I'm real proud that he's going to be a U.S. Marine and I sure would be proud to see him when he gets through his training and walks across that parade ground you told me about. But that ain't likely to happen since I can't go as far from home as Parris Island is from here. I ain't never been off this farm. But when Gerald does get home I can see him in his uniform. Thank you again and God bless you and keep you. Tell your husband he is a lucky man to have a fine Christian wife like you.

Mrs. Pearl Rawlings
Gerald's grandmother.

Norma flushed with pleasure, but Harry's stern expression quickly curbed it. Yet he spoke softly. "Honeychild, the Rawlings matter was not your business; it was Marine Corps business, for me to handle however poorly you may think I handled it. Our aim is to make men out of boys. Telling them to write home doesn't quite achieve that end."

"I just thought if she knew the reason she wouldn't bother you any more. Men just don't understand how a mother, or a grandmother, feels."

"And you don't understand how I feel. Therefore, I must tell you. Please, stay out of Marine Corps business." Norma lowered her head in misery and didn't see his look of amusement as he left the room. He returned with a highball in a glass decorated with a red fox chased by three white hounds. She had heard him tell Jesse that when he'd had a good day, he started with bourbon to the hind legs of the first hound. If his day had gone badly, he put it to the hind legs of the second hound. From the color of his drink tonight, he had put bourbon up to the fox.

"Don't be mad at me," Norma implored, "What I did was wrong, and I'm truly sorry. Please, forgive me. Tell me you forgive me."

He studied her for a moment over the glass top while she squirmed. Then, his gaze softened, "Of course, I forgive you. And since this is your first offense, there won't even be a court martial! Come here, you little busybody," and he held out his arms, "how can I stay upset with you?"

She ran to him with a joyful little cry and he gathered her to him. "Mmm, nice. But let's make a deal, Honeychild. You take care of the house and Anne and I'll take care of the recruits in Company B."

August set out to break July's heat record. Just as Norma decided to forego the Friday graduation parade Harry's call changed her mind. She was wrapped in a towel straight from a cooling shower. "There's a crowd of relatives here for the graduation. Col. McCormick thinks it would be a good idea to invite them for chow in the mess hall after the ceremony. He suggested having wives sit as hostesses, one to a table. Would you be willing, in spite of the heat?"

"What will I do with Anne?"

"Suppose I come home and stay with her?"

"You could do that? Col. McCormick will let you?"

Harry laughed, "Then you'll do it? I'll come for you in about an hour with a fact sheet on the mess in case you're asked any questions. And thanks, Honeychild. I told the Colonel we could count on you." He didn't tell her that the base photographer would be at the mess hall or that she would be hostess at the table with PFC Gerald Rawlings' platoon.

Norma floated on air to the car when Harry came for her after lunch. He listened attentively to her chatter about the number of meals served every day in the mess hall, the quality of the nutrition, the frequency of menu changes, and the number of recruits that went through the training program every twelve weeks. Then she came to the good part. She had actually met Gerald Rawlings, PFC Rawlings now, and had her picture made with him---" She stopped in mid-sentence. Harry's face was one big smile. "You knew!" she cried, "You knew."

He only raised his eyebrows and looked sideways at her. In the back seat, Anne clapped her hands.

"You *told* Colonel McCormick? You did! And he --Oh, that makes me love the Marine Corps even more. It does have a heart. And what good food they serve. I wouldn't mind eating there every day.You should instead of coming home to eat..." Suddenly she asked, "What did you have for lunch?"

"Never mind about me," he sighed, "I'm only the baby sitter minding the house while you were out taking care of Marine Corps business."

Through the base grapevine, Norma heard there was a shipment of hand soap at the commissary, with a limit of one bar per family. She and Hilda pushed their baby carriages, along with dozens of other wives, to pick up this scarce treasure. The sun beat down upon the long line of women waiting for the doors to open, hoping the supply wouldn't run out before they got their bar. Major General Hart's big black limousine came into sight, stirring up a breeze. The car always caused excitement when it passed, sometimes the general's stern patrician face could be glimpsed through the back seat window, sometimes the broad-brimmed hat of his wife. Today the car stopped. Mrs. Hart stepped out through the door held open by a Marine who followed her as she swept past the wilting women and babies toward the commissary door. The women gaped, and Hilda commented dryly, "I guess even she has to have soap."

"This is the second time in six weeks I've seen her up close," Norma said, "Isn't she a handsome woman? I wouldn't think she'd use ordinary soap on that skin of hers, though. It looks pampered."

Minutes later Mrs. Hart reappeared, sweeping by again without looking any way but straight ahead. The Marine carried a box filled with soap, and a notice went up in the commissary window: NO MORE SOAP.

All through supper, Norma fumed. "Now I understand why she is called 'Mrs. General Hart'. She won't have to worry anymore that I'll address her with a title of respect. It's not for myself that I'm disgusted. We have a car and can go hunting for soap, but most Marines can't. They have to depend on the commissary or the PX. Just because Quarters One has five bathrooms is no excuse for her buying all the soap. Why did they let her? Does General Hart know she does things like that? Does he know what that does to morale?"

"I understand your indignation, Honeychild, and I share it, but superiors are not criticized, and the penalty for gossip is severe. Denial of quarters. If we want to stay in quarters, please keep your opinions between the two of us."

"I will, I promise, but I don't have to like her." Norma noisily cleared the table of supper dishes. She plunked down dessert plates and poured more coffee. Seated again she asked questioningly, "Harry?"

"Yes, my little champion of justice. What is it now?"
"I've been thinking."
"I'm afraid to ask---" He braced himself with a grip on the table edge.
"I want to learn to drive the car. I'm tired of pushing that buggy everywhere I go. Will you teach me?"

Norma's lessons began, first on paper then on the road. When she felt ready, Harry drove her to Beaufort to apply for her driving license. She got it, they ate at the Ocean View, and she began the drive home. "I'm driving!" she exclaimed. "See, Anne, Mommy's driving.!" Along Bay Street she drove, on to Ribault Road and across Battery Creek Bridge. The sentry station at the main gate of Parris Island loomed ahead, and she panicked, "Oh, my goodness. What do I do?"

"Signal to stop, and then stop," Harry answered. "Put your foot on the brake NOW!" Instead of slowing, the car accelerated and the sentry, stepping from the guard shack, jumped aside. Harry's foot came down on the brake pedal just as Norma's reached it. The big black Packard came to a rocking halt. She slumped over the steering wheel, her hands over her face, wondering what would happen next. Nothing happened except the sentry inside was red faced from suppressed laughter and the sentry outside was nervously saluting. Harry returned it and said calmly to Norma, "Shift to first and drive on."

For a few times more, as Norma drove through the main gate, the sentries saluted from within. Soon neither she nor they had reason to feel even the slightest apprehension as the Kipp vehicle approached with her at the wheel.

22

The week before Labor Day, Harry was assigned to field officers quarters when Major Draper moved out. He was leaving not only Parris Island, but the Marine Corps. The Kipps had set a new record for themselves in MOQ 56, living there eleven months and loving the old house, one of several spared in the 1940 hurricane that nearly leveled the island. Their new address was 216 Tarawa, a street named for yet another battle Harry hadn't fought in, but it was only one house from the corner of

Nicaragua Street. In the living room of their new, modern bungalow, McDaniel's cottage could fit three times. Norma went from room to room, examining the windows. Yes, the curtains from 56 would fit, and so would the slip covers. The three bedrooms had large walk-in closets. In the central furnace room, she'd be able to dry Anne's diapers on rainy days instead of on the radiators as in 56. Behind the house was a maid's quarters and to the side, a raised rose garden with a dozen healthy bushes in various stages of bloom. She was delighted with everything except the filthy condition of the house. Major Draper's insolent stepson must have spent his days chewing gum and then grinding it onto the hardwood floors. The refrigerator had been left closed with the power off. The stench of rotting meat made Norma ill. "It's a pigsty" She held her nose. "Aren't quarters supposed to pass inspection when they're vacated?"

"True," Harry said, surveying the mess, clamping his teeth together.

"---and ours will have to pass inspection?"

"Still true."

"And I'll have to clean this mess, too? Don't say *true* to me another time," she slumped into a chair. "Can't we complain to somebody?"

"Honeychild, *somebody* is happy to be getting rid of Mrs. Draper at any price, except we're paying the price. If you think this house is a mess, it's nothing compared to Major Draper's life. Passing quarters inspection means qualifying for future quarters. Right now, that is not one of his concerns. And I couldn't bring myself to cause him any more grief. As for this," he waved his hand around to include everything, "we'll hire someone to clean it, and I'll help with 56. It won't be much of a job. You keep our home to inspection standard every day---"

Norma flashed him a look as he added, "Even the refrigerator top will pass white glove inspection on a moment's notice." He was referring to the day, almost a year ago, when they had their first supper guest, Jesse Griffin, in MOQ 56. In preparation, she had cleaned until the house literally glowed, so much that Harry was reluctant to touch anything for fear of mussing it. That noon, she had challenged him to find a speck of dust anywhere. Starting at the front, he inspected the window sills, tops of door frames, hanging light fixtures, bottoms of wash basins, drain pipes, as well as floors, window panes, and table tops, everything, as he made his way through the house and finally to the kitchen. Norma, jubilant with pride in her thoroughness, trailed behind. His face reflected equal pride in her as he dramatically, officiously played the part of inspector. At the refrigerator he reached to pass his hand across the top. It came away smeared with grime and they both looked with astonishment at the offending hand before he quickly closed it. Norma slumped in shame, "That's the one place in all the house I didn't clean! I never even thought of the refrigerator top."

"And why should you? You can't see up there, and neither can I, but Jesse's eyes would be level with it." He caught her and swung her up into his arms. "You're exhausted. Promise me you'll take a nap or I'll tell Jesse we'll be eating at the club tonight, and that would be a pity."

"Why a pity?"

"Because he'd not get to see your sparkling clean house. Promise?"

"Yes, but first I'll clean that dirty top."

"No, leave it, and I'll keep Jesse out of the kitchen."

The incident was often revived to support Harry's urging for Norma to get a maid at least until Anne was out of diapers. She always said she'd rather do the work herself. And she said it now, spending days on her hands and knees with a scrapper, steel wool, and paste wax until the hardwood floor was restored to its original beauty. Harry's appreciation came inside a manila envelope. Norma looked at it, her heart in her throat, "Official papers?" her voice trembled, "Oh, Harry, I'm afraid to look."

"Don't be. Go on, open it," his eyes twinkled in excitement.

She drew the paper out and began to read, "Request for leave approved beginning 29 September---"

Harry planned to celebrate their second wedding anniversary in Gatlinburg having arranged with Norma's mother to keep Anne. They entered the Great Smoky Mountains at Cherokee, North Carolina, taking the scenic switch back route which separated the National Park from the Cherokee Indian Reservation. "I'm eighth Cherokee on the Clinton side," Norma announced. "Daddy's grandmother was full-blooded. The rest of my ancestors were from England or Wales. You're all German, aren't you?"

"No, my father was Swedish, but I know nothing of him or his people. I think of myself as American--a Yankee, I believe your people call me," he smiled wryly, then pointed off to their left, "There's Clingman's Dome, the highest peak of the chain of sixteen for which the park is known. I don't remember seeing any of those peaks when we were here on our honeymoon," he looked at her sideways, eyebrows raised. "The only peaks I saw were---"

"You must remember The Chimneys!" Norma interrupted with a pretense of modesty, covering her breasts with both hands."You've certainly seen them in the photograph that's hanging in the dining room; two peaks so close together they're like lovers."

"As I was saying," Harry explained, "the peaks I saw were---like The Chimneys!"

"You weren't saying that at all, you're---I don't know *what* you are!"

"I'm in love, that's what I am. And I've got three days alone with my beautiful wife in this perfect place she found for us." He cradled her in his free arm and they rode on in serene silence, gazing at the mountain tops enveloped in mist until occasionally, when sunlight pierced through, the red and gold of tulip-shaped poplars and sumac seemed all the more brilliant. The highway descended to the quiet village of Gatlinburg, home to probably no more than five-hundred souls. They drove past the New Gatlinburg Inn, the town's pride two years ago, on to their stone cottage where behind it, their merry little stream still hurried on its way over the rocky bottom to wherever it was going.

After unpacking, they strolled along the five block main street then ate chicken and dumplings at the same cafe of two years ago. Returning to their cottage, they took a side trail to cross a stream by a narrow hand-railed bridge. Looking down upon the gurgling, clear water Norma murmured, "Bridges and streams; they make a good combination."

"Like us," he said, taking her arm, leading her to their cabin door, opening it, following her inside, then closing out the world.

The morning dawned brisk and colorful for their trip to Knoxville. They crossed the Tennessee River and took Hill Avenue to historic Blount Mansion, one of the first frame houses built west of the Alleghenies. "I know a Marine named Paddy Blount, no relation I'm sure," Harry joked, "but a swell fellow nonetheless. One day I hope you two can meet."

"Your friends must now be scattered far and wide," Norma speculated.

"That's for sure. Together for years, then within three months, dispersed to the four winds. We were the Old Corps---'a few good men'---already in the Pacific before the war, and when it began, we stayed to the end. A tight organization; everyone knew everyone else. Expansion to meet wartime demands created a new Marine Corps. But there's a few of us Old Salts around. Honeychild, do you know how Knoxville got its name? No? You want to know, don't you? Well, this James White Fort where we're standing was the first settlement and the home, originally, of General White. This should interest you: in 1791, when the chiefs of the Cherokee Nation relinquished all claims to the wilderness valley, the territory later to become Tennessee was formed. Our old friend, Governor Blount, chose this site as the capital and named it after Secretary of War Henry Knox. Do you suppose he was the grandfather of Frank Knox?"

Semper Fi

"Frank Knox? Should I know him? Is he one of your friends?"

"He was one of my bosses until 1944, Secretary of the Navy under F.D.R. You do know who he was, don't you?"

"You know I do, and I thought I knew all his cabinet members."

"Had enough history and sightseeing, Sweets?" Harry closed the guide book. "How about a matinee before supper. Look, "The Best Years of Our Lives" is showing across the street. It won the Oscar for best picture last year telling of three veterans returning home after the war to face an unsatisfactory job, an unfaithful wife, and for the third, a life without hands."

During their meal, Norma frequently felt Harry's eyes on her, attending to every feature of her face, reflecting an adoration that overwhelmed her. She closed her eyes against his soul on display. He reached across the table for her hand, "It was a powerful movie, wasn't it? Those men came home to great problems. And I? I came home to unbelievable happiness."

The movie had made her appreciate what they shared and she wanted to speak of her happiness; her heart overflowed with it! A million words wouldn't be enough. She could only whisper, "I love you, My Harry, I love you so much."

"Then all's well in my world." They drove back to Gatlinburg under the glow of a harvest moon, aware of each other, yet still absorbed in the pathos of the movie. At dawn Norma woke to an empty bed. On Harry's pillow lay a small gift wrapped box. From a chair by the window, he watched her untie the ribbon, lift the cover, sit transfixed for a moment before removing a pendant earring, a silver filigreed half-moon curved upward to support an oval moonstone. With a cry of delight, she fastened one in place, then the other. "So, this is why you wanted me to pack something blue!"

"Yes, Honeychild, to wear tonight for our second *anniversity* dinner."

She looked saucily at him, "What kind of man are you? One minute you give me the most beautiful pair of earrings in the whole wide world and the next you remind me of my ignorance?"

"Former ignorance! And what kind of man am I? Why, Sugar, I'm a deprived man, starved for you." Striding to her he pulled her into his arms, "Happy anniversary, my dearest wife, and may we have a hundred more!"

In La Fayette, Norma asked her parents if Julia could live with her and Harry. Daddy said no, but she could visit when school was not in session. So to La Fayette they went in December to bring Julia and Mary Lee to

Parris Island for Christmas. There they began to prepare for an old fashioned tree, stringing cranberries and popped corn into long ropes, baking gingerbread men cookies, and Norma made her famous fruit cake with the fruit and nuts soaked in brandy before baking. All week long the house was filled with delicious aromas, chatter, and laughter. After a Saturday matinee of "Song of the South", Zip-a-Dee-Doo-Dah was added to their caroling as they painted red and white spiraled canes and green trees on butcher paper for gift wrapping. When it was dry, they gathered around the dining room table to wrap presents. Holding a ribbon in place as Norma tied the bow, Harry said, "You're in demand again."

"Again?"

"Yes, again. You helped when Colonel McCormick sent out an SOS."

"Oh, that. Who needs me now?" she asked, fluffing the bow.

"The Enlisted Men's Club. We've been invited to their Christmas party. They'd consider it an honor if you would help Santa Claus give toys to the children." Norma knew that only mustang officers, those who had come up through the ranks, were welcome at the Enlisted Men's Club and the invitation was really a tribute to Harry. Of course, they would go.

The children's party began at 1800 hours on the twenty-third of December and Norma helped serve punch, cookies, and small bags of candy. Excitement reigned as the children waited for Santa Claus. They shrieked in glee when 'sleigh bells' sounded above the din and 'reindeer hooves' tapped on the roof top. But when a fat, red suited 'Santa' burst through the door, they stood in awe-struck silence. Without delay, he untied the cord of his bulging bag and reaching in, brought out a big stuffed teddy bear. Norma read the tag, "For David Austin" and a delighted five year old came forward to claim it. A second toy was brought out just as the door opened and Mrs. Hart swept in. Activity and talk ceased as her silky voice announced that she had come to help Santa distribute the toys.

Norma turned to leave. The costumed Marine reached out to detain her, his voice booming, "HO! HO! HO! Santa already has a helper."

Mrs. Hart advanced to the pair, turned her back on Norma, and smiled sweetly, "But I'm here now."

Santa boomed again, "HO! HO! HO! I can use two helpers." He gave Mrs. Hart the toy he was holding, the next to Norma. Alternating in this manner, both assisted until the bag was emptied. And for *The Boot* photographer, Santa posed with both ladies. When the photo session ended the general's wife departed, so did the children, and the adult party began with a buffet supper, then dancing. Norma took a seat at a corner table and declined Harry's invitation to dance. "You should, though," she urged, smiling, "It would please the ladies." As he waltzed away, she noticed a group of young Marines standing in a cluster on the far side of the room looking in her direction. Several shook their heads, making hand gestures of denial, their necks and faces red, shifting weight from foot to foot, eyes cast downward to glistening shoe tops. Abruptly, the oldest looking of the lot moved from the others, and glided toward Norma's table. She watched his self-assured approach, wondering if he came on a bet, dare, or of his own free will. *I'll know when I see his eyes.*

"Good evening, Mrs. Kipp. I'm Will Adams." His dark eyes flashed a challenge, "And I'd like the pleasure of this dance."

"Good evening, Corporal Adams, and thank you, but haven't you noticed? I'm not dancing, not even with my husband."

A fleeting expression of surprise widened his eyes and a slow flush rose from his collar to his crew-cut. Norma realized he had shown courage by asking in front of his comrades, and even if he were daring, or accepting a bet, she felt admiration, and sympathy, for him. She gestured to the chair beside her, "I don't dance in public, but would you care to sit with me?"

"Thank you, Ma'am." He sat, his back ramrod straight.

"Ma'am", Norma repeated the word into the air.

"I'm sorry, Ma'am---I mean, Mrs. Kipp. It's not because you're old, you're not, at least I don't think you are---any older than I am---it's because you're a lady, the Captain's lady at that."

She wanted to put him at ease, "Thank you. I commented because I remember once saying *Ma'am* to a very important lady who *was* offended. You shouldn't worry, I'm not."

From the dance floor, over his partner's shoulder, Harry saw the young corporal sitting with Norma, her skin pearly white against the rich brown of her hair and dress, looking reserved, yet approachable, her expression showing interest as she talked. The corporal stared as if in a trance. The music stopped and Norma extended her hand, Corporal Adams took it, bowed over it, and floated away. Harry reached her table a moment later. "Won't you dance with me, Honeychild, this last one before we go?"

"No, thank you, Captain, I'm not dancing tonight. But if you'd care to sit with me---" she indicated the chair.

"Are you playing musical chairs?" he asked still standing.

"Oh, you saw?"

"Yes, I saw you sitting there so desirable that I wanted to rush over and take you in my arms. If the music hadn't stopped when it did, I would have left Mrs. Kelly anyway." His eyes took on a suggestive gleam, "Shall we leave, Honeychild? Say our thank-you and good-by and get the hell out of here?" He took her arm, she rose; he bent to her ear, "And my darling, I hope you won't refuse my next offer!"

Christmas Eve, Norma brought out five red felt stockings she had made. Mary Lee filled them with little gifts, fruits, nuts, and candies, and Harry hung them from the mantel. Julia draped yards and yards of popcorn and cranberry strings on the tree and tossed on silver icicles. Norma lit candles and they sang carols in the semi-darkness. Anne's "Adeste Fideles" was accurate in melody but her words came out "Dusty Dayles". In bed at nine, the girls were asleep by ten. At eleven, Norma and Harry finished arranging toys beneath the tree, eating the cookies and drinking the milk left for Santa. "Morning's for the girls, but the Eve is ours," Harry said coming from his shower smelling of Neko soap.

Norma embraced him, sniffing at his freshness. "That smell," she wrinkled her nose, "How nauseous it made me before Anne was born."

"It worked in the tropics; mosquitoes and insects didn't like it either. You won't shy away from me now, will you?"

Moving closer, she pressed against him from head to toes, kissing his face and embracing the hardness of him. After a while she whispered, "A symphony---like Wagner's love-death theme from *Tristen*, the long crescendo, the summit, and then the melting. Do you suppose anyone ever dies from such ecstasy?"

"Often, I think I do, for just a little while, but Honeychild, what a way to die." He moved apart from her to lie on his side, his hand smoothing her shoulder, "I've read, or heard it said, that the most excruciating joy carries with it an awareness of death. At least a giving in to it, and the reverse. Men in combat threatened by death have been known to experience involuntary orgasm."

"Did it ever happen to you?"

"Yes, but---there's absolutely no comparison!"

They had slept only a few hours when squeals of joy sounded in the living room. Norma sprang up in bed, "Oh, my goodness! I completely forgot to write a note from Santa for the milk and cookies."

"Lie back; I wrote it. And stay put. Julia and I will prepare breakfast."

"Like what? Gingerbread men and hot chocolate?"

"Sounds good to me and doubtless will please the girls." And it did.

Semper Fi

The following day, Julia, Mary Lee, and all their 'loot' as Harry called it, and Anne and her crib were loaded into the car for the trip to La Fayette. As the car sped along, they sang carols and Zip--a-dee-doo-dah over and over in solos, duets, and trios. By dusk, the 'sung out' girls had gone to sleep one by one and Norma and Harry appreciated the silence. Theirs was the only car on Highway 27, driving in the twilight through the isolated pine country of north Georgia. Norma's eyes were on Harry's profile, her face awash with veneration. She heard his soft intake of breath as he glanced at her, " Don't look at me that way. I don't deserve it."
"You don't think so? You, the man who once said he didn't understand little girls. I don't know any man who shows better understanding. You must feel all the love that's in this car for you."

Home again, they were packing away Christmas paraphernalia. Stretched out in his favorite chair with his feet on the ottoman, Harry wound tinsel around cardboard. Norma, sitting on the floor beside him, read again Christmas messages and entered new addresses in her file. "Another girl for Ruth and Muggsy. Will I ever get to meet them I wonder? B.G. and Tom have a son and a new address. They've moved three times since he got out of the Marine Corps. Almost as much as we did our first year in. Butch and Dolly, still waiting for quarters on the base, and John has a wife! Juliette must have sent them our address. So, the two bachelor brothers are married, fathers, and uncles. A busy two years for the Kipp brothers, wouldn't you agree?"
"John wasn't a bachelor; this is his third marriage. The last time I heard from him he was on his second."
"When was that?"
"In March of '45. He wrote of flying in to Iwo Jima and Joe Rosenthal tossing him a bag of film to fly back to Guam saying, 'There are shots in here that will make history'. He was right. They were of the flag raising on Mount Surabachi."
"Really? John must be very proud of his part in making history," Norma acknowledged. "I'd like to take them up on their invitation to visit in Minnesota. I'd like to meet your brother. Does he look like you?"
"No, we're not at all alike." Harry laughed, " He's tall and I'm short."
"Short? of what? I can't think of a thing you're short of. But tell me more about John."
"There isn't much to tell."
"Didn't you grow up together?"

"I lived with my grandmother; he lived with his mother."
"She was your mother too."
"I didn't have a mother. I had a grandmother, until she died in 1940. She was already buried when word got to me on Midway Island."
"Oh, Harry, I'm so sorry." Norma moved to sit beside him, to stroke his shoulder, wanting to convey her sympathy though it was years too late.
"No need to be sorry," he said with sadness.
"Then I'm sad."
"Don't be sad, either," he said simply, holding her hand to his cheek. "I only wish the two women in my life could have known each other."
"Would she have liked me?"
"Honeychild, you bet your life she would."

23

1948 came in with unwelcome changes. The First Battalion's beloved Colonel McCormick was transferred to Marine Corps Headquarters in Washington, D.C. Before he left he told Harry, who had replaced Major Draper as executive officer, of the major's recent suicide by gun shot. After a nasty investigation, Mrs. Draper and her son returned to England. Harry was transferred to the Third Battalion as executive officer to Colonel Marvin Stewart. And Norma's terrible headaches began. Thinking her eyes were at fault since her hobbies required close vision, she gave them up to rest her eyes and turned her attention to Anne, now walking and a total delight, learning new things with every passing day.

Anne preferred singing to talking and was a walking soap commercial. All day long she hummed or sang "D U Z does everything" or "Rinso White, Rinso Bright, happy little wash day song." When she wasn't singing she was dancing to every recording she heard. As an infant she had enjoyed dancing in her mother's arms, breath drawn in, head back, hair flying and drawing big circles in the air as they whirled about the room. She had graduated to dancing on her own two feet and when the tempo became too fast, as in "The Hall of the Mountain King" from the *Peer Gynt Suites* she would fall on the floor and kick her feet in the air. At the weekly parades, she marched around the platform in perfect time to the martial music, delighting the spectators. She was everyone's darling, from her baby-sitters, to the waitresses at the Ocean View Cafe who had watched her grow from a baby to a charming little girl, to all her parents' friends, and the neighborhood children and dogs. Terry doted on her as did Grandmother Clinton who was quick to say, "That child's growin' up in the back seat of the car, like a gypsy. It's a million wonders she hasn't caught every disease goin' round but she hasn't; she's as healthy as can be."

Anne was healthy but her left eye, turned inward since birth, wasn't correcting itself as the pediatrician said it might. An ophthalmologist in Charleston recommended eyeglasses and Anne was fitted with them to be worn all her waking hours. It was difficult to tell whether or not they helped since she had never shown signs of impaired vision.

Norma's headaches were becoming intolerable. Resting her eyes had made no difference and an examination cleared them of being at fault. Her dentist found the cause: four impacted wisdom teeth. Removal was necessary to give her relief. He began with the right upper tooth, tugging, chiseling, and sweating as Norma lay in the chair, clutching the arm rests and bleeding. At last the tooth was extracted in pieces, and she left his office under sedation. She suggested that since they were in Beaufort, and it was supper time, they should eat at the Ocean View.

"The dentist expects you to go directly home," Harry reminded her.

"He expected me to be dizzy, too, and I'm not. I can wait for you to eat, if you eat fast." Norma giggled. She explained to the waitress why she wasn't eating. And rising to leave, she glided toward the door with hardly any effort ---never before feeling such lightness---almost reaching the door---passing the magazine rack---falling, falling---ever so gently to the floor along with the magazines.

Harry got her to the car and home to bed. She slept until noon of the following day and woke to tell of having dreamed of being at the Ocean View Cafe on the floor covered by *Time, Life,* and *Woman's Home Companion.* "That was no dream," he told her.

As soon as her gum healed, Norma was again in the dentist's chair having the lower right tooth dug out. Her headaches disappeared and she thought the pain of the extractions had been a good exchange, and like Scarlett O'Hara, she'd think about removal of the other two on another day.

On Midsummer Eve, the Kipps left for Minnesota. Harry drove across state borders with Norma making entries in her travel journal and Anne playing in her back seat cubbyhole made by her folding crib. In Northfield, Minnesota, on her birthday, Norma opened her eyes to find Harry propped on an elbow watching her. "What are you doing?" she asked sleepily.

"Sewing a button on a bar of soap," his usual answer to a silly question. Then relenting, he answered, "I'm waiting for my woman to wake. Today she's twenty-one and I have a present for her. Give me your arm, Honeychild," and he slipped a tiny-faced watch around her wrist, securing the clasp, then nodded toward the crib, "Our little daughter is waiting to make eye contact. Shall I bring her into bed with us?"

Norma looked to Anne, standing and watching in silent eagerness. As soon as their eyes met, she clapped her hands and squealed.

"Hello, my angel!" Norma squealed also, "Are you hungry? Do you want to sing "Happy Birthday" to Mommy? No? Oh, I know! You want to go to the bathroom---right away!"

Harry lifted her from the crib and Anne scooted to the bathroom then came running back to jump into bed with them. She put her ear against Norma's wrist and mimicked, "Tick, tock, tick, tock." then she pulled at Norma's hand, "Let's go, Mommy. Let's go!"

"We're going, all right. To the places where your Daddy used to play ...in basketball and track competitions...long ago before you were born, even before Mommy was born. Come on, let's get dressed."

Afterwards leaving Northfield, Harry pointed out St. Olaf College where Ole Rolvaag had been professor of Norwegian in the late Twenties. They remembered his book *Giants in the Earth* telling of the hardships and suffering of the first Norwegian settlers. Norma shuddered, "I didn't want to accept the ending, and to this day, I can still see in my mind, Per Hansa's frozen form leaning against a haystack holding his ski poles, facing west. Whatever happened to his family? to his wife?"

"When you were so sick before Anne was born, it all came back to me with full force. Remembering Beret's child birthing ordeal, I thought, My God, what have I done?"

"Is that why you were so protective of me?"

He nodded, "I just couldn't let myself think of you suffering the way she had. There were times I bitterly regretted that you were pregnant. When I got your mother's telegram that Anne was born and you were all right, I literally dropped to my knees in relief and thanksgiving. Norma, darling--if you had--hadn't made it--my life would have ended too."

"There is no way I would have died and left you! No, sir, I'm here to stay, you can bank on that!"

"Then I'm a millionaire," Harry said solemnly, his eyes meeting hers briefly before he gave his attention to the highway taking them to their destination. Rosemount. Hardly a town at all and Hazel and John lived a few miles beyond on Highway 3 going toward Minneapolis. Their address was really Southport. Norma looked at the flat plain stretching in every direction. Hazel had written that they should look for a high tower next to a hanger. In the distance she saw them rising above the horizon, then the airstrip, and a bit farther a new two-story wooden house glistening white in the afternoon sunlight. To the side a weathered farmhouse leaned ever so slightly toward a huge barn. A graveled driveway led them off the highway and up to the white house.

An attractive brown-haired woman, about Norma's age, came from the house carrying a pretty blond and fair skinned girl. "Hello, I'm Hazel. And this is Kathy. Jack's at the hanger. As soon as he sees your car, he'll come." She lowered the little girl to the ground and shook hands with them. Kathy and Anne gravitated toward each other immediately and could easily pass for sisters. Norma watched a tall, large framed man leave the hanger and walk toward them. His hair was light brown, his eyes were gray, his face, square. Harry was right; they didn't look alike, not like brothers at all.

He extended his hand, "Harry, good to see you. You've met Hazel?"

"Jack." Harry took his hand, "My wife Norma and our daughter Anne. Norma, my brother John."

John was making an appraisal of her, Norma felt, but his eyes gave no clue of his evaluation. She extended her hand which he took after a moment's hesitation. "I'm happy to meet you, John. You're the second of Harry's family I've met. Families are very important to me and I've looked forward to this meeting."

John nodded then moved his gaze to Harry, "Well, now that you're here, come in." He started toward the house. "We just finished painting the house and haven't got the screens back up. The mosquitoes are out like bombers so we'll have to keep the windows closed. It's too hot inside; we'll have to sit on the porch." He motioned to chairs placed to catch the breeze. While they waited for Hazel to bring lemonade, Norma watched a farm woman, large and heavy, coming across the yard with Anne and Kathy in tow. Anne was chattering and the old lady's pink face was beaming under her white hair. She heard John tell Harry, "Mother and Otto live next door. They help around the place."

Harry stood as his mother came up the porch steps, wiping her perspiring face with a white apron. He said, "I'd like you to meet my wife. Norma, my mother. You've already met our daughter."

Norma stared, her heart pounding, and the swelling in her head made the old woman's words seem to come from far away, "Juliette wrote me that you was a dear, sweet girl and I can see with my own eyes that she didn't lie."

"Thank you, Ma'am." Her own voice sounded strange. The ringing in her ears had turned to roaring and she felt dizzy. Then the pressure of Harry's hands on her shoulders steadied her, and her head began to clear. She sensed a tightness in him but no reaction from the others. Perhaps her confusion had gone unnoticed. Anne, animated as usual, broke away from the older woman's grip and ran from the porch to join a gaggle of geese waddling by. Norma welcomed the opportunity to follow her, needing to put distance between herself and this unexpected encounter with Harry's mother. *Had John purposely kept this for a surprise? Would Harry have come if he had known?* When she returned with Anne, Harry's mother had left and everyone acted as if nothing had happened--as if Anne had not suddenly gained another grandmother.

In the kitchen Norma asked Hazel, "What do you call John's mother?"

"Minnie," Hazel was slicing tomatoes.

"Just---Minnie?" Norma repeated.

"That is her name," Hazel said, giving Norma a tray of ice for the water glasses.

"But that's her first name," Norma said, then added, "She's an old lady, older than my mother. I wouldn't think of calling her by her first name." She took the glasses to the dining room table. Returning to the kitchen, she said, "I'm going to call her Mother Minnie. That is, if she doesn't mind."

Hazel seemed pleased that she and Norma were alike in marrying older men, Marines, brothers, having daughters within a year of marriage, were Southern (Hazel was from Maryland), were small, blue eyed and brunette, and almost the same age. She was disturbed by the differences, that she was the third wife, not the first, and that John had another child. She didn't mention directly that she was college educated with a commission in the WAVES. But she did mention that Norma had more power in marriage than she had.

John was retired on a disability from the Marine Corps, teaching flying to veterans on the GI Bill. Hazel was eligible as a student and John insisted she take lessons. "I'm terrified," she admitted to Norma, "I shake for hours before and after every lesson. John says it's a silly fear and I'll just have to get over it. Do you think he's right?"

"No, and if I were that afraid, I wouldn't take the lessons."

"You don't know John," Hazel said. "He makes all the decisions."

Norma remembered Harry's words: "We're not alike."

John had two planes, two cars, a truck, a tractor, and a motor boat. On the Fourth of July, he took the six of them on a cruise of Crystal Lake, telling Harry, "What I really want is a 30 foot Chris Craft and an ocean to take it out in." But Anne liked the boat he had. With Harry holding onto her legs, she leaned over the side and paddled her hands in the water as the boat raced along.

The following day John and Harry went off together and Hazel suggested a shopping trip to Minneapolis, without the girls, if Minnie would keep them. "Why not take them with us?" Norma asked.

Hazel grinned wickedly, "Silly, my plan is to get away from them!"

Mother Minnie willingly agreed, even on such short notice. "You dear girls go on and do your shopping and have lots of fun in the city. I'll have my fun with Anne and Katy." Her plump face glowed in anticipation.

Hazel fumed all the way to Minneapolis. "Minnie can't even say Kathy's name right. I've told her a million times her name's *not* Katy. You'd think she'd learn, wouldn't you?"

"I think she has trouble saying the 'th' words," Norma ventured.

Hazel looked at her, as if considering what she said, then changed the subject. She parked the car and their shopping spree began, each looking and finally buying a summer skirt and blouse. Norma bought a photograph album to give Mother Minnie for the pictures of Anne she planned to send.

Over lunch, Hazel leaned intimately toward Norma, "Now that Anne's almost two, do you plan to start another baby?"

"No, " Norma responded decisively, smiling and shaking her head.

"Doesn't Harry want a son?" Hazel pressed, looking at Norma over the brim of her iced tea glass. "To carry on the name?"

"No," Norma repeated. "He says not."

"Jack says that by the time Kathy's three, he wants a son. And we'll have one. He gets what he wants." Her expression, a mixture of exasperation and resignation, shifted to intimacy, "Is Harry very demanding about sex?"

"Actually, Harry's not demanding about anything," Norma answered.

"Really? Well, Jack is. He says---"

"Hazel," Norma interrupted, "How much should I pay Mother Minnie for baby-sitting?"

"You don't have to pay her anything. Jack pays her for the work she does. That includes keeping Kathy." Hazel said emphatically, spreading butter on her bread with equal emphasis.

"But not Anne," Norma said, "At home I pay a dollar an hour." Seeing Hazel's frown, she asked, "Isn't that enough? I don't want to insult her, either way---too little or too much."

"Let it be, Norma. She doesn't expect pay."

"Maybe not." *How can Hazel know what Mother Minnie expects?* "But I'd feel better if I did something to show my appreciation."

"Jack's right when he says you have a mind of your own. I'll bet you and Harry have knockout, drag-down fights!"

"Heavens, no! I'd die if we did. Besides Harry wouldn't fight with me. He says mature people don't fight, they negotiate."

"Then we must not be mature. We fight all the time. Jack can say the most hateful things and be so cold. Sometimes I think I hate him. I told him that and he has never forgiven me. I didn't really mean it, I just wanted to hurt him as he hurt me. But he doesn't believe me. I was just mad when I said it."

"Don't you think that what you say when you're angry is what you really mean?" Norma asked bravely, but cautiously.

"Funny you should say that because Jack said the same thing."

"It sounds like you're both just making each other miserable, but if John wants to have another child, don't you think that's a good sign?"

"He says he will not have another divorce, absolutely not." Hazel said.

For a while they concentrated on eating. Then Hazel's mood changed and she asked suddenly, "Norma, have you ever dated a cadet from VMI?" She toyed with her two-carat diamond ring.

Norma smiled humorously, "I don't even know what VMI is, Hazel."

"It's the Virginia Military Institute, Silly." Hazel's eyes brightened. "They have the best looking cadets in all the world!"

What is her point? She knows my background. But her voice didn't reflect irritation, only amusement, "Hazel, I doubt that a VMI cadet would have looked for me in the hills of north Georgia to ask me for a date." *I'm not as educated nor cultured as you, but I'm not a snob.* Then she added with a bright smile, "Still Harry found me there, and he did more than ask me for a date. He married me!"

"I could have married a cadet," Hazel said wistfully, "but Jack was a better catch." She folded her napkin with care, placing it on the table.

Then you and John deserve each other. Norma crumpled her napkin and let it fall on the table.

Back at Southport, Norma talked with Mother Minnie, telling her about herself, her family, and Anne, from birth to the present, about their life at Parris Island, and their visit with Juliette and Charley, avoiding any mention of Harry's past before their marriage. Mother Minnie was loving to her and Anne, smiling and cheerful, even childlike. And with a childish lack of discernment, she spoke of what Norma had purposely avoided.

"Dear girl, what has Harry said about his papa?" Her eagerness signaled a desire to reveal what Norma didn't want to hear...not from her.

"Only that he never knew him," she answered simply.

"Oh, dear girl, he was so handsome, and a real good talker. He was a real ladies man. All the girls was after him, but it was me he chose," her face was alive in remembrance.

Norma didn't comment nor ask for elaboration, but the old woman's joy was not lost upon her and her heart opened to Mother Minnie. Harry wanted the past left alone; he had said he would not talk about it. If he changed his mind, he would tell her. So far, he hadn't. And this visit would be the perfect time. She might never know what happened, because if she couldn't hear it from him, she wouldn't hear it from anyone.

One thing Harry did want was for her to meet his Aunt Bertha and Uncle Ernest for whom he was named. All their children, Harry's cousins, and their children were at Princeton to meet Harry's wife and daughter, all gathered around the long, cloth-covered dinner table to eat bread and butter and drink milk in solemn silence. No matter how polite they were, Norma still felt like an outsider. She had difficulty swallowing the bread and hoped she wouldn't cough or choke from nervousness. She wanted so much to measure up in their eyes as a good wife for Harry, knowing she didn't measure up with John. Maybe she was the only one who was tense, because the others sat easily in their straight backed chairs chewing and drinking. But they weren't on exhibit. Thank goodness for Anne. She made the situation less tense with her antics.

At leaving time, and while the men said farewell to Harry, the women brought to Norma jars of home-canned pickled beets, watermelon rind preserves, and fresh apples and for Anne a little corn husk doll. Amazed, Norma nodded and smiled, touching each hand in gratitude. *They are short on words, but I feel their good will. They don't try to be more than what they are. And genuine is what they are.* Harry looked so pleased she knew she had passed the test.

Driving back to Rosemount, Harry told of a boyhood experience at this same farmhouse. It had happened on a Sunday afternoon when he was eight years old. His aunt and uncle were away and only his cousin Matilda was home. "She was the woman sitting directly across the table from you," he explained, "the one with the very curly hair. Her hair was just as curly when she was sixteen. Several young men from the neighboring farm came courting. I didn't know about courting then but Matilda said that was what had brought them there, and she wouldn't go outside. They called to her, sang to her, threw stones at the house, but still she wouldn't go outside. One of the boys took off his hat and hung it in front of his overalls and walked back and forth across the porch. I asked her how the hat stayed there without falling but she didn't answer and began running from room to room yanking down the shades and closing the curtains. It wasn't until years later that I understood," he looked at her with mischief in his eyes.

She didn't take his bait, instead said wistfully, "I'd like us to be alone again."

"Then shall we leave?"

" Rosemount? Yes. From Minnesota, no. There's more I want to see."

"Can you wait until after tomorrow? John wants us to take in an auction. I said I'd check with you."

"Then go, and I'll get our clothes packed and we can leave Saturday."

After dinner, John lounged in his recliner, his eyes traveling over the others, finally settling on Norma. In a taunting voice he asked, "Have you given your permission for Harry to accompany me to the auction?"

Harry winked at her and answered, "She gave it, and then we'll be heading out on Saturday."

"Make that Sunday. You've got to take a spin with me before you go."

Harry's eyes sought Norma's, saw agreement, "All right. Sunday."

John snorted, "Do you always have to consult her?"

"If it affects her, yes." Harry replied, his voice a bit sharp.

"What about that taxi ride? I believe you did that on your own."

Norma bristled, "It wasn't a taxi ride, and we decided together to go by car."

"Don't be so touchy," John laughed, "for awhile you were a national mystery."

"I rather liked the story," Hazel smiled. "Jack hadn't heard from Harry in months, then suddenly he was front page news for more than a week. I was sorry it died down so soon."

"I wish it would die in everyone's memories. Please, let's put it to rest." Norma's voice was as firm as the lift of her chin.

"Now that we've settled that," Harry said, "I'm ready to hit the sack. How about you, Norma?" To John he asked, "What time should I plan to leave in the morning."

"Ask her," John answered disdainfully, nodding in Norma's direction.

Upstairs, Norma stood at the closed window staring out into the night, "See the tiny sliver of a moon, just above the barn, hardly any moon at all. I was hoping for a full moon over Minnesota, but I know that couldn't be. I was hoping your brother would like me, but he doesn't. I'm not imagining it, am I?"

"It's not you. Jack thinks I'm not the master of my house as he is. When I said I'd like to check with you before making a commitment, he said I should tell you, not ask you. He thinks I'm hen-pecked."

Norma turned to face him, "Do you think that?"

"I call it consideration. Never mind the label Jack puts on it."

"You are considerate, the most considerate person I've ever known. Not just to me, but to everyone. But a lot of people say you spoil me."

"Perhaps we spoil each other," he kissed her lips then touched his forehead to hers, "and I love it, don't you? Our job is to please each other, forget what Jack says. He never has approved of the way I conduct my life. I didn't expect that he would change now. Can you bear up until we leave on Sunday? Then we'll have a week to find all those places you want to see and be on our own 'schelude'." Before she could fire up her indignation, he covered her mouth with his.

On Saturday, John gave them all a ride in his high-wing monoplane, and on Sunday they said good-bys. The hardest for Norma was to Mother Minnie; she couldn't help loving her just a little bit. Her smile, coloring, and eyes were the same as Harry's. The resemblance between son and mother was as strong as between father and daughter. Three generations---worlds apart.

24

Leaving Rosemount they drove to the Falls of Saint Anthony, the birthplace of Minneapolis, where in 1823 the first grist and flour mill were built using the power of the falls. Harry pointed to the General Mills site where Betty Crocker got her start.

At Minnehaha Park they explored the first frame house built west of the Mississippi River and looked down on Minnehaha Falls. Upstream, Norma stared, spellbound, at the huge bronze statue of Hiawatha lifting Minnehaha in his arms. Harry touched the tears falling down her cheeks.

She whispered, "My heart is so full. I cut my teeth on "The Song of Hiawatha." I learned it from Daddy. He told us it was the first thing he learned to read." She quoted softly, breathlessly, her voice breaking:
By the shores of Gitche Gumee, By the shining Big-Sea-Water
Stood the wigwam of Nokomis, Daughter of the Moon, Nokomis...

Smiling through tears, she said, "Oh, Harry, I love your Minnesota," and both laughed as Anne babbled "Gitche Gumee, Gitche Gumee."

They crossed Stone Arch Bridge that joined Minneapolis to St. Paul and walked the campus of Saint Thomas College. Seeing the statue of Saint Thomas Aquinas, with the stone dove on his shoulder, Norma knew why Harry had once suggested Thomas as a name for their son.

Where the Mississippi River junctured with the Minnesota, they saw the ivy-covered limestone remains of Old Fort Snelling, the northern most of the military outposts of the early 19th century. Driving south, Harry cautioned, "Careful, Honeychild. If you blink twice, you'll miss Buffalo where I went to high school. Blink once and you'll miss Silver Creek where I was born. Just beyond is Annandale where I was baptized."

At Little Falls they visited Charles Lindbergh's home and then continued northwest to Itasca State Park and its 157 lakes surrounded by virgin Norway pines. From the parking lot a trail led to the source of the Mississippi River. A plaque at the edge of the lake gave credit to Henry R. Schoolcraft for its discovery in 1832. A few feet beyond, the clear sparkling water left the lake, tumbling over a stretch of smooth gray boulders, and began its long journey to the Gulf of Mexico. About twenty feet downstream a huge log, cut lengthwise and smoothed across its cut, spanned the ten foot width of shallow water. From the log, Norma dangled her bare feet in the Mississippi River, giggling as Anne looked on. "Do you think Mommy is being silly?" and looking up at Harry, "I don't care if I am. This is an experience I'll cherish all my life."

*   *   *   *

The Kipps were home from a wonderful vacation to find a new commanding general and new neighbors. Major General Alfred H. Noble had relieved Major General Franklin Hart who was moving up the coast to Camp Lejeune, North Carolina to take command of the Second Marine Division. Captain and Mrs. William Earney had moved into 217 Tarawa across the street. Jerry, a former Navy nurse, had joined Bill at Parris Island as his bride.

Semper Fi

As they were dressing for the farewell reception for the Harts, Norma said, "I'm not sorry she's leaving and I hope you don't expect me to say I am." Seeing Harry's warning look, she promised, "Don't worry, I'll say something nice, but truthful." The receiving line moved slowly since all base officers and their wives were in attendance. When the Kipps reached the honored pair, Norma with her glove still on her hand looked Mrs. Hart in the eye and intoned politely, "Good-by, Mrs. Hart. I hope your days at Camp Lejeune will be happy ones." The general's wife thanked her as graciously as Norma had extended her remark, and that was that.

The Harts left, the Nobles came, and so did a hurricane. Harry was the officer of the day when it hit; Anne and Norma were home alone. The air felt stifling until the wind came up suddenly blowing at gale, then hurricane, force. Norma went from window to window watching the palmetto fronds being striped from their mightily swaying trunks, listening to the torrential drumming on the roof as rain pelted the creaking house. Feeling cozy and safe inside, prepared with supplies in response to the storm alert, she wasn't afraid. The steady downpour and the howling wind lulled her to sleep. She woke suddenly around midnight to find a sudden quiet, then the ringing of the phone. Harry called to say they were in the vortex and while it was now calm, she should be prepared for another blast of wind and rain, perhaps worse than before. "I'm glad you're not afraid. Sit tight, Honeychild. I'll come home tomorrow--or today, rather, as soon as I can get away."

By daylight the storm had passed; the house was sitting in a lake. Marines paddled by in dinghies and Harry came home that way at noon. He had left their car on high ground at the Third Recruit Battalion parking lot. Cars parked in the quarters area were sitting in salt water up to their doors.

Parris Island was a stinking mess; dead fish and other animals were scattered about the land. Rattlesnakes swam over from uninhabited islands and were a threat, especially the baby rattlers which children mistook for big worms. Norma was careful where she stepped when she went outside to hang clothes and Anne was kept indoors.

The humidity was terrible. Everything in the house was damp and musty despite electric lights kept burning to combat the creeping mildew. Norma decided it was time to protect their books. She spread a thick layer of newspaper over the dining room table and brushed the book covers and inside spine with a liquid solution recommended to combat mildew. She propped them open and left them to dry.

"Company for dinner?" Harry asked when he came home from work. "A new recipe, perhaps, --- a tasty dish--,'books a la carte'? "

"Sorry to disappoint you, but it's beef stew served on the kitchen table."

The books were dry the following morning and Norma congratulated herself on a job well done. She returned the books to the shelves. Removing the newspaper from the table, she was horrified to see that its beautiful finish had turned an ugly, milky white. In dread she snatched away the remaining paper. It was the same all over. The tabletop was ruined. How could she have been so stupid? How could she explain to Harry? The truth was so condemning. At lunch time he looked at the table without comment, went to the phone, had a short conversation, and returned. "It's not as hopeless as you think. But we'll be eating in the kitchen for a while."

A driver in a Marine Corps truck came to take the table away. For a week the empty dining room reminded Norma of her carelessness, and when the table was returned, it looked as if it had never been damaged. She felt she had escaped a deserved punishment, but Harry acted as if she had done nothing wrong.

*   *   *   *   *

Election Day 1948. Norma waited in the main lobby of the base dispensary for her annual checkup. Her name was called and she followed a corpsman around a corner to wait still longer. A row of Marines stared in surprise as she walked past. From around the corner she heard their voices. "Did you hear her name?" one asked. "Yeah, they called her Mrs. Kipp," another answered. "Could that be the Captain's wife?" asked a third. "Nah, must be his daughter," said a fourth. "Has to be his wife; they called her *Mrs*," decided the first. "Nah, couldn't be; she's not even twenty-one," said the second.

Norma felt a devilish urge to set them straight and turned the corner to stand before them. "Oh, but I am twenty one," she told them, "and a fourth!" She let them squirm a bit before returning to her seat. Thirty minutes later, with her examination completed and a prescription for a new diaphragm in her purse, she passed the row of still waiting, and very embarrassed, Marines. After supper with the radio news predicting a landslide victory for Thomas Dewey, Norma complained to Harry, "I'm twenty-one, old enough, but not allowed to vote."

He shook his head, "Just another sacrifice you make being married to a Marine. If it's any consolation, I can't vote either, haven't since 1924. We're both disfranchised, Honeychild."
"If you could vote, who would you vote for?"
"Servicemen aren't political animals; they're warriors."
"You must have a choice of who you'd want to send you off to war."
"No, I don't."
"Well, I do! It's Truman!"
"He's the underdog."
"He's the Democrat," Norma countered, "My Daddy would disown me if I voted for a Republican."
Governor Thomas E. Dewey of New York was expected to win easily, but when all the votes were counted, Norma's choice had been re-elected president of the United States in the biggest political upset in American history. On a personal level, November third was Butch Condo's birthday and Betsy and Jim Moore had a baby boy.

The Marine Corps Birthday Ball, held each November tenth, was the biggest social event of the year, one the Kipps had never attended. On the tenth, in 1945, they had moved from the beach apartment into the Quonset hut. The following two years Harry had been Officer of the Day. This year in anticipation of going, Norma bought a Ceil Chapman gold lamè formal.

Once again they missed the Ball; they were at Roper Hospital in Charleston. For weeks Norma had said she would agree to an operation to straighten Anne's eyes only if she could stay with her. The ophthalmologist was suddenly free to perform the surgery at the same time a private room was available, on the tenth. Three days later, Anne went home with both eyes bandaged, yet able to navigate through the house unassisted, clinging to her dolls, wanting them with her always. Too young to count at twenty seven months, still she knew when any of the nine were missing. Her bandages were changed daily at the dispensary on Parris Island and a week later in Charleston, Dr. Hope removed the stitches.

After her long confinement, Anne was eager to resume their daily walks to Harry's office. After her afternoon bath of soaping, splashing, rinsing, drying, and powdering--a ritual Anne expected--Norma dressed them in one of their matching outfits and they were ready to go. As usual they stopped at the PX for an ice cream cone to fortify them for the long walk across the parade field. Arriving on the other side, they met Colonel Stewart getting into his car. He came to fold and put the sulky into the trunk of the Kipp Packard. He closed the trunk lid with a bang,"Mrs. Kipp, I just performed a most pleasant duty,"

"Sir?" Norma asked, looking at his smiling face.

"Yes, a most pleasant duty. On behalf of the Secretary of the Navy, I presented your husband with the Bronze Star medal...in my office...in private. He wouldn't agree to a public presentation nor allow me to pin it on his blouse. He's the most modest man I know." He paused, then added, "Perhaps you should let it come as a surprise when Harry tells you himself. He didn't exactly swear me to secrecy, but I believe that was what he had in mind." He winked knowingly then returned to his car and drove away.

Harry joined them a bit later, drove them home, had dinner, and read Anne a bedtime story, as if it were an ordinary day. And at bedtime, Norma found the medal and citation on their dresser beside her hair brush.

The President of the United States takes pleasure in presenting the
BRONZE STAR MEDAL to

CAPTAIN HARRY E. KIPP,
UNITED STATES MARINE CORPS,

for service as set forth in the following CITATION:

"For meritorious service as Commanding Officer of Battery B, Seacoast Artillery Group, Twelfth Defense Battalion, and subsequently as Commanding Officer of Battery A and later Battery B, Ninth 155-mm. Gun Battalion, Fleet Marine Force, during operations against enemy Japanese forces on Woodlark Island, New Guinea; Cape Gloucester, New Britain, Solomon Islands, and Okinawa, Ryukyu Islands, from 7 July 1943, to 21 June 1945. Demonstrating initiative and an outstanding knowledge of artillery, Captain Kipp skillfully directed his Battery throughout long months of arduous training and combat operations and contributed materially to the success of his Battalion in combat. His technical skill and leadership throughout were in keeping with the highest traditions of the United States Naval Service."

Captain Kipp is authorized to wear the combat "V"

For the President,
John L. Sullivan
Secretary of the Navy.

Harry came from the bathroom toweling himself dry and sat on the bed to dust his feet with powder, a nightly routine since his jungle fighting days had left them subject to fungi infection. No part of his body was ever neglected, but his feet got royal treatment. She watched him finish, then lift his legs onto the bed and stretch out the magnificent body she loved to look at, touch, and feel close to hers. It bore not one blemish, no sign to show of the many times it had been in peril. In the beginning of their marriage, in looking over his ribbons, she had asked if he had a Purple Heart. "No," he answered, "being a good dodger, I was never wounded in battle," and laughing, added, "fighting was my job and with experience I got good at it." She remembered that now as she held the Bronze Star.

"How long have you known?" she asked, gazing at the medal.

"Oh, somebody said something about it some time back."

"...and you never told me!"

"Honeychild, there was nothing to tell until it became a fact."

"Well, it's a fact now, so tell me about it."

"What's there to say? I had a job to do, and I did it. That's what they pay me to do."

"But the citation says *meritorious* service." She was on her knees beside him on the bed with shining eyes upon him, "You've always been my hero. This means the Marine Corps thinks you're one too."

"There were many heroes," he said staring up at her. "Not all of them got medals, dead or alive."

"Butch told me that you're the bravest man he has ever known, and he says he's not the only one who thinks so," her voice was laced with awe. "He said your men would die for you."

Harry's eyes took on a distant expression and for some moments he seemed to be somewhere else. She knew there were things he couldn't, or wouldn't, share with her. Once she had asked him to tell her about those times that took him away from her. He had shrugged and said, "To live through it once is enough." She had never asked again.

His eyes returned to the present and he reached for her. "That's all in the past, Honeychild. Let's leave it there...live for now, this moment."

She touched his chest, smoothing it with her palm, moving it across his shoulder and down his arms to lace her fingers with his. "All right, we'll live for this moment! But I want you to know that I am SO PROUD of you I'm going to walk around with my head so high all I'll see is the sky!"

He rolled her to her back, "Come down to earth, Honeychild. That's where real living takes place."

25

Harry's choice for the evening's musical fare was Rimsky-Korsakov. Having danced herself tired to "Capriccio Espagnol", Anne was in bed. Her humming could still be heard, but finally even that gave way to sleep. As the overture to *Scheherazade* ended, Norma paused in her knitting of a cable stitch vest to rest her head on Harry's shoulder. "Now that it's December, you'll soon be choosing Christmas music."

"And whom will you be choosing to spend Christmas with us?" He asked, placing a finger on her lips, "No, don't tell me. Let me guess. Mr. and Mrs. Max Scoggins. Right?"

"Right! Since their 'secret' marriage is secret no more they've had to live apart, the way both sets of parents want it. If they came here, while Max is on school vacation, they'd have a bedroom all their own with their own bathroom. Remember when we rode across country for four nights in the back seat of the Martin car, huddled under your uniform blouse suffering from desire? Imagine having to live like that for weeks! Do you remember what you said you'd buy if we ever got rich?"

"Yes, all the No Vacancy signs between Mississippi and California."

"I expected you to say all the motels between them," Norma laughed, "and speaking of motels--the Kipp Motel--can I invite them?"

"Affirmative, and I'll drive to La Fayette to get them."

The two week visit of the newlyweds seemed to pass all too quickly and on New Year's Eve, the car was being loaded for their return to La Fayette. Harry told Norma to ignore the ringing of the telephone unless she wanted to welcome in the New Year on the road. "It may be important," she said, hurrying to answer. Colonel Stewart's authoritative voice boomed across the line, "Is Major Kipp there?"

Norma knew at once that Harry's promotion had come through, but she answered, "I'm sorry, Sir, you have reached Captain Kipp's quarters."

"Mrs. Kipp, this is Marvin Stewart. I called to speak with MAJOR Kipp and by God, I want him on the phone, on the double!" His voice rang with mirth.

"Yes, Sir!" Norma replied crisply and with a telling look, called to Harry. "It's Colonel Stewart. He wants to speak with MAJOR Kipp."

As he listened, Harry's face creased into the grin she loved so much. Finally he said, "Thank you, Colonel, and Happy New Year to you, Sir."

With mock restraint he said to Norma, "The Colonel couldn't wait until Monday to give me the word. In addition, he's taking command of the First Battalion which leaves me the CO of the Third through its deactivation, then it'll be the First for me as well, as his executive officer."

It was a jubilant crowd that left Parris Island in the early afternoon to arrive at La Fayette thirty minutes into the New Year, 1949. When everybody was finally bedded down, and Norma and Harry were alone, she embraced him eagerly, "I can't wait until we get home and I can make love with a major."

"Honeychild, there's something I should tell you about majors; they don't wait for anything."

"Not even for me to make a trip to the bathroom?" She slipped from his arms, laughing gaily.

"Well, perhaps this once..."

She returned ready, slipping into his waiting arms, whispering, "Now let's see how a field officer does it!" How could it be better than it always was? How could it even be as good after a twelve hour drive, a strange bed and fear that it may collapse as it had one night after they returned from their honeymoon, and with others in the house to hear their moans of pleasure? But it was better, it was exquisite! He made her wild with desire, then tantalized her with slow love, thrilled her with swift love, and then stopped to smother her body with hot kisses. It was as if she were walking beside a long, long banquet table spread to overflowing with delicious edibles, darting about in hunger, sampling each and every one--a bite here, a bite there--unable to eat all of the mouthwatering morsels her hands could touch. Suddenly, the tablecloth was snatched away, and all the food with it, and she fell to the floor in a heap. Everything spread over her and she began to take in all the goodness through every pore, weeping softly with satiety. And Harry was kissing her mouth to quiet her sobbing, asking, "Honeychild, my Honeychild! Are you pleased?"

"Oh, Harry!" she sighed, breathless against his shoulder, "If they make you Lt. Colonel, I won't be able to stand it."

On January 4, Norma invited the Griffins, Moores, and Earneys to a small dinner party at their quarters to celebrate Harry's promotion. Betsy and Jim brought baby Paul since he was breast-feeding. Linn Griffin toddled around behind Anne until both were put to bed. Jerry and Bill looked on all this offspring activity with interest since within a few months they too would be parents. After a toast to Harry, Hilda rose to make another toast to Linn's expected brother or sister, due in August. Turning to Norma, she said, "You're next. Anne should have a brother or sister, don't you think?"

"No," Norma gulped, "and you and Jerry stay away from me; it might be contagious!"

When their guests had gone, Harry helped gather glasses and dessert plates for washing, "That was a swell party. You know you make me the happiest man alive, don't you?"

Norma took the dish towel from him, draped her arms around his neck and pulled his mouth to hers. After a long, moist kiss, "But are you *completely* happy?"

"*Completely happy*, from the first time I took you in my arms. If I haven't made that clear, then you haven't been listening."

"Some people think it takes babies to make them feel complete," she said testily.

"Was that your reason?" He asked with interest.

"No, I loved Julia and Mary Lee as babies and I wanted one of my own with you. We have our one, and she's enough for me. But don't you want a son? Sometime in the future? Your brother wants a son, the Campbells want a son, the Moores have a son, even Jesse and Hilda who already have a son are having another baby..."

"If we had a son, I'd want it. But to say I must have one, the answer is no. Anyway according to Jesse, it may be taken out of our hands."

"How? Who could take it out of our hands? I just took measures to see that it doesn't happen."

"You saw Commander True, didn't you? Jesse says the rumor is that most of his patients are getting pregnant, even menopausal wives. He's against birth control; his wife has had three babies in as many years, so he's giving Marine wives a chance to catch up!"

"I don't believe that. I saw him more than two months ago and I'm not pregnant. I just had my period."

*   *   *   *   *

Norma would soon see the inside of Quarters 1, more than the brief glimpse she and Harry saw when they made their courtesy call to General and Mrs. Hart upon arriving at Parris Island and later when General and Mrs. Noble came. She had seen the new general's wife around the base, and liked her at first sight. Mrs. Noble had great dignity, kind eyes, and extended an easy smile to whomever she met. Once, Norma had observed her courtesy to a clerk in the post exchange when she was buying bed linen. And at the children's Christmas party, she had greeted every child with a smile and a handshake. "She's worthy of respect," Norma concluded as she showed Harry her invitation to a tea for the wives of the Third Battalion officers and a tour of the sprawling two-story quarters.

After the tour, tea was served in the downstairs reception room which opened by three French doors onto a veranda half encircling the first story. During the warm afternoon, while the ladies sat munching on tiny open-faced sandwiches and cookies, a huge black cockroach entered from the open door and crawled to the middle of the room as if it owned the place. Breaths were held, sandwiches were poised in midair, chewing and tea-sipping ceased. All eyes focused on the approaching insect. Mrs. Noble calmly rose, moving to engage it. The cockroach retreated but too slowly. With a quick step, Mrs. Noble's small slipper came down upon it, making a loud pop. With a shrug of her shoulders, she returned to her chair not even hesitating in the story she was telling. A lift of her hand brought an orderly who scooped the remains into a silent butler with a tiny broom. Audible sighs of relief accompanied his departure and once more the ladies relaxed and attended to their refreshments.

Cockroaches were permanent party on Parris Island, annoying everyone from generals to recruits, hardly affected by the continuous spraying intended to discourage them. After months of losing battles with them herself, Norma concluded that this was one war the Marines would never win. There would never be a Cockroach Street on Parris Island.

At the end of January, Anne had her second operation to correct the strabismus. Since no private rooms were available, she was assigned to the nursery ward. She didn't cry at being left there, but going home her parents did, and they returned every evening to Charleston to visit her. Four days after the surgery, Dr. Hope removed the bandages, stiffened Anne's arms with cardboard cylinders to prevent scratching fingers from reaching her eyes, and released her. She was unable to play with her dolls or feed herself, but she never cried nor complained. Not even when medication was applied to the stitches. They knew it burned, since Harry had tested it in his eyes, and were amazed at the bravery of their little daughter.

Just when the stitches were healed, Anne developed a severe case of tonsillitis which required penicillin injections. At sight of the doctor in his white jacket her bravery disappeared. She went into hysterics and reacted the same to the butcher at the commissary--to anyone in a white jacket. The strain of the surgery and recovery began to take its toll on everyone. Norma could hardly keep from crying herself. "I feel absolutely drained," she told Harry. His arms encircled her in a powerful embrace until she struggled to free herself, pulling back, her hands to her chest. "My breasts, they're so sore! Oh, my goodness! It's the middle of February. I've missed my period. Could I be pregnant? No, it can't be. We've been too careful."

March came and still no period. Dr. True said she wasn't pregnant. He thought she had instead, a tumor. In April, she demanded a pregnancy test. Positive. Along with a tumor, according to Dr.True. Norma was bewildered, angry, and disconsolate. What was happening inside her body? She felt perfectly well and wasn't getting any bigger. Maybe Dr. True was mistaken. She couldn't be pregnant; she had been faithful in using the diaphragm he had fitted for her. It was simply unbelievable. So was the result of Anne's surgery. Her eye still turned inward. Dr. Hope explained that he had never expected to correct her strabismus in one, two, or even three operations. It sometimes required five. And they were only intended for cosmetic purposes. Eyeglasses were for improving her vision and she would probably need to wear them all her life.

Norma felt betrayed. Dr.Hope had never before presented the prognosis in those terms. "We trusted you," she told him, her voice shaking in pain. "You were not honest with us. Our child is your victim; you just wanted to practice on her eyes. Maybe the Navy doctors were right after all; they didn't want to do anything." She wept all the way home from Charleston. Anne sang and Harry drove.

The unexpected was happening all around them. John Campbell, Bill Godwin, and Bill Earney all got orders to Camp Lejeune, North Carolina. At the end of May when the Earneys gave up quarters across the street, Jerry and their three week old daughter moved into the Kipp's guest room until Bill got a place for them in Jacksonville outside the Marine base. Suddenly, Harry was ordered to Camp Lejeune. A specific request from General Hart; he wanted Harry to straighten out a 'fouled up' battalion. For the first time in his Marine Corps career, Harry questioned his orders, asking instead for an assignment in his speciality: artillery. It was denied and Norma started packing for a transfer. One thing made them happy. At last they would live near the Condos.

Two days after the Fourth of July, and a farewell visit to Hunting Island--this time Terry drove her new Ford convertible with Anne standing in Harry's arms, her long blond hair blowing in the wind--the Kipps left Parris

Island for Jacksonville to move in with the Earneys. Surprise! The Condos had orders to the West Coast! At their final dinner together, Butch indulged Anne with all the ice cream and oyster crackers she could eat, her choice of a perfect meal. Dolly hoped the unborn member of the Kipp family would be born on her birthday, October sixth. "We can hope for that, " Norma told her, "but the due date is the fourteenth."

"From the looks of you, even that would be early," Dolly exclaimed. "You're the smallest sixth month mother-to-be I've ever seen."

She's right, and she doesn't even know about the tumor, and I'm not going to tell her or anybody. Maybe it's just a figment of Dr.True's imagination. It just has to be, because if it isn't...

On 22 July, the Kipps moved onto the base. MOQ 2511 was the address at the entrance to the long paved driveway leading to a huge, two-story white wooden house with green shutters surrounded by an expanse of immaculately groomed lawn. Maid's quarters separated the garage from the house. The living room, painted pale pink, had a fireplace flanked by built-in book shelves. Norma said the deep blue walls of the dining room would surely give her ulcers, and she wanted it changed to pink. That could be done, they were told, after a year in residence. "Then for a year, I'll eat with my eyes closed or on the large screened porch." She made couch slipcovers from the jade colored drapes and bought pink and gray floral brocade for chair covers. A gray wool rug and a painting of a sailing ship on stormy sea, Harry's purchase, completed the decorating. At last, the Marine Corps supplied a desk for Harry's ebony letter openers.

At Norma's seventh month prenatal visit, she weighed in at one hundred six pounds, with low blood pressure, and tiring easily. Dr. McClellan, one of three obstetricians on staff at the Naval Hospital, told her all was well and she could expect an easy delivery.

"But the tumor..?" Norma asked anxiously.

Dr. McClellan looked at her strangely, "I beg your pardon?"

"The tumor Dr. True said I have..".

"Your records haven't arrived from Parris Island, but I saw no evidence whatsoever of a tumor...only a baby and a big one at that, despite your low weight gain. I can't imagine why you were told that."

At hearing those words, Norma let go of the terrible image that had haunted her for weeks: that of her baby being crowded unto death by an ever expanding growth, a non-existing growth. Darn that Dr.True! But so relieved she couldn't be angry for long, she dressed quickly and rushed to Harry's office to tell him the good news. He wasn't there; he was out looking for tanks and trucks he had signed for when he took command of a very slipshod outfit according to his evaluation. General Hart's as well. Harry had confided to her that he might have signed their life away for materiel he didn't even know existed and he wouldn't have a moment's peace of mind until he had located and documented its whereabouts. That's what he's doing, she surmised, out getting peace of mind. Well, her news would certainly give him peace of mind. Once he heard it. The wait was longer than she anticipated. Harry's long, but successful, day kept him away until supper time. Finished with eating, she led him to the porch. "No, don't turn on the light," she said, "leave it dark."

"Leave it dark? Honeychild, it can't be dark with all your radiance. I haven't seen you like this in months."

"That's because I haven't felt like this in months. I saw my new doctor today and he said..." she couldn't remain seated, jumped up, and stood before him, her hands on his shoulders, "...there is no tumor!"

Harry sat very still while her words took hold. Relief, then joy, surging in his eyes, "He's sure? Really sure?" He too jumped up, to take her in his arms, "Thank God. So many months of unhappiness for my Honeychild. You've been like a little lost soul, almost remote at times. I felt so responsible that you were pregnant, and I haven't known what to say...or do."

"And I felt the same way..."

He stepped back, shaking his head and grinning, "Then shall we each stop feeling to blame? No one is to blame! We're simply going to have a baby, not one we planned, but it's all right. What do we have to be unhappy about now that we know there is no tumor?"

"Not a thing, and I'm beginning to be very happy. We can begin to talk about our baby. Do you think it will be another girl or a boy?"

"Let's not speak of 'girl' or 'boy', just wait to see. Now, will you tell your family?"

"I've waited this long, I may as well wait until it's here. Then we can tell them which it is, a grandson or a granddaughter. Will you help me address the announcements?"

"Of course, but that's two months away. Right now, I'm bushed. Let's call it a day--a red letter day--wouldn't you agree?"

They climbed the stairs arm in arm. At the top landing Norma stopped, listening, "I hear talking, loud talking. Where is it coming from?"

"That *talking*," Harry informed her, "is the loudspeaker of the outdoor theater. It's behind our quarters beyond that stand of trees."

"It certainly is a *loud* speaker. And we're going to have to listen to movies every night?"

"No, not every night," Harry chuckled, "only four nights a week."

She stood by the open window. "Listen! It's "The Third Man". Hear the zither?" She turned from the window to find Harry waiting. She came alive at his touch, as he did to hers. And the last thing they heard before falling asleep was the melody of the "Third Man Theme" floating in with the night breeze.

*   *   *   *   *

Some nights after Harry was asleep and the noise from the outdoor theater kept her awake, Norma went downstairs to read, write letters, or listen to the radio. One such night, as she started upstairs for a book left on her bedside table, glorious music poured from the radio and she paused on the landing to listen. Then she sat--for two hours--entranced by *Madama Butterfly*. The opera ended and still she sat. She felt Harry's hand on her shoulder and heard his sleepy, surprised voice, "So, this is where you are?" He sat beside her drawing her to his warm chest.

"I couldn't move once the music began, it was so beautiful...and so sad, the heavenly duet of pure love when they met, the passionate duet after the wedding, and the waiting music. And when at last he returned, it was with a wife. He was heartless!" She stiffened with indignation.

"I think Heartless was another character, Honeychild," he laughed, "Besides it's just a story."

"But a story about life. And when I think that it could have happened to me. But NO! It couldn't have happened to me, not with you."

He lifted her from the step, "I'm taking you where you should have been hours ago. Sitting on the stairs until one o'clock in the morning," he scolded her softly. "What must our baby think? Do you feel it moving? He wants his Mommy to stretch out and give him room to do the same."

"*He*? You said he!"

"Did I? Yes, I suppose I did. How 'bout that?"

"Then you do want a boy?"

"Don't you think that would be nice?"

"Yes," she agreed. "If it should be a boy, I'd be very, very happy."

26

Anne had celebrated her first birthday at Quarters 56, her second at 216, and now her third at 2511 with the Earneys as dinner guests. Bill poured champagne for a toast and Anne ran to the kitchen for a knife and fork; French toast was her favorite food. When the others lifted their glasses instead, she looked so puzzled they broke into gales of laughter. Sympathizing with Anne's confusion, Bill gathered her into his lap to tell of another birthday incident that happened back at Parris Island when he was in charge of a plan to convert some old, little used buildings into a recreation center at Hilton Head where the Marine Corps had control of one end of the island. Eleven civilian families occupied the other end.

"When the accommodations had been improved sufficiently for use, General Hart told me he was bringing a party of six for the weekend, but the fifty-foot launch arrived with ten aboard. The sedan I had procured for transportation was too small and Mrs. Hart wouldn't hear of making two trips. So I volunteered my jeep. Her idea of who should ride where conflicted with the general's and for half an hour people were shuffled and reshuffled between the jeep and the sedan. I could've had them transported in two trips by that time, and General Hart said as much, but Mrs. Hart paid him no mind. Finally, when everyone was seated as she preferred, she pondered over which vehicle would be safest for carrying the three-tiered birthday cake she had aboard the launch for their son's birthday. Another verbal foray ensued only to be settled once again in Mrs. Hart's favor. That was the good part," Bill laughed. "Things got worse. At the buildings the power was off, the generators couldn't be made to work, nor the antiquated refrigerator. And the mosquito netting had gone back with the launch. The general was convinced that I was not on top of my job, and it took a long time for him to forgive me for that disastrous weekend." Bill reached for the champagne, poured another round, winked at Harry and raised his chalice, "No matter the duty, it all counts on thirty! Right?"

General and Mrs. Hart were indeed colorful people, and here they were all together once more. And Norma would again find herself seated at a table with her when General Hart presented the team championship trophy to the winning team of the Officers Club Bowling League at a banquet in their honor. Another guest was Felix de Weldon the sculptor casting the Marine Corps War Memorial, a seventy-eight foot, one hundred ton portrayal of the flag raising on Iwo Jima's Mount Surabachi.

Early in September, Norma hired a maid in anticipation of her confinement. Generally, Anabelle was competent, but she and Norma disagreed on a few things. She applied furniture polish until it dripped, dumped cigarette butts in the fireplace, and never changed the bag in the vacuum cleaner. It became a contest and one Norma lost until the day Harry got polish from the armrests on his shirt sleeves. That day Norma established who was the maid and who was the lady of the house.

October sixth came and the baby did not arrive. Downstairs, at midnight, Norma was writing Dolly of her disappointment. At the sounding of the doorbell, she hurried to answer, finding at the door a small man with a large mustache in civilian clothing, smelling of whiskey. "Good evening, Madam." He bowed slightly, "Or should I say 'good morning'?"

"Good morning, I suppose. How can I help you?"

"I saw the lights on...and I stopped to see Harry."

"I'm sorry, but he's asleep. Could you call again tomorrow?"

The man stood silently for a few seconds, then, "I think he will see me if you would be so kind as to tell him Sammy Taxis is calling."

Norma hesitated, sensing in his manner an expectation of compliance. And she complied, going upstairs to shake Harry awake. "There's a man at the door asking to see you."

"Tell him I'm asleep," he muttered.

"I did, but he said to tell you that Sammy Taxis is calling."

Harry's eyes flew open and he jumped to his feet, grabbing for his robe, "My God! Colonel Taxis, or is it General by now? Honeychild, tell him I'll be down on the double." And he was, just a few steps behind her, fully awake and smiling with pleasure, "Sir, come in and meet my wife Norma and..." grinning broadly, "our baby in waiting."

After the introduction, Norma excused herself and went upstairs to bed. At dawn, Harry joined her, very happy and very sleepy, but talkative. "That Marine you just met is from the Old Corps and absolutely tops in my book; he was about to leave the base when he saw my name on the driveway marker. We haven't seen each other since '44. He recommended me for promotion from platoon sergeant to gunnery and then to Marine gunner; that was in the early '40's. He was a captain then and the best CO I ever had." The last thing he said before he fell asleep was, "By the way, Honeychild, he told me I have a beautiful watch dog."

*   *   *   *   *

As the birth of the baby drew near, Norma felt guilt at not preparing her parents for the arrival of their second grandchild. And she felt an unusual longing to have Mama visit in her home. Daddy hadn't allowed it when they lived at Parris Island, saying he needed her at home. Norma and Harry thought the arrival of a new grandchild might just do the trick. She wrote the invitation, then settled down to wait for the baby to be born. Everything was ready; there was nothing to do but wait. And waiting was the hardest thing in the world for her. On the evening of October 13, with not even a hint of discomfort, and to Harry's astonishment, Norma wailed, "I cannot wait another day for this baby to be born! Harry, speak to it."

He put his hands on her swollen stomach and spoke softly to the baby, "Your mother is desirous of your making an appearance. So am I, but I can wait. I'm not sure she can. Do what you can, please." He winked at her, "Let's see how much influence a mere father has."

They woke early the next morning, the predicted date, still with no sign of labor, but a showing of blood. "You did it, Harry! You can take me to the hospital on your way to work!" And there, the nurse whisked her into an elevator and Harry was left standing in the lobby like a frozen statue, clutching her suitcase.

It was Dr. Reece's day for delivering babies. The nurse introduced them and said, "Mrs. Kipp has no contractions, but she's dilated. The baby's crowning." An hour later when contractions began, Norma let herself go with them, welcoming them, each meaning the baby was closer to being born. Across the room, the eyes in a very young face, big brown beautiful eyes, seemed to be merging into one giant eye which grew and grew until it filled the room and Norma was encompassed within it, feeling herself a part of it and it a part of her. Suddenly a voice broke into this beautiful world. Dr. Reece was asking, "Mrs. Kipp, please tell us why you refuse the spinal block. We need to give it now. You're ready to deliver."

Norma resented the intrusion and in a foggy voice answered, "It's in my records. Please, just let me have my baby." They took her to the delivery room without the block. The room was flooded with blinding light. The one great eye was gone; instead a corpsman hovered above, blocking the light with a halo of golden hair. The serene face showed no sign of beard; the arms were bare as well. Was this a male or a female? The uniform was that of a corpsman, and the form inside it seemed to float from the foot to the head of the table and her eyes followed him, or her, back and forth, and around. Dr. Reece's voice, once more, saying gently, "One hard push should do it." With the next splitting pain, she heard a lusty, angry wail. Raising her head, she saw her stomach disappearing as the doctor received the infant beneath its arms. She saw first a tiny backside, then a scrotum hanging between scrawny little legs. "It's a boy!" She cried in delight and lay back on the table. The clock read 10:47 A.M. Her work was done, an eight pound one ounce boy. She couldn't wait to see Harry's face when she told him. But first she would sleep a while.

At noon, she woke to see Harry standing in grim silence at the foot of her bed. Her arms reached for him, "Darling, we have a son. Why aren't you happy?"

"I'll be happy when I know you're all right. The nurses tell me you're bleeding excessively and they're trying to stop it. I had to see you, if only for a minute. I'm going now to call your parents." He bent to touch his lips to hers and whisper, "I love you much more than you could possibly imagine. Take care of yourself for me." He looked as if he might cry.

The nurses worked in shifts kneading Norma's abdomen. Off and on she roused from sleep and remembered bleeding profusely after Anne's birth when her shivering had made the wheeled table slide around on the bloody floor. It had taken many hours and many blankets before she had gotten warm. Finally, now, she was beginning to feel warm, and the nurses stopped their massage and left her alone to sleep. She slept through dinner and visiting hours. Harry came and sat, watching her sleep. Before leaving, he arranged with the nurse to make a phone available with the provision that when his wife awoke, no matter the hour, he wanted to hear from her. Norma called at one in the morning. "Thank you for the beautiful flowers and I'm sorry I slept through your visit, but I think I deserved it, don't you? How about that boy of ours, an eight pounder!"

"You did a great job, Honeychild, and your parents are pleased also with their new grandchild. Your mother is leaving Monday morning on the bus, arriving around midnight. It's a seventeen hour drive, but she wouldn't consider flying. You two can have a grand visit after you've both had a rest. I'll say good night now and let you begin yours."

It wasn't to be as Harry thought. The next morning Norma was told to get up, shower, dress, and take the elevator to the cafeteria for breakfast. Doctor's orders. Afterwards a nurse brought the baby in his little hospital crib and placed it beside her bed. He was now her responsibility, and she joyfully put him to her breast even though there was as yet no milk. He suckled as if there were, sighing and yawning and falling asleep. Returning him to his crib, Norma glanced across the room to see the girl with the lovely brown eyes which had helped her so much in the labor room. She wanted to thank her, but after the initial lock of eyes, the girl turned her head away to face the wall.

At Harry's afternoon visit, Norma gave him a completed order form except for one blank space. "This is for the birth announcements we must order right away," she looked at him expectantly, "when you decide on a name for our son."

He hesitated only a moment, "What do you think of 'Charles'?"

"Somehow I expected you to choose that name. And I'll add Eric....Charles Eric Kipp...an excellent name for a German Viking."

After Harry left, Norma returned Charles to his crib, meeting the eyes of her roommate again, eyes filled with pain. *Could her baby have died? It had not been brought to its mother.* This time, their eyes held. "Hello, I'm Norma. We were together in the labor room."

"I know," the girl said softly, "My name is Peggy."

"I'm happy to meet you, Peggy. Shall we go to supper together?"

They took the elevator and ate with the other new mothers who chattered about their infants. Peggy only listened but back in their room, her words came tumbling out. "You haven't seen my baby because I'm not taking him home. They say they will find a good home for him, maybe one like yours." She lowered her gaze from Norma's shocked expression."We have another son, a year old. My husband is home with him, on leave, for the three days I'll be here. We don't have money for a baby sitter and Victor says he doesn't want to see the baby...I haven't seen him either..."

Norma closed her eyes against Peggy's anguish, trying to comprehend, finally asking gently, "Your parents...do they know?"

"Victor's parents are dead and the Corps is his family. Mine? The way they'd want to help, I couldn't handle. They didn't want me to marry at all, much less to a Marine PFC. Our first baby was born too soon for them to believe I hadn't been expecting when we married. I wasn't though." Peggy clasped her arms around her knees. "I was just seventeen the month after Vic Junior was born. My parents said they'd take me back--with the baby--if I divorced Victor. They'd raise my son and send me to college. They thought Victor had talked me into marrying him and because I was a minor, I wasn't responsible. They didn't believe I was the one that didn't want to wait. But now, if they knew about the new baby, they'd just say double what they said before...that Victor can't take care of me. He can take care of me and one baby, but two...or three...or.." Peggy's voice was bitter. She got out of bed. "I won't be having any more, my tubes were tied with this one." At the door, she turned to Norma, "I'm going for a walk. Thank you for listening to me;I had to tell someone, someone not involved. Swear to me that you won't tell anyone what I've told you."

While Peggy was gone someone who was involved came to their room, the nurse who had assisted at Charles' birth. Lt. Reynolds got right to the point, "Mrs. Kipp, I need your help."

"My help?" Norma asked, puzzled. "How can I help you?"

"I'm going out on a limb to ask, but I feel I must. You must have noticed that the Owens baby is not with his mother." Seeing Norma's nod, she asked, "You know the reason, don't you?"

Again Norma nodded.

"Mrs. Owens has declined to talk with the hospital staff about the adoption placement she has elected for her son. I hoped she might have confided in you and that you would be willing to tell me."

Norma saw the genuine concern in the nurse's eyes, but she replied, "You know I can't tell you; she told me in confidence."

"Do you also know why her husband doesn't come to see her?"

"I do, and I can't tell you that either."

"We aren't permitted to question her about her motives or decision, only to supply the forms and witness the signature of release. If there were something, anything, that I, we, could do to make a different outcome possible, we should do it now. Perhaps all she needs is financial assistance. Can you tell me this much, would that make a difference?"

"I don't know. Honestly, I don't know. There should be someone to counsel her about such a drastic decision...she's so young... eighteen."

"She's planning to sign the release papers before she leaves tomorrow. Before then, would you talk to her about accepting assistance?"

Norma promised, and when she asked, Peggy responded crisply, "No, thank you. I didn't tell you with the idea of asking for help. We don't want or need help. Vic says a man makes his own problems and solves his own problems. Please, I beg you, don't try to get help for us. Vic would die if the Marine Corps got involved; he thinks it would go against him. He wants to be a Marine more than anything in the world. His dad was a Marine, killed in the war. His mother died a few years later and Vic joined the Corps. I want him to have what he wants. Don't think he's being selfish and running our lives. He loves me and our little boy very much. We're a happy family and the three of us have a chance. Four, no. We'll all have a better life this way..." Peggy's eyes were tightly closed but tears escaped and slid down her face. She dried them with her hands, lifted her chin, gave Norma a determined smile, and went to do what she had to do.

Sunlight streamed through the window on this beautiful autumn morning. But not for Peggy, Norma thought. A hand touched her shoulder. She turned and a nurse pressed a folded paper into her hand: "Care for Your Newborn Baby". Norma looked at it, sadly, then laid it aside.

"Look on the back," the nurse instructed. "Mrs. Owens asked me to be sure you got her note."

> To a Nice Southern Lady,
> I will always remember you every October 14 and wonder how your little boy is and I will also think of another little boy and wonder how he is.
> Your friend, Peggy Owens

During Harry's afternoon visit, Norma's eyes returned again and again to the empty bed across from hers. "Are you tired. Honeychild? Have I stayed too long?"

"No, please stay. I'm just very sad." She felt so close to tears.

"I can see that. I know it upset you that the baby cried himself hoarse when they cut him, but he's over it now. See how contented he is after his satisfying meal? Let me put him in his crib." He took the bundle from her and laid him in his bed, turning to find Norma standing. "Hold me, oh, please, hold me." She pressed against him.

"What's wrong, Honeychild?" he murmured, his arms encircling her.

"I just need your arms around me," she breathed against his shoulder, "I can't wait until Tuesday when I can leave this room."

On Tuesday Jerry played chauffeur, coming to the hospital for Norma and Charles, bringing Anne and Mrs. Clinton. Riding home Anne, sitting in her mother's lap, peered at the baby in grandmother's arms. Norma said, "See, there's lots of room for you now that baby Charles is no longer inside me." During the last month when she stuck straight out, she tried to prepare Anne for the arrival of the baby, telling her where it was and letting her feel its movements. Anne had looked and touched and Norma thought she understood.

Norma also thought she and Mama would have long talks, exchanges as mothers, women, housewives, but that never happened. Mama was fatigued from the long bus ride and dreaded the return, still refusing to take a plane. Their only serious conversation centered around Mama's concern about fuzz growing on Norma's arms and face. "I hope you're not going to start growing hair all over you," she said in alarm, "You've got two peaks already on the nape of your neck. They're goin' to ruin the look of that upsweep hairdo you like to wear."

Examining the back of her neck in the mirror, Norma said, "Why, I can barely see that little bit of fuzz." *I've never known Mama to be vain, though she has often grieved at her rough hands and fingernails from hard work, and nothing pleases her more than a bottle of Jergens hand lotion. She seldom buys a thing for herself and last year when we bought her a nice dress, hat and gloves to match she told me not to do that again, she didn't need such things. It made me cry.* Turning from the mirror she examined Mama's plain face with the tired lines around her mouth, the straight black hair pulled back and held with bobby pins, the unadorned dress on her slim but broad-hipped body. *What then was causing such concern over a little bit of hair? Mama's a mystery to me.*

On the morning of Mama's last day, her long stay in the shower alarmed Norma. Knocking on the door, she asked if there was a problem. "Come on in," Mama said "I'm just drying off the tile; it was like a mirror when I started and I want to leave it that way. You told me Harry always rubbed it dry after his shower."

"He thinks a little work all along saves a lot later on, but that doesn't mean you have to do it."

"I wish Clarence could see the things Harry does for you. I'll declare, I never saw such a considerate man. I believe he'd have had that baby for you if he could of!"

"I think you're right, Mama. Now do you see why I think he's the greatest man alive?"

Jerry, Bill, and baby Liz came for a farewell dinner for Mama. Later, they were eager to know how she liked her visit. "I think she was bored," Norma sighed, "Anne was in nursery school all morning and napped in the afternoon. Mama couldn't give Charles a bottle since I nursed him, and except for his bath he slept all the time. She said she didn't have anything to do with a maid here, although she did the cooking." Norma began to laugh, "What upset her most is that she's afraid I'm going to grow hair all over and turn into a man!"

"Why, Honeychild, you're just maturing," Harry teased, rubbing a finger down her jaw line, "and I like this tiny bit of fuzz here and down the back of your legs."

"Down my legs! Oh, no...You don't suppose she could be right?" Norma cried. Charles was nursing and as usual nearly drowning under the rushing flow, swallowing in great gulps that could be heard all over the house, his eyes blinking from spattering milk. Anne's eyes were as big as saucers and Jerry was laughing so hard she nearly lost her breath.

"Little Gah-noma," Bill used his nick name for her, "You don't have to worry; you're absolutely the last woman on earth who'll turn into a man!"

Gifts for Charles began arriving from friends and relatives. Included with Hazel Kipp's gift was a little blue suit from Mother Minnie and a note expressing surprise at the name given to her first grandson--Charles--it was the name of Harry's father. Had the baby been named for him? Norma wrote that he might have been. Thus began her correspondence with Mother Minnie. It was hers alone. "Write to her if you wish," Harry said, "but please, leave me out of it."

Dr. Reece had given a lecture and a set of exercises to the new mothers on how to get back in shape after delivery. From the day Norma left the hospital she had faithfully done the pelvic tilt, the chin to chest, cat stretch, and situps as well as reading the evening paper on the floor on knees and elbows with her *derriere* in the air. Harry told her it was only because Anne was around that she was safe from attack. "Remember how I boasted a year ago that majors couldn't wait?" he chuckled. "I didn't know then how much waiting was ahead of me, and I never expected to be happy to go on maneuvers, but now I confess that in one respect that's true."

Norma came out of her cat stretch, "You're going on maneuvers?"

"November 14-18."

"And you'll be happy about it?" She stood before him with her hands on her hips, "Explain that please."

"How much more do you think I can take? Seeing that lovely thing in the air and watching that boy nurse, pressed so close to you, his nose hidden in your breast and his mouth where I'd like mine to be! Honeychild, is it wrong to be jealous of a little baby?"

"Oh, my darling, I know how long it's been and how hard it is to wait. You can't possibly know what torture it is for me when he nurses and excites me with those delicious uterine contractions. And sometimes when I'm knitting and the ball of yarn unrolls in my lap against my thighs, I have to stop and find something else to do."

"You too, huh?" He pulled her down into his lap. "Norma, I don't know how we're going to avoid it, but I do not want you pregnant again. Your tendency to excessive bleeding really concerns me."

"Me, too. And we've simply got to find an absolutely fail proof way of contraception. I can't explain what happened before unless I was fitted incorrectly for the diaphragm. Doctor Reece says that's unlikely. He thinks I was careless and won't admit it. Well, I wasn't. But we have a baby. I'm not sorry about that now, but I'm terrified for the future if we can't find some way to keep it from happening again."

"There's always abstinence!" Harry joked, quickly shielding himself from her mock attack.

A week later he returned from maneuvers, hauling in his gear, with Anne running about examining every pack he brought inside. Finally she asked, "Daddy, where's your baby?"

"Charles? Why, I suppose he's in his crib, Anne."

"No, he's Mommy's baby. Where's yours?"

"He's my baby too, just as you are mine and Mommy's little girl."

"No, he's Mommy's baby. She went away and came back with a baby. you went away, where's your baby?"

Norma and Harry looked at each other in amazement, realizing that Anne hadn't understood at all where babies came from. And at Norma's postnatal checkup with Dr. Reece, she found out where Charles came from. An incorrectly fitted diaphragm by Dr.True. Her new size after delivery was smaller that the size he had prescribed. She was both enormously relieved and furious on her drive home. Dr.True had played God with their lives and with the lives of many others. She remembered Peggy. Had some careless or vengeful doctor played God with her life as well? There was nothing to do but accept it. The bright side was that now they had a reliable method of birth control--one that had worked for two years until Dr.True came into their lives. And after her visit to the pharmacy she and Harry would have a night they would never forget...with many more to follow!

27

Christmas 1949. The perfect holiday. And the perfect family in the perfect house in a perfect world celebrated it around a perfect tree. Santa had left a miniature car and baby carriage for Anne and a savings bond for the little tyke. Norma had wrapped a set of backup lights for Harry's new dark green Lincoln sedan, two Kaywoodie pipes and a walnut pipe holder, and a pair of hand-knitted argyle socks. Harry had wrapped two packages for her. One held two records of the opera *Madama Butterfly* and the brand new Broadway musical *South Pacific*. The other was an almost never ending surprise. A large black leather envelope purse which, he said, would hold diapers for the baby when they went out, but what held now, hidden in its various zippered compartments, a lacy silk petticoat, a bottle of perfume, a gold ostrich pin with a small pearl for an eye and a larger one for a body, and a transparent nightgown even shorter than the one she had worn on their honeymoon. The Condos sent Savings Bonds for both children, a cowboy suit for the little Bronco Buster and a lifelike doll with its own bottle and diaper for Anne.

The Earneys came for Christmas dinner; Thanksgiving dinner had been at their home. These were the happiest of times; sharing holidays, watching the children develop, listening to music, playing canasta, cooking and eating together, and growing in friendship. Small problems like waiting for quarters for the Earneys and Anabelle's growing unreliability could be endured. After weekends off, she was sending messages of a death in the family and returning a day or two late. By Christmas, three members of her family had died. When Norma mentioned these unfortunate happenings to her neighbors, they laughed, saying Anabelle was known for giving this excuse to everyone for whom she had worked. And true to form she used it after Christmas, even with having been given two weekends off in a row.

"She's taking advantage of you," Harry told her.

"I know," Norma admitted. "I'm not very good at being a boss. The better I am to her the worse she treats me. All I ask is that she live up to the agreement we made, and be civil about it. She gets the same pay as the other maids and she does less work. She hasn't sat with the children since Charles was born. Other maids baby sit three or four times a week."

"Perhaps it's time you took a break from the twenty-four-hour-a-day motherhood role you've been playing for two and a half months."

"I'm just explaining, not complaining," Norma answered.

"Perhaps not, but I am. Let's put Anabelle to work and attend the New Year Eve Ball. Can't the Bronco Buster spare you for four or five hours?" He reached for the nursing boy, raised him to his shoulder, burped him expertly, then returned him to his mother's breast. "Make the necessary arrangements, Honeychild, because I'm taking my girl out on December 31st, and that's for sure."

On New Year's Eve, Charles emptied his mother's breasts at eight then she dressed in her Ceil Chapman original, the one she had bought in Beaufort the year before, and they left for the Officers Club. One minute after midnight and a toast to a new decade and the New Year, they rushed home. Turning into their driveway, they saw the house ablaze with lights and heard music so loud it seemed to shake the house. Downstairs swarmed with dancing couples, colored Marines and maids. Pinching her nipples to hold back the milk, Norma took the stairs two at a time, calling back to Harry, "Dismiss Anabelle. She is to be gone tomorrow before I come downstairs."

The house cleared in less than five minutes and by nine the next morning the maid's quarters was empty of everything belonging to Anabelle except the horrible stench from her constant smoking. Word of her dismissal circulated quickly. No one had ever dismissed Anabelle no matter what her indiscretions; she had been considered the maid of choice."If she's the best, heaven help us," Norma said, "and I will get along without a maid," she declared.

Every day at least one girl came to apply for Anabelle's former job. "Word has gotten around, I suppose, of what an easy mark I am," Norma said, still holding out not to hire another maid. But after two weeks of seeing her exhausted and then finding her shivering in the cold garage one rainy day feeding diapers through the washer wringer, Harry told her, "Hire someone to help you, or I will." That night, moaning with engorged breasts and having to use the breast pump between Charles' feedings, Norma agreed with Harry.

The next day two women came to the door. One talked for her shy friend who had never worked on the base, but was a good worker. Norma looked at the sad-faced woman wearing men's khaki clothing and a turban wound around her head, and hired her. Rebecca George came to work on Monday, January 16, and spent the first day scrubbing every inch of the room and bath that Anabelle had vacated. The open windows and door allowed circulating air to chase away the foul air and by sundown the place had a fresh, clean smell just like its new occupant. Rebecca could neither read nor write and while filling out her health questionnaire, Norma learned her age was twenty nine, much younger than she had appeared at first.

Tuesday morning Norma woke to find Rebecca's six-foot, khaki-clad form looming at the foot of her bed waiting to be told what to do. Each morning thereafter, Norma rose to spend the days demonstrating how to use electrical appliances, how to wash dishes in a sink instead of a pot, and even how to flush the toilets. Rebecca was afraid of the washer wringer and wouldn't use it, instead twisting diapers free of water in her powerful grasp, breaking the fibers. She didn't vacuum the rug; she swept it, after dusting the furniture. She answered the phone with 'Miz Kipp's quarters' instead of 'Major Kipp's quarters' as she had been repeatedly instructed to do. She could neither raise nor lower the blinds. In fact, Rebecca had never before cleaned nor even lived in a modern house.

Telling the Earneys on Sunday evening of her two dreadful weeks with Rebecca, Norma groaned, "Instead of relieving me of work, she's adding to it. Still, I like her despite her lack of qualifications. I really hate to let her go when she returns tomorrow. But I can tell you that after I find a replacement, I'm going to sleep for a solid week."

Norma woke late on Monday morning, not finding Rebecca standing as usual at the foot of her bed. Relief flooded over her; probably the poor woman quit of her own accord. She rose and went to Anne's room to find it empty and the bed made. Harry must have gotten her off to nursery school. Downstairs the kitchen was spotless, the blinds were raised and on the clothesline, diapers were flapping, untwisted. Rebecca, in a starched white blouse and gathered skirt, was starting the vacuum cleaner. She looked like a teenager striding around the room in a light, swinging manner, smelling like a fresh scented breeze in springtime. Hardly believing her eyes Norma cried joyfully, "Good morning, Welcome back!"

Rebecca glanced over her shoulder, without a break in her stride, "Mornin', Miz Kipp. I's glad to be back."

Freed from housework and training Rebecca, Norma resumed the afternoon tea parties with Anne, their special times together. Harry's times were when he shampooed her hair and read her bedtime stories. Time alone with Charles came after his late night feeding when Harry, holding him high with extended arms, 'dive-bombed' him through the air toward his mother, around and around, up and down, swooping, until they all lost their breath from laughing. Expecting those nightly romps, Charles wouldn't go to sleep without them. When Harry was OD, Norma did the honors. Fortunately, Charles wasn't heavy. Actually he was scrawny--only four pounds over his birth weight. Yet he now slept through the 2 A.M. feeding, and wanted to eat only four times a day.

Rebecca had her special times too. Norma and Anne were teaching her to read. Anne recited nursery rhymes and Rebecca followed in the book. Her affection for the children grew daily and she showed it in many ways. On rainy days, even though Anne had rain boots, coat, and umbrella, Rebecca, who had none, carried her the three blocks to nursery school. And when she took 'Chasey Boy', her name for him, for a ride in his carriage, she strutted like a queen. Norma invited her to eat with them; Rebecca firmly refused, "No'm, I jes sits here on my stool," placing it in the doorway between the kitchen and dining room, then sat balancing her plate on her knees. She ate with them and conversed with them, but not at the table with them.

With the onset of her menstrual cycle, Rebecca suffered horrible cramps, bent double and ashen in pain trying to do her work. On these occasions, and over Rebecca's protests, Norma would send her to bed with a heating pad and hot ginger tea. At meal time, she served hot soup and insisted that Rebecca stay in bed until relief came. Hardly a day passed that Rebecca didn't say, "Miz Kipp, ain't nobody ever been as good to me as you." She had spoken of a marriage and of having had several babies born dead before term. She said an old woman had looked inside her and said she would never have any more, dead or alive."That's why I loves yo babies so much, Miz Kipp, 'cause they's my babies now. I's not like them other maids what's got jitney babies."

Norma had inquired of Anabelle about that term. "They's babies of men, mostly Marines, that you not married to. I got me two," she had boasted.

One afternoon as Norma sat at the dining room table shelling peas for supper, Rebecca came to walk around and around the table touching the top with the fingertips of her big right hand. Clearly, there was something on her mind. Norma waited while she made three turns around before speaking. "Them other maids, they don't like me. No'm, they don't." Around the table again. "They says I 'sociate with you and not them." Around and around she went. "What I do, Miz Kipp? You tell me."

"Do you want to be friends with them, Rebecca?"

"No'm, I don't. They sez, you loves Miz Kipp." Rebecca stopped walking and looked at Norma. "I does. I done told my mammy that. She wanna come see you, but she's afeared to cross them bridges. So what I do, Miz Kipp?"

"What happened to your husband, Rebecca? Do you mind telling me?"

"That no good man! Lawsy me, Miz Kipp, I done run him off a long time ago. I got fed up with him beatin' me up."

"Who told you to run him off?"

"Nobody done told me. I got that right outta my own head."

"How do you suppose that idea got there?"

" 'Cause I knowed I had to take care of mysef."

"Then do you need me to tell you what to do now?"

Rebecca stopped suddenly, her stiff-fingered hand poised in midair. "No'm, I reckon I don't. I sees what youse sayin', Miz Kipp. I sho do."

Norma liked to share happenings of her day with Harry at bedtime when they were alone. Often he had told her, "There's something about the prone position that incites your brain to action, then it sends messages to your tongue and ..." Some nights he drifted off to sleep in the middle of her talking. So, tonight she began before he finished dusting his feet with powder, telling first of Rebecca's plight with the other maids, then getting to her own. "Mrs. Saunders called today."

"And?"

"And she asked me to co-hostess the March Officers Wives Luncheon with her." He waited, she continued, "I told her I couldn't because of Charles. She wasn't too pleased."

"Nursing him ties you down, doesn't it? How long do you plan to continue?"

"As long as I have milk, I suppose."

He pressed his head against her full breasts, "That could be a long time. Couldn't you give him a bottle when you want to go out?"

"It doesn't work that way. Milk comes at feeding time whether he's with me or not. And why should I bother with formula and sterilizing bottles when it's so easy to unbutton my dress? But Mrs. Saunders reminded me that I had responsibilities as a Marine wife that I was neglecting." Apprehension colored Norma's voice, "Is she right?"

He looked at her lazily, "Perhaps from her point of view. She's twenty years older than you, her children are grown, and Colonel Saunders is bucking for brigadier general."

"What about your point of view?"

"Mine?" He looked at her thoughtfully, "Honeychild, as I see it, your only duty is to be a decent, moral wife and keep your Marine happy. And you do that wonderfully well. But, I leave it to you. Do what pleases you. Nurse Charles, head up a committee, join clubs, do volunteer work. Whatever. Remember, I, and not Mrs. Saunders, give you your rating and in my book you rate four point oh."

*   *   *   *

Rain started early Friday morning, pouring in torrents without letup. It was Rebecca's weekend to go home. Harry and Norma drove her to the main gate, but the bus had left. They had no choice but to drive her home across the many bridges over Wolf Swamp and White Oak River to Pollocksville, twenty-five miles north of the base. Norma noticed Rebecca's knuckles almost white from gripping the arm rest. "'T's afeared of them bridges, Miz Kipp, ain't you?"

"No, Rebecca, they're safe and I'm thankful we have them, else how would we ever get to the other side of the river?"

"You tell that to my mammy, Miz Kipp, when we gets to my house."

Rebecca's mammy laughed in toothless joy at meeting Norma, and the two stood outside her shanty talking beneath the dripping umbrella until both were drenched from waist down before the old lady loosened her grip on the handle and Norma was able to leave. Going home, her shivering made Harry shake his head in worry, "If this doesn't make you sick, it will surprise me." At home, they drank mugs of hot chocolate and ate leftovers. When the children were in bed, Norma and Harry cuddled under blankets and listened to the downpour, wondering how Rebecca and her mother were keeping warm and dry.

Monday morning Rebecca didn't come to work. At nine a sentry called from the main gate, "We have a Rebecca George here wanting to come aboard. She says she works for you."

"Yes, she does. Is there a problem?" Norma asked.

"Ma'am, her name is on a contact list for venereal disease. We can't let her pass without notifying you. She'll need clearance to continue working on the base. Can you come for her and take her to the dispensary?"

"I don't have a car. Would you please call Major Kipp at..."

"Ma'am, you're at 2511? Yes, then someone can bring her."

Rebecca was crying when the MP brought her to the door."Miz Kipp, it be a lie. I ain't been with no man. I don't never leave the house 'cep with Missy Anne and Chasey Boy.You knows that. They's jes mad 'cause I don't do what they wants. I ain't got no bad disease. I wouldn't touch yo babies if'n I did." Wringing her hands, Rebecca looked imploringing down on Norma who reached up to touch the white tear streaks on her face. "I believe you, and the tests will clear you, and Rebecca, Chasey Boy needs his bath."

"But, Miz Kipp, that be yo job."

"I think today's a good time for you to do it."

Comprehension flashed across Rebecca's face, "Yes'm," she said taking the stairs at a gallop. Henceforth, bathing Chasey Boy was added to her daily chores even before her good name was restored.

*   *   *

Toby and Bill Godwin bought a cattle ranch in Tennessee and wanted Harry and Norma to see it, certain they would consider the area as a retirement possibility for themselves. The Kipps took a short leave and spent two days in La Fayette showing Charles off, then went to Crossville.

It was everything the Godwins claimed. Clean, orderly, scenic, and the county seat of Cumberland County, located just west of the Crab Orchard Mountains of the Cumberland Plateau. On the main highway between Nashville and Knoxville, it was one hundred twenty-seven miles north of La Fayette.

Norma and Harry were convinced they had found the perfect place to settle and build their home when he retired in two years. With less than a year at Lejeune, Harry would probably retire from there. They purchased blueprints for a large, one level country style home with a four columned front porch. "We're in the home stretch," Harry told her, "Dream with me, Honeychild. Look up on the hill. Do you see what I see?"

"Oh, I do!" she assured him, "I do, and I can even smell the roses!"

One mid-May afternoon, Harry had a visitor at the front door who didn't wait to be invited in. Gunnery Sergeant Bullet shoved past Norma to greet Harry with a hearty slap on the back and a "By God, it's great to see ya, Skipper!" After Harry's introduction, he nodded to Norma, "Pleased to meet you, Ma'am," and then turning to Harry, "I heard you got yourself hooked up, Skipper. By God, you sure picked a looker. Yes, sir, a real genuwine lady." And back to Norma, "And you, Ma'am, you got the best goddamn gyrene in this man's Corps."

He seated himself on the couch, crouching forward, speaking in short bursts, swearing at the beginning of every sentence. Norma winced each time and hoped his loud voice and bellows of laughter wouldn't wake Anne from her nap. The two leathernecks dug in to hash over their Old Corps' past in Nicaragua and China with liberty in Managua and Shanghai when both were corporals. They worked their way into World War 11 cursing the jungles of Cape Gloucester where they had endured soakings for weeks on end, their feet so infected with jungle rot they could barely walk; and the blue bottleflies, rotting enemy corpses, and blistering hot coral of Peleliu, calling themselves raggedy-ass Marines. And to Norma's horror, Harry was slinging his share of goddamns. She clinched her teeth and tried not to cover her ears, but the endless swearing almost made her sick. Neither seemed to notice when she left. As always when she was upset, she began cleaning even though the bathrooms were already spotless.

When Gunny 'Bully' Bullet departed, Harry came upstairs looking for her. He said simply, "He's gone."

"Good, I'm glad he left before the kids woke up. What a loud mouth and that awful language...I'd rather not have him around them."

Harry looked as if she had struck him, his eyes widened, then in a barely audible voice he said, "That comment is beneath you. I'm going to forget you made it. But think on this, for all you know I might not be here today if it weren't for him--and others like him.You may owe him more than you know. Remember that the next time you judge any of my friends who may come to this house." His face was white, his eyes filled with disappointment in her.

She recoiled at seeing it, losing her haughtiness at once, feeling shame and regret. Harry had never judged nor condemned anyone in her world. And he could have, with justification. Living with him, how could she have been so narrow minded and unkind? He was not angry; that would have been bearable. He was impersonal. She felt reduced to nothing and could not bear his eyes without their usual warmth and acceptance, or his face without the softness that spread over its granite hardness when he looked at her. The Rock of Gibraltar, that's what Butch said Harry's men called him. What had she done with her thoughtless and cruel words? All because of that boorish man. She almost hated him. No, she took that back! She hated herself. It was because of the swearing. She had taken Daddy's condemnation of it as her own and condemned Harry's friend. His friend in battle when life and death were separated only by bullets. She had wanted to know before, and he hadn't told her. Today she had the chance to know, really know, and what had she done? She had judged them by the swearing and retreated. If only she could do it over again and welcome Harry's friend. So he swears; so Harry swore. It doesn't mean what Daddy says it means. Her voice struggled in repentance, "I apologize to you and I will apologize to him, or do anything you ask."

"You won't have the opportunity. He's just been retired, going back to start life as a civilian--a warrior no more--a warrior with a heart as big as the Montana sky under which he'll be living. He came to say good-by."

Norma stared across the two foot chasm that separated them, "Then how can I make it up to him, and to you?"

His features softened and he said, "I hope you learn from it."

"I have, oh, Harry, I have. You must believe me." Her eyes begged him to open his arms to her. Slowly she moved toward him and cried against his chest. "Please, forgive me."

He raised his arms to encircle her, "Everyone makes a mistake every now and then. It's allowed. Yes, Honeychild, of course, I forgive you." In his embrace Norma felt the return of his acceptance and silently she vowed that from now on she would guard against petty behavior that could keep it from her. The world was nothing without his love and respect, with it she had everything.

*   *   *   *

As the summer temperature rose, Charles' raspy breathing worsened and Norma was afraid he would die in his crib during the night as Major and Mrs.Shaw's baby boy had died at Parris Island last year. The Navy doctors said Charles had asthma, but she didn't believe them. She got an appointment with Doctor Sidbury, a specialist who treated rare childhood disorders, in Wrightsville Beach, fifty miles south of Camp Lejeune. His diagnosis was an enlarged thymus gland which usually decreased with age; Charles' had not. He prescribed X-ray treatment to reduce it which the Naval Hospital administered and Charles was cured after two treatments.

Bill Earney drew a six-month cruise in the Mediterranean aboard the USS Salem, the captain in charge of Marines aboard, just as his name got near the top of the quarters list. Jerry could move in since Bill was on temporary duty. His good-by to the Kipps was loving and brief; he'd miss their good times and would they please look after his family while he was away? Jerry expected to be settled on the base by the time Bill returned and confided to Norma, "Then we plan to start another baby. Maybe Bill will have a son--like Harry--and our life can be as happy as yours."

"Yes, our life is happy, but I have an uneasy feeling about the news coming out of Korea."

"You're just borrowing trouble, Norma, and if it worries you, stop listening to the radio."

None of the wives who gathered at the neighborhood playground with their children seemed to be bothered by news reports of the Asian conflict. Life was peaceful and routine, and a country called Korea, on the other side of the world, was of concern only to the missionaries, they said. But Norma had a premonition that all their lives would be affected by the happenings on the slender peninsula bordered by the Yellow Sea on one coast and the Sea of Japan on the other. She continued to listen to the reports of military raids being made into South Korea by the North Korean Communist forces. Then came the full scale invasion on June 25 provoking a cease fire order from the United Nations Security Council which the North Korean forces ignored. Next, military action was invoked against the aggressor. Norma listened with such fear that Harry tried to reassure her. On June 30, he gave her a gift-wrapped box of stationery bordered and monogrammed in royal blue, "It's your birthday, Honeychild, lay aside world affairs and celebrate with me."

"I'll celebrate with you," she said solemnly, "even without gifts--your sweet presence is enough for me...if it lasts."

Three weeks later their year was up in Quarters 2511.The dining room blue could be changed to pink. But it would never happen. One month and one day after the invasion of South Korea by North Korean Communist forces, the United States became involved in the conflict. Norma and Harry heard the announcement on the radio Wednesday during their nightly cribbage game. Thursday, he came home to tell her in his calm, controlled voice that their life in MOQ 2511 had come to an end. Suddenly having a pink dining room seemed quite trivial. Friday they put Rebecca on the bus to Pollocksville begging until the bus drove away to stay with them, her long arms reaching from the bus window toward Norma and the children. And within three days most of the Second Marine Division was en route to the Far East via Camp Pendleton. Saturday noon Harry was en route to Camp Pendleton via La Fayette with his family, their car loaded with personal belongings. All else was left in the care of military packers to be shipped to a Chattanooga warehouse. They drove away from their happy home, leaving the key with Bunny Edwards their neighbor who promised to witness the quarters check-out scheduled for 8 August.

They drove from Camp Lejeune to La Fayette in eighteen hours, looking throughout the night at the full moon and listening to the radio to keep awake. Every station seemed to play only two songs, "Good Night Irene" and "Bewitched, Bothered, and Bewildered." For the rest of her life, Norma never wanted to hear either song again.

Charles woke at six to nurse from his mother's milk supply that had satisfied him so well. A supply that had disappeared overnight. He suckled furiously, then cried furiously, until he decided, Norma supposed, that just to suckle was all the comfort he could get. When Sunday's sunrise blinded their bleary eyes, Harry stopped to take a slug from his Jack Daniel's bottle. Before he could replace the cap, Norma reached for the bottle to take a burning gulp, and since she was a teetotaler, this shocked them both into laughter which woke the children. It was a frazzled foursome that arrived at the Clinton home just in time for breakfast.

Julia took Anne under her wing, Grandmother gave Charles milk from a cup which he drank greedily, and Norma and Harry went to bed to sleep until dark. After supper, she explained why they were there. And later, she and Harry held each other through the night, not wanting to spend their last hours together in sleep. In the morning, like marionettes with some unseen force pulling the strings, they stepped apart and Harry walked to the car and drove away. And Norma, like a marionette with strings detached, watched him go. She had been catapulted into a desolate world, a world untouched by Marines going into combat in far away Korea. The people in La Fayette seemed as unconcerned as the wives at Camp Lejeune had been, but were no more. Anne and Charles knew only that their daddy no longer came home at night.

Anne's birthday, her fourth, was celebrated once again at a different address, this year without her daddy. Julia took charge, baking a cake and making favors to give her a happy birthday.

28

With Anne's birthday past, Norma set out to put order into their lives. Within a few days she had rented a little house and located a storage place for the things that wouldn't fit into it when they arrived from Camp Lejeune. Harry's wire on August third let her know he had arrived safely. His first letter came four days later.

Camp Pendleton, Calif.
4 August, 1950

My dearest, dearest Norma,

The full meaning of this separation did not penetrate my thick skull until after I had left you, and then it hit me like a bomb. What a heavenly little home we had with the kids, and you made it so. Believe me, Norma darling, I realize now how very much I love you. The months ahead, away from you, will be one long night-mare. I swear now, before God, that when this is over I'll never, never leave you again. I'll clean cesspools if I have to, to support you, but I'll always be near you. My heart feels as if it is breaking when I think what a hard time you are having in getting some semblance of a household together. I guess no woman ever married a worse kind of man than you did. I wouldn't blame you if you divorced me, but please, honeychild, don't do it!

I was so upset the morning I left that I forgot the pictures and the lock of hair you gave me. I must have left them on the radio. Please send them to me when I get a more permanent address. I want them so very much but don't send them until I ask for them; they might get lost.

According to rumors we are going to Yokosuka, Japan but don't know anything definite yet. We are supposed to leave next week. I'll send you a telegram when I find out for sure. If there isn't time to write send me a wire and let me know if you have an apartment and a storeroom for our things, and if the things arrived OK. Also if you heard from Bunny Edwards about the house checkout.

The trip across wasn't bad except that I didn't get much sleep. I arrived in San Diego sixty-three hours after I left La Fayette. The car did wonderfully well. When I leave, I'll store it at the Tenth Avenue Garage, 843 10th Avenue, San Diego. The place is owned and operated by A.C. Buss and H.G. Buss, father and son, nice people. The son is in the Air Force Reserve and may be called to active duty. I'll bring the car back to you one of these days and then we can make some *pleasant* trips.

Gee! Our little daughter is four years old now. Wish I could have stayed for her birthday. Tell her "wup de do" for me. And give the Bronco Buster a pat on the fanny. And give my sweet, lovely little wife the biggest and longest kiss in the world, and all my love to have and keep forever. Your lonesome Harry.

Tuesday, 8 August

My Dearest,

This is the day they were to check us out of our happy home back in Camp Lejeune. I wonder how everything came out. Have you heard from Bunny Edwards, or have you called her?

How I long to get your first letter. Honeychild, are you getting along all right? Can you see an orderly routine coming out of all the chaos I left you in? Oh! darling mine, I hope you are not too unhappy. I am, and will be so very worried about you until you tell me that you have managed to straighten out everything and that you and the children have a nice place to live in. A month ago I didn't dream that I'd be away from you all so soon, and that I'd miss you so much.

Did I tell you about the pictures? I found them in my map case. Norma darling, you are so very beautiful! And your note on the back of your card made me as happy as it is possible for me to be until I am with you again. I love you too, more than anything else in this world, and I always will.

I saw Muggsy Geiser for a few minutes. He is assistant to the Provost Marshal here. Went by our old place on Bougainville Street this afternoon. Couldn't resist going in to look at it but my look was short. I had to look away quickly because my eyes got dim and watery when I saw it.

Don't know yet what I will do when I finish with the C.S.G. Think they have me slated for an Artillery Training Command but that is not yet definite. Everything here is in turmoil. Men wander around wondering what they will be assigned to and an hour later they are gone. Life was so beautiful, so perfect, with you. Norma, the minute I can retire from this Marine Corps nothing in this world will keep me in it. I'll find some way to make up for the difference in pay and I'll be with you and our children.

Keep on writing to me % General Delivery, Oceanside, until I get a permanent address. The camp mail is all fouled up. No one has gotten any mail yet. Good night, my sweetheart. I love you.

Harry.

Camp Lejeune, N.C.
Thursday, August 10

Dear Norma,

The inspection on Tuesday was a breeze. As you predicted, they couldn't find a thing to complain about. Your Rebecca kept your house immaculate. She came back on Monday after you left and sat all day on the porch outside her room. She also came back for the inspection and told Capt. King she was your maid. I'm worried about her. She can get a position with any one of the families remaining here after your recommendation, but she says she can't work for anyone but Miz Kipp.

Jerry Earney came by on the 8th to see if she could help. She is waiting to see if she'll have to vacate quarters. Scuttlebutt says the Marines on the Salem will be sent directly to Japan. Here, everything is at a stand still. The busiest people are the quarters inspection team and the moving people. Your things got packed on the 7th. The next day the packers ran out of supplies.

Good luck to you, Norma. My best to Harry when you write him. We don't know how much longer we'll be here, but someone has to stay or Camp Lejeune will fold up.

Bunny

Friday, 11 August

Hello Darling!

Another day has passed and we are another day nearer to each other. The days are not so bad with so much work to do and so many things to keep our minds occupied, but the long lonesome nights are something to struggle through. If I ever go out of my mind it will be some night when I don't have to work. Writing to you helps so much. It seems to bring us closer to each other. Remember how I used to abhor letter writing after we were married? I love it now. I still can't enjoy writing to anyone else but I do get much pleasure from writing to you, even when I have nothing of unusual interest to say. It is the only way I have of letting my love go out to you.

Still no assignment for us. There are nearly 200 officers here just doing odd jobs here and there and who have no regular assignment. Rumor has it that 2000 Marines and 175 officers are coming here from Camp Lejeune this month. Maybe another unit of some kind will be organized.

Norma, if by some miracle I should get an assignment with a possibility of staying at Pendleton for a while, would you care to come over here? I know it would be a very difficult trip for you and the two youngsters and there would be no assurance that I would stay here, but darling mine, I miss you so, and I want so much to be with you. I guess this is just a dream, a hope, like the straw that the drowning man clings to.

Would you care to come over here? Nothing in this world could stop her! Already in her fantasy--this separation wasn't bearable without her fantasy--she had contacted American Airlines in Chattanooga for flight and fare information to San Diego. Without a word to anyone she had mailed her 'hope' letter. And her fantasy was coming true!

Haven't written to Butch and Dolly yet. Maybe I will tomorrow night, if I don't get a letter from you.

Real estate seems to be fairly reasonably priced here. What do you think about making this our home? This climate is wonderful, it is everything that the East Coast climate is not. I have slept under blankets every night since I've been here. Last night I used two and in the daytime it is just pleasantly warm. Everything seems so clean and orderly, and the people are so accommodating and friendly.

I am rooming with a chaplain, a Navy Lt. who used to be an enlisted Marine. He is a swell fellow, about 35. His name is Piggot. He doesn't know where he is going or when, either.

Gee! Hon, we've been apart only ten days; it seems so very much longer. Does it seem like a long time to you too? Darling mine, you are so sweet and lovely. If something should happen to you or our love my life would be ended. The world would be too empty to keep my body alive. But nothing will happen to any of our little family nor to the love that binds us. God wouldn't let such a thing come to pass because He is kind and I know He answers my prayers. This separation is painful and hard to endure but because of it our love may grow even more great and strong. Oh, Norma! you do love me, don't you? You will never be tempted to let any one else take my place ever, will you? Forgive me the question dear, I guess I go part way insane at times with lonesomeness and longing for you.

Good night my dear sweet wife. I just can't write any more tonight. I love you,
Harry.

On August 14, their household effects arrived in Chattanooga and Norma had them brought to her little house in La Fayette. Day time, she was preparing a home here. Night time, she was writing to Harry that she would join him at the earliest possible moment.

Wednesday, 16 August

My sweet little Wife,

Gee! Hon, you ought to be getting more letters from me. I've been writing almost every night. Do you notice the numbers on the envelopes? I number each letter on the outside of the envelope flap.

This one is number 5 since I started numbering them.

Tell Anne Daddy said, "Be a good girl and be good to Mommy and one of these days we'll go back to Anne's house again." So Charles finally decided to grow a tooth. The little rascal! Guess I'll have to send him a toothbrush for his birthday gift.

Yes, Honeychild, sell the buggy, scales, and anything else that you think we won't need anymore, but don't sell *everything*. We'll need most of our things again, dear, and for a long, long time.

Yes, Norma darling, this does seem like a bad dream. Let's pretend it *is*, and one of these days it will turn out to be just that, and we will forget it and be happy again. I, too, relive the happy, wonderful times we had together, not in imagination, but in memory. Don't know if that is good or bad. I haven't been able to sleep during the last several nights. I lay in bed and toss around, smoke cigarettes, sit up, lay down and toss some more. It is generally three or four in the morning before I fall asleep. I get up at six and I don't feel tired or sleepy because I start thinking of you as soon as I wake. Hope I don't become a nervous wreck before I can come back to you, but I guess there is no danger of that. I eat well and this old frame is still rugged enough to take a lot of punishment. If only I could be sure that you are all right and not too unhappy, it would be easier for me.

And I must confess that I am a little afraid too--afraid of losing you. You are so sweet and lovely and desirable and alone with all those wolves back there. I know there are men who will take advantage of your circumstances and will outdo themselves to help you and to win your confidence and gratitude. Darling mine, there is no woman on earth in whom I have greater faith and trust than in you, but your very dearness makes me afraid of losing you. Forgive me, sweetheart mine. I love you so!

Harry.

While the people in La Fayette, with the exception of Norma's family, seemed untouched by the turmoil in the lives of military people, the airlines knew. Military personnel were given priority in across country flights, but on August 20, American Airlines put Norma's name on standby for a flight to San Diego.

Saturday 19 August

My Wonderful Wife and Children,

I am having a family reunion tonight--you in the middle, Anne and Charles on either side of you, propped up against the lamp, all looking at me and smiling. What a precious family! If only I could be with you! Oh, how I love you--and miss you.

No letter today. The Post office closed at noon and it won't be open at all tomorrow so it will be two more days before I'll know how you are getting along and if anything has happened.

I saw some interesting real estate ads in the San Diego *Tribune* today. Some of the places are open tomorrow so if I don't have to work, I'll go and take a look and write you about them tomorrow night. What do you think about having a house in or near San Diego? I'd have a better chance of getting a good job there than I would in Oceanside when I retire.

I found out today why we here are all wondering what is coming next. General Noble himself doesn't know. He sent a dispatch to the Commanding General, FMF, Pacific requesting clarification of our orders and mission. He meant "Why are we here and what are we going to do?" The classic hurry up and wait. Maybe we will find out soon.

I saw Dick Schutt today. He and his family, car and all, got to Pearl Harbor just before Korea broke loose. Just as they moved into quarters he was sent back here on detached duty-- and his family is out there. He doesn't know when he is to go back or if he'll go back at all. What a life Marines and their families have to live.

I had chop suey for supper tonight at the old White Front. It has been remodeled and is now called "Marty's". I generally eat there after I go to the post office. I can get a meal for an average of about $1.10. At the mess, the evening meal is $1.50 and isn't any better. Norma darling, are you eating well now and getting enough rest? I'm so afraid you worry and lose weight. Please don't worry, little sweetheart, everything is going to be all right. All we have to do is wait. It may be a longer wait than we want it to be but one thing is certain; it won't be more than twenty months and twelve days, and then we won't ever be apart again. And don't worry about me, Hon, I'm beginning to sleep better now and I'm always hungry. I miss you, my dearest one, and think of you the last thing at night and the first thing in the morning, but I think too of the happy days to come when we will be in our own home, always together and with no fear of ever being suddenly torn apart. We can wait for that, can't we, darling? I couldn't think of anything in the world that could be better to look forward to or more worthwhile waiting for.

Say "Nighty night" to Anne for me and tell Chasey Boy I'll bring him a cowboy suit to do some real bronco-busting when I see him again. Nite my dear wife, I love you.

Harry.

21 August

Honeychild!

The die is cast! We'll have our home--permanent type--before Christmas! I deposited $100 to bind the contract this evening. Will have to add $400 in a month, after that $72 per month beginning three months after the house is ready for occupancy. The location is one of the best in San Diego. Fifty-seven building sites were put up for sale yesterday morning and this evening there were only four left unsold. I got one of them and I like it better than those that were already sold. I had them change the plan to a double garage to provide for washing, extra storage, workshop, etc. Total cost of the house and lot is $11,600. That includes water, sewer, and electric connections, concrete walk and driveway, bathroom complete with Kohler fittings, double sink in the kitchen, lots of storage cabinets, water heater and laundry tub in the garage. Does not include stove and refrigerator. But does include house heating unit. I saw a completed house and it is beautiful. The bathroom and kitchen are partly tiled with glazed colored tile. The bathroom fixtures are also in colors. I chose pink for ours! And there are hardwood floors.

We may have to sell the car to furnish the house. I hope not, but if it gets to a pinch, the house takes precedence.

Dennstedt Heights is the top of a spur from a big hill flattened out with bulldozers and is about five miles northeast of downtown San Diego. The surroundings are clean and nice and the view is good. It is cool compared to the lower surrounding area. I believe that in a few years these properties will be much more valuable than what they are selling for now. Schools, markets, bus lines, etc.

are within a stone's throw and still the Heights are secluded and aloof from the hustle and bustle of the business sections. Although we have a corner lot there won't be much traffic--only that of the residents of the immediate area, probably less than we had at 2511. Several Marine officers have bought places in the settlement. It's near enough to the coast to get the cool breeze and far enough inland to be away from the fog. Honeychild, it's just perfect and by the time I can retire we'll have a beautiful home.

Do you want to come out now and take a chance on my staying here? I have rented a house in case you do decide to come. 512 North Tremont, Oceanside. I'll send instructions regarding freight and expenses for shipping our things as soon as I can get all the information together. Have you heard from the airlines yet? The whole thing hinges on getting my discharge as an enlisted man certified for a GI loan. I hope it comes tomorrow.

Norma darling, I hope you think this is all right. The whole thing seems good to me. If only you will like it too, then I'll be very, very happy. The house plan isn't much like the one you had your dear little heart set on, but it is nice and I think you will become fond of it when you see it. Nite, sweetheart, I'm going to say a thank you prayer tonight.

Harry.

American Airlines had two seats available on a 10 A.M. flight to San Diego on August 27. Did Mrs. Kipp want them? Yes, she wanted them! Somehow, someway, she would get done what needed to be done and get to Chattanooga with her children to make that flight. She sent three wires to Harry. One to the house he had rented. Another to General Delivery at the post office in Oceanside. The third to the BOQ at Camp Pendleton. On Friday she packed two barrels to be shipped to Oceanside along with the crib. Republic Van Lines from Chattanooga picked them up before noon on Saturday and stored the rest of their things until further notice. She charged it to the Marine Corps. Whether or not they would pay, she would deal with later. Or Harry could.

Saturday night Western Union reported that none of the telegrams had been delivered. "Keep trying," Norma requested. Sunday morning the message was the same. "Hold them in Oceanside," Norma advised, "He'll be by." Not until the plane departed could she relax...finally on her way. Every minute, every mile carried her closer to Harry. Her heart sent out a message to him, "Be there, my love. I'm on my way, coming to you. Please, please, be there." Across the rivers, the plains, the mountains, across the desert they flew. When the plane descended in San Diego, from her window seat, Norma saw Harry's beloved form, leaning with both hands on the chain link fence, as close to the incoming planes as he was permitted. "Thank you, God," she sighed, stepping onto the stairway platform. He saw her and raised his hand. She breathed in the warm, moist air of San Diego and looked up at the moon. It was full, the same as on that night they left Camp Lejeune four weeks, a lifetime, ago.

They met at the gate and his arms crushed her to him, baby and all, his lips devouring hers. Then he stepped back, his hands on her elbows, to look at her, his eyes as consuming as his lips had been. "Ma Ma," Charles broke the silence. Then Anne's voice pierced the night, "Are we going to Anne's house now?" Harry dropped to his heels, eyes level with hers. "You bet we are!" Then to Norma, "Can you hold the Bronco Buster for just a little longer while I get your luggage?" Minutes later, Norma sank into the comfort of the Lincoln, resting her head against the seat back as Harry maneuvered the car out of the parking lot and onto Pacific Highway, driving north toward Oceanside. His hand reached to find hers, "You must be exhausted, Honeychild."

"It has been a long day. We left La Fayette at seven this morning and now it's nearly midnight by my watch."

"Were you able to rest on the flight?"

"No, but the kids did. I was too busy sending messages to you, and my darling, you received them!"

"Let me tell you how it happened. Yesterday, I got to the PO in Oceanside after the window closed. I returned to the base to work. This morning even though the PO was closed, I felt a pull back to Oceanside so strongly I couldn't ignore it. Walking down Hill Street past Western Union the hair suddenly stood up on the nape of my neck and I felt drawn inside and stood in the doorway, dazed. A girl behind the counter asked if I was Major Kipp. She had your three wires for me!"

Norma shouted in delight, "I knew I'd get through to you! Just like August 27 in 1944! Six years later to the day. Mama didn't want me to leave since you didn't know I was coming, but wild horses couldn't have kept me off that plane. I didn't know when I'd get another flight."

"That was some miracle you pulled, Honeychild. You amaze me." His eyes sparkled with praise. "What about our things? Will your folks get them shipped to us?"

"Another miracle! I got the crib crated and two barrels packed with kitchen things and linen, and they left before we did. The rest are in storage in Chattanooga."

"How did you manage all that in only two days?"

"By throwing myself on everyone's mercy."

"And I'm sure they knocked themselves out to be of service," a grin played around his mouth, "What price did they exact?"

"Only a handshake and a smile! Everyone was so nice and seemed to think that was payment enough along with a ten dollar bill."

"I hope you saved a few for me. Nobody here has been paid; the pay records are either lost or misplaced. The Paymaster has promised to have everything squared away by the first of the month. That's when I planned to pay the house rent. I never thought you could arrive here before then. But when I got your wires, I asked for the keys early, otherwise we'd be sleeping in a motel tonight...with you paying."

"No, if you hadn't gotten them, I'd be at the airport with the kids and you'd be at the BOQ. Why didn't you get the telegram I sent there?"

"Perhaps they tried, but I was OD and slept at the barracks. Today I got bed linen and towels from the BOQ to use at the house. I also did a bit of shopping until you could do a proper job of it. I'm about out of cash."

They were in Oceanside now and Norma recognized Hill Street. Harry turned west to drive past the Municipal Pier, then east to Tremont. He parked in the street in front of a house not much larger than the one she had in La Fayette. "Here it is, Honeychild, your new home in California."

The children slept through being carried inside, Anne to a bed, Charles to pillows in the corner of their bedroom. Norma noticed that Harry had made the bed. "I was doing that about the time you were flying over the Rockies and now here you are!" His arms held her to him like a vise. "Mmm, how I've missed you!" His voice was almost a sob. Her eyes were closed and her knees seemed to buckle. He lifted her and laid her on the bed. She didn't move except for the gentle rise and fall of breathing in and breathing out, asleep. He brushed her face with kisses and watched her in the peaceful sleep of one whose task is done; she had come home to him.

Charles woke at six, the usual hour, and his fretting woke Norma with a start. She sat up in bed looking frantically about the room. "He's on the floor, Honeychild," Harry spoke softly, "I'll get him."

Norma turned startled eyes in the direction of Harry's voice, suddenly wide awake. Her face brightened and she cried in joy, "You *are* here! I'm not dreaming."

"Not now, but I think you have been, and I hope it was of me; you were holding me very close."

A dry diaper and warm milk satisfied Charles and he went back to sleep. "Food is not what I want, what I'm starved for," Harry was almost savage as he pulled her to him. His eyes were blue electric sparks, charging hers, and his roving hands were like flames. His hard urgency found its home, and when after a few strokes he paused, quivering, she whispered, "Go ahead, this first one is for you." He went to work a very happy man.

29

At long last, Norma met Ruth and Muggsy Geiser and their girls. Gloria Jean was four, the same as Anne; Betty Jane was a year older than Charles. He and Muggsy drew together like magnets and Charles remained on Muggsy's lap throughout the visit. "Uncle" Muggsy was short and blond, the same age as Harry. "Aunt"Ruth, a youthful-looking woman with snow white hair, was in her early forties. The Geisers were from Minneapolis. Christmas, 1942, on a six-week leave from duty in the Pacific, Muggsy went home to marry Ruth with Harry to be best man. But he could only be a witness since he wasn't Catholic. After the wedding, the two Marines returned to the Pacific. When the war ended, both returned to brides and ten months later each was the father of a baby daughter.

Master Sergeant Gilbert J. Geiser, assistant to the Provost Marshal, had quarters on the base at Camp Pendleton. Within a month, so did the Kipps--in a barracks converted into seven apartments. Theirs was 17-B-5, Apartment F. From outside, the building looked exactly what it was: a plain ugly structure, but inside it was beautifully and comfortably furnished. And Norma was running up and down stairs once again.

Their first week in quarters, Harry was away fighting brush fires so common in October in dry, hot southern California when the strong desert winds raced down the coastal mountains toward the ocean, bringing fierce .temperatures. By mid-October, the fires had been extinguished and Harry was home in time for Charles' first birthday.

Norma and Harry lived in daily bliss within the walls of Apartment F. The house sparkled under her care. Meals were prepared and served with devotion. From him she lacked nothing that she needed to make her the happiest wife in all the world. And she didn't forget that they owed it all to General Hart. If Harry had been in artillery as he requested, he would have left for Korea with the first wave of Marines instead of staying in Pendleton to train future artillery men.

Their only cloud, except that Harry could still be sent away, was Anne's continuing visual problem. The base ophthalmologist had her wearing a patch over the strong eye to force the use of the weak one. Anne submitted without complaint except that she didn't answer to her name, every day choosing a new one for herself. "Why don't you want to be Anne anymore?" Norma asked after two weeks of trying to guess each day what Anne's new name might be.

"Because," she answered, "if I'm Anne, I have to wear the patch."

Those pitiful--but true--words made Norma cry. She removed the despised patch and hugged her daughter tightly, "You don't have to wear it anymore. I want my little Anne back."

The ophthalmologist was visibly displeased. "I wish you understood, Mrs. Kipp, that we have only a short time to save the vision in your daughter's weak eye--a year at most. If the brain continues to disregard the imperfect images it receives from that defective eye, in time it will disregard them all together and for all practical purposes, the eye will be blind. Covering the strong eye is the accepted method of achieving this. You must convince her of its value. But even if she doesn't accept it, you'll still be doing the right thing for her eye."

"What about the rest of her? and her attitude toward me? The one who makes her cover the eye that she sees with?"

"I'm not certain that will become a problem. And if it does, you have the rest of her life to straighten that out."

"Can you promise that if she wears the patch for a year, her weak eye will be strengthened?"

"I can't promise that for certain, but in many cases it has proven to be successful."

Norma sat for a moment, then said quietly, "It seems to me that you're not certain of very much." She opened her purse and removed the black patch, held it for a moment, then placed it on his desk. Rising to leave, she said, "Good-by, Doctor Powell. You won't be seeing Anne again."

*   *   *   *

Semper Fi

Ruth fed the Kipps at Thanksgiving and Norma promised Christmas dinner in their new home. But heavy rainfall had forced delays and the house wasn't completed and ready for occupancy until February. So it was a Valentine Day celebration at 6551 Estelle Street. By then Harry had temporary duty at the Marine Corps Recruit Depot in San Diego. He enclosed the large back yard with a six foot redwood fence, made a swing set and picnic table with benches, and Norma made curtains again. They bought an electric range with two ovens, a refrigerator, and a dining room set. The children had their own beds; Norma and Harry slept on a mattress and box springs until they found exactly what they wanted for their bedroom, a modern headboard in limed oak with matching chests and a large sit-down dresser for Norma.

When Harry selected the large corner lot he was unaware of the care required to maintain a lawn in southern California. It must be hand watered several times a day until the grass grew enough to be mowed. After that, daily watering. Mowing, and clipping around the house and curb, took hours every Saturday. Fertilizer kept it green, water made it grow, and clipping made it neat. They were slaves to the beautiful verdant carpet that surrounded their house.

Jerry Earney wrote that Bill was in Korea. Muggsy got orders to go. The Geiser girls and the Kipp children got chicken-pox. When all were recovered, Ruth brought her girls to San Diego and they all went to the zoo in Balboa Park. Returning to Estelle Street along the six lane El Cajon Boulevard, Harry drove to a new kind of restaurant that sold hamburgers, five for a dollar, that were made almost instantly. The place was called Jack in The Box and looked just like its name. He drove through a lane beside the 'Box', spoke his order into a microphone, proceeded around the building to pick up and pay for their supper. Charles observed the procedure and when Harry had the food in his hand, he chirped, "Daddy, that's faster than praying!"

Finally, Norma and Harry found the living room set that pleased them completely, a huge, modern couch and two matching chairs covered in dark brown looped chenille, from V.J.Lloyds on El Cajon Boulevard. They had also the perfect coffee table. It was round, solid oak, and had four pie-shaped footstools, covered in deep pink looped chenille, which slipped underneath when not in use. It was an original Sherman/Bertram of California, the only one to be sold in San Diego, the salesman confided with pride. "That's not why I want it," Norma told him. "I like the way the grain forms heart designs on the top, and its solidness. It's a very stable

table. The price is the problem. Two hundred dollars! It's worth it, every penny," she affirmed, "it's just that we don't have the pennies."

They visited it from time to time, always happy to find it there, unsold. This went on for months, until the day came when it was gone. Norma had almost decided to take the plunge and obligate themselves to a debt. "It's been taken out of our hands," she sighed in resignation. "I'll just have to dream of it." And she did until her birthday, when Lloyds' delivery truck stopped at their front door, and the dream table set became real again.

Their living room was complete in July when Juliette and Charley came for their first look at Harry's children, both as yellow haired as he had been in his youth. Anne's hair was long and wavy; Charles had a mass of corkscrew ringlets covering his head. "Just like mine when I was young," Charley said. He also told of his lifetime allergy to cow's milk. Norma said, "Ah, ha. Perhaps if Charles the younger had inherited curls from Charles the elder, he might have also inherited an allergy to milk. Could that explain the rash Charles had gotten as soon as he quit nursing?" Doctors blamed it on detergent, but an allergy test for milk proved positive.

On August first, Anne celebrated her fifth birthday at yet another different address. In September, she started to kindergarten and Bill Earney returned from Korea, disembarking in San Diego harbor two days after Jerry arrived by invitation from the Kipps to make it a grand reunion in their home. Bill was so gaunt and hollow-eyed it hurt to look at him. He looked half starved, and indeed he had been. His outfit had been cut off for days, lost, suffering from severe cold, and hunger. Almost without hope of survival when they were rescued at Choshin Reservoir.

*   *   *   *

Harry wasn't as delighted with Charles' golden curls as Norma. Yes, they were beautiful, but he was a boy. And they were causing family disharmony. Norma insisted on combing them into perfect order every time the family went out together, then the naughty boy would shake his head until they were once again in disarray. She refused to leave with him looking like a frazzle-head when he could look so nice. So back into the highchair he went for another session with the comb while the others stood and waited. After a few repetitions of the mother and son contest, Norma made a pact with Harry, "Let him keep his curls until he's two, then he can have a burr cut." It was now payoff time and the curls were shorn with her collecting them as they fell from the barber's shears and Harry proudly escorting Charles from the barber shop.

"This calls for a celebration," Harry said, driving in the opposite direction from home. Thirty minutes later he crossed the Mexican border into Tijuana and parked on the dusty downtown *Avenida Revoluciòn*. It was crowded with dark-skinned, dark-haired men, women, and children, colorful in their native dress, with *huaraches* on their feet, and for the men *sombreros* on their heads. The long thick braids of the women were sometimes hanging, sometimes wound around heads. All gave lingering stares at the fair haired, blue eyed Anne and Charles.

Burros, also wearing sombreros, swatted flies with their tails and waited patiently for someone to climb into their *carretas* to have photographs taken. Anne bubbled with eagerness, but her 'scaredy-cat' brother balked. She was fearless; he was fearful, not only of burros, but most things, unless he was in Harry's arms. Then he was brave and agreed to a photograph. Afterwards he explored with Norma the storefronts open to the street whose delightful, colorful wares, hanging and stacked in long narrow stalls drew them inside: pottery animals, tableware, stacked pots; *piñatas* shaped like fruits, vegetables, animals, and stars; paper flowers of every color and design; bird cages; and miniature tables and chairs painted in outrageous hues. Shopkeepers in all the stores, and even on the sidewalk, called out their bargains. *Muy barato,* very cheap, one would shout. *Màs barato*, cheaper, another countered. Norma's Spanish study of years ago was useless now, but she enjoyed listening to the lovely sounds that Harry translated for her.

In a street side cafe under a giant canopy, they ate rice and beans, and a Mexican-type sandwich called a *taco,* meat seasoned with hot peppers and stuffed inside thin, folded corn cakes called *tortillas.* "Daddy would love this food!" Norma smacked her lips and licked her fingers. Strolling musicians serenaded with lively melodies. "Ask them to play *La Paloma,*" she whispered to Harry. Before he could request it, the lovely melody filled the air and she was delighted at being understood. Afterwards she couldn't get the haunting tune out of her mind and hummed it all the way home.

On Halloween night, Norma dressed Anne in red pajamas, devil mask, and a pitchfork, her choice, for the Lutheran Church costume party. Charles went as an Easter Bunny in white pajamas and white terry cloth helmet with floppy ears, one falling forward, the other backward. The big cotton fluff ball, sewed onto his diapered seat, bobbed back and forth as he ran around on little mincing steps. He was so adorable with his enormous blue eyes and fake whiskers that he won first prize; fiercesome Anne won second.

Colma, Calif.
5 November, 1951

Dearest Butch:

    I wish to take this early opportunity to write and thank you for your thoughtfulness in remembering me on my birthday. I appreciate your card very much and I'm awful, awful proud to have a grand pal like you. How did you make out with your evening at trick or treat? I'll bet you had lots of fun. I had lots of little girls and boys here during the evening--but no Bunny Rabbit--Why didn't you stop here and see me? Maybe next year, huh?

    Well, Butch, I want to add a few lines to your parents, so will be saying good night now. Give your sister Anne a big hug and kiss from me. I think of you both often. Your pal, "Butch."

Hi Norma:

    I could never tell in words how the card made me feel--I got goose bumps, choked up, then dropped a few tears--believe me I felt awful proud. Thanks.

    Thanks too for adding a few lines about you folks. Truthfully I feel awful ashamed for our negligence on our Butch's birthday. Since last year Dolly and I have been planning on a Hopalong Cassidy suit with two big revolvers for Butch and what happens? Dolly goes back East on an unplanned trip. I even had to write for your address (I don't know where she keeps her address book). To date she has never sent it only gave me h--- for not taking care of it. Anyway we didn't forget him and we will make it up as soon as she gets back from Pennsylvania.

    I will be glad when she gets back for this living alone isn't very good. This is the most lonesome house I have ever been in. Boy! and this coming home to do my own cooking! I can destroy more good food accidentally than a field cook can on purpose. I finally gave up the fancy dishes like steak, ham, bacon, pork chops, mashed potatoes, fried potatoes, boiled potatoes, etc., and have drifted back to the good old standby 'eggs'. By the time Dolly gets back I will be in shape to lay eggs in competition with the best hens in the country. The balance of my housework isn't too bad, excepting I never make the bed each morning--just pull the sheets and blankets up over--so much for my domestic life.

Everything else in general is OK or as good as can be expected. I like my job here quite well, but 'Frisco itself I cannot say much for. Of course, it is still better than Korea, so better not sound off too much.

Harry:

I saw Pitts several months ago. He'd just got back from Korea. He was OK. Thanks for the news about Muggsy. Sure hope he makes the trip back OK. Does Tom remember me? Tell him I send my regards.

Give Anne a hug and kiss for me--if ever our past two years of tough luck changes to better, we hope to see you folks. My plans have gone haywire since coming out here, so I no longer plan a darn thing. Anyway to all of you my best of wishes and love.

Always,
Butch

Tommy Clinton quit high school in his senior year, joined the Navy and took basic training in San Diego. His Christmas Day liberty was spent with Norma and her family, then they left for Colma, California where at last Butch would see his namesake, and he and Dolly would officially become godparents to both the Kipp offspring. During the baptismal, five year old Anne stood quietly, her hand in Dolly's. Two year old Charles squirmed unceasingly in Butch's arms, chirping throughout the ceremony, "Lookit the Kitchmas tree, Daddy. See the lights, Mommy. Anne, lookit the Kitchmas tree!"

Afterward Butch, red faced and perspiring, delivered Charles to his father, "Damn, Harry! It may not be appropriate, but I think this calls for a beer. A BAR's easier to handle than the Bronco Buster." He pulled out a handkerchief and began to mop his brow, "Hell, that must be our penalty for waiting until he's half grown to get him baptized!"

At the Condo home, Harry accepted the proffered beer and Charles scampered to the bathroom only to return shortly, struggling with his clothes, trying to remove his jacket and overalls. "Gotta go, gotta go, Mommy," he whimpered in distress.

"I'll take him," Butch rose. "Come on, you little parrot." Hand in hand they disappeared into the bathroom. Norma and Dolly, placing sandwiches and potato salad on the dining table, complimented Anne on her sterling behavior as she lay napkins beside the luncheon plates. The calm was shattered when Butch's voice thundered down the hallway, "I don't believe what these astonished eyes just witnessed! Where in the hell were *you*, Harry, when this boy was potty trained?"

Harry's eyebrows rose in surprise as a glowering Butch strode toward him, "You don't know that the hell I'm talking about, do you?" Then he lowered his voice to a rasping whisper, "You've left it to his mother, haven't you? That's what happens when you put a female in charge of men's work."

Norma and Dolly raced into the living room where Butch stood with his hands on his hips and Harry looked bewildered. Charles stood in the bathroom doorway, trousers at his feet, eyes big and round looking back and forth from Uncle Butch to his daddy.

"You've got me, Butch," Harry said, "I'm probably guilty of something, but be good enough to tell me what it is."

"It's Butch, here," the indignant Marine's voice was full of scorn. "He will not permit me to put his gizmo back into his pants until I take a tissue and blot it! Damn, to think manhood has come to this."

Norma flushed and turned to escape into the dining room as Harry's twinkling eyes met hers and a slow grin spread across his face. Turning to Butch, he snapped to attention, "Sir, I stand denounced, humiliated, shamed and condemned before the eyes of all near and dear to me," bowing his head, "I am indeed derelict in my duty...and a disgrace to the Corps."

Butch winked at him, "It's a damn good thing I nipped this in the bud; I think you'd better take command of this detail and teach Butch how a Marine takes care of such matters."Then he shouted, "At ease, dismissed," with such authority that everyone, except Harry, jumped.

The cold, damp air of San Francisco chilled Norma to the bone and she was relieved to return to San Diego's pleasant temperature. Even if it meant that she was faced with the removal of her last two impacted wisdom teeth. Harry extended his leave to care for the children while she recovered. Her face swelled tight enough to burst, her skin turned black, blue, then to green and finally yellow. When she ate at all, she took food through a straw.

On her third night of recovery, Harry shook her awake. "Forgive me, Honeychild, but you'd better have a look at Charles. He's been lethargic all day and his breathing is labored. I wouldn't disturb you, but I think he's very sick." Norma looked and listened to the shallow, rapid breathing of the listless child then went quickly to call the pediatrician at home."Can you please see my little boy right away, I'm afraid he has pneumonia." To Harry, "Get Anne up and dressed. Dr. Laney's meeting us at his office."

The doctor looked sharply at Norma as he took Charles from her arms. She spoke through clenched teeth, "I've been the patient already. It's our son we're worried about." Dr.Laney's examination confirmed pneumonia in the boy's right lung and started penicillin treatment at once, advising that their home be kept warm and moist, and to bring Charles again in two days.

On Harry's final evening of leave, he took a supper tray to Norma's bedside. Sitting beside her, a dish towel draped over his shoulder, he lit a cigarette. "Enjoy your supper, Honeychild. Your last day of being served." He watched as she ate solid food for the first time in five days and asked, "How do you do it?" with wonder and respect in his voice.

"It's not as painful as I expected. At least I can open my jaws."

"I don't mean chewing. I mean running the house. I get no more done than meals cooked and dishes washed. Yet you keep the house immaculate, clothes washed and ironed, meals prepared, lawn watered and mowed, you even have time for dressmaking. Honeychild, I salute you."

She reveled in his praise, but remembered certain comments in times past. With a straight face she explained, "It's because, I think, that I start everything at the same time and run from one thing to another like...I think you termed it...a chicken with its head cut off."

His face crinkled into a smile, "I have said that, haven't I? Well, the next time I complain that you start too many things at once, remind me of this, won't you? I've had my eyes opened these past five days, and I can tell you I'll be thankful to get back to men's work. That I can manage with a degree of competence."

With treatment and the house like a giant steam bath, Charles recovered. So did Norma, and her headaches were a thing of the past.

February was Anne's month for attention. Her beautiful blue eyes needed another operation. Dr. Werner, a renowned ophthalmologist from Austria, was at the Balboa Naval Hospital as a consultant and took Anne as a patient. She came through the surgery with relative calm and comfort. Norma stayed with her as much as was permitted. Anne's eyes were never bandaged and she went home on the third day. For the first time in her life her eyes were in perfect alignment. Janie Lutmer, her best friend from across the street, was a daily visitor. Her mother wanted a coffee table like

Norma's, but Lloyds Furniture Store refused to sell another like it in San Diego even after she called the store manager to give her approval. "We simply cannot, Madam. You paid for a one-of-a-kind and that is what your table shall remain. Our reputation and integrity are at stake. We shall not jeopardize them."

"Now, that is a good place to do business," Norma told Harry.

30

In March, Harry was ordered to serve on a promotion selection board at USMC Headquarters in Washington, D.C. "If there are no military flights East when I'm due to leave, I could ask for mileage and drive. Would you consider going with me?" he asked Norma. "It would have to be a fast trip, driving almost straight through to La Fayette. You would like a visit with your folks, wouldn't you?And perhaps you might fly up to D.C. and join me the second week. How about it, Honeychild? Would you be willing to undergo such hardship just to be with your old man?" He picked her up, swinging her high in the air.

"You know I would!" She cried from up high, "Put me down, Tarzan, the kids are staring."

Harry drove the two thousand two hundred miles in eighty-four hours, stopping to sleep only twice, arriving in La Fayette at sunrise on Friday morning. He and Norma fell into a 'sleep of the dead' for twelve hours and woke refreshed. Harry ate and left immediately for Washington, D.C.

Norma gave her family first hand news of Tommy who was still at the Naval Training Station in San Diego, happy and twenty pounds heavier. So was Joan; she was five months pregnant and ecstatic. Mary Lee was about to celebrate her ninth birthday. Julia, fifteen and a half, had blossomed into a beautiful, exotic young lady, but her underlying sadness and timidity were still present. Norma raved over her glowing beauty, but Julia said, "It's because you love me; that's why you say it. I'm 'Frog Eyes' to the rest of the family."

"Could be they're envious." Norma tried to console her, "You're the only one with big brown eyes, our exception! Be proud of it." Sincere as her words were, they didn't convince Julia.

2000 hours, 17 March

Dearest,

The first day is done. Reported at 0800, was briefed on the procedure of the Board, got paid ($135) and was off from 1000 until 1300. Went to work then and really hit the ball until 1630. Saw Bill Earney at the cafeteria during lunch hour. He said Jerry will want to see you if you can make it up here next week. Have you inquired about plane schedules and fares yet? I am pretty sure we will be through with this job on the 29th. Colonel Cook, the senior member, said he'll schedule the working hours so that we will be, if we have to work 16 hours a day, so you can plan definitely that we'll be ready to leave from here on Sunday the 30th.

I'll send you a money order by registered mail as soon as I can get to a post office. My address is: Analostan Hotel, 1740 North Oak St., Arlington, Virginia. Phone number is "Chestnut 3343". As far as I know I'll be in every evening by 1900.

I love you and miss you. Always, Harry.

2100 hours, 19 March

Darling,

This selection board deal is really a sweat shop. My thumb is sore from turning pages and I can hardly see when we get through for the day. The clerks are really efficient; before we finish with one folder they are standing at our elbows waiting to hand us another. We have 1500 records to review and classify--each record contains about 150 pages. There are eight of us on the board. We have completed 400 up to now.

Saw my official record today during the noon hour. It looks all right--could be picked up for promotion by the next selection board but am not sufficiently optimistic to plan on that. Opinion here seems to be that we will not get a pay raise--they need to save all the money they can so there will be more to give to Yugoslavia, etc. But after all, we shouldn't complain--we are getting enough to get by on.

I'll call you Sunday night and then we can make definite plans for your coming here. I'll be very happy when I can be with you again. If you can arrange to arrive at the airport after 1730, I can meet you there, otherwise you'll have to take a taxi because I can't get away any earlier.

Hope the kids aren't driving you all to distraction. Bet they are having a good time--at everyone else's expense. The little rascals! I love them.
   Can't be sure of getting mileage back to San Diego, but will try to work some angles. The disbursing office seems to be quite cooperative. Hope there aren't too many flights to the West Coast. Good Night, Darling! I love you! Harry.

Norma left Chattanooga Monday afternoon on a small plane bound for Greenville, South Carolina to connect with a jet into Dulles Airport. Four of the twelve passengers were commercial pilots and when the plane began lurching, heaving, and dropping, Norma overheard them exchanging ideas of the cause. "It's a tornado," and "Yeah, he's trying to fly around it", and "Hope he has plenty of fuel." They were excited, but for Norma the combination of fear and turbulence translated into instant air-sickness.

The pilot sitting beside her supplied a sick bag and moved; Norma curled up in two seats. After what seemed hours of bouncing around, the plane was brought down at its destination. Only Norma, though too sick to stand, and the pilots were willing to continue the flight. Two of them half-dragged, half-carried her aboard the jet just minutes before it departed for Dulles. By the time the plane reached Washington, D. C. and Harry saw her, though green as a leprechaun, she was walking under her own power.

They stayed with the Earneys in Falls Church, Virginia. Bill looked great; seven months of Jerry's good cooking had filled out his six-foot four frame. During the days, while he and Harry labored at Marine Corps Headquarters, Jerry and Norma saw the sights of the capital and exchanged news of mutual friends. The worst was that Rebecca George had died of cancer the year before. Memories of her days with them swept over Norma. One in particular stood out sharply. On a steamy summer day in the midst of a fierce electrical storm, she, Anne, and Harry returned from a trip to Wilmington, to find Rebecca in the nursery with the blinds drawn, huddled in the closet, clasping Charles against her chest, surrounding him with her arms. Norma rushed in, asking, "What's wrong?"

"It be the lightning, Miz Kipp," Rebecca explained, "It hunts out little naked bodies and Chasey Boy, he jes wearing his diaper like you wants. I's afeared it finds him, so I hides him." *Dear, dear Rebecca, I will never forget that show of love for my little boy.*

More heartbreaking news was that Dick Granger was in the Veterans Hospital with throat cancer, unable to speak. Jerry and Bill had been to see him. "He was so pitiful, Norma," Jerry's eyes filled with tears. "You wouldn't recognize him, so thin, so haggard, having to write everything he wanted to say, walking the halls, distraught over Marilyn. His confinement sent her over the edge and she's been committed to a mental hospital. Their two little boys, both under three years, were found covered with sores, near starvation, in a filthy crib when the social worker visited Marilyn. She just sat staring straight ahead, not knowing who she was, where she was, or who anyone was. Do you remember what an immaculate housekeeper she was at Parris Island?"

"I remember," Norma said. *How long ago was it? Five years?...to the month. Yes, it had been in March. And today she and Jerry were eating ham sandwiches on rye bread with mustard and pickles....*

"Marilyn's mother went insane too," Jerry added. "That's why she can't take the boys. Isn't this the saddest thing you ever heard of?"

On March 30, the Kipps bade farewell to the Earneys and drove to La Fayette for Anne and Charles. No one but Harry could understand the fervent embraces Norma gave her children when she saw them. On their almost nonstop trip back to San Diego, Harry saw tears spill from Norma's eyes many times. Even the crossing of the Mississippi River at Vicksburg couldn't revive her spirit. He comforted her, promising, "You'll feel better when we get home. You draw strength from it, Honeychild, as I do."

*   *   *   *

Easter Sunday, Harry stayed with Anne and Charles while Norma and Marie Lutmer went to a sunrise service on the aircraft carrier *Bonhomme Richard* anchored at North Island. Looking beyond the landing deck to the fog that framed the ship, Norma remembered another Easter Sunday sunrise service. Was it only seven years ago that she rode down Missionary Ridge in a similar mist and heard of the Marine landing on Okinawa? And today, happy today, Harry was not half way around the world but only ten miles away--at home with their children. The Navy chaplain was speaking of the Resurrection. New Life. New beginnings. She thought of the times their lives had been disrupted, turned upside down, and the new beginnings. At times she had wondered about the ways of God, but He had cared for them and kept them together; and her heart was filled with gratitude and love for Him. As the service ended and all rose to sing, "Christ the Lord is risen today, Al----le--lu--ia!", the sun appeared above the horizon sending bursts of light through the disappearing mist, creating a sunpath on the water and heralding a new day.

Tommy got liberty the following Saturday and with the Kipps, taking their own popped corn and lemonade, got in line at the Campus drive-in for the 8 P.M. showing of *Quo Vadis*. Harry inched the car along until second in line only to be told, "Sorry, the lot is filled. Come back at eleven." Harry bought the ticket and they went home to wait. Anne and Charles went to bed, Norma and Tommy started on the popcorn and lemonade, and Harry smoked his pipe as they listened to recordings.

The informality loosened Tommy's tongue and inhibitions."I don't want to make you mad, Sis, but at first I was afraid of you. Mama told me you'd probably make me use the back door. She says you're the most particular person she knows. That when Anne was born you got a book and raised her by it and wouldn't listen to her or anybody else, and you haul your kids around the country like a pair of gypsies." Tommy laughed nervously, chomping on the popcorn.

"She's right," Norma laughed with him, "I haul them to La Fayette to see their grandparents every chance I get. And it's true about the books; they've been my teacher many times."

"I guess you're the only one in the family that loves to read," Tommy said, "except Julia. She reads all the time. But I'd never thought you'd go barefoot or sit on the floor and eat popcorn, like now...or go to the movies at midnight. You're not at all like the folks say you are."

"They don't really know how I am. Mama and Joan have been in my home only two weeks of my married life. But in fairness to them, I *am* different, but so are you. I remember as a kid you were out in the woods or on the creek bank most of the time."

"That's where I was happiest."

"I've wondered why you left home to join the Navy."

"Oh, I got along okay with Joan, but I couldn't do anything to suit Mama," Tommy frowned. "And with Daddy...well, once in a while he'd take me hunting or fishing. I know he didn't pay much attention to you girls, but I was supposed to be the son Mama said he always wanted." He stared at the floor and Norma wondered if he would mention the shooting accident. The family never spoke of it among themselves, but people in La Fayette always reminded her of it every time she went there. Tommy's voice grew bitter, "For five years I lived with the business of the accident with Mack Mahan. And in my last year of high school, I'd had enough. When the Navy recruiter said they'd take me without a high school diploma, I joined on the spot. Besides, I always hated school. Reading was the hardest thing I ever tried to do. But I didn't get away from it in the Navy! Ha! Ha!"

Norma smiled,"I remember when it fell to me to help you with reading. You guessed at the words, made up stories to go with the pictures, squirmed until you fell out of your chair...and Julia caught on in a flash. How is she? Not too happy, I gather. Still not allowed to date?"

"Nah, Daddy's just as strict as always. He's all the time preaching to her, but she won't believe the way he wants her to, and he punishes her, sometimes with the belt...other times by making her stay at home."

"He used to preach to me, too..." Norma shivered. Suddenly the popcorn was tasteless.

"I never stayed home long enough for him to preach to me, but Julia can't go anywhere except to school and church. Every other place is a 'den of iniquity'. "

"Poor Julia. What are her plans after high school, do you know?"

"Go to work somewhere, I guess. She's working at the five and ten cent store now, on Saturdays."

"Just as I did. Joan, too." Norma said, "It must run in the family...like having babies. Do you know that Joan's expecting? In early July, but I'm hoping it will be born on my birthday. Oh, look, it's ten-thirty. Let's get the gypsies up; they can sleep in the back seat while we watch the movie!"

*   *   *   *

In May, Harry's temporary duty at the Recruit Depot ended and he returned to Camp Pendleton and daily round trips of eighty miles. Right away he went on maneuvers for a week to Yucca Flat, Nevada, where for the first time ground troops walked over the site of an above ground nuclear blast within forty-eight hours after the explosion. Later, he spoke of the overwhelming, awesome sight of it: the incredible brightness, the intensity and charge in the air, and the blackened earth with all the desert wildlife burned to identifiable crisps. It was like black death spread across the land, a horrifying sight in its implications and he hoped to soon be able to erase the flashbacks from his memory.

Retirement was within reach, also a promotion to Lt. Colonel and a stint of duty in Korea. "Which shall it be? More pay or more freedom?"

"And a year apart?" she asked. "Can we live with that?"

He looked into her eyes, into her soul, "No," he said simply.

"Then it's retirement," she said. On that they were agreed. Where to live had to be determined. Harry favored San Diego or Santa Fe, New Mexico. Norma wanted the children to grow up near at least one set of grandparents. And in a small town. And near Julia and Mary Lee. One thing was certain: mileage was fast accumulating on the already ninety thousand mile odometer of their 1949 Lincoln. Harry thought they should buy a new car and try to have it paid for by the time he retired.

"This is my time to choose," Norma said, "and I'm choosing a good economy car." They went looking. In a stroll around a Lincoln, Mercury dealership, Norma spied, over in the far corner almost hidden, a 1952 Lincoln Capri, two door, pale yellow with a dark green top, the interior upholstered in soft yellow leather imported from Scotland. It was the most beautiful car she had ever seen. It wasn't for sale, having been ordered especially for the owner, but it was the car she wanted. There was a red and white one she could have, they said. Let the owner take that one, she said. Harry looked on in amusement as she, the salesman, and the sales manager carried on dealing. At suppertime, Norma herded the hungry, fretful children toward the door with the salesman in close pursuit. "If we can't have that car, we won't buy any," she said, and casting a backward glance, added, "We'll be back in an hour for your answer."

Two hours later, driving home in the yellow and green Capri, Harry shook his head in bewilderment, "Instead of the good economy car you said you would choose, we drive away with the highest priced car on the road, yet for supper you wanted to go to Jack In The Box!"

"Not because it's cheap, but because the food is good and quick. As for the car, I couldn't help myself. To see it, is to love it. You think so, too, or else you wouldn't have let me buy it." For the first time she understood how Harry felt about cars. She was trembling with joy. "This car is magnificent, a thing of pure beauty. I'm going to give it a special name," she exclaimed, "when I can think of one good enough!"

Harry drove the car to Camp Pendleton on Monday and returned home with a suggestion. "The fellows in the office thought *The Mayflower* would be a good choice."

"May Flower?" she asked, puzzled, "But we bought it in June. Why didn't they suggest The June Bug?"

"It's not for the month, but for the ship," Harry explained, grinning. "You know. Get in and come across."

Semper Fi

"Oh, I see," Norma nodded. "Like the Pilgrims. They got in and came across...but what has that got to do with us?"

"Honeychild!" Harry gave her a look of mock exasperation, "You are so damned literal! Come here, Woman," and he pulled her to him, close, then closer, "See what I mean?" he whispered. "Get in and come across."

Suddenly she understood and with a cocked head, she purred, "And which are my days to drive the Mayflower?"

"Well, now on second thought, perhaps we ought to choose another name..."

"No, I like Mayflower," she said decisively. "That's its name."

The first step toward retirement had been made. Next the house was listed for sale. On July seventh, Joan's boy was born and a week later Tommy sailed for Japan on the aircraft carrier *Kearsage*. "Please don't cry when we say good-by", he asked. "I don't think I can stand it. Everybody always cried when you and Harry left after a visit home. Dreading those good-bys almost ruined your visits for me."

Norma held her tears through the last words and last embraces. She watched him walk down the hill to the bus stop, turn to wave, then disappear into the early morning fog; then she cried.

Their house had been on the market nearly two months when Harry left for a week of desert training at 29 Palms at the Marine Corps Artillery Training Center, "That's when we'll get a buyer for the house," Norma predicted.

"Then you'll have to deal with it," he said. "You won't be able to reach me there." But she did reach him, on his second day away, with the aid of a resourceful and cooperative long distance telephone operator and pure luck. Harry's voice crackled over a bad connection. "What's up? An offer for the house?"

"How'd you guess?"

"Didn't you predict it? And the timing is unbelievable. I came into the command post from the boonies for only a twenty-minute stop. I think that if I were in Hell, you'd find a way to reach me."

She thought she heard him chuckle. "Then you're not mad? I debated for a whole day about whether or not to bother you, but I didn't want to make the decision alone."

"No, I'm not upset, actually I'm pleased. And you can accept the offer if it's within the limits we set. If that's all you called for, I need to get off the line. I'll see you on the 29th."

The house was sold on August 27th which convinced Norma there really was something magic about the date. When Harry returned he found all arrangements made for their move to 1015 Oak Drive in Vista, California, a pleasant little town near Camp Pendleton which they knew well since Ruth and Muggsy had bought a home there. It was a perfect place to wait out the final months of Harry's duty in the Marine Corps.

November 4th Norma broke her vow never to vote Republican and along with Harry and thirty-three million other Americans elected Dwight D. Eisenhower president of the United States. Before Butch shipped off to Korea in February, he and Dolly came for a weekend visit. Muggsy was back from Korea and "The Three Musketeers", as their wives called Harry, Muggsy, and Butch, were together again for the first time since 1945 when they parted on Okinawa. They had one swell weekend of 'chewing the rag'.

*   *   *   *

Harry grew nostalgic on his last night of active duty, "Looking back over my career," he mused, "it seems that March has always brought orders or unexpected events--things out of the ordinary--and this year..." He gazed at his glass, tilting it with a sober expression, then took a long sip, "...and this year is no exception. This March, I'm mustering out, stowing my gear, wrapping it up, hanging up my uniform. Over the years, no matter what duty I pulled, I always consoled myself with 'it all counts on thirty'...and here it is." He emptied his glass, set it on the table, looked at Norma whose eyes glistened with tears. "Cheer up, Honeychild," a grin beginning to form on his lips, "As of tomorrow you will be married to a civilian. How about that?"

Norma tried to steady her voice, "You think so? Don't forget the Marine Corps slogan. *Semper Fidelis*! Once a Marine, always a Marine. I will never be able to think of you as anything else."

WAIT FOR ME
PART THREE

ON THE OUTSIDE

On April first, Lt. Colonel Harry E. Kipp, USMC Retired, pulled out of the driveway ahead of Republic Van Lines, carrier of his household effects, and with his family drove away from Vista in a gentle rain. Taking US 80 in San Diego, he drove the beautiful yellow Mayflower across the southern United States to Fort Lauderdale, Florida in seven days.

John Kipp had a proposition for Harry and wanted to show him his new waterfront home, a thirty-foot Chris Craft anchored just outside, and a son John Junior five months younger than Charles. Norma still laughed at Hazel's frantic plea when Charles was due and she was four months pregnant, "If your baby is a boy, you won't name him John, will you? If you do, John will never forgive Harry, or me either, for not giving him a son before Harry had one."

As they suspected, John's proposition was a job offer. The same one made to Charley when he retired. "He didn't accept it," Harry said, "He wanted to remain independent."

"And you?" Norma asked. "You just got your independence. Do you want to give it up so soon?"

"If it were just myself to consider, I'd turn him down flat, but I think you should have a part in the decision. It could mean financial security, so consider it carefully."

"Other than loss of independence, what else would it cost you?"

"Oh," he laughed and shrugged, "only my soul." His eyes held a plaintiveness she didn't miss. For three days John had explained his diversified business endeavors to Harry while Norma helped Hazel with her spring cleaning. Anne and Charles played with Kathy and Johnny and begged to go to the beach. On their fourth morning, their final day, and last chance at the beach, Norma asked Harry to take them. The sand was pure white and beautiful, the water deep blue and warm, the sun bright and burning, and Norma got a first class sunburn. At bedtime, smoothing sunburn lotion on her shoulders, he said, "John wants an answer. I told him I'd give him one after we had a chance to discuss it, perhaps in the morning."

"Then tell him no thank you. You can't get along without your soul, and we can live well enough without his offer. If you want my opinion, tell him we're heading back to the mountains."

John said Harry was a fool to listen to Norma, and he wouldn't even speak to her. On that happy note, the Harry Kipps returned to La Fayette and there bought a newly built house on a level, pine-studded quarter acre site in a development north of town. Harry began at once laying carpets, installing built-in bookshelves, and window valences which Norma covered to match their drapes. He papered one end of the living room with a mural of Pebble Beach's Cypress Point and repainted the other walls deep green. On the long wall opposite the picture window, he installed a twelve foot display shelf at eye level and topped it with mirrors. He painted the bedrooms dusty rose.

Behind the house, near the edge of the property, he dug and cemented a two-foot deep wading pool fifteen feet across, and hung two swings from tall tree limbs nearby. For Norma he built a wide, curved flower bed along the back of the house and next to it, a patio deck, picnic table and benches. Bordering the deck he planted a row of small cedars. Anne and Charles named them "B I N G O" after the game they played with neighborhood children in the Kipp kitchen. From the front lawn, he cut down and dug up a dozen pines to give the sun entry into the house. These labors took all summer.

In September, Anne entered first grade and Harry found employment in Chattanooga in the parts department of Lawrence Brothers Lincoln, Mercury Motor Company. He bought an English Ford for commuting and left the Mayflower for Norma's use.

An older couple from Duluth, Minnesota moved into the house across the street. Mr. Hoff came as vice-president of Barwick Carpet Mills which employed most of the people in town. His wife Mildred was a pleasant, silver-haired woman of many talents. In awe of her vast knowledge of home economics, Norma became her willing student in house management and meal preparation. And the Hoffs shared with Harry the stigma of being the only Yankees in this southern town. It made for an immediate bond.

Joan's second pregnancy was coming to an end. She went into labor on September 19 and Norma volunteered to accompany her to the clinic. She hadn't intended to witness the birthing, only to encourage Joan at the head of the bed, but as the delivery progressed she gravitated to the other end and was available to receive the eight pound boy as soon as his cord was cut. He was named Gregory Norman.

18 September, 1953
2030 Hours

My dear Kipps,

I'm one h--- of a poor correspondent, however I'm enclosing a small ransom payment for being delinquent in the form of Korean currency.

First of all, Dolly mailed me the recent pictures of Anne. Boy! if any guy was proud, surprised, and shocked, it was this one. That girl is getting to be more darling than ever, honest I didn't recognize her. She is lovely. Kiss her for me, a big hug too, and tell her that I love her. Dolly is nuts about the pictures too.

I really enjoyed Harry's letter. Boy, I have a bad memory. Did he write since I came out here? Anyway, I am sure happy to hear that the breadwinner is on a job that he likes.

Norma, if that brother of yours gets out here, he better look me up. No doubt he would anchor at Inchon. We are about 40 or 50 miles away. He should have no trouble 'hitch hiking' that distance over a dusty road.

How's that boy Butch? Growing like a weed I bet, with such a big yard to play in. Tell him I asked about him.

I'm trying to write a letter and there are four guys in the tent arguing the old and the new Corps. I stopped writing to add my piece to their conception. Somehow they believed me.

Harry, spent an evening with Tom Randall. Boy, we both had a gab session. He said, you, Muggsy, and me are the choice of his Corps. Made me feel good. Muggsy is in the 3rd in Japan. Lt. Col. Barnes reported in for duty last week.

In conclusion to all the Kipps, my love and every good wish.

Butch.

"Poor Ruth," Norma said sadly, folding Butch's letter. "Muggsy was home from Korea only a year and now he's gone again. Poor Dolly too. I'm so glad you're out and I know you can't be sent away. But in time, they will reap the rewards we now enjoy after all their years of service."

"So, you're still happy we got out?" Harry asked, "Even with the cut in pay?"

"Yes, still happy." She was definite. "I have what I want most in all the world, having you with me, knowing that every night you'll be with me...until death do us part."

"Until death do us part," Harry repeated, "Yes, Honeychild, about a hundred years from now."

Mid-October was bulb planting time. Anne came, eating a peach, to watch her mother. She looked curiously at the bulbs, "They look dead."

"That's because they're dormant. Sleeping. When the ground warms in Spring and the rains give them water, they'll wake up and grow into beautiful red, yellow, and purple tulips!" Norma explained.

"How can pretty colors come from such ugly brown things?"

"A miracle of nature. Look at your peach seed. It's hard and brown, but if we planted it, it could grow into a beautiful tree and bear sweet juicy peaches like the one you just ate. Where would you like to plant it?"

"In the BINGO row." Anne pointed with her toe to the exact spot. Norma dug the hole, Anne dropped the seed in and covered it with earth. "How long will it take?" she asked, pressing the soil firmly.

"For a peach tree, probably a long time. But the bulbs will grow into tulips by April or May. That's not very long to wait, is it?"

At supper, Anne carefully examined her tomato slices, "Will these little bitty seeds make tomatoes if they're planted?" Then, "Does everything start from seeds?" she giggled. "Even me? and Charles too?"

"You surely did." Norma answered.

"Where did we grow?"

"Inside my body."

Anne finished eating the tomato, "Will these seeds grow into tomatoes inside me?"

"No, only baby seeds grow inside their mother's bodies."

"How did we get planted?"

"I know!" Charles shouted, "Let me tell her."

Harry swallowed, raising his eyebrows, "Yes, you tell, Charles."

"It's like at Jack In The Box. You just put in the order and God sends a little baby," he said, looking very pleased.

"Where did you hear that, son?" Harry asked.

"Aunt Joan told me. She said God had sent little Gregory to them." He looked triumphantly at Anne, "That's how we got planted."

"Does that explanation satisfy you, Anne?" Norma asked.

But Anne's attention was elsewhere. "Mommy, can I go home with Carolyn tomorrow night? She wants me to. Please let me. I'd get to ride on the school bus."

"I'll have to call Carolyn's mother to see if it's all right with her."

"Can I go too?" Charles begged.

"No, she's my friend." Anne answered. "You can go to Stevie's."

"Hush, you two," Norma said. "If you go tomorrow night, we can come for you Saturday," then to Charles, "And you can go with us."

On Saturday afternoon, Harry turned off the highway onto a dirt road and inched through a flock of turkeys, parking in the side yard of a small farmhouse. Carolyn's mother came out to greet them, offering Norma her pick of the lot for Thanksgiving dinner. Just then the big bird Charles was chasing turned on him and he ran crying to Harry, "Daddy, they won't play with me."

"Turkeys aren't pets, Charles. They're grown for food, for people to eat. Help us choose one for our Thanksgiving dinner."

Five days before the big day, the Kipps returned for their turkey. On the drive home Charles chattered of how he would feed and care for his new playmate. Realizing that Charles still misunderstood, Harry explained the tradition of the Thanksgiving turkey with Anne adding what she knew of Indians and Pilgrims. Charles listened, but another mile down the road, he announced, "Daddy, I know a good name for him! Checkers!"

"Charles," Harry's voice was commanding, "the turkey has already been named. It's 'Dinner'. It isn't a pet, it was not meant to be a pet, and it will never be one. You may feed him, but only to fatten him so we'll have more to eat on Thanksgiving Day."

By the time Charles woke on that day, the bird was already roasting, filling the kitchen with a delicious smell that mingled with those of breakfast fare. His first concern was the turkey's breakfast, not his own, and he rushed through the kitchen to feed his five day charge. Almost at once, he returned, stumbling through the door, his eyes blinded by tears, "Daddy, Daddy, Checkers is gone! He's not in his pen or in the yard. Help me look for him!"

Harry pointed to the window of the oven door and Charles saw the plucked bird turning to a golden brown. He threw himself onto the kitchen floor in a crying fit and later refused to eat a bite of 'Checkers.' Harry and Norma felt helpless, and he said wisely, "That's the last time we'll go that route."

Charles' grief lasted until he received his very own letter a few days later addressed to Master Charles "Butch" Kipp. Reading it to him, Norma smiled at seeing the familiar globe, anchor, and eagle on Marine Corps stationery once again.

15 November, 1953
2100 Hours

My Dear Butch:

This is to thank you for the nice birthday card, the three proofs, and your good wishes that you were so kind to send me. I think you write real well for a four year old impish looking little rascal and now that I know you can write, I will look forward to having more nice letters from you.

As I look at your pictures here before me I can hardly believe how big you are getting. I like all three and it is difficult to pick which I like best. If you was here I'd give you a hug for all three.

Hope by now you have those darn old tonsils taken out and that you won't be bothered with those mean things anymore. I bet you even help your Daddy wash the car and assist him with chores around the house. (Ho Ho). You continue to be a good boy and as soon as I get back from Korea, I hope I can see you. We will have a beer together and talk over old times. Okay?

So long, Butch, with love from the other Butch.

Hi Folks:

Thanks for all the news. This is Sunday morning and I have devoted it so far to Dolly and Butch, so I'll ease in a few lines to the rest of the Kipps before I do the endless odd jobs there are always to be done. Have my sox on 'cooking' now. Dolly sent me a little washboard so will try it out for the first time. It looks like a handy little thing.

The pictures are really swell of Butch. It was wise of you not to send the finished ones out here. I don't like to keep anything I value with me in this dump.

It was swell to hear that Anne is doing so fine in every way. Does she like school? Be sure to tell her that I send my love and am proud of her for the progress she is making.

My girl is still doing fine at last report which was yesterday. She has done a grand job of being alone to handle the house and work at the same time.

Everything is still going as usual out here. The weather now is down to freezing and the 'long handles' are the vogue with most of the troops. We have plenty of warm clothing though and so far I actually like it. I feel much better in general in cold weather.

How are the Kipps doing? Fine I hope in every way. Sure would like to hear more about that part of the country and everything in general for I want to get out of the MC and settle down somewhere so bad I can taste it.

Well, Folks, time to tackle my laundry. So, for this time, every good wish and love to all.   Butch.

Very soon, Anne made her acquaintance with death. One evening at dusk a noisy commotion coming from the carport-- screeching yowls and thuds against the car and house-- jolted the family from the enjoyment of their radio program. Harry rushed to investigate with Norma at his heels; Anne and Charles peered cautiously out the side window at the strange animal thrashing about with its teeth locked into the throat of Anne's tomcat. Fur thickened the air and animal feces was landing everywhere. Charles began crying in terror; Anne shrieked encouragement to Tom. Harry was in the middle of the fracas swinging a baseball bat, his blows falling indiscriminately on the rotating mass until one sure hit dislodged the bobcat and Tom streaked up a tree. The intruder lay dead and Tom was mortally wounded. He died in the local animal clinic a day later and Anne somberly helped her daddy bury him in the back yard, placing a poem upon the grave, "Tom, you were like a rose to me."

On New Year's Eve the Kipps hosted an after dinner Open House for their friends and family. Norma served her famous fruitcake, candies, popcorn balls and two huge bowls of eggnog, one with rum, one without. Max came for a refill as she was serving from the rum bowl. From across the room Joan shouted, "Max, no! It's spiked." Norma held the ladle poised in midair, waiting. Max moved the cup forward and Norma filled it as Joan charged toward them. She took his arm, pulling him toward the kitchen, with Norma looking after them in wonder. Still they, along with most of the guests, remained late into the evening, enjoying the refreshments and admiring the many ways Harry had improved their new home. All in all, Norma believed the party was a success.

A few minutes past midnight, as Harry was about to turn off the lights, Dolly Condo called from California, "Happy 1954...at least it's the New Year where you are. I've two hours and fifty-five minutes to go, but I just couldn't wait."

"Happy New Year to you too, Dolly, even if it isn't there!" Norma exclaimed, "And you give me the chance to thank you in person for the portrait of Anne and Charles that Butch sent from Korea. It's beautiful."

"Is it a good likeness?"

"Exactly like them. It's painted on a white silk square, a scarf, but I wouldn't think of wearing it, to soil it. We're going to frame it and hang it in their joint bedroom for now. Later, we'll add on to the house to give them their own rooms...if we stay here."

"You might not?" Dolly asked in surprise.

"We're not sure...let me just say the honeymoon is over."

"Do you think it's being civilians?"

"Maybe, but I don't feel like a civilian. That could be part of the problem. Everyone expects me to be the girl I was before I married, ignoring the fact that I'm now a mother and wife with my own home to manage. They still ask Mama why she lets me do some of the things I do, like wearing slacks. They don't ask *me*. I wish she would tell them to mind their own business. But, they think it is their business! Pants on women are absolutely taboo here and I am expected to honor it. And the lax way of doing things here drives Harry crazy, as you can imagine. It took him two weeks to get the parts department squared away where he works. Now they know what they've got, how many, and where it is. He got a raise the second week; the big boss thinks he's some kind of genius."

"I know two others who'd agree with that rating," Dolly laughed.

"Make that three! We know we're out of step here, and we're not sure we want to get in step. This is the buckle of the Bible Belt, and that rules every area of life; we don't follow the narrow, dogmatic rules and we pay the price. Harry was automatically expected to join the church where Daddy joined me as a kid and where I take the kids. I had forgotten how unrelenting religious zeal can be after getting used to the Marines' 'live and let live' attitude on personal beliefs. The preacher has come to see Harry three times already in nine months. The deacons have come as well, and in pairs. They send out their big guns, Harry says. He just looks at them, saying nothing, when they start in on 'preparing to die'. He never mentions his own experiences with death and seeing his men, his buddies, there one minute, dead the next. And the hordes of dead Japanese, bodies sprawled unburied on the jagged coral with no soil to spade over them, flies swarming--the unbearable stench in the jungle heat. Death all around, even raining down from the sky. If they would only ask him what he's seen and lived through...they know he was a military man... but it's out of their world and therefore counts for nothing."

"I'm sorry to hear it's not what you hoped it would be."

"I did have high hopes, didn't I? Even though everybody warned me," Norma sighed. "I thought I was coming *home*, but I feel almost like a foreigner and you can imagine how Harry feels. I guess time will tell how well we two fit in. The kids love it here of course with the huge back yard, like a playground, and the neighborhood children coming to use it, and that pleases us. Anne and Mary Lee spat just like sisters. Charles is begging for a little brother because Joan's oldest boy Phillip has one. Mama and Daddy are settled in the brick house Daddy built...on the right side of the tracks! Mama's working in the school cafeteria and she's learned to drive! We're really proud of her."

"You should be. How about Anne? Is she still loving school?"

"Yes, everything about it, especially her teacher. I'm room mother for her class and was chairman of the Halloween Carnival. I worked for two solid weeks getting it organized and set up, and Dolly, we made enough money for a two hundred dollar gift to the school! The PTA president wants me to do it again next year. She told Anne's teacher that if they could get me to take on a project, their worries were over. But that's enough about us. Tell me about yourself. How was your Christmas?"

"As good as could be expected with Chick away. There were several parties at work and I wore the beautiful black stole you sent. I love it and I'll bet you knitted it, didn't you?"

"Yes, and I'll bet you looked gorgeous in it, black suits you so well. Dolly, Harry wants me to say that you and Butch are too generous with the kids. All those toys and savings bonds too; how can we thank you?"

"None are necessary. They're our kids too, remember. Kiss them for me, Harry too. When Chick comes home from Korea one of the first things we want to do is see you folks either here or there. Agreed?"

"Agreed--and Dolly, take care of yourself, and write me soon...we love you."

"It's mutual. But you know that, I'm sure. Until later, good night and again Happy New Year."

Anne returned to school and Harry to work. Norma and Charles set about to 'un-decorate' the Christmas tree as he described it, packing silver globes into cartons and winding the much used tinsel on cardboard. Norma answered a rap on the door to encounter a carpenter hired by Mrs. Harmon the sheriff's wife to make a copy of the coffee table set she saw at the Open House party. Norma burst out laughing, "My coffee table! Always liked by everyone who sees it. "Come in and take a look, Mr...?" Norma hesitated.

"Louis, my name is Louis."

"And I'm Mrs. Kipp. And *this* is my much sought after table."

He squatted to rub his callused hand along the grain forming heart shapes at the joints of the nine panels spanning the forty inch table top. He examined the two inch curve that bordered it and tilted the heavy table to observe the support which formed right triangles extending into legs. Four pie-shaped ottomans fit underneath and their curved connection, joining two outside legs, followed the curve of the table top.

"It's a mighty handsome piece of work, Mrs. Kipp, mighty fine. I can't say as how I'll be able to copy it exactly, but I think I can approximate it. Who ever made this one had some special equipment and skill that I ain't got." He straightened up and folded his scale. "Well, all I can say is that I'll give it my best, but I ain't got no way of bending wood like this here. She'll have to settle for straight supports for them little stools. I'm obliged to you, Ma'am. Mind if I come back if I need to?"

"No, I don't mind, Mr. Louis. The table will be here, and I'd like to see yours when it's finished."

A few weeks passed before Norma was invited to see the finished table, a good job but no copy. The wood was walnut with no distinctive grain, like hers, and the top was less than an inch thick and its edge was finished in a narrow brass strip. The stools were so small without the curve that they wouldn't accommodate more than a child's bottom. That didn't bother Mrs. Harmon; she was as proud as a new mother, and Norma understood. Even as a poor copy it was a beautiful set.

*   *   *   *

Springtime brought a tulip crop beyond Norma's belief. Red, gold, and purple cups, the size of Harry's fists, on stems two feet high, filled her flower bed. On Sunday morning she was admiring them when Harry took the telephone call from John Kipp at the Barwick Mill airstrip. Flying home from Minnesota, over La Fayette, he remembered that Harry lived there and dropped down for a visit. "I told him we'd pick him up and treat him to breakfast. Okay?"

But John wasn't interested in breakfast. Instead, he took them up for an aerial view of La Fayette, Queen of the Highlands, one at a time, then went on his way. Looking down from the plane before breakfast made Norma airsick. Not Anne and Charles. They thought their Uncle John, the pilot, was pretty wonderful.

*   *   *   *

On the Outside

Most housewives in La Fayette ordered their groceries by phone, had them delivered, charged to an account, and paid for by their husbands. But in her home, Norma handled the household money. And she shopped for food the same way she shopped for clothes, driving to the town square and walking from store to store looking over all the selections before buying, always searching for the best price and quality. Merchants were in contest for her exclusive patronage, offering discounts or bargains, even outright gifts. She declined all of them; wanting freedom in her shopping. She also wanted produce not available in the local markets such as papayas, mangoes, kiwis and avocados that Harry liked so much, but were to be found in Chattanooga. When she brought this to the attention of the local merchants, they supplied those fruits for her along with broccoli, brussel sprouts, and artichokes. These were not popular food items in La Fayette, but Norma introduced them to her parents and sisters on her menus when it was her turn to prepare the meal on family get-togethers. As on this Mother's Day.

After the leisurely meal, the women gathered in the living room and the men sat on the patio. Julia volunteered to clean up the kitchen and, when the horrendous chore was completed, asked to go for a drive with school friends. Joan said it was disrespectful of Mama for Julia to leave on Mother's Day, but Norma said it couldn't be much fun for Julia to hear three married women discuss the trials of motherhood, so she was allowed to go. On that drive, Julia met a soldier home on leave.

Some months earlier, in despair over the severe social restrictions imposed by her parents, Julia had contemplated leaving home. In return for her promise to 'stick it out' and complete high school, Norma agreed to sign for Julia's enlistment in the WACS. She never had to keep her promise. Julia became a June bride with Samuel Edward Brown as Norma's second brother-in-law, but not Joan's. Ed was a divorced man and in her eyes, and in God's, he and Julia were living in sin.

After Ed's discharge from the Army, he became purchasing agent for Barwick Mills and attended night school to study law under the GI Bill. He also drank beer and on occasion he and Harry paid a visit to the local bootlegger in dry Walker County. However, none of the 'evil drink' ever passed the lips of their wives. Ed had seen combat in Korea and admired Harry's military record. He told Norma, speaking from his lofty six foot four height, that Harry was the first short man he'd known who didn't have to try to prove he was a man. "He is a man, plain and simple. He knows it and everyone else knows it." She shared his opinion.

32

In late summer the Geisers, en route to Camp Lejeune, stopped by for a visit. Muggsy was a 'short timer' on his final assignment before joining the ranks of the retired. In September Anne entered second grade and Charles enrolled in a private kindergarten. Norma took charge of the PTA fall carnival and was room mother again for Anne's class. Christmas messages brought news of a son for the Earneys, and Butch home from Korea got duty at Barstow, California, USMC Supply Depot. And the Kipps and the Condos were still coasts apart.

And Tommy was coming home from Japan! He had been writing regularly to Norma, but not to their mother. When Norma offered to share his letters, Mama said she didn't want any more second hand reports. When Tommy's letter came from the Naval Hospital in Bremerton, Washington, where he was recovering from a foot injury sustained in a motorcycle accident, Norma felt it must be shared. Mama burst into tears and refused to read it. However, the following day she made contact with Tommy's doctor by telephone complaining of his neglect of her. Tommy, already in disfavor with the Navy due to the cause of his accident, wrote Norma that Mama's call got him a 'royal chewing out'.

"It's your own fault," Norma wrote him, "I asked you to write to *her.*"

"I was writing to her until she wrote that your drinking was having a bad influence on Julia. I knew it wasn't true, that you didn't drink at all, but I didn't know what to do about it."

Norma did know what to do; she went to her mother for an explanation. Mama's eyes blinked, but her chin jutted forward as she complained, "You're trying to take Tommy and Julia away from me and for all I know, Mary Lee will be next. You do it with kindness, but I'm on to you."

Speechless, Norma stared into her mother's accusing eyes and a memory long buried flashed across her mind:

She was sixteen and working in the mill. It would close for Labor Day and with the weekend she would have three days off before school began. This would be her last chance for a vacation until Thanksgiving. She wanted to go to Rockmart, sixty miles away. Mama had encouraged her to go and together they began sewing new clothes for her to wear, talking excitedly of the bus ride and

the good times she would have with cousin Flora and Aunt Louise. Friday night after the dress, skirt, and blouse were finished and ready for packing, she said to Mama, "Keep your fingers crossed that Daddy will let me go." She approached Daddy's chair to ask for permission. Without taking his eyes from the newspaper he said one word, "No."
"Sir?" she asked, waiting for more. He neither repeated his answer nor looked at her. Dazed, she stumbled back into the bedroom where Mama waited, crouched forward in anticipation, "Well, what did he say?"
"He said, 'No'."
"I knew he would," Mama looked triumphant, with a lift of her chin, "I told him not to let you go."
"But why? You helped me get ready, you said I could go..." she choked out the words.
"I know I did," Mama smiled strangely, "but I changed my mind."
It took a long moment for Mama's betrayal to sink in and was like a knife in her heart, cutting away trust, making her feel sick.

It had happened again, another betrayal. The first had been pushed down deep, almost forgotten--though never understood--no more than now. Sabotaging an eagerly planned trip was one thing, but slander was another. What was behind this malice? Her mind struggled with it as well as the fact that her parents never came to her house except by direct invitation. And when she took Anne and Charles to their house, Daddy was as distant and unresponsive to them as he had been of her as she was growing up. They didn't understand why they couldn't run to granddaddy, jump into his arms or sit in his lap as they did with their daddy, Mr. Hoff, Uncle Charley, Uncle Butch, and Uncle Mugsy. They didn't understand why he turned them away without a word. It hurt her more now than it had when she was growing up, but she made the same excuses for him as she always had: "He's tired," or "He's got sinus problems," or "He's got a lot on his mind."

Today it was clear that the way things had been was the way they would always remain, no matter what she did. She felt sick remembering that it had been her idea to move here; and it had been a terrible mistake. Part of the problem came from her and Harry's desire for religious freedom, their resistance to the practices and expectations of the church, accepted by everyone else without reservation. But it had always caused tension between her and her family. They had smarted when Anne and Charles were baptized in a Congregational Church in San Francisco and then horrified when Anne went to a Catholic kindergarten in San Diego. Now they were embarrassed that she and Harry didn't attend church services regularly and were defensive when Norma spoke of first hand knowledge of a 'wife-swapping' circle within the church, after she and Harry had been approached. Daddy said she shouldn't condemn the entire church for the indiscretion of a few. She had agreed and tried to put her feelings aside, but couldn't, and stopped going to church.

No one could understand why she and Harry opposed preachers being allowed into the schools to give devotionals. Several times Anne had come home sobbing after being branded a sinner and doomed to burn in hell fire forever because she went to the movies and the swimming pool. Norma had protested to the school principal whose solution was that Anne could be excused to the office on future visits of those God-fearing men.

And then someone in 'authority' from the church had looked over their bank account to determine the amount of tithes they should contribute. When that amount was not forthcoming, they received duns through the mail. Harry ignored them and moved their banking to Chattanooga.

Furthermore, the church building suddenly became unsafe for worship. A wealthy member had noticed a sag in the ceiling so great that he feared it would fall in upon them as they prayed in the pews and he generously donated a plot of land for a new structure. Many in the congregation thought they could also see the sag, but the Kipps couldn't. So when pledges were requested to finance the new building, they declined to participate, but enough came rolling in to permit construction to begin. Daddy, now returned to the First Methodist fold, was hired to lay the brick. And the old, 'unsafe' structure was sold to a shouting, foot-stomping sect who apparently had more faith in their God to protect them from falling timber than the Methodists had.

There were just too many problems. They weren't getting solved, they were growing larger. She believed they had tried long enough to make it work here. And soon their good neighbors, the Hoffs would be leaving, maybe the Kipps should be leaving too. Well, she'd find out what Harry thought about that. Tonight.

At supper, Norma pushed her food around on her plate, eating little and rising to clear the table as soon as the others finished their chocolate pudding. The children went out to play and when Norma finished with the dishes and took up her knitting, Harry watched her fingers knit and purl, back and forth across the sleeve of a sweater until "One Man's Family" ended on the radio. Stilling her busy hands, he said, "I'm ready to listen if you're ready to talk."

Without preliminaries she said, "I made a mistake in wanting to live here. It's not working out. Visiting was one thing, living here is another. Why did you give in to me?"

"Honeychild, why should I tell you what I had to learn the hard way? You had to find out for yourself. You returned for the best of reasons, but your expectations were more than the town could live up to."

"In San Diego, I thought the people were unfriendly, but they were just leaving us alone, letting us live our own lives. Here our lives have to be an open book with every one turning the pages. I caused us to leave the very place I'd like to go back to..." Norma raised apologetic eyes to Harry.

"We can go back," he grinned, "I'm ready; I've been ready for some time. At first everything appeared to be just right and I was happy since I hadn't expected it. The townsfolk welcomed us and were friendly--on the surface. But within a few months it became apparent that we couldn't be happy here. The aggressively religious people have not been too Christian in their daily behavior and the animosity among the various sects belies true charity. The gossip and prejudices are stifling. Then, there are the differences between us and your family. I've watched the conflict building little by little and I knew that in time you would have to resolve it."

"And you never said a word..."

"I'm saying it now. What are we doing here?"

She looked at him sharply, then her surprise turned to thoughtfulness. "That's a good question...maybe what we're doing is getting around to the idea of leaving..."

Juliette and Charley came from New York for a vacation and to look for a house in La Fayette, wanting to live near Harry. "Don't plan on doing it here," he advised. "We aren't staying. We've encountered more problems than we want to tackle. As soon as school ends and we can sell the house, we'll be moving back to San Diego. Why don't you join us out there?"

"We will." Charley said. "Until then, we're looking for a warmer place than New York." And they went to St. Petersburg, Florida for the winter.

On a crisp February morning, after she left her children at school, Norma in her red wool flannel slacks drove through the streets of La Fayette for no purpose except reflection. Turning onto Cherokee Street, she stopped for a long, fond look at the three story brick high school. Culverson and Chattanooga Streets took her out of town to Cove Road, now paved, and up Reservoir Hill which had seemed so very steep when she had climbed it on foot as a girl. The old home place looked much the same except that the elm was gone. She parked the Mayflower at the bottom of 'her' hill and walked up to where she used to go for solace. A sizable colored population lived on the hill, segregated still, with their separate school and church. She remembered that the colored adults always called her 'Miss Norma', even when she was a child. And now she insisted that her children address them with the same title. She smiled, remembering the time Charles had asked their neighbor, "Miss Lillian, Miss Susie is always helping you clean your house. When are you going to help clean hers?"

Lillian had asked in disbelief, "What is he sayin'?"

"What it sounds like," Norma had responded." He wants to know."

Lillian had sputtered, "Why, I don't believe it. Haven't you *told* him?"

Norma had asked in all innocence, "Told him what, Lillian?"

"Why, that ...you know...here...they...," she faltered.

Norma had smiled and said, "No, I haven't told him, Lillian. Why don't you tell him?" But Lillian hadn't said another word.

Incidents like that had not endeared her to the people in La Fayette where segregation and Protestantism, suspicion of strangers, resistance to change, disdain if not hatred of Northerners still ruled. She saw with adult eyes the solidly drawn levels of class structure she had known as a child, still just as tight. The poor white trash at the bottom and the genteel wealthy and professionals at the top. In between were the colored, mill hands, farmers, tradesmen, and merchants. It did not matter how much one owed, it was the appearance of material possession that mattered.

Where did she and Harry fit in? The enigmas. They were thought to be wealthy by the car they drove, but not by the home they lived in. Harry had position, but Norma did her own cooking and housework. Worse than that, she washed her own car right in the driveway. And they never had given information on the three topics of most interest to the locals: amount of income, personal business, and method of birth control, not even Norma's doctor knew that Harry had a vasectomy. If he had known the whole town would have known, for nothing was confidential in La Fayette.

Harry hadn't become 'one of the boys', going hunting or fishing, or to ball games with them. Instead his leisure time was spent with her and their children, even helping with the housework and spoiling her rotten, many said. And here, couples didn't do things together as they had in the Marine Corps, dining together, playing cards, and visiting back and forth in each other's homes which the Kipps had enjoyed so much. Here, it hadn't been all bad, but the bad was bad enough. Then the Supreme Court ruled that school segregation was unconstitutional. Petitions were circulated to return the public schools to private. She had been asked not only to sign but to circulate one. She wouldn't do either and at the end of January, they listed their house for sale. It was final; they were leaving.

Resolutely, Norma left her hill, retracing her route to the town square. She circled past Mitchell's 5 & 10 cent store where she had once worked on Saturdays, past Kitchen's Clinic where Anne was born, and the Greyhound Bus Station which now had a cafe the Colored could use--through the back window. Next stood the Palace Theater with its balcony for colored people, unless an overflow crowd of whites needed it. Finally, the Walgreen Pharmacy, the long ago dispenser of free sodas to straight A students on report card days. A right turn, then another, and there loomed the huge court house with its revolving door. South Main Street took her to Rays Lake and the city park where the community swimming pool was still for whites only. Returning home, she turned left on West Main which took her to the Hosiery and Cotton Mills. Her past. Almost nothing had changed from as far back as she could remember. Even the population was the same, around four thousand committed citizens-- less two, she and Harry.

The months passed with no buyer for the house--not even a nibble. Harry shrugged and gave a hollow laugh, "We may have to pay someone to buy it." In the middle of May all the family attended the kindergarten graduation ceremony and saw Charles march across the stage to *Pomp and Circumstance* to get his little diploma in long white pants and a red, white, and blue blazer Norma had made. The end of May brought a visit from the Earneys with their two children, Elizabeth Ann and little Billy. Jerry helped with an end-of-school-party Anne gave for her second grade class. In the midst of it, a prospective buyer came to look at the house and walked among the twenty-five children eating cake and drinking juice on the patio deck and among the rooms in total disarray with four house guests and four permanent occupants living together, temporarily. He was impressed with the house and wondered if the Kipps would consider selling the furnishings as well. And could he have immediate occupancy? He said the wading pool had been the deciding factor; he had a little boy who liked to float sailboats.

The sale was made on May 27. Harry quit his job and sold his English Ford. Norma gave her last luncheon at 103 Circle Drive for the children's teachers. The coffee table, sewing machine, cedar chest, and their personal belongings were shipped to Chattanooga for indefinite storage. Mama cooked a birthday dinner for Harry on June third. On June fourth, Norma made an entry in their new travel book as Harry drove out of the carport: Evacuated this position at 1545 hours. Destination: California.

And so began another odyssey for the Kipp family, going once again across the United States, this time from east to west. They had no ties, no schedule, only a few things held in storage until they found a place to call home, cash from the sale of their home, and Harry's monthly government pension. Ah! yes, they had one more thing: a sense of adventure and hope for the future...back in San Diego, California.

They drove south to see the Hoffs in Decatur, Georgia, turned north to visit the Smiths and Geisers in Camp Lejeune, on to Virginia for a few days with the Earneys, a weekend in Cleveland with Tom and B.G. Ellis, Sheree and Tim. In Chicago they strolled along Lake Michigan and Anne and Charles climbed on Abe Lincoln's lap in Lincoln Park. Charles was introduced to Mother Minnie and Otto in Minnesota. Lincoln was viewed from afar in South Dakota's Mount Rushmore. On Midsummer day they played in the snow at 9032 feet elevation at Granite Pass, Wyoming. Old Faithful and grizzly bears thrilled them in Yellowstone National Park. Supper on the boardwalk at the Million Dollar Cowboy Bar and Grill in Jackson Hole. The Tetons towered over them, the Great Salt Lake floated them, and the Grand Canyon awed them. Looking down over the rim, five year old Charles said, "I'll bet if I fell, I'd be twelve years old before I hit bottom."

"Then you'd better hold Daddy's hand tight," Anne said.

In Nevada they toured Boulder Dam where Harry had worked as a time keeper in 1934 between Marine Corps enlistments. When the guide boasted of only eight fatalities during the entire construction of the project, Harry said to Norma, "I was here the day fatality one thousand occurred. That man should get his facts straight or not mention death at all."

After three weeks on the road, the Kipps arrived at the Condo's quarters in Daggett, California for a ten-day reunion before departing for San Diego. In their rented duplex at 4474 Clairemont Mesa Boulevard, they received three letters. One from the church in La Fayette, asking for back tithes, which was thrown away. A second from the Chattanooga office of Prudential Insurance Company with a receipt for the July payment on Harry's life insurance policy. The third from the manager of Lawrence Brothers in Chattanooga.

July 18, 1955

Dear Harry,

Just a few lines in reply to your letter received this morning and I will get this VA form back in the mail.

Harry, I can never express in words how much all of us here think of you. The association with people like yourself is what makes it a pleasure to live. If there is ever anything that I or any of us here at Lawrence Bros. can do for you, please don't hesitate to call on us.

Give my regards to your wonderful family and here's hoping I'll have the pleasure of seeing all of you again. Good luck to all of you.

Best regards,
Bill.

For their new home, the Kipps bought a tract house up on the mesa seven miles from the Pacific Ocean, near Miramar Naval Air Station whose facilities were available to them as a retired military family. The newly developing section of San Diego called Clairemont spread out to the northwest, isolated for the most part. One end of a wide paved road, Clairemont Mesa Boulevard, connected to the city below. The other end stopped at a canyon mouth one half mile west of their house site. No bus nor telephone service was available; both were promised within six months. The nearest market was two miles west; three miles farther a small shopping center boasted several stores, a doctor, dentist and pharmacy.

The Kipps and their future neighbors met in the streets to watch their houses rise from a concrete foundation as wooden skeletons dressed in tar paper, wire, and finally stucco. All in three months. On October sixteenth the Kipps moved into their four bedroom, two bath, double garage house.

Harry, enrolled in San Diego Junior College, was unable to use his new Shopsmith power tool except on weekends. In an adult education class, Norma was learning to make pleated drapes. Anne and Charles went to school one mile away.

Because of the Cold War, the mushrooming population of expanding San Diego lived under the threat of possible air attack. So said the builders of underground shelters. A few people built them. Community alert sirens were installed in all neighborhoods and tested each Monday noon. Their alarms pierced ears and nerves for one long minute and all activity and conversation ceased for that length of time as all contemplated their destiny. Car gas tanks were kept half filled in case of possible evacuation and the procedure was announced frequently on television, radio, and in the classrooms. Fearing his scattered family might never be reunited if evacuation became necessary, Harry left the car with Norma and made the one mile hike to the nearest bus stop to get downtown to college.

Living almost within the flight pattern of the Navy fighter planes subjected the residents to the noise of night training exercises, yet gave comfort as well in those nervous times. Other night creatures, those that prowled on land, intruded right up to the front doors and could be seen scattering under the headlights of homecoming cars.

After Christmas, the Kipps planted their holiday four foot live cedar on the east side of the front lawn to keep company with the elm and maple put there by the developers. "It takes seven trees for each of us to balance the carbon dioxide we breathe out," Norma informed her family. "I think we should plant live trees until we reach that number."

Julia wrote that she and Ed were expecting a baby in June. A girl would be named Norma; a boy, Kipp. "We can't lose either way," Norma wrote back in delight, "but why did you wait until we moved away?"

Harry began his second semester of journalism classes. As time permitted he built furniture. Norma was assistant leader to Anne's Brownie troop and a chaperon on field trips with Charles' class. Saturday mornings, Harry drove the kids to a pony ring in Mission Valley where Anne was becoming an accomplished and fearless rider. Charles couldn't be coaxed to even mount a pony. Soon Anne's friend Paula went instead and Charles stayed with his friend Dusty Best whose family was one of very few with a television set. Without the knowledge of his parents, Charles entered a television contest by mail and won an appearance on the Captain Jet show in Los Angeles. They were obliged to take him since his friends knew of it from television. He was the neighborhood celebrity until Norma's advanced sewing class gave a style show of handmade creations which was filmed and shown on television. She modeled a stole made over from her fur coat and a dress of natural raw silk and matching pill box hat. Anne exclaimed, "Two down, and two to go!" and to Harry, "You can be next, Dad."

There was no celebrity status for Harry. Instead, two summer school classes and the shared work with three neighbors of installing a five foot redwood fence to enclose their respective lots. Just as final exams fell due, John and Hazel Kipp arrived for a surprise visit, towing a small trailer behind their station wagon. In San Diego he bought a new trailer, twice the size and half the price of his little one, and was delighted with the prospect of a great profit on a resale in Florida. He wanted Harry to deliver the used one to him later, but Harry said he had no plans for a trip east for years. Nevertheless John placed the old trailer's tags on the new one in preparation for towing it to Florida.

Everyone but Harry spent the following day in Tijuana enjoying the sights and sounds of Mexico. At day's end when Anne and Charles had purchased nothing, John asked if they hadn't found anything they liked. "Yes, but we've already spent our allowance," Anne answered.

"Then let me buy it for you," John offered.

"No, thank you," Charles said, "Mom said we shouldn't ask for anything."

"You're not asking," John said, "I'm offering."

"Thank you, John, but they aren't accustomed to buying every time they go somewhere. The trip is enough," Norma explained.

After supper when the children were in bed, the grownups were having coffee and seconds on peach pie and ice cream. The conversation was pleasant and Norma thought the visit had gone well until John spoke of his regret that Anne and Charles, and even Norma, led such a stringent existence, living with hardly any furniture and not being able to buy even a simple souvenir in Mexico. He reprimanded Harry for not accepting his job offer of three years ago and summarized by saying Harry had wasted his life and was a failure as a husband and father.

From across the table Harry looked at John, his facial expression unchanging except for a strange glint in his eyes. He reached for a cigarette, tapped its end on his thumbnail and put his lighter to it. He took a deep pull then leisurely expelled the smoke, all the while studying his brother. Norma watched for a moment then sprang from her chair so quickly it overturned and hit the floor with a crack. Leaning toward John, she hurled her words at him, "Maybe Harry is going to take that from you because you are a guest in his home, but I am not! You are not going to sit at his table and sleep under his roof and insult him. You don't know what you're talking about and the reason behind the way we are living now. You don't have the least idea of what Harry does for us. We don't make judgments about you and you are *not* going to say another derogatory word about him, do you hear me? I will not allow it." She glared at him, shaking in rage, until he dropped his eyes. Harry left the room, followed by Hazel and then a white-faced John. Norma noisily gathered the dishes from the table, piled them in the sink and then joined Harry in their bedroom, still shaking in anger.

"You shouldn't let him get to you, Honeychild." Harry held her quivering body in his arms. "He baits you, me. I'm used to it. And from his point of view, I am a failure. But making and keeping money has not ever been as high a priority with me as it has been with him."

From her safe place in Harry's arms, she implored, "Please tell me how things were with you... and your mother... and John when you were growing up...is it responsible for what happens every time we see John?"

"I've told you before that I'm not going to talk about it. Trust me, talking wouldn't change a thing. It's your opinion that matters to me, only yours. If you are satisfied with me, John can say whatever he wishes; it runs off me like water off a duck. Now, let's call it a night, Sweets. I've got two finals ahead of me tomorrow."

Harry was gone when the others got up to eat the breakfast Norma prepared, returning just as John and Hazel were leaving, in time to say good-by. And the little trailer was left behind in the street. A week later a policeman said it would have to be moved since it wasn't licensed. Harry moved it into the back yard and it became a play house for the neighborhood children.

33

The Condos bought four acres at Hinkley where Dolly was Postmistress and were building a ranch style house.

Sunday morning
July 15, 1956

Dearest Norma,

Last week I took your letter along to work hoping I might get a chance to answer it during a lull (big laugh) or on some lunch hour. Well, I didn't get to it--and the letter is still at the office. I hope I don't forget to answer anything that was important.

You people's schedule seems to be about as full as *ours!* It certainly was good to hear the latest on every one. And we were thrilled over Harry's good marks for the year. Chick said, "That damn Harry! *He's smart!"* I agree!

We want to thank Anne and Charles for the lovely Mother's Day and Father's Day cards. They mean a lot to us.

Absolutely! We still want to take our obligation as god-parents seriously. Of course our *first* hope and prayer is that Anne and Charles will always have you and Harry. But if things aren't meant to be that way, we'd be happy to take them and stand by them as long as we live. But before you have it legalized, there's one thing we'd like you to change. Under no circumstances would either Chick nor I want any kind of reimbursement for ourselves. The only times that your money would be touched would have to be for educational purposes or any luxuries that *we* couldn't *afford* to give them. But we wouldn't want any payment for ourselves. Maybe I'm putting this badly, but if there's any question in your mind, do ask about it. Too, Chick suggests that you might name an alternate, in the event that *we* should pass away before you folks do, which could easily happen to all four of us before they are grown-up. We too would like to know that they'd be cared for in any possibility.

Anyway, as long as we are living, we'd be glad to share with them whatever we have and do the best we could for them. I suggest that the next time we get together, it would be a good idea to discuss with you their futures and what you would like the future to hold for them in the way of education, etc. Oh, and while we are on the subject of the children, this might be a good time to ask you: after Chick retires, and there will be one or both of us at home at all times, would you consider allowing Anne and Charles to come up for awhile each summer? We could all get to know each other better, they might enjoy it, and I know it would be good for us to have them around. By then, we'll have more time too to do things for them by way of recreation, such as trips up to Big Bear camping and all sorts of things.

Before closing and tackling the ironing, I want to tell you again how much we appreciate your trust and faith in us. And we promise that *knowingly,* at least, we will never abuse that trust, or let you down.

Much love to all,
Dolly

Harry and Norma exchanged looks through misty eyes, humbled by this commitment from Butch and Dolly, friends without parallel.

*   *   *   *

Norma's brother, discharged from the Navy, came to San Diego and moved into the Kipp's spare bedroom. After some months of riveting in the nose of an airplane in the General Dynamics plant, Tommy wanted something better. Harry suggested that he work days and finish high school in night classes, then start college. By spring this was accomplished. Harry made another suggestion: that Norma join them. It was her first semester, his last. She took three classes, he took five.

While three classes kept her away from home only nine hours a week, they required twice that many for preparation. In admiration she asked Harry, "How did you manage to get A's and B's for three semesters without studying?"

"Oh, I studied," he answered, a sly look covering his face "...in the library on campus. I gave up trying to study at home."

"I'm sorry," Norma said ruefully, "I didn't have any idea..."

"See how smart you've become in only one month," he said, his eyes twinkling. "Think what an intellectual you'll be by June!"

Norma sat in Dr. Miller's office with the results of her Kuder Preference Record Tests taken by Psychology 1 students. "Are there areas with which you disagree?" he asked in their follow-up conference.

"Only two," she answered. "I scored high on dislike of routine and neatness. I'm puzzled since I live by a strict schedule and keep an immaculate house. I don't see how that score can be accurate."

He looked at her over his glasses, "Perhaps," he said finally, "the behavior you describe is acquired, not intrinsic."

"Why would I acquire a behavior?"

"For many reasons. Perhaps to please or impress someone. Who might that be?" He asked with a knowing smile.

"My husband, of course!" Norma exclaimed. "He's the neatest, most organized person I know and I do want him to think well of me. You mean, I'm really a slob at heart?"

"No...just that you have an aversion to putting things away once you've finished with them...and you probably have a great many things going at the same time!"

"Have you been talking with Harry?" she joked. "But, you're right, I do have a lot of projects going..."

"In art, I'd say, from your high rating in artistic interests. So did he. I found that interesting in a combat veteran."

"You did? Well, he certainly didn't court me as a combat veteran, even though he was, but as a sensitive romantic man...what a way with words! As well as great taste in jewelry, beautifully gift wrapped with his combat hands. He's something else, I tell you. Helps decorate the house for holidays, helps selects our Christmas cards. Now, making furniture. And his love of music is beyond measure. The first thing he bought for our house was a record player and his greatest extravagance is buying recordings; we must have over five hundred. He even enjoys listening to our children practice their music lessons. You know, Dr. Miller, combat veterans are more than killers who fight the wars less sensitive people get us into." A hint of scorn edged her voice.

"Touché, Mrs. Kipp. And you've just supported your Persuasive rating. It almost goes off the scale!"

"I can't be that persuasive," Norma replied with a touch of skepticism.

"I'd say you are," Dr. Miller laughed. "Tell me something. How often do you get your way?" He leaned forward, eyebrows raised.

"More often than not, but..."

"I rest my case," Dr. Miller used his hand like a gavel on the desk top. "One more thing, from observing you and Harry on campus, I conclude that he approves of you highly and for reasons other than your proclaimed and defended organization and neatness...acquired to be sure."

At home, Norma shared the conversation with Harry. "Persuasive?" he asked with raised eyebrows, "*You,* Honeychild? Think about it. How did you get our first alarm clock, and the house in Vista from the man who didn't rent to people with kids, and the Mayflower, and the avocados and such in the markets in La Fayette? I could go on and on..." he grinned, drawing her to him vigorously.

She pushed him away, playfully. "How about going on and getting the paper you wrote for Dr. Miller. I want to read it before I start on mine." Persuaded, he got the folder from his file. She opened it, immediately engrossed in the thirty pages, scanning the Personality Traits, Interest Inventory, Vocational History, Family Tree, Biography, and Vocational Selection. *He'd written all this and at the same time met her requests to do things at home! But that would change.* Tonight they studied together at home. He used the dining room table, spreading his materials in neat piles, his cigarettes and ash tray nearby, reading and thinking, and organizing in his head, then writing non-stop. She used the couch, books and papers spread over it spilling onto the floor, making note cards, then shuffling through them again and again before beginning to write. She had only begun when he was finished. He went to the kitchen for corn flakes and milk in his blue bowl. She stopped to peel a banana and slice it into the mix, then sat beside him as he ate, her gaze falling on the paper he had just finished.

Kipp, Harry E.
Pol.Sci. 10
09:10-10:00
20 Feb., 1957

The Ten Most Important Things in Life

1. Opportunity to learn the truth about any matter.
2. Freedom to speak the truth, as one sees it, without fear of reprisal.
3. Physical security. (safety)
4. Freedom from want of material needs.
5. Recognition, not necessarily remuneration, for any contribution one may make toward the welfare of mankind.
6. Elimination of competition for common material necessities of life.
7. Removal of the causes of war.
8. Recognition of the immorality of possessing more than a reasonable share of material things by certain individuals or groups at the expense of others.
9. Friendly and cooperative association with members of one's family and community.
10. Measurement of man's prestige by his contributions and worth to mankind rather than by his ability to accumulate wealth.

She read the list thoughtfully, then raised her eyes to follow when he took the empty bowl to the kitchen sink. He returned to stand behind her chair, resting his hands lightly on her shoulders. "What are you thinking, Honeychild?" he nodded toward the list.

"I was thinking... how idealistic you are," she answered, placing her hands over his.

"That's all?" he probed.

"Well, I thought I was more than a 'friendly and cooperative' force."
"You did, huh?"
"Yes." She looked up at him, bemused.
He dropped to his knees, "In this assignment, I was aiming for mankind in general. Surely you wouldn't want me to reveal in a Political Science class my subjective description of you. If I did you know what would be at the top of the list!"
She rolled her eyes coyly, "You mean you want a 'friendly and cooperative' relationship with me?"
"You know damn well that's not what I want," Harry rose, picked her up and started down the hall.
"I want to hear it," she whispered, "I want the opportunity to learn the truth..." And he whispered the truth in her ear.

*   *   *   *

Everyone was giving the same reading in Norma's Oral Interpretation class. Robert Brownings's "My Last Duchess". Most of the students were drama majors, actors in the college productions, and they were good. Norma listened to them render their interpretations, watching as they portrayed the Duke's rage at the flirtations of his duchess. At home she practiced for Harry, taking on the cold, vengeful, imperious attitude and posture of the Duke who felt justified in 'doing away' with his *last* duchess for the humiliation he had suffered at her hands.

Harry's praise was genuine, but more generous than her teacher's. Mrs. Jenkin's praise would come after Norma's final oral report. She had discovered an appealing quality in Norma's lower register which surprised and pleased them both. Together they worked to develop it for her final presentation. On that day, flooded with excitement instead of her usual dread, and bolstered with new confidence, Norma strode to the podium and began speaking in her new voice on the life of Tennessee Williams, surprising her classmates into rapt attention. Her skill and passion in readings from "The Glass Menagerie", "Mooney's Kid Don't Cry", and "Streetcar Named Desire" brought the entire audience to its feet, applauding. At last she gave an admirable performance and at lunch with Harry, she tried to be modest when fellow students stopped to offer praise.

*   *   *   *

Tommy's romance with the dark-eyed beauty who lived up the street had increased in fervor to the point that he asked Norma to help him select an engagement ring. On April 7, Joyce Wyatt became his bride at a formal ceremony at the Naval Training Center chapel.

The spring semester ended Harry's tour of duty at SDJC. He had earned an Associate in Arts degree and membership in the honor society Alpha Gamma Sigma. Finished with school, he began full time on a twelve foot built-in buffet in their dining room. Norma enrolled in a summer school class and Joyce announced that she was pregnant with twins! "I must say that when you two do a thing, you do it in a big way," Norma exclaimed. "Are you absolutely certain? Maybe the thrill of it will soften the surprise for Mama."

"Or double it!" Tommy frowned. "Do you think we'll ever convince her that they just came early?"

"Haven't you heard of the saying: The first baby comes anytime. After that it takes nine months?" Norma teased, trying to lighten the tenseness of the situation.

"I think now we'll definitely wait until they're here before we bring up the subject. No need to do it twice, " Tommy said in a dead serious tone.

"Pun intended, Tom?" Joyce asked. And everybody laughed.

Tommy shook his head, "To think that four months ago I was just a lonely bachelor."

*   *   *   *

"Happy birthday, Honeychild!" Harry's words and the smell of toast and soft-boiled eggs greeted Norma. He placed the tray of food on the bedside table and smiled down at her, "My wife has finally reached the ripe old age of thirty. Congratulations, Sleepy Head."

Anne and Charles came into the room laughing and juggling three gift wrapped packages and a bouquet of carnations. "One for each decade", Harry explained.

"And one from each of us," Anne added.

"Open mine first," Charles begged. "It's the largest one." He helped her remove the paper to reveal a vase shaped like Aladdin's lamp in hand-decorated weeping gold glaze. Anne's vase had the same finish on a teardrop shape, and Harry's was the classic pedestal. "They're for the buffet when it's finished," Harry said, "And promise me you'll discard those bottles of tinted water."

"Oh, I will," she promised with tears brimming over as she embraced each of them. Anne and Charles loved surprises as much as Harry, and they had certainly splurged on this one. He must have cut back on cigarettes because money had been tight since they returned to San Diego. What they had gotten from selling their furniture had not gone far enough in replacing it, and this house was nearly twice as large as the one in La Fayette. Mahogany for furniture had been very expensive. Anne needed new eyeglasses, a violin and a Brownie uniform--things she couldn't make. Charles would soon need a Cub Scout uniform and was begging for a piano. Fed-Mart Corporation was awarding scholarships to qualified members in college. Perhaps she should apply. Her grades were good enough. After getting another 'A' in summer school, she was given something else--a new name. Harry was now calling her Norma A.

Anne's birthday cookout was cut short by an encounter with a stingray in the surf at La Jolla Shores. Her bravery on the rush drive to Balboa Naval Hospital prompted her parents to promise an extra trip to the pony ring and another picnic. This one at Presidio Park on Saturday with the Geisers who recently had returned to live in Vista after Muggsy's retirement from the Marine Corps. Butch also had retired and now the three long time warriors were all masters of their own fate and living in Southern California.

At 4840 Aberdeen Street, house improvements continued. Norma believed there wasn't anything Harry couldn't do to beautify their home and when her savings from preparing economical meals was sufficient to pay for a wallpaper mural, they went to buy it. Looking through the catalogues at Frazee Paint Company, their search ended with a replica of beautiful Orton Plantation of Wilmington, North Carolina. The ante-bellum mansion and extensive terraced gardens expressed the grandeur and elegance of the South at the height of its Colonial culture. So said the papers that came with the mural. Three background colors were offered, rose, beige, and aqua. They chose aqua.

Harry said that Norma's confidence in him to hang the wallpaper was misplaced as he faced the eight sections to be matched across the eighteen foot living room wall. But being a Marine with the attitude that anything was possible, he pitched in. After preparing the wall, pasting and applying the felt undercoat, he found the mural hanging to be easy, though tedious and time consuming. As each panel was added, Norma's joy heightened and Harry's confidence increased. At sundown the entire mural was in place. They stood in awe looking at the magnificent scene spread before them, the huge mansion partially shadowed by the massive live oak bearded in moss, an expanse of lawn, and the sculptured gardens. It seemed as if they could stroll among the dazzling floral display of camellias, azaleas, Japanese quince, magnolias, and flowering peach trees and take the banistered board walk over a lagoon to look out on Cape Fear River.

The living room seemed to have expanded and when the other walls were painted in matching aqua and Norma made drapes of a slightly darker hue to cover the floor to ceiling windows, the room took on an atmosphere of calm beauty. Two modern couches in beige sat beneath the mural with a matching couch on the adjacent wall. Harry's huge Philippine mahogany television and music cabinet occupied the opposite wall. And of course Norma's coffee table had the place of honor in the center of the room.

Outside, in the back, Harry planted bougainvillea vines to climb the patio roof supports. Their Christmas trees had been named by the years they were planted; but the three shade trees Harry planted in back were named Faith, Hope, and Charity. Faith had lived when the nurseryman said it would die, and replaced it. Norma named the replacement Charity. Harry named the third one Hope because its roots were in adobe soil. Only one thing marred the beauty and order of the back patio. John's little trailer. Its tires had rotted and its interior was water-damaged and moldy. Harry hauled it to the city dump, expecting to be cited because it was still unlicensed. Despite repeated requests, John had never sent the papers and when informed of the trailer's demise, he soundly denounced them by mail for destroying his property. "He lost his sick cow," Harry said, laughing as he tossed John's letter aside. They both thought back to a conversation with John on his last visit. He had asked, "If you had a valuable cow and it got sick, what would you do?"

They had answered, "We'd call the vet."

"What if there was no hope of recovery?" John had pressed.

"Then we'd wait for it to die or put it out of its misery, whichever the vet recommended. What would you do?"

"Calling the vet is the last thing to do; I'd sell it before it got any sicker." John had answered.

34

Instead of a summer vacation trip, the Kipps took in the local offerings: Starlight Opera's renderings of Broadway plays in the outdoor bowl, priced so that everyone could afford them; historic Old Town; Balboa Park and the Zoo; the Cabrillo Lighthouse on top of Point Loma; and the swimming pool, stables, and theater at Miramar. Parks were spacious and convenient to get to, beaches were free, and there were good friends to enjoy them with. Clairemont Mesa Boulevard extended east to intersect Highway 395 which went to Vista and Hinkley, and gave another exit in case of bomb attack. Mountains at six thousand feet were sixty miles east, the desert forty miles farther. Mexico was twenty miles to the south. Life was good in the unbelievable climate they enjoyed all year. Paradise! That's what San Diego was to the Kipps.

Juliette didn't agree. She and Charley had followed them there. Harry helped them find an apartment. They stayed one month. The sea dampness worsened Juliette's sinus condition and they relocated to Tucson, Arizona.

Friday, September 13. Norma and Anne were packing a picnic lunch to take to the beach this last day before school began. Tommy called from the hospital. Joyce had been in labor all night. He called again at noon. The babies had arrived, a boy and a girl, hale and hearty--a combined weight of thirteen pounds and born thirteen minutes apart! With Joyce's permission, Norma gave the story to a *San Diego Union* reporter if he promised to keep the facts straight. Tommy called his parents and they couldn't believe *he* had the facts straight. Speechless for a moment Mama finally cried, "But you've been married only five months!"

Julia wrote that Mama took it badly, calling and wailing, "You'll never guess what Tom's got!" Julia imagined it was some dreadful illness and was relieved to learn it was only twins.

A month later, on Charles' eighth birthday, Norma removed a Cub Scout uniform from her cedar chest where it had been stored in anticipation of this long awaited occasion. To add to his joy, Harry became assistant den leader. Anne joined the school orchestra as a beginning violinist. Norma car-pooled to Junior College with a classmate, Jeanne Morton, who had a son the same age as Charles and a younger daughter. Jeanne was another Alabama girl, one who didn't want to lose her southern accent.

In January, Norma collected three more A's, another B, and a scholarship. "The A's please me, the scholarship thrills me, and the B keeps me humble," she confided to her family.

As winter ended, the cold, ugly asphalt tile floor of the living room, dining room and hallway was covered by a warm, cushiony beige wool carpet. Harry made mahogany bookcases to hold their expanding book collection, re-located the washing machine and dryer from the kitchen to the garage and built a snack bar in their place. He painted the outside stucco a rosy beige, the wooden trim a mushroom white. Beneath the kitchen windows, he built a window seat to hide the faucet and hose. Norma decided the ledge top was better suited for clay pots filled with geraniums than for sitting.

The house faced south and in winter the kitchen and living room were filled with warmth and light; in summer they were shady and cool. The children's bedrooms were bright with morning sunlight, and in the afternoon the master bedroom was filled with the glow of the setting sun. Norma thought it had been a happy accident getting a house with a southern exposure, but then the kind hand of fate was always at work in her life. Fate--and hard work-- had earned her four more A's, the lone B, and yet another scholarship.

Harry had finished their bedroom suite, a four-foot high headboard with matching chests which filled the end wall. Its smooth clean lines made the bedroom look like a ship-captain's quarters. Harry painted the walls ivory white and Norma made drapes of striped chintz, in cocoa, ivory, and peach colors. It was a room befitting an officer and his lady.

Throughout the house Harry's furniture of Philippine mahogany, with surfaces finished to mirror smoothness, glowed under the soft sheen of seven hand-rubbed coats of varnish. Norma sometimes wished that John and Hazel could see it now; Harry had turned the house into a palace. But others would see it. Her parents, Joan and her family, and Mary Lee were braving the heat of August and driving Daddy's great, black Buick across the southern United States for a week long visit. They came to see the twins and meet Joyce, but they headquartered at the Kipps and Norma was responsible for the meals.

When the group of fifteen went out to see the sights, they traveled in a three car caravan. They saw everything San Diego had to offer and even went to Mexico. In Tijuana, the three generations climbed into a single *carreta* behind a striped burro for a family photograph. The big regret was that Julia, two year old Kipp, and Ed were not there.

Norma started the fall semester with classes in Physical Geography, Physical Science, Sociology, and Modern European Drama. She enjoyed the first three; the fourth she loved, reading not only the assigned plays but all other works by the playwrights they studied. Once Professor Newman scolded her as she labored under the weight of an armload of books, "Mrs. Kipp, if you're not careful your head will grow so big Harry won't love you anymore."

Anne's sixth grade class went to school camp, a week-long study of conservation, in the east county mountains at one of three camp sites. Hers was Camp Cuyumaca where the dormitories were named North Wind, South Wind, East Wind, and West Wind. The nurse's office was called Ill Wind! The camp program paired a white school with a black school, San Diego's way of complying with the Supreme Court ruling against segregation. Students were taught socialization along with the conservation of natural resources and a skill such as pottery-making from local clay, rock polishing, basket weaving or wood carving. They played games, hiked, and crossed streams on rope bridges. Food was delicious and plentiful. Anne returned home full to overflowing with tales of her five days and four nights at camp. The highlight was falling into a cold mountain stream from a 'monkey' bridge. Later Harry signed a release for the photograph, taken just before her fall, to be used on the cover of next year's camp brochure. "Now, you're a celebrity," Charles said proudly.

Another sixth grade offering was a voluntary course on human reproduction, an hour a day for one week. Through the cooperation of parents, doctors, and teachers, a text was developed which classroom teachers were obligated to follow. On the final day, the school nurse answered written questions submitted by students. Afterwards Anne said, "I didn't learn anything new. You'd already told me all about it; it was boring."

"You are sure, now, how babies get 'planted'?" Norma asked.

"Yeah," Anne laughed, "But don't tell Charles. Let him think Aunt Joan's right...you just give an order like at Jack in the Box and God sends a baby."

*   *   *   *

Norma breezed through three final exams at the end of January, but in Modern Drama, her mind refused to release all that was stored there. Staring at Mr. Newman's test questions, she hoped her class participation would save her. She remembered her initial reticence since once again her young fellow classmates were drama majors who acted in the plays she only read. In time, she realized they didn't always grasp the playwrights' point and when they floundered, Mr. Newman called on her.Today, as they wrote and wrote, she could fill only half the pages. Feeling more and more blocked, she turned in her test booklet and left in shame to spend a dreadful weekend of self doubt and condemnation.

Spring semester began immediately, Norma's last at Junior College. She was elected president of California Student Teachers Association with Jeanne Morton as vice-president. At their first meeting, an Open House, Norma and Jeanne served a huge cake they had baked and decorated themselves. Mr. Newman came by for a slice and asked Norma to meet with him after class. At two, outside his office, she took ten deep breaths, expecting a lecture on her poor test performance. He talked instead of his class in public speaking she'd taken two summers ago."Your speeches always had such point," he recalled. "I enjoyed them all. One, in particular. You called it 'The Unpardonable Sin of Hum-Drum Cooking'. Do you remember that speech?"

"Yes, and I'm surprised, but pleased, that you remember. I have to tell you the idea wasn't original; I just agreed with it."

"And so did I. That's why I asked you here today. You can help me, if you will. The Drama Lab is doing *As You Like It* in April. I'd like to actually have a wedding feast and serve food to select members of the audience, those who pay extra for their tickets. I wonder if you would plan a suitable menu and ...prepare it?" His tone was hesitant but hopeful.

Caught by surprise and relieved that her test performance wasn't mentioned, Norma hesitated.

"Can you give me an answer soon, say, within a week?"

"Oh, my answer is yes! But give me a week to think about the menu."

At home, Norma opened her grade notice. Three A's and the lone B she'd come to expect, but the B was in Physical Geography, not in Drama! "How strange," she said to Harry, "You don't suppose Mr. Newman's making me earn the A he gave me with this menu request, do you? I think I really goofed on that exam..."

"What's that saying you often quote?...isn't it from *As You Like It*?"

"Sweet are the uses of adversity... And you're right, I'm glad I told him I'd do it. Now I must get busy and think of an *A* menu."

At each performance, the 'wedding feast' was served to sixteen paying 'guests', who sat at four small tables placed around the stage. For eight nights, Jeanne and Norma worked backstage, fashioning 'birds of paradise' from fresh pineapple halved, scooped out, then stuffed with fruit and nut morsels. Plywood heads, made and painted by Harry, were placed opposite the tail-feathered foliage. On four Lazy Susans, a pair of 'birds' nested on a bed of endive, surrounded by bite-sized glazed ham squares, cheese, fresh coconut meat, sauteed banana slices rolled in ground nutmeats, and tiny muffins. The play and the feast were a rousing success.

The two women worked together in other ways. For their Biology class they memorized such things as the reproductive systems of flatworms and the excretory system of the protozoan. Dr. Moffit seemed obsessed with test questions based on minutia instead of broad principles of plant and animal life. The very sight of the textbook made them ill. Their Shakespeare class was another matter. They loved to fit quotes from the plays under study into their own life situations such as Iago's "Put money in they purse" after getting change in the cafeteria line. Or King Lear's "Nothing will come from nothing" when they didn't get around to studying. From Hamlet, "Oh, that this too solid flesh would melt" if they gained a pound or two. MacBeth's "Out damned spot! Out I say!" when their sons came home with grass stains on their trousers from playing in the ice plant.

The Shakespeare final was scheduled at the same hour as Anne's sixth grade promotion. Norma asked if she might take it early. Mrs. Fitzpatrick had another solution and asked her to identify quotes on the spot, then excused her from taking the exam. Norma exclaimed to Harry, "It was as if she'd been there when we studied. She asked the quotes I knew best."

Harry smiled, "I think it was because you knew them all."

Six nights after Anne's promotion, Norma marched to *Pomp and Circumstance* to receive her Associate in Arts degree in English and the permanent gold pin and certificate from Alpha Tau Chapter, Alpha Gamma Sigma for excellent scholarship. Her name was one of two from SDJC placed on the Alpha Gamma Sigma State Honor Roll which included recognition for extracurricular activities. She thought Harry might explode from pride, Anne and Charles cheered, and she smiled out to them with joy and gratitude. She couldn't have done it without their help.

With no more than a weekend of rest, she matriculated to San Diego State College, declared a major of Elementary Education, and took a summer school class. When it ended, she began extending the back yard patio deck with cement blocks, widening it by a foot every week. Each Saturday they bought a supply of blocks for her next week's work.

In September, instead of joining Norma at State College as planned, Harry took part-time employment at the two Clairemont shopping centers as a security guard and to control the kids who sped though on bicycles and skateboards. The business manager, a former Marine, had advertised for a retired Marine expecting brawn to do the job. Harry soon gained the friendship of the offenders and the problem ceased. The job extended to other duties with an appropriate increase in salary. Harry bought a new Hillman and once again Norma had the exclusive use of the Mayflower.

On December 4, 1959 Norma drove home from State College thinking of Julia's new son born just ten days ago: Clarence Cort Brown. Her mind was on her new nephew but her eyes followed the dark smoke cloud hovering in the sky so close to where she would turn north to go home. She hoped it wasn't from a fire, a house fire...her house! Suddenly alarmed, she made the turn and met a road block two streets from home. A policeman let her pass after seeing proof that she lived in the neighborhood. Arriving home she saw a note taped to the front door. It directed her to a neighbor's house where Charles was resting. He had witnessed a jet from Miramar crash into the canyon just beyond the school fence and burst into roaring flames. He had been alone putting up the volley ball nets when the plane swooped low enough for him to see the pilot's face as it passed over the school playground. Weeks later, he still had nightmares and told his parents he didn't want to be a pilot anymore when he grew up.

The community, shocked, afraid, and grateful, had high praise for Lt. Albert Joe Hickman, the Navy flier who had stayed with his plane, guiding it away from homes and school at the expense of his own life. The Board of Education passed a resolution to name a future school in his honor.

35

1960. A new decade, but the same old grind for everyone. School, school, school, and work. Norma had four classes as usual. Two were a snap for her, being a wife for fifteen years and a parent for fourteen made her somewhat of an authority in "Marriage and Family Relations" and "Child Growth and Development." The music class was her downfall; she couldn't play the tonebells nor flutophone which every elementary teacher was expected to master and teach to students. Theory, she knew up one side and down the other, but to play anything other than the record player was beyond her ability. Yet her children were excelling in music. Anne played the violin in the school orchestra and sang with the Girls Advanced Chorus in Hale Junior High School which had cut a record for San Diego City Schools. Charles, new to the piano, was already in a recital. Norma justified her musical deficiencies by saying, "I gave my musical talent to Anne and Charles!"

Her fourth class was Advanced Shakespeare, and because of the reputation of Dr. Johnson's unsurpassed expertise, Norma had planned her semester schedule around this course. However, she wasn't privileged to see the professor for almost three weeks; he didn't appear at the first class meeting nor the second. He was ill and rumor said that the class would be canceled; but students attended class, even without a teacher. This had worked in the past. Everyone said that, in time, Dr. Johnson would return and he was worth the wait. Two weeks passed: six class sessions. Students came and remained, signing attendance sheets, sitting and waiting. The third week Dr. Johnson shuffled in. A large grizzly man, in need of a haircut, his suit wrinkled and baggy, hoisted himself upon the edge of the stage platform and sat with his legs dangling. Crossing one arm over the other, leaning back to balance himself, and gazing across the room to some spot over the heads of the breathless students, he began to speak. His deep sonorous voice poured forth words like a steady stream of precious jewels. The hour was magical and when it ended, Dr. Johnson slid from the ledge and shuffled out the door. No one moved until he was gone. His lecture had been a feast for the senses; it couldn't be described, only experienced, though Norma tried to share it with Harry.

Every class meeting was the same. Dr. Johnson never acknowledged the presence of anyone. Norma wondered if he knew they were there. He entered, gave his lecture to the spellbound students, and left. At exam time, he didn't appear. Test papers were laid on the stage ledge, where he usually sat, to be picked up, written, and turned over to the lady who sat ready to collect them at the end of the hour.

Norma wasn't sure whom she admired more: Dr. Johnson or William Shakespeare. From the mouth of one the pen words of the other took on a meaning and life unthought of before and evoked a near religious experience in the listeners. Once she had thought that people who revered the great Bard were a bit 'off'. Well, now, *she* was a bit 'off' herself. Her enjoyment was further extended through discussions with Harry of the broad, comprehensive impact of this sixteenth century genius on humanity, whether or not it was recognized or acknowledged.

Admittance to the Education Department required clearance by two staff psychologists. Norma's interviews were scheduled with affable Dr. Strom and the much feared, meticulous, unfriendly Dr. Singer. "How could you be so unlucky?" her fellow education majors asked with obvious sympathy for her, "He hates women you know!"

Don't let that influence you. Judge for yourself after you meet him.

She met first with Dr. Strom, a short, jovial man who was comfortable with himself, and Norma felt comfortable with him. His first question: "Are you a native Californian, Mrs. Kipp?"

"No, I'm a transplant from Georgia, born in Alabama."

"Alabama, you say! So, what do you think of George Wallace?"

"Not much," Norma laughed.

"Is that so? May I ask why?"

"Because of his stand on segregation...of all the southern governors, he's the worst." *I hope he doesn't like George Wallace.*

"Aren't you a southerner, though?"

"Yes, but not a typical one. I moved from the south a few years ago because of it. I never understood why colored people had to be treated differently than white people. As a child I lived near and played with colored children and I was embarrassed by the way they were treated. No one ever explained the reason to me...at least not to my satisfaction."

"Then you must be following the events in Arkansas with a great deal of interest," Dr. Strom asked.

"Yes, and in Tennessee also. Up until now there haven't been any riots in Alabama because the colored there are so cowed they wouldn't dare oppose white rule...so far. But I think that when there is a showdown, it will be even more violent than what we're seeing in Arkansas, Tennessee, or Mississippi. I don't know what will happen in Georgia. And I'm disappointed that there is segregation here."

"How do you mean?"

"Well, colored people can't buy houses where they want to. When we bought our house five years ago, the realtor noticed our Georgia car tags. He said we didn't need to worry that we'd have black neighbors because they weren't selling to them in Clairemont. Isn't that illegal?"

"It's only segregation in schools that's illegal," Dr. Strom reminded her.

"Doesn't segregation in housing result in segregation in schools?"

"Of course, and that needs to be addressed sooner or later."

"The sooner the better then," Norma said heatedly. A pause followed and she wondered if she had been too outspoken.

Then, "How far into the program are you, Mrs. Kipp?"

"I lack thirty units. I'm late getting interviewed through no fault of my own. I'm counting on being accepted." She looked at him confidently.

"And you have no reason to think otherwise. I wish you every success in your teaching career, Mrs. Kipp."

Norma thanked him and floated out of his office and down the hall to Dr. Singer's office. *One down and one to go!* The door was open and she went inside to sit in a chair beside a desk with a completely bare top. Dr. Strom's had been covered with papers! Minutes later, Dr. Singer strode in, frowning, waving Norma back into her chair on his way to a filing cabinet. Removing a folder, he stood thumbing through its contents. She noted his exceptional good looks, tall and lean, classic features...but why such a scowl? He closed the folder with a snap and placed it upon his desk. He sat. "It's *Mrs.* Kipp, I see." His intense brown eyes settled on her.

"Yes, I'm married." *He wishes he didn't have to interview me.* "For fourteen years."

"Twice the seven-year itch," he said with a twisted smile.

"I beg your pardon?" Norma asked.

"Nothing..., just thinking out loud. Any offspring from this union?"

"Two". *How very formal. Let him ask the gender.* He didn't.

Instead, "Tell me why you think you want to be a teacher," sitting with a straight back, hands before him on the desk, fingertips touching.

He's more nervous than I am! "I don't think, Dr. Singer, I know. Wanting to be a teacher has been a goal for as long as I can remember. My younger siblings were my first students, as well as their playmates and mine. And now my own children. It's been almost a compulsion..." she laughed at the quick lift of his eyebrows, "I should be careful with that word, shouldn't I? I'll change it to *certainty,* a given, that someday, I would be a teacher for hire, although it's taken an unusually long time to arrive at the point of sitting in this chair. Other things intervened, equally important things." Her voice was as steady as her eyes.

"You refer to marriage and a family? And you believe you can manage both along with a career in teaching?" His voice was almost challenging.

"Teaching can't be more demanding than college, can it?" she asked earnestly, breaking into a confident smile. "And I've managed so far, thank you."

"I see." He said it slowly. "Tell me, how does your husband feel about this goal of yours?"

"He's in agreement with it." Her smile widened.

"How does this agreement manifest itself?" He leaned forward a bit.

"Actually, it was his idea that I started when I did, while our children were so young. He's retired and his help has relieved me of some parental responsibility. Our children are in no way neglected or deprived by my absence in the day or my studying at night. On the contrary, I think it proves to them that it's not just rhetoric when I say education is important."

"What is your husband's educational background?"

"Three years of college in all and..."

He interrupted, "No degree, then?"

"Yes, an Associate in Arts in English and when I finish my education, he plans to return for a Bachelor's degree."

"Until then, do you think he might feel...threatened?"

She burst out laughing, "We don't threaten each other! And you don't know my husband. With all the education in the world I could never get smarter than he is, or even as smart. Every time I learn something new and tell him, I discover he already knows it."

"I see." Interest replaced indifference in his attitude, and he shifted his position to lean against the chair back, placing his arms on the side rests. "Well, good." He cleared his throat. "Now tell me what you expect to be doing ten years from now."

"I expect to be teaching during the school year, baby-sitting my grandchildren, and traveling in the summer months when I'm not taking classes. But we won't wait until I begin teaching; we're already planning to spend summers in Guadalajara, Mexico. My husband speaks Spanish, our daughter is studying it, and our son and I can learn on the spot, so to speak. But first, we'll go to the Hawaiian Islands, a place my husband has been promising to take me for a long time."

"A cruise, perhaps?"

"Oh, no. We'll fly. Definitely."

"Definitely, you say. Why so emphatic?"

"Because I'm afraid of ships!" she shivered.

"Afraid?" He studied her. "Why?"

She frowned, "I don't know. I honestly don't know. It's silly, but about ten years ago when my husband hung a picture of a sailing ship in stormy waters under heavy clouds in our living room, I couldn't bear to look at it, even though I'd never been on a ship or even seen one."

"What happened to the picture?"

"We replaced it--with the scene of a colorful fishing village."

"A safe harbor?"

"I suppose."
"And you're not afraid of flying?"
"No."
"Many people are," he said thoughtfully. "Now tell me what do you do for recreation?"
"Would you believe I read, despite all my classes?"
"What book has had the most impact on your life?"
"The Bible," she laughed at his surprised expression, "although not for the reasons you might suppose. But for good or bad, it's the book that has touched my life more than any other."
"What are you currently reading?" His gaze fell on the book beneath her purse. She gave it to him. "*Wind, Sand, and Stars* by Antoine de Saint Exupèry..." His voice caressed the words. He looked up to meet her eyes, "Are you enjoying it?"
"Very much, but I'm returning it to the library. I've renewed it once; now I must give it up." She blushed, "I like having it in my possession. Exupèry takes me along with him into the heavens as he shares his bond with the natural elements, his aircraft, crew, comrades, and devotion to his mission."

Dr. Singer held the book lightly, his eyes upon it, then on her. "You're extremely introspective, wouldn't you agree?" His voice did not seem at all disapproving.

"Yes, I am guided by my feelings. Whenever we have doubts about something, my husband will say, 'Don't tell me what you *think*, tell me what you *feel*'. My feelings have never let me down; he trusts them, too."

Returning the book, he asked, "I wonder, Mrs. Kipp, is there a single cloud in your sky?"

Norma looked at him thoughtfully, "Not unless you put one there, Dr. Singer."

"I shan't," he replied, his eyes friendly.

"Then, I'm grateful." She stood, shook his hand, then left his office.
He isn't to be feared, and that expression he wears: it's pain. I saw it lift when we were talking of Saint Exupèry. I wonder if Dr. Singer is a pilot.

36

Norma thumbed through the mail for her spring grades. The same story: A's and the lone B. "I can't break the jinx," she groaned. Another envelope was addressed to Norma A.

"Go on, open it!" Harry commanded, an impish grin creasing his face.

She pulled out a road map of the United States with Route 66 drawn in a wide red line going east until it ended in a circle around Gatlinburg. "I've managed to talk my way into four weeks off, beginning around the middle of July. Do you think we could be ready to leave by then?"

They were ready, even before. On the night of July 10, under the light of the waning full moon, the Mayflower was sailing along Highway 395 en route to Hinkley, and a few days later, it began its second voyage to Georgia. The Democratic Party National Convention was in session and every night in their motel rooms, they watched the highlights on television. Harry reminded Norma of John's prediction in 1948: Keep your eye on the mayor of Minneapolis; he's going straight to the top.

That mayor was now Senator Hubert H. Humphrey and one of four candidates nominated for president from the Democratic Party. Norma and Harry hoped he would win, but he didn't. The youngest of the four, John F. Kennedy of Massachusetts, was chosen with Lyndon B. Johnson of Texas filling the number two spot. The Kipps arrived in La Fayette to hear Daddy ranting and raving, "A Catholic *and* a Yankee representing the Democratic Party for the president of the United States of America. What is the world coming to?"

Mama was on the telephone summoning the Browns and Scoggins to the 'home place' as everyone called the Clinton house. Julia arrived first with her boys. She and Norma rushed to meet in the driveway, catching each other in a tight embrace, rocking back and forth in joyful greeting. Eighteen month old Cort hung on his mother's legs. Norma stooped to look into his little face with its wide-set eyes and broad forehead, the set of his jaw, and thought he could pass for her son. Then she saw Kipp, a tall boy for his four years, the very image of his mother at that age. He stole her heart just as Julia had.

Max and Joan arrived and Phil and Greg jumped from their Volkswagon Beetle, as soon as the doors were flung open, to greet their California cousins. Joan was heavier, saying she had put on the weight

Max had lost. She explained that cotton mill work was sapping him of his strength and he needed a rest. Except for the vacation two years ago when they went to San Diego, he hadn't had any time off work since Greg was born seven years ago. When Norma and Harry had a chance to talk alone, they agreed to invite Joan and Max to accompany them to Gatlinburg if Mama would keep the kids, and if Max could get a day off from work.

Daddy showed off the 'new' Methodist Church he'd helped to build, though it was now four years old. Norma supposed he had forgotten that she and Harry had opposed the building of it. And she wasn't surprised to see the 'old' church still standing--intact, roof and all--and still housing the worshipers of the group that bought it. The stately old brick building looked the same except that the huge white columns in front, four of them, needed a coat of paint.

Norma was surprised to see Mary Lee's brown hair bleached to a golden blond, a decided improvement, and almost identical to Anne's natural hair color. At seventeen, Mary Lee had three interests in life: her hair, clothes, and boys. Clothes were almost an obsession. She had dozens of dresses, skirts, and blouses Mama had made for her. Sometimes she changed outfits twice a day. And boys. Yes, she was permitted to date even though she was still in school. But times had changed. The Sixties were not the Forties, and Daddy's ideas must have changed also, Norma decided.

Mary Lee's interests held scant fascination for Anne. Although three years younger than Mary Lee and nine than Julia, it was to Julia that Anne turned for companionship. Both loved swimming and dancing and neither was concerned with getting her hair wet, and both were feather light on their feet.

One evening the Browns and the Kipps picnicked at Lake Winnepesaukeh, afterward taking canoe rides on the lake, then climbing aboard the Madd Mouse, a giant roller coaster, that snaked its way over a course leading ever skyward and then after a sharp turn plunged downward with such speed that it took their breath away. Norma screamed like a teenager and to everyone's delight it got them a few extra turns. The children were thrilled, never realizing her genuine terror.

Next came the three day trip to the Smokies for the Kipps and the Scoggins. Gatlinburg was crowded with tourist attractions, and tranquillity and beauty were to be found only within the park where commercialism was prohibited. The long drive among the dense trees and beside the rushing stream to Cade's Cove soothed their ruffled spirits. The well preserved remnants of pioneer life were pleasing to see, but it was back to the crowded restaurant they had to go for dinner. Harry insisted on individual rooms, hang the expense. What was a vacation for, he asked Norma, if they couldn't be alone, especially here where it had all begun for them nearly fifteen years ago? So the couples were together by day; at night they went separate ways. And when Harry closed the door behind them he said, "Well, here we are, Honeychild...now what?..." his face wearing a rakish grin, his eyes promising as he drew her to him.

With downcast eyes, she replied demurely, "Oh, my, I can't imagine..." as her fingers began to unbutton his shirt.

At breakfast, Norma, dressed in flats, shorts, and a sleeveless blouse, was surprised to see Joan in heels and hose and wearing a dress. "Have you changed your mind about hiking?" she asked, inspecting the menu.

"Oh, no," Joan smiled, "I'm still goin'. I don't get many chances to really dress up. I thought this would be a good one."

Norma looked at Harry and knew what he was thinking. Some hike this was going to be. Heels and hose on the trail. It was already hot at nine in the morning and Joan had a problem with heat, yet her dress had a high collar and three-quarter length sleeves. Joan explained, "Our church forbids bare legs, bare arms and throats." A half hour into the hike, she found a shady spot near a stream and sat while the others continued on the trail. In the afternoon the four explored the air-conditioned art galleries and gift shops where Joan bought for Norma her choice of a little brown Pigeon Forge ceramic wren and Norma bought for Joan her choice: a colorful ceramic rooster.

After an early dinner, and alone again, Norma and Harry took another flight into glory. Later, glowing in the pleasure of each other, their hearts calm again, she exclaimed, "It does get better, doesn't it? I can't believe that my love can grow bigger and bigger with each passing year, but it does! It almost frightens me. Do I deserve this much from life?"

"You deserve all you can get, and the wonderful thing is that your happiness spills over to me. Our happiness increases by what it feeds on." Gentle laughter lifted the corners of his lips." Who said that, Honeychild?"

"I'll give you three guesses!" She challenged, sitting on her haunches on the bed, extending three fingers.

He stood, drew his 'six-shooter', and took aim, "Mr. Dillon?"

"Oh, Harry! No!" She exclaimed, lowering one finger.

"Chester?" He limped around the bed with one leg stiff.

"Be serious! I know you know. And this is your last guess."
"I've got it! It's Zorro," with an imaginary sword making a Z in the air.
"No, and your three guesses are used up." She sprang toward the head of the bed.
"Just one more! It's my rival...that man, what's his name? Spearhead? No, I've got it. Don't throw that pillow! It's Shakespeare!"

On Saturday evening the two couples saw "Unto These Hills" telling of the eviction of the Cherokee Nation from their homeland, by order of President Jackson, and the thousand-mile forced march from Tennessee to Oklahoma. The performance evoked such rage, shame, and sorrow that at the end, the four walked to their hotel rooms in silence. Inside, Norma looked from their balcony one last time for the moon. "There isn't one, not even the tiniest little sliver." Turning to Harry she asked, "Do you know where the moon goes when it's hidden from us--according to Indian lore?"

"No, my little Cherokee, but I know you're going to tell me. Right?"

"I am. The Moon is wife to Sun Man, but they are usually apart since he travels by day and she travels by night Only once a month do they come together. And at the time we call New Moon, she is being filled with the potency of his light in order to grow full and give her own light to earth creatures at the Full Moon. When they are finished communing, the tiny crescent can be seen beside a faint image of that full moon disc. That's what I was looking for tonight."

Harry eyed her with interest, "And you didn't see it?" He asked.

"No."

"Then don't look any more. What's good enough for the Sun and Moon is good enough for us earthlings. Come here, Moonchild, I want to commune with you!"

On their return to La Fayette, Harry planned to go by way of Dayton, Tennessee where *Inherit the Wind* was premiering. Joan said she and Max couldn't possibly go to a movie, certainly not on Sunday; that would be a double sin. "I'd really like to see the movie," Norma said, "Do you think you two could find something else to do while Harry and I go? It's historical, you know, about the Scopes trial that took place there in 1925 in this very month too. It would be a shame to miss it since we're here where it actually happened."

"You mean it's about the monkey trial?" Max's interest picked up.

"It's sometimes called that," Harry answered, and with a wink at

Norma he took the road to Dayton. Joan and Max talked it over in the back seat and by the time Harry parked near the theater, they had decided that God would approve of them seeing this movie. It would be like going to church to see the trial of the heretic who had taught in public school that man had descended from monkeys and lost.

Spencer Tracy as Henry Drummond (Clarence Darrow) was magnificent and Fredrick March as Matthew Harrison Brady (William Jennings Bryan) was brilliant. Brady's answers to Drummond's skillful questioning discredited fundamentalist dogma and severely weakened the literal interpretation of the Bible on which Joan and Max based their faith. When the movie ended, Norma dreaded to hear their reaction. To her amazement, they were not offended. Instead they thought the film defined and substantiated their belief. Their elation was unlimited. With emotion Max thanked them, "It was truly God's will for us to see the movie. You were His hand servant making it possible."

Norma accepted their thanks with relief but wondered how four people could see the same movie and interpret it so differently, asking Harry about it later. "That was the film's message," he explained. "Bryan said, 'I am more interested in the rock of ages than the age of rocks', and he had quite a following in his opposition to scientific findings which appear to challenge that dogma. Drummond's quarrel was with sects like that which keep knowledge from their members, telling them precisely what to think, setting boundaries on the human brain. But people are sometimes lazy and see only what they want to see."

"That's scary," she frowned, "is that what 'bending the truth' means?"

"Possibly. Most people tend to define truth from their own experience and need. What else can they do?"

"You mean that truth is not absolute? It depends on..."

"If you had taken that Philosophy class you avoided at all costs, you'd have someone besides Shakespeare to quote. Voltaire, for instance. He said something like 'there are truths that are not for all men nor for all occasions'."

"Do you believe that?"

"I think one has to search for the truth, not take anything on face value or accept anything unconditionally." He was silent for a time, as she was, then he sought her eyes, a twinkle in his, "Can you bear another quote? This one from your man Truman who said, 'I never give 'em hell. I just tell the truth and they think it's hell'."

*   *   *   *

Departing for San Diego, the Kipp's stop in Crossville was saddened by Toby Godwin's news that her dreaded fear was now a reality; she had breast cancer, the disease that had taken both her sister and mother. Everyone placed great hope in her treatment soon to begin at Bethesda Naval Hospital. There was good news in Memphis. Tom Ellis was now five-state district manager for General Motors' Oldsmobile division; B. G. was teaching elementary school.

Crossing the western deserts, Norma and Charles became ill from the searing heat and they decided then and there to never again buy a car without air-conditioning. In Tucson, Charley's swamp cooler revived Norma but Charles required medical attention. Along with heat prostration, he suffered from a poison ivy rash acquired from rolling in the vine along the creek bank behind Grandmother's house on a dare from Phil and Greg. By the time they arrived in Hinkley, Charles presented a pitiful sight as he climbed from the back seat of the car covered from head to foot with calamine lotion and eyes swelled shut. At the end of a week he was recovered and Butch gave the credit to Hinkley well-water spiked with a dab of home brew. Anne said it was from Aunt Dolly's good chow. Norma and Harry thought it came from Condo love so liberally given. Charles said that wherever it came from, he wanted more.

On the drive home, Harry caught Charles' eye in the rear view mirror. "It's been a rough trip, hasn't it, Bub?"

"Kind of," Charles agreed, meekly, hunching forward in the seat. "Dad, I've been wondering...could God be punishing me with the poison ivy rash?"

"No, Charles, I think you got the rash because you took a foolish dare. We all must assume responsibility for our actions and not blame hardships and suffering on God."

"Is that why we don't go to church anymore?"

Norma waited for Harry to answer, but he remained silent. Charles added, "Phil and Greg say we don't believe in God."

"And what was your reply?" Harry asked.

"That we do, that we pray to Him."

Anne spoke up, "They said that if we really believed in God, we'd go to church to worship Him. And because we don't go, we're gonna burn in hell when we die, just like that preacher said that used to come to my school in La Fayette."

"That's what their parents are teaching them," Harry pointed out. "But we aren't teaching you that."

"But aren't you afraid of going to hell?" Charles asked nervously.

"No. Hell's right here on earth."

"It's not a place, but a state of mind," Norma added.

"State of mind?" Both asked, "What's that?"

"It's the way you feel about yourself, life, and other people. And as long as you can talk to God, you don't have to fear hell," Norma explained.

"Phil and Greg say that the only thing that keeps people from going to hell is believing in Jesus Christ, and you learn that only in church," Charles repeated.

Norma asked, "Who brought up the subject of hell? They? or you?"

"They did, 'cause they couldn't go to church when Aunt Joan and Uncle Max were in Gatlinburg with you," Anne said.

"But they could have gone with Granddaddy," Norma reminded them.

"I know, he asked them. They said it wasn't their church."

"Then, it's just their church that offers protection from hell?" Harry asked.

"I guess so," Charles concluded.

Norma turned to face Anne and Charles, asking softly, "Do you want to go to church? Is that what this is all about? Of course you may go, to any church you choose. We want you to learn about all the ways people believe, that's why we encourage you to go to church with your friends, why we bought *Great Religions of the World* for you to read. We don't want to limit you to our beliefs, and by the time you're on your own, you should be able to choose a faith for yourself. Right now, you say prayers. Do you think they are heard?"

"Yes," Charles said. Anne nodded.

"May I add my two-cents worth?" Harry asked. "There are three kinds of people: those who go to church and enjoy the comforts of the teachings, those who go to church and tell everyone else they and they alone have the answers and all others are wrong, and the third kind is like your mother and me. We don't belong to a specific group, but we nevertheless have beliefs we live by. You have been taught those beliefs. There are many paths to God. I won't tell you which to choose, but I will tell you this: Beware of those who tell you their path is the only path."

"And remember," Norma added, "You live in a country where choosing for yourself is possible. It was founded on the freedom to choose, and we want you to use that freedom."

"I'm hungry," Anne said. "Can we stop and eat? You know, food for the flesh, Mom, now that we've had food for the soul!"

"Yeah," Charles laughed, "Do they have a Jack in the Box in San Bernadino?" and looking around he said, "There!Up ahead...I see a pointed cap. Good timing, Anne, " he said, wiping his forehead.

"Smart alecks!" Norma said.

37

On January 20, 1961, in twenty-two degree weather in the nation's capital, John F. Kennedy was inaugurated as the thirty-fifth president of the United States. And in seventy degree weather in San Diego, Harry planted a five foot Monterey pine, their 1960 Christmas tree, in the northeast corner of their back lot. They were told it would grow to forty feet. In the northwest corner, he built a low terrace from which to view the patio. He joined the two corners with his United Nations planter of trees from Africa, Italy, Australia, Japan, and the United States. There were now twenty trees growing on their property and two bougainvillea vines climbing to the patio roof. Norma's patio deck was now twenty by twelve. She planned to add ten feet more to the twelve, then connect the finished deck to the terrace with a curved walk way.

An Easter visit to Twenty-nine Palms found the Earneys 'warming' up to their new duty station in the desert where Jerry's cactus garden was in brilliant bloom. Bill and Harry debated over the length of time each thought Fidel Castro would remain in power after his takeover in Cuba. Bill gave him one year: Harry said four. They made a bet of five dollars and in 1965 one or the other would collect.

"So, you've taken up gambling?" Norma teased on their drive home.

"And I'm making another bet," he nodded, "You'll get your straight A's before you finish college."

"And I'll bet you're going to have sore hands from gripping the steering wheel so tightly," she observed.

"It's this awful vibration. And it's getting worse with every mile, especially at freeway speed. You haven't noticed? It's unsafe, and if it can't be corrected, we'll have to scrap it."

"No! not my Mayflower!" Norma cried. "I want it to last until I finish college and get a job. Then we can use it for going to the market. It's really a good car."

"Good, yes," he agreed, "except for the vibration, probably resulting from the accident we had four years ago." At an intersection near Junior College one morning on their way to class, a driver had run a red light. Harry's swerve to the right had avoided a serious collision, but their left bumper had caught the right one of the offending car. The Mayflower's radiator was cracked and the car had to be towed to a garage. Its new radiator was paid for by the insurance company of the sailor from Tennessee. They had thought that was the only harm done to the car. Now, it was not repairable. Norma continued to drive it to State College, but not on the freeway. She found another way to go.

Charles went to sixth grade camp in April and returned in time to scratch his initials, along with the others, in the hardening cement Harry had poured for a sidewalk in front of the newly completed foyer addition. And Norma had her picture taken for the 1960-61 yearbook as a new member of Delta Phi Upsilon, National Honorary Fraternity of Early Education.

Last semester, Norma's student teaching had been in a first grade class; this semester in a gifted sixth grade class. She was asked to teach poetry to a group whose response was giggling and hooting. She didn't mention foot, line, and stanza but focused on feeling, telling the uncooperative students: "Think of poetry as the record of an experience the poet wanted to share."

It was helpful having her own sixth grader who said, "If they give you a hard time, Mom, remind them that songs are really poems and play some of my Presley records; that'll win them over for sure." Anne sat down and dashed off a Haiku: Poised on a fence top
my cat sits in silent pose
staring down at me.

Encouraged by their help, Norma gathered books of pioneering ballads, sea chanteys, and Negro spirituals to read to her class. Afterwards she primed them with stories evoking emotional and sensory reactions on which to base their own poetry. Exquisite verses poured forth from her students with an ease they hadn't expected, and Norma's cup of happiness overflowed. Her cup was about to overflow a second time. She was invited to go to school camp the first week in May. There, she was treated not as a student teacher but as a real teacher, bunking in the dormitory with them, supervising a table at mealtime and cleanup in the galley, planting seedling trees and helping construct an earthen dam, even taking a role in the talent show. For her the week was a peak experience and she couldn't wait to share it with her family.

On the Outside

The school bus returned ahead of schedule on Friday afternoon and Norma accepted a ride home from a parent. She was struggling with her camp gear in the driveway when Harry drove up. He leaped from the car calling, "Wait!" just as she raised the garage door. There sat a big Mercury Monterey in gleaming white splendor. Blinking in astonishment, she cried, "Where's my car? Harry, where's the Mayflower?"

In a few quick steps Harry was beside her, touching her arm, "Honeychild, I didn't want you to find out this way. I planned to prepare you, but you had left when I got to the school." His expression changed to joy, "But now that you've seen it, what do you think of your new car?"

She didn't trust herself to speak. *He's pleased. Pleased with this new piece of...machinery...but I'm not! I want my car...and it's gone...* Fumbling in her purse for the house keys, she unlocked the front door and ran inside, down the hall to their bedroom. Harry was close behind, his hands on her, drawing her to him, "Speak to me, Honeychild, if only to chew me out. I'm sorry. I never dreamed you'd react this way."

Anne and Charles came home from school running in to see their mother's reaction to her Mother's Day present. Harry herded them to the living room, explaining that she had been a bit more surprised than he expected and needed time to herself. They remained there until their mother came out to start supper. Harry intercepted her in the kitchen, "I'd planned to take us out to eat to celebrate your homecoming and ...the new car." He lifted her chin to look into her face. "Will you let me do that?" His voice pleaded, "Forgive me. It seems I've been thickheaded again."

Norma met his eyes looking disappointed, helpless. She had ruined his surprise, but darn it, he had no right to get rid of her car while she was gone. She couldn't hide her feelings and pretend to be happy with the new car, but she went to supper with him and the kids. No more was said about it until they were home alone, then Norma cried angrily, "You promised not to do anything about getting a new car while I was gone.You promised!" She hit the pillow with her fist, "If we had to get a new one, didn't you know I wanted us to do it together?"

"Believe me, Norma, I know it now. But also knowing how pressed you are for time, I thought I'd spare you some hassle. And I see also that I don't feel about cars the way you do." He took her face in his hands and looked into her eyes, and his were very serious. "Honeychild, the mechanic showed me the cause of the awful shimmying, where the frame was worn. He said it was a miracle that it hadn't broken apart. It was absolutely unsafe and I couldn't let you drive it another mile. And frankly, darling, I don't think you would have believed him. You think the Mayflower has special powers, but it's just a car. It's time had come. I'm thankful we discovered the problem when we did or perhaps," he drew a deep breath, "...the outcome could have been something I don't even want to think about..." He caressed her cheek with his fingertips, "Forgive *me,* Honeychild, and give the *car* a chance; it's a good one and it's safe for my precious wife to drive."

She forgave him, and quicker than she could forget her beloved Mayflower. And Harry was right, the new car was a good one and drove ever so smoothly. On June four when it was one month old, she noticed her initials beneath the handles of both front doors.

Norma's next teaching was a health unit on the body systems and their care. She took a projector and filmstrip home to show her family the harm that comes from cigarette smoking. The graphic pictures of damaged and diseased lungs had a sobering effect on everyone. Harry had already reduced his cigarette smoking and agreed to stop entirely. Anne and Charles vowed never to start.

In June, Norma was initiated into Kappa Delta Pi honorary education fraternity and awarded the Delta Phi Upsilon state scholarship. The family saw Charles promoted to junior high school. Jeanne Morton graduated from Junior College and moved to Marietta, Georgia where her husband would work with Lockheed Aircraft. In July, Tommy and Joyce, now living in Baldwin Hills, had another son. After a summer school class, Norma completed the rear patio paving and then wanted one corner of it dug up for a fire pit.

"I'll make a raised one, but I'm finished with digging," Harry held out his hands. "See these blisters? They're from digging through adobe for the eugenia hedge at the end of the patio and the trench for the Italian cypresses beside the west fence. That should do it for trees," he informed Norma with a salute. "We now have sufficient number to consume all the carbon dioxide we could possibly exhale." They compromised. Norma agreed to a raised fire pit and Harry built it in time to celebrate Anne's fifteenth birthday on August first with a wiener and marshmallow roast.

Two weeks later Mary Lee got married. She telephoned Norma an hour before the ceremony and cried all through the conversation. "I wonder if it's bride's jitters or something else," Norma asked after she hung up. "I had the feeling she wanted me to tell her not to do it."

"You think you should call her back?" Harry asked.

"No, if I did, Mama would say I'm trying to run her life. Besides I don't know where to call. Mary Lee said the ceremony was being held at a nearby ranch where Jimmy works. I'm hoping Mama and Daddy or Joan will see how upset she is and know something is not right."

In the fall semester of 1961-62, Norma's final student teaching assignment was at Eugene Field Elementary School where Anne had been a student for four years. It was a fourth grade class and as part of the study of "Living in Mexico", a native-speaking specialist taught Spanish an hour a day. Norma, along with her students, was learning the language she would use when her family spent summers in Mexico. *Oh, Fate, how kind you are! And please let my December seventh appointment with San Diego City Schools result in being hired for the coming school year.*

Harry insisted that she buy a complete outfit for the interview and on the seventh, he watched her dress in the dove gray suit and fasten the beaded choker that curved along the round neckline of her white silk blouse. Adding the matching earrings, she stood ready for inspection, "Well, do I look like a proper school teacher?"

He nodded approval, "That you do!" His eyes gleamed as he stepped close, "How about ditching that interview and staying here with me...I've a job offer that might interest you."

"I can feel it," she laughed. "But you can't be serious!"

"I am, damned serious...but my offer can wait...Come, *Maestra*, I'll drive you."

Four people at the Education Center were interviewing applicants for teaching positions, taking turns going down the list posted on the bulletin board. Norma sat upright in her chair, watching as names were crossed off the list, waiting her turn, anxiety dampening her hands. For five years she had worked for this moment, to be here in this room waiting to be interviewed. What would she be asked? Would she have the right answers? If she were hired, they'd have the summers free to travel and the money to fund it. Harry could return to school. They could enlarge the house. The kids would be assured of college if they wanted to go. And she would be a teacher! *Oh, please have a job for me.*

She heard her name! Startled, she looked at the tall, distinguished man standing at an open door with his hand extended. Like a robot she rose, walked into his office and sat in the chair he indicated. He smiled down at her with friendly eyes from his perch on the corner of his desk. "I'm Lester Warenbrock, Mrs. Kipp, and I'm very happy to be interviewing you."

I've heard of Dr. Warenbrock; he's assistant superintendent of San Diego City Schools. Am I dreaming?

"I've just been on the phone with Mrs. Clarke at Field School where you're doing your final semester of student teaching. She's very pleased with your work in Mrs. Swain's fourth grade class, and you could do us a big favor if you would take the class when you graduate next month."

I am dreaming, but what a wonderful dream! "Dr. Warenbrock, the class has a teacher."

"Only until the winter break. Mrs. Swain will be leaving the position and San Diego December 20. We'll hire a substitute to finish the semester. After that, the class can be yours."

I wondered why Mrs. Clarke came to observe me teach, now I know. I've prayed for a job, any job, but to be offered the class I already know... and love...this is incredible.

Dr. Warenbrock continued as if she needed further persuasion, "You could turn an unfortunate situation into a good one for the children. They've known you from September, and if you took the class, there would be a continuity, and they wouldn't suffer at all from this unfortunate set of circumstances. So, Mrs. Kipp, will you accept the position?"

"Will I?" Norma found her voice at last. "But I had no idea Mrs. Swain was leaving. Although I was wishing she would go somewhere...I won't say where..." her face flushed and she added quickly, "You see, she had required me to make lesson plans for the next Social Studies unit along with ordering films, filmstrips, and textbooks that I wouldn't even be there to use."

Dr. Warenbrock laughed heartily, "That was Mrs. Clarke's idea. Mrs. Swain felt badly to ask that of you. But now that you have done part of the work, will you do the rest and teach from those materials?"

"It will be my pleasure, my absolute pleasure!"

"We hoped to persuade you, so I took the liberty of making an appointment at the clinic for a physical tomorrow at four. Can you keep it on such short notice?" Seeing her nod of acceptance, he extended his hand. "After that, we'll issue the contract; you should receive it very soon. Good afternoon, Mrs. Kipp. Thank you and welcome to City Schools."

Norma almost ran from his office to the car where Harry waited. "We could have saved the expense of this new outfit." She kept a blank face for a full minute, then let joy burst through. "They planned to hire me all along!" She kissed him right there in the parking lot. "And guess where I'll be teaching? Right where I am in Room 29 at Field School."

At home, Harry watched with increasing interest as Norma removed her new suit and blouse and hung them in the closet. Next her slip and bra. With a flip of her foot, one black suede pump was off, then the other. He was undressing also. Her eyes were upon him as she bent to remove her hose and then she moved very close, almost touching him, in only her choker and earrings. Eyes locked, she knew before she asked what his answer would be, "Now about that offer you made earlier..."

With three deft movements of his hand, she was free of the jewelry. He closed the space between them, "I shouldn't tell you this, but I've always wondered what it would be like to make it with a school marm!"

"Oh, really?" She pressed into him, "I think you're about to find out."

On January 26, Norma completed the course work for a Bachelor of Arts degree and a general elementary credential. Harry won his bet; her grades for the first time were all A's. She was a full-fledged teacher, and construction on an addition to their house was in progress, soon to be completed. All her goals had been attained. The family was well and happy. For certain, all was well in their world.

In Room 29, the transition from Mrs. Swain to Mrs. Kipp went smoothly, only a matter of Norma going from half day to all day teaching and by putting into practice her personal philosophy of education: Responsibility, Relevancy, and Involvement. Her responsibility was to make the classroom environment conducive to learning and her lessons relevant to the students' lives, to promote visits in the children's home by the teacher and visits to the classroom by parents, and to send home weekly newsletters of classroom happenings. The children's responsibilities were to help make rules that insured fairness and harmony in their classroom relationships, to abide by those rules, and to know that something reasonable would happen if they did not. She asked that they perform daily tasks in classroom management, making it truly their own.

Another means of involvement was through her daily reading of literature, from classics to contemporary works. This reading and listening became a time of mutual involvement, a cohesive force developing and extending all the good things hoped for in a school relationship. Since the experience was non-evaluative, it showed her in another role and provided many topics for class discussion. It expanded awareness to vicarious involvement with people, situations, and places and the understanding that all people have problems and that problems are solved in many ways. Norma knew the value of reading to children, having seen it turn Anne and

Charles into avid readers. And her first choice, for the students in Room 29, had been their best-loved book *Little Britches* by Ralph Moody.

Other activities included the making of hand puppets to use in the Little Theater that Harry constructed. Her class gave shows for other classes who came to see stories from their reading books come to life. Valentines were made for blind children from textured wallpaper sample books and their verses were typed by two Braille transcribers who came to the classroom with their machines. From the school publication *Newstime*, her class performed for other classes adaptations of Shakespeare's "Hamlet" and "Julius Caesar", and Norma added almost a hundred new disciples to followers of the Bard.

At home, the house extension brought a visit from the next-door neighbors who from across their fence had watched with curiosity as the ten foot addition was framed, tar-papered, and stuccoed. When the huge corner fireplace was finished, they wanted to see it from inside. "Why, it dominates the room!" Cynthia exclaimed. "Where did you get such an idea, Norma?"

"From Frank Lloyd Wright," Harry answered for her, "he's Norma's current idol and he thinks a fireplace should be a family gathering place, a place for warmth of two kinds. That's what we have here; we all can sit on the raised hearth and be warmed by the fire at the same time."

Cynthia nodded absently, then moved from the fireplace to peer out the sliding glass door opening to the newly poured concrete deck that extended to Harry's landscaping. "Another Wright idea," Norma said, "to merge the inside with the outside, having a view of nature from every window and door..."

But the wood paneling covering the long wall had captured Cynthia's attention and she gave it the 'once over' before leaving for the master bedroom. There, Bill was examining the stretch of high, louvered windows on a side and end wall, the built-in closet with sliding doors, the plastered walls, the concrete floor...and questioning Harry, "Are you pleased with their work? and their price?"

"Completely," Harry responded with eagerness, "Baird's bid was the most reasonable one we got, and his terms were good. Twenty-five percent initially to cover materials and the balance thirty days after completion when the work passes city inspection."

"Then you would recommend them?" Cynthia asked.

"Definitely," he answered, puzzled by all the questions. Two days later, he understood. Work on their house stopped and began on the house next door. A week passed with not one workman coming to the Kipp job. The unfinished rooms were unusable, cold, and full of scrap material. Day after day, Norma came home from school to find the workman gone from next door and Harry gone to his job. After a week her anger mounted to spill out on Harry as he came into the house from work. "Why can't you do something to make them come back and finish *our* job?" she exploded. "I'm sick and tired of the mess and the cold air coming from those rooms. Their promised completion date is weeks overdue, as you well know!" She even stamped her foot.

Harry looked at her in surprise for a moment then answered, "I'm just as upset as you, and I can't make them do anything. I have tried. Baird doesn't return my phone calls; what more can I do? If you think you can do any better, you're welcome to try." His icy tone stopped her tirade on the spot. She went straight to the kitchen to put supper on the table. For the first time in their lives the Kipp family ate in silence.

Then Mother Nature intervened. Winter rain started and the work next door stopped. The workmen returned to finish the Kipp addition and by the 21st of February, the day before a school holiday, they cleared away their tools and scrap material and left for good. On George Washington's birthday, Norma and Harry began their work. She painted the walls and he painted the ceilings in the cold rooms. Next, he put a coat of Deft on the wood paneling. Two days later, and three more coats of Deft, the Philippine mahogany glowed with a soft luster. Norma hung drapes and Harry built the first fire. Everyone waited anxiously, but the chimney drew well. Not a whisper of smoke came into the room.

Soon it was cozy warm and "Gunsmoke" was showing on the television screen. Norma brought hot chocolate and date bars. All together, they toasted the new rooms then Anne and Charles toasted the 'truce' between their parents. "It really wasn't a war, just a skirmish," Harry said. "I guess we both overreacted to a bad situation. It's a poor excuse, but I just haven't been feeling my usual charming self."

"I don't have an excuse, except impatience," Norma said, "I'm truly sorry. Forgive me, everyone?"

Charles lifted his mug again, "At least now we know our Mom and Dad are human!"

Anne touched her mug to his, "And all's well that ends well. I beat you to it, Mom!" She laughed gleefully, quoting her mother's oft-used saying.

38

Norma went to school on Monday leaving Harry in bed, nursing a very painful back. Tuesday the pain worsened. "I guess it's from painting the ceilings," Harry concluded. The family doctor agreed and prescribed a muscle relaxant. Within a day the pain disappeared, along with February. March had arrived. The month of change and new beginnings. Norma recalled that last March the vibrations in the Mayflower precipitated the buying of a new car. It was now almost a year old and tonight would transport them to a nice restaurant for dinner. They wouldn't be going to the Stardust Room next to the Clairemont Bowling Alley for the corned beef and cabbage special at a dollar a plate or to the Tamale Factory in Old Town where they could look right into the kitchen where the tortillas were being made. Not that there was anything wrong with those places, but tonight they would splurge and she would pick up the bill. Because this March was bringing her first pay check!

By her orders, the others were waiting to climb into the Mercury when she drove into the driveway after work to take them to their favorite place in all of San Diego: the Cabrillo National Monument. There the old Point Loma lighthouse stood 462 feet above sea level, the highest point in the city. They often ate picnics in its shadow on the cliffs overlooking the bay. But not today. Today they only climbed the circular stairway to the top for the most spectacular harbor view in the world, and to watch the sun set. Carrying the sight with them, they began the downhill drive through Fort Rosecrans National Cemetery winding among the thousands of small, white headstones, marching in arrow straight rows over the hillsides on both sides of the road, silent sentinels in tribute to the sacrifice of the nation's fallen warriors. From the back seat Charles asked, "Dad, do you know anyone that's buried here?"

"Not personally, Charles, at least not that I'm aware of."

"Will you be buried here? I mean...when you die...uh, if you die..." Charles stammered. "You're a veteran so I thought...no offense, Dad."

"None taken, Son. But no, I won't be buried here, dead or alive!" Harry laughed softly.

Norma shivered, and Anne glared at Charles, "He wants to be buried with Mom, silly."

"She could be buried here, as well as you and Charles," Harry said. "If I applied for it, I'd be assigned a plot and whoever of us died first would be buried first, and then so on..."

"You mean we'd be buried in layers?" Anne asked incredulously.

"That's the way it's done, but your mother and I have decided to be cremated when we check out about fifty years from now. It's all been arranged so you and Charles won't have to deal with it in your old age." Harry winked at Norma, "Right, Honeychild?"

"Right. So you can relax for the next fifty years." Norma gave Anne a reassuring smile. They were out of the cemetery and back on Rosecrans Street. At the intersection of Midway Drive, Norma turned right and parked at the Chuck Wagon. Inside with menus in hand she said, "Don't even look at the price. It's steak for everyone, and I'm paying!"

Harry raised his water glass, "Here's to the new wage earner, and to Guadalajara. Perhaps, if we don't eat up your mother's first pay check, we can start our savings for a visit there this summer." Turning to Anne, *"Hija, quieres ir conmigo y tu Mamá a Guadalajara en julio?"*

"Sí, Papa, yo quiero ir."

Then to Charles, *"Y tú, Carlos, quieres ir tambien?"*

"Sí, padre, me gusteria mucho." Charles was in first year Spanish.

"Entonces, nos iremos." Harry nodded to Norma who rebuked them laughingly, "Show-offs!"

While Anne and Charles made selections on the jukebox, Harry asked solemnly, "Honeychild, can you possibly know how proud I am of you?"

"Enough, I hope, to make up for my causing us to move back and forth across the country, selling two houses, bringing financial loss."

"There was nothing to forgive. We were just searching for our happiness...and it was worth any price. And speaking of happiness, I'm happy that my back pain is gone. I didn't want to worry you, but I was plenty worried. I thought many times of Senator Sam Rayburn; his back pain turned out to be fatal."

Harry's was a prophetic thought because when the muscle relaxant prescription ran out, his pain returned, more intense than before. Doctor Morris wanted to examine him again before renewing the prescription. Instead Harry went to Balboa Naval Hospital. Norma came home from school to find him waiting, sitting at the dining room table, staring into space. "Did you get something for the pain?"

"Yes," he sighed deeply, "I got something for the pain." He leaned his head against her breast and his arms encircled her waist.

She stroked his forehead, moist from perspiration on this cold day. "Good. What did the doctor say was causing it?"

Harry raised his head and looked at her with the saddest expression she had ever seen on his face. "What is it? Harry, what's wrong? Don't tell me it's a slipped disk?"

"Sit down, Honeychild." Pain dulled his usual bright eyes and his voice sounded flat. "The doctor wants me in the hospital; he's ordered all kinds of tests. And a deep needle biopsy."

"A biopsy?" Alarm spread over her features and her voice rose with every syllable. "Why? What for? Where? Tell me, what did he *say*?"

"He said he was sorry," Harry replied grimly.

"He's *sorry*?" She repeated, then screeched, "*He's sorry*?"

"That's all he said." Harry handed her a folder of papers. "Here. You can read what he wrote."

Dr. Craven had written, *I'm afraid it's Big C.*

"Big C. What on earth is Big C?" But she knew. Every cell in her brain screamed CANCER and her throat swelled shut. Her tongue couldn't say the hateful word. *And I won't think it either.* She became a walking, talking, cooking, eating, teaching robot, her mind frozen--refusing to thaw.

At school, Norma's class made kites and flew them one windy day from the playground. March! That month of change. Norma felt the kite string, pulled and tugged at by the wind, and she felt pulled and tugged herself by some invisible force. The kite remained aloft, dipping, rising, soaring. Last month her spirit soared; would it ever soar again? But maybe, the doctor was wrong. He had said only, "I'm afraid".

Easter came early with school vacation the week before. Harry spent four days in the hospital and then they made their promised visit to Hinkley. Norma looked forward to the comfort they always found with Butch and Dolly, their very dearest friends, and the healing power of the desert sun. They needed healing; but first they would have to reveal the reason for their need of it. Harry broke the news of his probable prostate cancer; she couldn't speak the words. The biopsy report was not back, but X-rays and manual examination indicated cancer with metastasis to the spine; it was inoperable and terminal, prognosis six months. Butch and Dolly were as stunned as they had been. Nobody could believe that Harry's life was so threatened; he looked the picture of health, like that of a man much younger than his fifty-nine years.

They waited three weeks more for the biopsy report. It came back positive: advanced adenocarcinoma. Harry's acceptance was stoic; like that of the farmer whose crop is ruined by locusts or storm. It wasn't done 'on purpose' to annoy him; it is neither for nor against him. He accepted it as he would any other occurring event of nature. His objectivity allowed him to remain apart from it. His body might be ill, but his mind remained healthy. But Norma could not be objective. For the farmer whose crop is ruined by disaster, there is another year, another crop, another chance. To accept Harry's imminent death meant there was no further chance.

While Harry took on quiet resignation, one would have thought Norma was the one who was ill. Knots developed over all her body, the worst on the soles of her feet. She walked as if on marbles. Rage and despair surged through her; one minute she was in denial, the next she felt trapped and powerless. Her outward appearance never betrayed her inner turmoil except that she never laughed anymore, and before, she had been full of laughter. Anne turned inward and suffering settled on her shoulders like a terrible weight. She took refuge in her school work as Norma did in teaching. Charles acted as if he had never been told. On the subject he was unapproachable. At times he was cocky or belligerent over nothing at all. They all seemed to be walking on separate paths.

Life went on. They had to eat, so Norma shopped and cooked. Clothes got soiled and had to be washed. The house had to be cleaned and the yard work done.Those were safe activities and in doing them together they were a unit once more. Everyone took long showers and Norma decided the others cried as the water splashed down upon them as she did. No one ever mentioned the red and puffy eyes of the others. Then one night Harry asked Norma if he would ever see her smile again. She cried openly in his arms; she cried herself to sleep. After this open admission of grief and suffering, she was able to smile again, even laugh, to please Harry. And the others did the same.

Norma's class hatched a caterpillar through all the stages, then released the butterfly on the school lawn and watched it fly away: THE CYCLE OF LIFE, she explained to them. Yes, the cycle of life, and with it comes death. She told her students that the butterfly might live but a day. But for that day, it would bring great beauty. *Another lesson, somewhere. Always look for lessons or meaning. There must be a meaning to things. But what on earth could be the meaning of Harry having cancer?*

In her daily classroom reading, Norma had come to the last chapter of *Little Britches,* the story of the young boy growing up in Colorado where his family had moved from Vermont looking for a cure of his father's lung disease. A cure had come, but now his father was dying from an accident.

In this last chapter, "So Long, Partner", the boy was called to his father's bedside to be given a new name: the man of the family. Always a poignant story, it now took on added poignancy for Norma. Her voice wavered as she came to the father's parting words. She handed the book to her best reader, claiming to have something in her eye. The student finished the chapter and there were others who also had something in their eyes. Norma told them there was a sequel to the book, titled *Man of the Family*, and she just happened to have a copy. Tomorrow she would begin it.

In May, Norma received a letter written on behalf of the local alumni association of Phi Beta Kappa extending congratulations on her forth coming graduation with highest honors from San Diego State College. The announcement had been made in advance of the June 8 ceremony. On that morning City Schools would provide a substitute teacher for her, and Anne and Charles would also be excused from school.

June 8 arrived. Norma woke as usual to the cooing of the doves. Today she could lie beyond seven to enjoy it. Dozing between sleep and waking, she felt Harry's arms pulling her close and the long absent stirring of the sleeping tiger against her hips. For weeks she had not pressed close to arouse him or let her hands roam his body or lay resting at his groin. By day she had caught the look of sorrow in his eyes at the loss of an important part of their expression of love; by night they lay with only their hearts touching. Now, every fiber of her responded to his ardent caresses, hungry kisses, and love making as tender and passionate as before; completed as before. She felt somehow shy as a bride, yet she had shown her urgent need of him, knowing the price in pain he would pay. Knowing also it was his gift on her special day. She rose from bed with a greater love than ever expanding her heart for this man who had always placed her needs above his. She trembled with the wonder of it and when their eyes met she saw a softness in his, replacing the emptiness of yesterday.

Exactly at nine, Harry let her out of the car at the Book Store on campus to walk to the bell tower to take her place in line. Soon the procession of graduates would cross the courtyard and follow the worn path through the trees and down the gently sloping hillside to the back entrance of the outdoor theater. In the fresh morning air of June, the first beat of Richard Wagner's *Homage March* started the line moving forward into view of the audience waiting in the tiered rows of the bowl-shaped amphitheater. The power of the music and the meaning of the ceremony swelled her heart to near bursting and joy surged through her like a river. Her eyes scanned the rows of seats until they found sitting side by side her world, Anne, Harry, and Charles. As the music filled her being, so did hope. Dare she embrace it? Yes, she would hope, would fight! She had too much to lose not to fight. Until the last breath left her body, or his body, she would hope and fight for Harry's life and for their world. She would not be afraid of that wretched word, that robber of life. She would say it, shout it to the world, shout it down. It would not take her man. There must be a way to conquer that word, and she would find it.

Harry Steele Commager, historian, writer, member of the War Department's Committee on the History of World War 11, Professor of History and American Studies, Amherst College, gave the commencement address--something about the dangers of worldwide chauvinism--but Norma's mind was busy formulating a plan of attack on the threat to Harry's life. He told her later it was a great speech befitting one whose degree read in the lower left hand corner: Graduated with Highest Honors and Distinction in Elementary Education.

Harry's second gift was a gold wrist watch and from Anne and Charles the album *Camelot*. For some reason the movie "On the Beach" flashed across her mind. She likened her former hopelessness to that of the film whose message intended to show the danger of blind devotion to chauvinism as Commenger's speech predicted. And the theme of *Camelot* reflected her new attitude toward Harry's illness. Yes, it was a new day!

Back at school in the faculty workroom she disclosed Harry's condition with the words, " My husband has cancer."

Janet Hudson called her aside to say, "Norma, there is hope; come to my house tonight and I'll tell you where to find it." They went, and she told them of a medical clinic in Tijuana, Mexico where miracles were happening for cancer patients. Harry objected to spending their money on a doubtful treatment when one was free at the Naval Hospital, telling her, "I want to leave you with as much as I can."

"I want you to *not* leave me at all!" Norma answered. "The Navy doctors are dealing with surrender; I can't accept that. There must be a way to fight it, perhaps this is it. Please give it a chance. Let's at least investigate. If you won't do it for yourself, do it for me. Indulge me. I'm begging!"

On July 31, they went to the Cancer Clinic of Dr. Jose' Jesus Barbosa a well known plastic surgeon, one who often donated his time and services to local hospitals. His associates were Dr. Anton R. Schenk and Dr. Jorge Estrella. Dr. Schenk, a German, was recently from the City of Hope Hospital in Duarte, California where he said Laetrile and Krebiozen had been used on imminently terminal patients. The small success in the amelioration of symptoms had convinced him that treatment would be significantly more beneficial if begun earlier. Thus, he had joined Dr. Barbosa in Mexico where use of Laetrile and Krebiozen was legal.

In their initial examination of Harry, the doctors described him as being a well nourished, youthful appearing, muscular male Caucasian whose weight was stable at 170 pounds and had been unchanged all his adult life. Except for the cancer, there was no health problem, but a mild case of gum infection which would make their treatment hazardous. Therefore all twenty-eight perfect teeth would have to be extracted. Vitamin therapy and a rigid diet must be implemented: whole wheat or rye bread, natural brown rice, fresh fruit and vegetables in abundance. Any meat consumed should come from animals no larger than a rabbit, and be fresh and unprocessed. No smoking, alcohol, sugar, commercial ice cream, or pork. The hormone treatment started at the Naval Hospital would be continued. Weekly visits would be necessary, at a cost of twenty dollars to include all services except tests and X-rays to be given periodically.

Norma talked with patients in the waiting room who were eager to tell of the efficacy of the treatments. One lady told of walking in now, up the stairs, when originally she was brought in on a stretcher. Another told of coming formerly with her own oxygen supply; now she was without it. One man whose left jaw had once been an open sore, kept covered, was now almost healed.

The doctors were hopeful of at least arresting Harry's disease and giving him relief from pain since his cancer had not been interfered with by surgery or radiation. He agreed to begin treatment and was given an injection to begin the cleansing process. It would induce a fever to begin the destruction of harmful cells, leaving the body invigorated and able to begin self-healing.

Hope was surging in San Diego; turmoil was raging in La Fayette. Mary Lee's marriage had collapsed and she was heartbroken and home with her parents, refusing to eat and weeping constantly. Nobody there could comfort her. In desperation, Mama and Daddy brought her to Norma. There, with the Kipps, Mary Lee improved to the point her parents were able to return home alone. On Mary Lee's first wedding anniversary, she received a written plea from Jimmy to give their marriage another try. And a reconciliation by mail began under Norma's guidance.

Mary Lee found a job as a waitress in a family style restaurant. Unhappy with wearing white uniforms, she prevailed upon Norma, as before on Mama, to make her flattering, gingham dirndls of pink, yellow, and blue with ruffled-edged aprons, and Norma made her three. Bus service was not convenient so Harry drove her to work always getting her there at the last minute since she took so long arranging her hair. Punctuality was his middle name and he hated this morning rush. "I don't know what to think of anyone who spends so much time primping that she travels with a three-way-mirror. Why don't you council her on that?" But Norma was thankful Mary Lee was eating and not crying anymore.

Harry was half way through the teeth extractions and continuing with the cleansing treatments in Tijuana. All molars had been removed without the aid of anesthesia. Instead, he drank herbal teas and took massive amounts of calcium and magnesium supplements for pain, to help with blood clotting and reduce nervousness. His body seemed to be as resistant to the cleansing process as it had been to revealing symptoms of cancer. Even with taking ever larger doses, no fever occurred. And until it happened, Laetrile treatments could not begin. The doctors were hesitant to give larger and larger dosages since Harry couldn't be properly monitored as an outpatient, and he couldn't be admitted into the hospital in Tijuana while the teeth extractions were in progress.

At last, in the first week of September, when Harry's incisors had been extracted and dentures put into place, the fever came. It raged on for hours with Harry in a state of near delirium and Norma in telephone contact with Dr. Barbosa in Tijuana. Finally, at dusk, the fever broke and Harry slept peacefully, drenched in foul smelling perspiration. Around midnight, he woke calm and alert. After a hot, sudsy shower he felt better than he had in months. At his next visit to the clinic his jubilant doctors began Laetrile treatment. With each weekly injection, Harry improved in stamina, freedom from pain, and in a feeling of well-being.

Clairemont's newest high school, the James Madison, opened to an onslaught of sophomores with Anne among them. When the newly formed Warhawks played their first football game, the Kipps were in the bleachers cheering them to victory. Norma was teaching during the day and in the evening making shirts for Harry and Charles in subtle plaids of blue and brown. For herself, sheath dresses in bold bright pink, orange, and chartreuse. Anne chose pastels for hers, and with her coloring, she looked like an angel. Whenever she went along to Tijuana, the Latin boys touched with their eyes her long blond hair and golden skin, smiling and uttering, *Que linda!* until she refused to go. Unlike her childhood daring, she had become a shy young lady.

Charles became a teenager on October 14 to the news breaking story of the Soviet ballistic missile build up in Cuba. On October 22, President Kennedy launched a sea and air quarantine as twenty-five Russian ships moved toward Cuba. For seven days the world lived in dread of armed conflict between the United States and Russia as each readied its armed forces for action. October 28, Premier Khruschev backed down and ordered that the missile sites be dismantled. Four days later, President Kennedy announced it was indeed in progress and eighteen days later, he removed the quarantine but continued United States aerial surveillance over Cuba. Thanksgiving Day was celebrated with truly grateful hearts.

At Field Elementary, Norma assumed chairmanship of "Project Amigos", a school-wide gesture of friendship extended to an orphanage in Tijuana, Mexico. She supervised the after-school activity of sewing towels into 'kits' to hold toilet articles and small toys donated by charitable organizations. The enormous response required a moving truck to transport them; Norma and three other teachers went along to help with their distribution. In addition, Norma's class made three large mobiles for Children's Hospital in San Diego. They collected and delivered a trunk load of magazines to Juvenile Hall where the number of gates that separated the youthful inmates from the outside world convinced her students that this place was not the place to be, except on a mercy mission.

Three days before Christmas, the Kipps loaded Mary Lee, her three-way mirror, three suitcases stuffed with clothes, and twenty pounds of country western recordings into the car and drove her to the airport. After twenty minutes of tearful farewells, the two sisters parted and Mary Lee flew out of Lindbergh Field bound for La Fayette and a reunion with Jimmy. "Norma the peacemaker," Harry remarked, then added, "You love your family quite a lot, don't you, Honeychild?"

"Yes," she sighed happily, "Quite a lot. It's good to know that roots can spread all the way across this wide country. Despite our differences, I'm part of them and they're part of me."

On Christmas Eve, the Kipps drove to Tecate, Mexico, forty miles inland from Tijuana, a typically Mexican *pueblo* unmarked by tourism. The cobbled streets were overrun with playful children, dogs, and squealing pigs. Women, carrying water jars on top of proud heads, glided from the town well; others patted *masa* into *tortillas*, heated them on *braseros* set up at the edge of the central *plaza,* and filled them with delicately seasoned beef, lettuce, tomatoes, and shredded cheese. The *tacos* were served with *frijoles* and *arroz*, beans and rice, and the Kipps ate to the strains of Christmas carols played by strolling *mariaches*. At dusk the traditional *posada* began: a couple posing as Mary and Joseph passed from door to door in the houses bordering the street asking for shelter, being refused time after time, but at last welcomed inside. Then festivities began with singing, dancing, feasting, and the breaking of a piñata. The decorated clay pot, filled with candies and fruit, was raised and lowered from the ceiling by a rope. Blindfolded children took turns swinging at it. The 'wise' rope-puller finally allowed a child to strike the jar and when it broke, goodies fell upon the upturned and expectant faces of children who then scrambled on the ground for what had escaped eager, reaching hands.

It wasn't Guadalajara in July as the Kipps had planned; it was Tecate in December. And at Christmas they were celebrating the amazing result of the Laetrile treatment. Harry was taking nothing for pain because he had none. The prostate gland was softening and decreasing in size and in January his visits to the clinic would be at two week intervals instead of weekly. Total cost had been five hundred dollars for five months of treatment. Not that a price could be placed on Harry's health, but critics of the controversial treatment said it cost gullible patients their life savings and offered nothing. That wasn't true. The Kipps wanted the world to know and their Christmas cards to friends and family carried the happy message. Even to Mother Minnie. When his illness appeared, Harry had asked that she not be burdened with it since her own health was poor--poorer than she realized, according to Juliette. Over the years when Norma had written on special occasions, sending photos and news of Anne and Charles, she always said in regard to Harry, that he was well. As he always had been, until last spring. Since then, she had written nothing of him until she could be truthful in saying he was well. Mother Minnie had always seemed satisfied, even joyful, in her brief and infrequent replies.

39

March again. In this one, Harry's improved health permitted the construction of the office-sized desk Norma wanted and needed. The little desk from her childhood was still in Georgia, and much too small for her purposes now that she was a teacher writing lesson plans, making worksheets and other materials for the classroom. Harry was strong enough to move the heavy desk about as he worked on it in the garage, but when it was completed two men were required to carry it inside. In place in the den, Norma sat at it caressing its smooth mahogany top under Harry's usual seven coats of hand-rubbed varnish. Pull-out boards above the side drawers, along with the desktop, provided an ample work area. The center drawer had a secret compartment so well concealed that Harry had to show her where it was. The desk was Harry's masterpiece, according to Norma, and proof that he was getting well. They celebrated the Easter message of the Resurrection with the Condos in Hinkley.

The students in Room 29, in answer to a newspaper article, began corresponding with a seventy-four year old gentleman, the proud grandson of 1851 Stockton pioneers. A month before, Mr. John C. Crowe had stationed himself at Fourth and Broadway in downtown Los Angeles offering dollar bills to anyone who answered his questions on California history. Starting with fifty crisp one dollar notes, he went home with forty-three after two days of effort. Saddened by the ignorance of local citizens, he urged that the coming September be designated as "Read California History Month". Governor Edmund "Pat" Brown gave his support and a statewide committee was appointed to plan the observance with Thomas J. Hammer, Jr., President of Sacramento County Historical Society, to serve as chairman.

Norma had requested Mr. Crowe's list of questions so that her students might answer them. Over several months, he replied to three batches of thirty letters answering each individually in his bold handwriting. He sent eight by ten photographs of himself appearing before the Los Angeles City Council on behalf of his proposal as well as numerous newspaper articles telling of his survival as a seventeen year old youth in the 1906 San Francisco earthquake. In a letter published in the *San Diego Union,* Mr. Crowe described his contact with Mrs. Kipp's fourth grade class at Eugene Field School.

Her delighted students sent an autographed class picture and an anniversary card to Mr. and Mrs. Crowe on the occasion of their fifty-second year of marriage. His gratitude at the outpouring of their love filled two handwritten pages to Norma. At the end of school, Mr. Richard Oliver, regional director of San Diego City Schools, came to read Mr. Crowe's letters and sent a letter of appreciation to him. Norma received one as well. A wonderful way to end her first year of teaching!

Harry's treatments at the Barbosa Clinic were now scheduled at four week intervals and the doctors approved his request for a cross-country drive to Georgia. There, for two weeks, the Kipps were catered to by Mama and Daddy, Joan and Max, Julia and Ed, and Mary Lee and Jimmy at fish fries, ice cream socials, barbecues, and good southern meals. Charles tried his hand at water skiing on Chickamauga Lake. Up on Sand Mountain, Julia taught Anne hoedown steps. Norma and Harry spent a weekend in Crossville to comfort Bill Godwin whose Toby had died in the spring. On their way home, they stopped in Leeds, Alabama where Harry met Norma's eighty year old Grandmother Butts. At home, a sad letter awaited. Mrs. Crowe had written in her shaky script that her dear husband had died in his sleep on July 20 from a year-long illness. She thanked Norma for the great happiness her students had brought to both of them.

"It's hard to believe," Norma sobbed. "In his letters he was so vital, so enthusiastic. How could he have been so ill? If only I had known."

"It was better the way it was," Harry said soberly, "the way he wanted. Who can ever know how big a little seed of kindness can grow? You did a wonderful thing for Mr. Crowe and your students, Honeychild."

His praise pleased her since on their trip to Georgia she had faced their derision, as if she were out to ruin their vacation by her frugality. She had kept expenses low, but the others seemed to have forgotten their agreement to travel on a shoestring in order to afford another trip--to Oregon in August--if Harry felt well enough. Now, home from one vacation, with clearance from his doctors, they were ready to leave again. And she was their heroine!

They traveled north through the agricultural central valley of California, the blast furnace Harry called it, to visit Sequoia National Park. They roomed there in a cool and rustic lodge built along side a shallow stream just perfect for wading. The surrounding countryside was majestic and, except for the lodge and restaurant, belonged to the ages. Redwood and giant sequoias were awesome; and they drove through the tunnel tree twice. The long steep climb to the foot of Moro rock was slow and strenuous. Theirs wasn't the only car to stop at the pullouts to let engines cool. From the summit the view was far and wide. They looked down upon the serpentine highway they had followed upward, watching the 'ant-sized' vehicles in their ascent. In Kings Canyon they felt like ants themselves standing at the base of the rising canyon walls on all sides.

Half Dome and El Capitan, at Yosemite, deserved salutes and many photographs which they were awarded. In downtown Sacramento, the grounds of the state capital were isolated at sunset. Norma peered through the locked doors of the golden-domed capitol to get a glimpse of the life sized portraits of former governors. At Sutter's Fort, a few blocks away, Anne and Charles bought gold nugget souvenirs.

Near the northern border of California, beautiful snowcapped Mount Shasta loomed to the east. Shasta Dam on the Sacramento River formed a tremendous lake to the north. "The dam's spillway, dropping four hundred eighty feet, makes it the highest overflow dam in the world," Norma read from her travel guide, "Its reservoir extends thirty-five miles from the dam up the Sacramento, Pit, and McCloud Rivers."

"I wonder," Charles queried, "Do teachers go to all the places they teach about? I thought they just got it all from books."

"It starts with books," Norma conceded, "but think how much better I can teach about California after seeing all this first hand."

"And that's why you go to Mexico?" Anne asked, "Because you teach about it?"

"That's part of the reason. But I've been fascinated with Mexico ever since I heard Gene Autry sing "South of the Border" in a movie I saw when I was ten years old."

"Gene Autry was the first cowboy your mother fell in love with," Harry winked at Anne.

"Who was the second?" Anne asked, laughing at her daddy mimicking a horseman. "Not *you,* Dad. I've heard about you being a wrestler, circus strong man, sailor, and Marine. Don't tell me you've been a cowboy too!"

"It's true," Norma confirmed. "Remind me when we get home to show you pictures of him on his mount, 'Old Fifty-seven' ".

"Dad, you should write a book," Charles challenged.

"I intend to," Harry responded, "in my old age."

Fifty miles up the highway, Harry crossed the Oregon border and Norma soon exhausted her supply of adjectives in describing the verdant lushness bordering the freeway that sliced through the central part of the Beaver State. She proceeded to explain how the state got its name. Anne and Charles sniggered behind their hands and Anne whispered loudly, "I guess we're never going to get away from school, even on vacation, with a teacher for a mother!" and seeing Norma's head turn toward them, she added quickly, "No offense, Mom. We're really glad you're one."

In Springfield, Norma introduced her family to Uncle Bob and Aunt Thelma, Mama's oldest sister, the one she took after, Mama always said. The Bruces had moved from Alabama years ago because Uncle Bob favored logging to farming. He didn't look like a logger, but what he lacked in size he made up for in grit. He soon captivated all the Kipps with his collections of rocks, coins, stamps, guns and old photographs. His son Robert, about twice the size of his dad, took Charles home with him to let him try his hand at logging. Robert's little sister Mary Ina--only five feet tall-- and her husband Chet, a former Marine, came to meet Harry. After a few hours, her awe of him finally broke down and she exclaimed,"Why Aunt Ann had us dreading to meet him; like he was a prince or duke or even a king! But he's easy to be around, he's just like us...common."

He was a good fisherman as well. When the men and boys went fishing, they came home with twenty-two lake trout which Aunt Thelma cooked in a southern fish fry. Norma didn't want to boast that Harry caught fifteen, but she was quick to say that Charles and Robert didn't have any luck, Uncle Bob broke his pole, and Chet brought in seven.

Of the many natural sights they were shown, Crater Lake impressed them most. From the thirty mile Rim Drive, which encircled the caldera, they looked down upon the lake's incredible blue water. Richly forested slopes descended to the lava cliffs bordering the lake's twenty mile shoreline. One large dike rose out of the lake's surface; back lighted by the sun, it did indeed look like a ship under sail as Uncle Bob said it would.

Aunt Thelma wouldn't let them leave until she loaded the trunk of the Mercury with three dozen jars of canned fruit and vegetables, tucking them among Norma's lava, obsidian, pumice stone, driftwood and their luggage. Harry warned that the car shocks would never survive such weight, but Aunt Thelma didn't listen; she added a few more jars.

Going home they took the coast highway from Grant's Pass stopping at Redwood National Park and Fort Ross, the wooden-enclosed former Russian fort Norma's class had learned about from Mr. Crowe. A little farther south, Anne and Charles asked to see the location site of Alfred Hitchcock's recent film, "The Birds".

They crossed the fog-shrouded Golden Gate Bridge, drove through the Presidio and Golden State Park while listening to Norma's running commentary. Soon they were once more on the winding scenic coast highway where cliffs dropped many feet to the ocean surf. Charles was lying in the back seat, green from car sickness, rising only briefly at the exclamations of the others for a look at the downward views. Then Norma took Anne's back seat so she too could lie down. "I'm glad I'm strong," Anne boasted, "like Dad." The car shocks were not so strong, but they lasted until the car stopped in their driveway at home.

The following day the Mercury went into the repair shop for new shocks and Harry drove the Hillman to Tijuana for his treatment. Norma went along to shop for the Mexican market she planned to set up in the classroom again this year. Last year she bought clothing for their study of Mexico: *serapes, rebosos, sombrero, huaraches, huipil,* and *ponchos* in sizes to fit her fourth grade students. This year she chose household articles: *matate* and *mano* for grinding corn, *canastas* for carrying things, *molinillo* for frothing chocolate, *olla* for storing water and *taza*, a cup for drinking. For herself she bought a book of Mexican folk songs and set out to learn the lyrics of Harry's favorite song *La Paloma.*

> *Si a tu ventana llega una paloma,*
> *Trátala con cariño, que es mi persona,*
> *Cuéntale tus amores bien de mi vida,*
> *Corónala de flores, que es cosa mia.*
> *¡Ay, chinita, que sí!*
> *¡Ay, que dame tu amor!*
> *¡Ay, que vente conmigo, chinita,*
> *¡ A donde vivo yo!*

"I can read the words," she said, "But I don't know what they mean. Help me! Harry, stop grinning and translate it for me."

"Well, its about this Marine who gets orders overseas and has to leave his little darling behind..."

"No! It isn't! Stop teasing me and tell me the truth."

"That is the truth--essentially--a man, some man, must go away, leaving his lover behind. He tells her that when a dove comes to her window it comes to remind her of his love."

"Really?" She looked at him quickly and saw that he was serious.

"*La verdad*" he answered. "The truth, *chinita!*"

"All this time I've loved the song without knowing what it meant....of course, *La Paloma*, the dove, symbol of loyalty and love."

*   *   *   *

Friday, November 22, almost a week until Thanksgiving. Sitting in the teachers' lounge, Norma was thinking of the sculptured paper turkeys her students would make in the art lesson when recess ended. The bell to summon all to classrooms had not yet rung, but she rose to go. At the door she met the principal, white-faced and solemn, who had shocking, unbelievable news, "A radio bulletin says President Kennedy has just been shot in Dallas. He's being rushed to Parkland Hospital. It sounds bad. Don't say anything yet to your students, but be prepared to tell them something by lunch time. By then there should be...good... or bad...news. I'll send a monitor around as soon as I hear something more." The teachers, mute with the shock of this unthinkable occurrence, left to collect their children and escort them to their classrooms.

Mechanically, Norma distributed art materials to her students and demonstrated the making of a sample turkey, then sank into the chair at her desk. A position unusual for her since she always circulated among her students as they worked. Minutes dragged by. Her attention was on the window looking out to the flag pole, the lunch tables, and beyond to the door of the principal's office. The clock hands seemed to be standing still as her thoughts raced...waiting...hoping...waiting...one completed fowl was brought to her for pinning to the bulletin board, then another. She was pinning a third when the door opened and an office monitor entered carrying a message mounted in black. Norma reached for it, read it, checked her name off the routing list and returned it to the white-lipped messenger. She walked slowly to her desk and leaned against it. "Class..." she began, hardly recognizing her own voice. The children looked up, waiting. She began again, "Class, I have some very sad news. President Kennedy has been shot. You know he went to Dallas today. That's where it happened. He was taken to a hospital, but it was too late. He has died."

The children didn't move; they sat like frozen statues with scissors poised, paste on fingers, crayons pressed to paper. Then, as one, their eyes turned to the window, looking through it to the flag pole where the patrol boys were slowly lowering the drooping flag to half mast; one was playing taps, rather badly. As the last note died, the noon bell rang.

Throughout the week it was as if the entire nation stopped. The only movement was what passed across the television screens: the succession of Lyndon Baines Johnson to the office of the president of the United States, eulogies to the slain president, comparisons of the two fallen presidents, Lincoln and Kennedy one hundred two years apart, preparations for the great state funeral, the procession of white horses bearing the coffin to the rotunda followed by the riderless horse, the muffled drum beats, and the visit of the first family where Mrs. Kennedy and Caroline kissed the flag-draped casket, and young John-John gave his little salute. Finally the burial at Arlington National Cemetery and the lighting of the eternal flame. It was over, and the grieving citizens returned to their daily tasks.

Norma had admired Mrs. Kennedy from the beginning of her public life, even looking upon her with some small envy as the woman who had it all: poise and breeding, stunning beauty, two precious children, and wife to the president of the country. But she envied her no more. In a matter of seconds a bullet had taken her husband and Jackie was a widow. Even though his life was under attack, Harry was alive sitting beside her, returning the pressure of her hand as they witnessed this shattering turn of fate. President Kennedy dead. Who could have imagined it a week ago?

The country still staggered from shock when, before the eyes of the world, via television, Jack Ruby fired upon and slew the accused assassin Lee Harvey Oswald. It was a most difficult Christmas for the nation. The Kipps escaped to Hinkley where they and the Condos made a vow not to mention the tragedies. Instead they talked of Harry's improvement. "Damn, Harry," Butch shouted as he greeted his friend every morning, "You old athlete, you look great. You just may lick this thing."

The New Year began with the people picking up the threads of their lives, moving forward even through the trial of Jack Ruby. For the teachers in San Diego that meant in-service classes to learn New Math. The young people of America saw their idol Elvis Presley crowded off the screen by a rock and roll quartet from Liverpool with Edwardian-styled clothes and soup-bowled haircuts calling themselves 'The Beatles'. Norma and Harry exchanged puzzled glances as they watched three guitar thwacking boys and a fourth pounding away on drums on the Ed Sullivan Show. "Is this some kind of joke?" Norma asked, astonished, "Do you think that at the end of the song, they'll yank off those funny looking hair-pieces?"

"No, Mom, that's their real hair," Anne hooted. "New style."

"It doesn't make them look like beetles, if that's their aim."

"Aw, Mom," laughed Charles, "they're Beatles, named for the b-e-a-t of their music. Listen." And he demonstrated on the piano with "I Want to Hold Your Hand." But they can't touch The King!" he asserted.

"Or the Kingston Trio." said Anne.

"Nor the New York Philharmonic Symphony," from Harry.

*   *   *   *

President Johnson declared war on poverty in his State of the Union address. Jack Ruby was sentenced to die in the electric chair for the murder of Lee Harvey Oswald. A violent earthquake struck Alaska near the Kenai peninsula, killing sixty-six. General Douglas MacArthur died after a brief illness. Charles played on the All-Stars team against the Einstein faculty in softball. Anne was a finalist on

Madison High School's debating team. Norma and her class gave an all-school assembly on National Brotherhood and Negro History. And Harry was taking Norma to a Mother's Day performance of the *Ramona* pageant given each spring since 1923 by the people of Hemet, California.

The pageant was held in a huge natural amphitheater at the foot of San Jacinto Mountain, an hour's drive from San Diego, the actual setting of Helen Hunt Jackson's novel on which the pageant was based. In the opening scene a dozen or so reveling horsemen galloped past the audience, down a trail, over a bridge, and circled to a dust-raising stop at the coral next to the ranch house. A fiesta was beginning in honor of Don Felipe's recovery from a serious illness. Norma sat engrossed in the action taking place before the ranch house, at the nearby spring where Ramona and Alessandro had their secret meetings, and up in the surrounding hills where the sheepherders lived. As the story unfolded, she lived it along with Ramona. When it ended, she exclaimed, "Oh, Harry, thank you; it was wonderful. I hope you enjoyed it half as much as I. You would have, if you had read the book."

"Since I haven't, perhaps you will read it to me," he said, "beginning tonight."

For weeks Norma had been preparing her class for their exhibit in the Field School Science Fair. The fourth grade theme was Water Power. Norma's class focused on Hoover Dam with a model of the dam, a dozen photographs Harry took in 1955 and enlarged by Charles in his photography class, and a thirty minute interview with Harry from home and the students from Room 29, using a 'spokesman' provided by the telephone company. Their questions related to his work on the dam during its construction in the early Thirties. And on the evening of the Fair, he was available for further questions and autographs which the students begged for. Anne acknowledged, "You're finally a celebrity, Dad!"

The school year ended with Harry escorting Anne to the Father and Daughter Banquet at Madison High and Charles to the Father and Son Banquet at the Boys Club where Harry was a charter member. Charles won merit awards in Math and Drafting and Anne held the cast party for the Drama Club at 4840 Aberdeen Street. Mrs. Clarke retired as principal of Field School. Harry renewed his California driver's license and sold the Hillman. And Norma began to notice subtle signs of his discomfort, sitting cautiously, favoring his left leg, sitting on his right thigh instead of flat, and when they went swimming at Miramar, he didn't dive anymore.

He made no complaints and they still took drives to the mountains, desert, and seashore for picnics and attended movies in the evenings. He began weekly visits to the clinic in Tijuana--just a precaution, he told her, nothing for her to worry about. But she was worried and once again the icy fingers of terror gripped her heart. Her senses became alert to the slightest change in him, seeing to it that his diet was as good as she could make it, filling his vitamin tray as he emptied it, and making no demands on his strength.

When the clinic in Tijuana lost its supplier of Laetrile and while it sought another, Harry grew impatient and went to the Naval Hospital for pain medication. He accepted their offer of a series of cobalt treatments in August while Anne and Charles were visiting the Condos. The side effects of nausea, dehydration, and debilitating fatigue were devastating and at the end of twelve treatments he had lost twenty pounds.

About this time, the Scoggins moved to California. Max's health had continued to suffer from mill work and Tommy helped him secure employment in Downey. They felt it was God's will that they live close to Harry in his time of crisis and came often for weekend visits.

In September, Charles joined Anne at Madison High and Field School got a new principal, Robert Ingrum, a six foot four genius in Math. "He's exactly what we need," Norma told Harry, "to help us with the set theory and binary numeration." The focus in education had shifted from Science to Math and New Math had been thrust upon the hapless teachers and students. Parents were confused and angry, unable to help their children with math homework; teachers were frustrated; and students were lost.

In October, a district music teacher was scheduled to observe Norma's music lessons. For her, it was an opportunity to show that those daily twenty minutes were a special time for her and the students. On Monday she taught a Japanese folk song from San Francisco and likened the key of G flat with its six markers sitting on the treble staff to little doves sitting on the temple rooftops. On Tuesday, rhythm instruments were added to the singing. Wednesday, they danced to the song becoming doves swooping down from the rooftops to light and eat *mahmay* (beans), flutter their wings, and return to their seats. First two, then four, then eight, then half the class, and finally all at once, graceful little doves eating daintily and fluttering wings in time with the music. Thursday they listened to the Standard School Broadcast featuring Japanese music and Norma displayed a doll, music box, fan, and kimono Tommy had sent from Japan. Friday's lesson was a songfest with rhythm instruments, dancing, and singing. The children became cotton pickers to "Pick a Bale of Cotton", sawyers to "Cutting Down the Pines", paddle wheelers to "Down the Ohio", and of course they were doves again to "Ha-to Po-po."

Norma pranced around the room as she told Harry, "The kids really put on a show for that teacher, playing the records, distributing then collecting the rhythm instruments, and putting everything away. All I had to do was sit and enjoy, along with her. I just couldn't be prouder of my class than I was today."

"And you have a right to be proud, Mother Goose. You've taught your little flock well".

Norma raised her eyebrows, "So now it's Mother Goose! Whatever happened to Norma A?"

"She's still around...somewhere," Harry reached for her, "Why, here she is. In my arms."

40

At last Harry was able to vote for the man from Minnesota, if only for the number two spot. President Johnson was re-elected on November 3, 1964 with Hubert H. Humphrey as his vice-president. Then, almost directly from the voting booth, Harry checked himself into the Tijuana clinic for a ten day stay. He was willing to endure the separation from his family in the hope that larger doses of Laetrile would once again rescue him from pain. Dr. Barbosa couldn't promise relief since the intervention of radiation, but Harry returned home with decreased pain, an improved appetite and food tolerance. Almost at once, he began to regain his lost weight.

Norma's parents arrived the week before Thanksgiving and with Joan's and Tom's families coming from Los Angeles for the big holiday dinner, there was a west coast reunion. Her parents visit gave immense relief to Norma. Mama did the cooking and housework and Daddy did the yard work. For the first time since she was a little girl, Norma leaned on them. Their physical presence, concern, and emotional support strengthened all the Kipps.

Harry resumed driving Norma to school in the mornings and returning for her at the end of the school day. Every afternoon, from her classroom window she could see him waiting as she prepared the room for the following day. Some days he came inside as he did the day he brought a letter from San Diego City Schools. "It looks official," he said, "from Ken Owens, District Music Specialist. I thought you'd be eager to read it."

"Funny," she said, opening it, "I wonder why it was sent through the post office instead of school mail,"

<blockquote>
December 2, 1964

Dear Mrs. Kipp;

A special group of classroom teachers is being invited to participate in a Contemporary Music Project next semester. You have been selected to be a member because of your interest and ability to augment your fine classroom music program...

Classes meet two Wednesdays a month from February through May from 4 to 6 P.M. Please complete the attached form and return it on or before January 8, 1965, indicating whether or not you will be able to accept our invitation...
</blockquote>

Norma shouted, "I've finally made it! I mean in music! I always knew that with my trusted pal the record player, I'd do a good job teaching music even if I can't read notes. I just needed a chance to show someone. Recognition at last! Can you believe this?"

"I believe it," Harry said, "it's no more than I'd expect from Norma A."

On Christmas Eve, Anne and Charles decorated a ceiling high blue spruce with flashing white lights and silver balls. It was their first cut tree and Norma and Harry told them of their little spruce of twenty years ago, the one they'd moved in the rain from the Quonset hut into Sterling Housing. They spoke of many other things, with words, as their eyes spoke also, silently and powerfully. His, steady and intent, glowing with love, were telling her, "We have this moment..."

Suddenly Anne's voice cut across time and space, "Hey, Mom, when are you going to take the fruit cake out of the oven? The smell's driving me and Charles crazy."

"I'll do it now, if you'll get *The Littlest Angel* album and start it playing. We can eat as we listen."

"Sure thing, Mom, how many years have we listened to it?" she asked.

"Since Charles' first Christmas," Norma answered.

"Really?" Charles perked up. "That's fifteen years! It's as old as me."

"Not quite; you're two and a half months older." Norma served the fruitcake, then hot chocolate as Loretta Young's lovely voice told of the humble gift of the littlest angel to the Christ child. Then came the reading from Luke, chapter two, verses one to twenty. Afterwards, good-nights were exchanged and it was off to bed.

Early Christmas morning Dolly Condo called from Hinkley. Norma answered with Harry on the extension."We can't bear to spend the holidays without you," Dolly said, "Chick and I thought of dropping over to San Diego then I thought that if you folks came here, you'd have a break from cooking, Norma. Do you think you could come...and stay until New Year's Day?"

Norma hesitated, then heard Harry's voice, "Sounds swell, Dolly. You bet we'll come. Holidays with the Condos is my kind of duty."

When they arrived in Hinkley, Butch greeted his long time friend with a mighty slap on the back, a firm handshake and words of praise, "Damn, Harry, you defy gravity, you know." Admiration and love flowed from him. He and Dolly were as aware as Norma of Harry's valiant determination to resist the insidious drain of cancer upon his strength. He seemed able to overpower it by sheer will.

During the magic week, the Kipps and the Condos reveled in good fellowship, savoring their time together. The days drifted by as the six feasted on tasty Pennsylvania Dutch fare and lazed in the sun. Harry and Butch shot the breeze about the old Corps and recalled mutual friendships. Evenings were filled with games of cribbage, hearts, and pinochle--teaming up males against females, couples against couples, kids against godparents, kids against parents. They sang crazy songs, acted out hilarious charades, finally toasting in 1965 without a word of the misery it might bring.

Home again, the Kipps settled into daytime routines and cozy evenings together before blazing fires in the grate, watching television or listening to recordings or Anne and Charles playing solos or duets on their respective instruments. Some nights they all enjoyed Scrabble, other times Charles and Harry challenged each other in a game of chess while Norma knitted a new sweater and Anne wrote poetry.

Harry's strength was waning, Norma knew, before he confided, "My spirit's strong, but my flesh is weak, as the saying goes. I think I'll just hang around the house and be close to the sack except for driving you to and from school." He continued cooking breakfast for the family, his 'duty' he called it when Norma objected after seeing him lean against the kitchen counter as he stirred the oatmeal or sitting while he waited for the toaster to release its charge. When he walked down the hall, she heard the drag of his foot and the sound stabbed her heart and caused her to break out in a sweat of fear. No more was he able to surprise her by suddenly appearing at her side as before when his tread had made no sound at all. Soon he was walking very little, spending his days in bed except for meals.

Being useful had always been a tenet of Harry's life and Norma intended that it remain so. She asked him to cross-index their extensive record collection, get their papers in order for income-tax filing, write the checks for all their bills, and make a list of things to be done for car maintenance. She sent Charles to him for advice on the hole-digging in the side yard for the installation of a set of highbars for his gymnastic feats, and counseling when she caught him sneaking a smoke with his friends and when he got his second pedestrian ticket for crossing against the traffic light. He helped Anne tune her violin and gave comfort when her midterm grades fell below her expectation. "But my middle initial really is an 'A'," Anne protested unhappily, "I should be getting A's not B's and C's."

"You must remember that your Mom can't play the violin," Harry reminded her. "We each have our particular talents."

And Norma thankfully let him take charge of making primitive musical instruments for her Contemporary Music Seminar. Using the instruction pamphlet and the materials she collected, he made a cigar-box guitar, bamboo flute, beans-in-box rattle, coffee-can and mop-pail drum, soup-can xylophone, and coconut-shell cloppers. Her students followed his examples and made enough 'instruments' to form a band, and they taped a medley of songs. Her seminar project was a hit, thanks to Harry. But his condition worsened and his activity ceased. He didn't leave the bed except for trips to the bathroom.

Norma hired a nurse-housekeeper three days a week who came as she left in the mornings and departed when Anne came home from school. Tilly was an excellent companion for Harry, but she was unable to give them more time. There might be another solution. Mary Lee, now living in Texas, wrote that her marriage was crumbling again and she would leave Jimmy if she had somewhere to go. She definitely wouldn't go back to her parents. Norma offered her a home with them saying that her acceptance would benefit everyone. Joan thought so, too.

The Scoggins were faithful in their weekend visits and on Washington's birthday, a Post Office holiday, the Condos came as well. They spent time alone with Harry and after leaving his room, Butch was inconsolable. Charley came at the end of February. His grief was the hardest of all to bear. His love for Harry had been lifelong, as an uncle, which he was, but also as a brother, and a father. On the morning of his departure, as Norma scrambled eggs for breakfast, he stood at her elbow in the kitchen with tears rolling down his stricken face, falling from his nose and chin without his notice, "I don't know what to do or say," he repeated over and over. "I've always meant to leave Harry everything I have, I never thought he's be the first to go. Now, I don't know what to do."

Charley's pain tore at Norma's heart until she almost lost her own composure on the drive to the bus station. But numbness saved her, as it always did; if she didn't feel, she didn't hurt. She just did her duty as Harry wanted, going to school and teaching her class, coming home and caring for the family. And in the evenings, taking her school work to his bedside. Grading and making worksheets, writing lesson plans, and filling out film requisitions. He rested and watched and the music played...from *Aida* to *As Time Goes By, Brigadoon* to *Barber of Seville, Camelot* to *Carmen, White Christmas* to *Where the Citrus Blooms,* and hundreds more!

Whenever he moved or reached for water, she'd stop her work to look up to meet his eyes. Sometimes they had a depth she couldn't fathom, sometimes an expression so tender it stopped her heart, other times a melancholy that made her turn away. At times he was amused, once calling her "Bushy Head" when after a shampoo her hair was all fluffed out.

Then March arrived. Fateful March. "At least I'm contributing something", Harry said as he endorsed his pension check. "So long as these come in, I'm not a total burden. You can be sure that if they weren't, I wouldn't still be hanging around." After her violent sobbing subsided, he promised never to say such a thing again, and later he dutifully drank the liver juice she pressed for him. He knew that some days she had to drive to several markets to find fresh liver. "You take such good care of me," he said, "finding the freshest foods in all San Diego." And he ate even if he had no appetite.

Whenever she spoke of staying home with him, he reminded her of the tenure requirement. This was her third year, and she'd have to teach three-fourths of it to qualify. "As long as you feel well, don't stay home on my account. It would make me very unhappy if, because of me, you had to teach an extra year. Besides, your students need you; it's enough to see your beautiful face when you return after a day with them." His crooked grin would appear, his eyes tease as he reached for her, "But once you have tenure, I won't object at all if you take some days off to be with me."

Two weeks later he said, "Honeychild, I want you to go to the bank, tomorrow, and get the forms to change our accounts into your name only." His voice was calm, the set of his jaw firm. His eyes determined.

"No, please don't ask me to do that! It would be like admitting..." She buried her face in her hands. He took them away, forcing her to look at him, "Honeychild, you cling to the merest thread of hope that I'm going to get better, and I'm not. We must accept that." He pressed her head to his shoulder, his arms around her. "I regret that I'm not going to get better, that I am leaving you, my beloved, that I'm leaving you with teen-agers to care for. Not that I think you incapable, but that you must, because I'm checking out."

Breaking his hold, she clasped him tightly, her heart screaming, *Don't say it; you're not going to die. I won't let you. Don't leave us. Don't..*

He whispered against her ear, "I used to look at you, so young and seemingly fragile, and think that it was my place to look after you. And now you are taking care of all of us. Honeychild, no man ever had a finer, braver wife."

Her heart felt pierced with pain and despair, yet it rejoiced at his praise. That's all she could do for him now, make him proud of her. He, so patient, never demanding, never complaining, not even when pain caused his mouth to tighten and perspiration to form on his brow. Never making a sound even when his face was contorted in pain. If he could be so brave, she could be no less. Shuddering in resolve, she lay upon his chest.

They lived in a private, family world treasuring every day as it began and ended. Until March 29, the day Norma came home from school, collected the letters from the mail box, and hurried to Harry. He was dressed, sitting on the bed. At her look of total bewilderment he explained, "I've called the Naval Hospital. I tried to wait until March ended," his smile was strained and he held her hand ever so tightly. "Forgive me, Honeychild, but it will be easier for you if I'm where you know I'll be looked after, and better for me where I can get something stronger for pain. I've asked Emil to drive us in his station wagon so I can lie down on the drive there. It's all arranged; he's coming at four."

She sank onto the bed, the air knocked out of her, contemplating the meaning of this move to the hospital. He was in charge, and this was his decision; the one she had known would some day be made. And here it is. Her gaze fell to the letters in her hand. The top one from his mother, probably a thank you for her birthday gift. No need to read it now. But it was time to ask, "Harry, let me tell Mother Minnie."

For a moment, she thought he was agreeing, then he said simply, "No." The doorbell rang. Emil, their neighbor, had come.

Norma went the following day to the ward to see Harry. He was in terrible pain and said the hospital staff would not break their rule of giving pain medication closer than every four hours. All he wanted was relief from the pain as they had promised when he agreed to come. He asked her to speak to the doctor; the doctor promised to attend to it. But two days passed with no change. On April second, Harry went into a deep coma. As she stepped through the door at home, Norma heard Anne on the phone. She hung up, saying, "It's bad, Mom. The corpsman said for us to come right away. Charles is locking the back doors."

After a quick call to Joan in Downey who promised to call Mary Lee, Norma and her children sped to the hospital. As they stepped from the elevator, her eyes went to the chart at the nurses' station: Lt. Col. Kipp, Critical. They rushed to the ward looking for Harry. A corpsman came and took them to a room with two other patients. Harry was in the bed nearest the window, lying so still. Norma went to him, touched his forehead, and in her mind she saw the hand of God, open, palm up, with Harry standing in it. When she opened her eyes, his were also open, shining bright and clear. "Honeychild," he breathed softly, looking around. "Hello, Anne...Charles. It's nice to wake and see you all here." He smiled at the corpsman, "Harley, might I trouble you for a glass of grape juice?"

Harley, staring in wonder, suddenly came to attention, blurting, "Why, Colonel Kipp, what's happened to you since your wife got here?"

The following day, Harry's room was filled with visitors. Joan and her family, Anne, Charles, and Norma. By noon there was one more; Mary Lee arrived on a morning flight from Ft. Worth prepared to remain in San Diego. Harry was alert, his pain much reduced even without medication. The four hour interval for pain medication that the staff continued to uphold didn't seem to be a concern for Harry now. He was relaxed and cheerful and he wanted Norma to return to work. "You're needed at school. I'm fine here with Steve, Glenn, and Harley who tend to my few needs. Please, go back to your little flock." To please him, she went back to work, able to do so with a sense of relief because every school day Mary Lee took the bus to the Naval Hospital to be with him.

The week before spring vacation, Norma had her year end evaluation. In Mr. Ingrum's office, she scanned the two page document with superior ratings in every category. "I'm terribly pleased," she blushed in happiness. "This means I'll get tenure.. when I've met the time requirement."

"I must say I am surprised with your concern over getting tenure. Surely you are able to assess your own competence. I can only say I'm thankful it's not the other way around...that you are evaluating me. I'm afraid your standard would find me lacking," he said, smiling.

"Oh, no, sir..." Norma stammered, "I hardly think so. Your leadership has been an inspiration, and please know how grateful and humbled I am by this evaluation." She paused, struggling with her emotions. "But I am very much concerned about tenure, if I am to get it. I need to know now, not later." She drew in a great breath, released it, and in a labored voice continued, "My husband wants to know. You see...he's very ill... and in the hospital; he has been for more than two weeks. His doctors tell me...he's not improving...it's going the other way...and..." She stopped to press her trembling lips together.

Shocked, intent on her words, Mr. Ingrum looked at her sharply.

With tears spilling from her eyes, Norma continued, "Please, forgive me, but I always cry when I try to talk about his condition. I wouldn't now, but you need to know that soon, after Open House, you will need to get a substitute for my class, because then I intend to spend the remaining time my husband has with him." She sat still, eyes closed, composing herself. "I will leave lesson plans showing all that I have taught along with what remains to be covered, in every subject. Both of us, Harry and I, are quite concerned that my little flock, as he calls them, doesn't suffer because of our...private ordeal." Now that it all had been said, Norma leaned involuntarily against the chair back, gripping its arms, and lowering her eyes against the sympathy lines etching Mr. Ingrum's face.

In a strained voice he asked, "Why haven't you told me this before?" He rose and walked to the window, his back to her for a moment. Turning, he asked softly, "Am I the last to know?"

"No," Norma sighed, "No one here knows. I can't talk about it without crying. Just like now. And I didn't want pity...nor my evaluation to be based on anything but my ability to do my job. Please, I ask you not to speak of this again, either to me or to anyone. I insist on it. The only way I can go on is by not talking about it."

"I wish you didn't feel that way. Can't you let us help, spare you some work, take your recess duty, anything..."

"Don't you understand," she said tearfully, "that's exactly what I don't want. Why should anyone else add some of my load to theirs? No, I can't allow that."

"No one would think if it in those terms," he assured her. "Isn't there something that I could do," and seeing the resistance in her eyes, he finished lamely, "something that you will allow me to do?"

"Yes, there is one thing," she said with certainty, "You can get the best substitute possible for my class three weeks from now."

Afterwards, Mr. Ingrum made excuses to come to her classroom to teach a math lesson which he said he sorely missed since he had become a principal. And when she had playground duty, he'd come to relieve her saying he needed some fresh air and why didn't she go and have a cup of coffee? Even though she didn't drink coffee, she would go. Mr. Ingrum was the epitome of discretion in his kindness and even though Norma knew his motives, she acquiesced. If she tried to protest, or express gratitude, she would cry. And once she started, would she ever be able to stop?

During spring vacation, Norma, Anne, and Charles took turns with Harry in his hospital room. The children visited in the mornings and spent the afternoons in Balboa Park and the zoo across Park Boulevard from the hospital. Anne shared her newly arrived graduation announcements and year book. She talked of the drama club productions she was a part of and rehearsed her debating position that soon technology would rule man instead of the reverse. Charles told of the neighborhood band he was starting with Lanny on lead guitar and Dusty on drums; he was playing bass on the new guitar he had bought with earnings from his newspaper route. His high bars were in place, and his traps in the canyon had caught a fox. Mr. Smith from across the street had helped him skin it and its carcass was in the school lab. With its fur he would make a collar for Mom.

The afternoons and evenings were Norma's time with Harry. They filled out their income tax return together. They talked of Anne's plans for college. Would she begin right out of high school? And would she go to the new junior college on the mesa so near home or to the old one downtown where they had gone? Could Norma resist Charles' pleas to drive the car before he was a responsible driver? Should she consider having him take private lessons? What about her music seminar, how many sessions were remaining? Three. Would she be taking her usual summer school course? Yes, she would be studying Spanish, and he could help her. And what about tenure? Had she heard anything definite? Yes, Mr. Ingrum said she would be granted tenure, it was just a matter of routine, now that she had met the time requirement.

"Then, you're all set," he said with relief and joy. In the soft darkness he gathered her to him, his hands resting lightly on her shoulders, his voice tender in her ear, "Norma, I've a confession to make. I've been thinking only of myself. I keep hanging around just to be with you, to have another day of seeing your beautiful face, sweet smile and holding you, like now."

He squeezed her shoulders gently. "On our honeymoon I thought you were the most beautiful, divine creature that had ever taken a breath, but you kept growing more beautiful, a precious bud opening to the world. And now you are a fully flowered woman, and when you reach your peak, Honeychild, you'll be more than I deserve...perhaps that's why..."

Norma's tears fell to his chest and she shivered in his arms. Apologetically he continued, "Please forgive me, but I was selfish from the start. I fell so passionately, so utterly, in love with you that I disregarded the natural order of things. I took advantage of your loving and trusting nature and wooed you, knowing the difference in our ages would hasten the day when I might leave you a widow. And now I am leaving you, not by choice, my dearest one, never by choice, but by the law of nature that takes the old and infirm. And the sooner I go, the sooner you can get on with living."

She raised to face him, her face anguished, "NO, you're not old. You've never been old! You've been young in heart and body until this cruel freak of nature intruded on our happiness. I hate it, hate, hate, hate it! And there can be no life for me without you. I know it. Don't say there can be! The sun will go down and never shine again, there will be total darkness." Her haunted eyes tortured him, but he answered calmly, "No, my darling, it won't be that way."

"Then tell me how I can live without you when you *are* my life?"

"Life doesn't end because we want it to, or because it's difficult, and when one is young and vibrant, as you are, life will have its way. And don't forget your dedication to duty. You will live by knowing and doing what needs to be done, a day at a time...attending to the needs of Anne and Charles, yourself...and to your little flock at school. They all need you, and you have so much to give. Duty is a friend, and there will always be more duty than you have time to perform..."

"I don't want duty, I want you!" She fell onto his chest, sobbing.

"Oh, darling mine. I know that, and knowing that gives me both exquisite joy and pain. I loathe myself for what I'm putting you through. but it is not in my power to change a thing. My heart is breaking at your unhappiness and despair." She felt him tremble, but his voice was steady and firm. "Norma, it was when you came into my life that I began to live, and I was older then than you are now. And my darling, my beautiful, beloved Norma, my baby, my lady, my woman, I have loved you so completely, and I will never stop loving you. Nothing on earth or beyond will ever change that. My love will surround you when I'm gone, but my fervent wish is that you will love again, a flesh and blood love. Perhaps, the best is yet to come for you. I pray that is true."

She was ready to deny his words, but he stilled her lips with a gentle touch, "Shhhh, don't talk, but think about and remember what I've said."

She sank into his embrace. What could she say? Her heart was breaking. He smoothed her hair and then his hand was still. "There's a Sanskrit verse I committed to memory long ago. Listen!" his voice was soft and low. "Look to this day! For it is Life--the very Life of life! In its brief course lie all the varieties and realities of your existence: the glory of action, the bliss of growth, the splendor of beauty, for yesterday is but a dream and tomorrow only a vision; but today well lived makes every yesterday a dream of happiness and every tomorrow a vision of hope. Look well, therefore, to this day."

*   *   *   *

Each afternoon at a quarter to three, Harry would say to Mary Lee, "Norma is dismissing her little flock." And at half past three, "Now, she's leaving the school." At three-fifty, he watched for the elevator doors to open when she would step out and walk into his room. She'd fill him in on the news at school, the news at home, bring the mail and messages from friends and family. After supper together, they had their talks. But no more did they talk of dying. Instead Norma had a list of questions to ask, such as: "When the Mercury needs replacing... it's nearly four years old, remember?...when it wears out, what kind of car do you suggest I buy?"

His answer, "I think perhaps a 'small economy car'," brought memories and laughter of that day long ago when she had bought the Mayflower.

"No, I mean *seriously,* what kind of car?"

"Perhaps a Dodge Dart," he told her seriously.

Or, "Should I pay off the mortgage or put the money in savings?"

He'd wag his head, "Don't, whatever you do, pay off a four and three-quarter mortgage."

And she asked, "In all of San Diego, what is your favorite place?"

"You know it well, my darling, the view of the harbor from the lighthouse on Point Loma."

And he always noticed the clothes she wore, that she had made in bold, bright colors--ruby red, sapphire blue, shocking pink, lemon yellow. "Honeychild, you love color so much. Don't wear black, promise me you won't wear black." And his eyes would scan the sunlight on her hair, and his finger would follow a wave, "It's still the same as I remember on our honeymoon, gleaming where the sunlight strikes it."

At half past three on Thursday, April 29, Norma left her room in readiness for the parents' evening visitation. Spring Open House was the high point of the school year for everyone: teachers, students, and parents. She drove to the hospital with great relief. After tonight, her work at school was finished. Her goal was reached, and from now on Harry would have her full attention. He had had it for nearly two hours when he pointed to his watch, "Go now and dress for your big night. In a little more than an hour the parents will be pounding on the door of Room 29. WOW them, Honeychild, and hurry back to tell me of another triumph."

She did, and remained until midnight. When she walked into his room the following morning with a big bouquet of roses, he asked in surprise, "Why, Honeychild, to what do I owe this unexpected pleasure?"

"Let me count the ways," she smiled, "your charming manners, your good looks, your kind words...no, I'm playing hooky. After Open House, I need a rest." Would he believe her? Did he know that last night the doctors had told her it could be any day?

"Rest well, then, because I have a request to make of you."

"Ask, my darling, and it is granted."

"I want you to do something special for Glenn, Harley, and Steve."

They both felt deep gratitude to those three corpsmen who often returned after their regular duty to see to Harry, an extra bath or shave or just to talk. Norma had already wondered how to show her appreciation. Butch had suggested a letter to Admiral Warden, commanding officer of the Naval Hospital, on behalf of the three specific corpsmen with enclosures for their service record. He was helping her draft it. But Harry wanted something now. "I think they'd like one of your great dinners. Grilled steak, corn-on the-cob, a big tossed salad with lots of avocado, crisp garlic bread, and for dessert home made ice cream. Peach. Is it too early for fresh peaches? *He's naming his favorite foods.* The weather's nice enough to eat on the patio, near the fire pit with a fire going." He was looking out the window at the bright blue sky. "I suppose the bougainvillea are still full of red clusters. And the acacias...Faith and Charity?"

"Both are flowering, dropping their golden blossoms on the patio, keeping Anne busy sweeping them up. And Hope still has her red berries that you saw at Christmas. Everything's in bloom, the geraniums and petunias in front and the cacti around the terrace wall. We're surrounded by color from the things you planted."

"It must be a sight to see," he nodded, his eyes misty. "We have a beautiful home, Honeychild."

She couldn't bear to think he'd never see it again. And if he saw her eyes, they would surely betray her terror, her sorrow. Taking his hand, she covered them with it and sprinkled kisses on its palm. *He had always made everything turn out right for them. She had grown to expect it through the years, but this illness that was robbing him of life, he couldn't make this turn out right.*

"Will you do it? Have them for dinner? Tomorrow evening?" Harry asked again.

Mr. Ingrum called, while Norma was preparing for her dinner guests, to say that the Board of Education would meet on May 4 and her tenure would be granted. She said to him, "Mr. Ingrum, you asked me once if there were something you could do for me."

"Yes, I did, and I still mean it," he assured her.

"Then would you visit my husband in the hospital and tell him about my tenure? Tonight? Please?"

"I would be happy to do that."

After the patio dinner, Norma drove the corpsmen to the hospital and had a midnight rendezvous with Harry. He was enormously pleased with Mr. Ingrum's news and very happy that the dinner had been a success.

Sunday. The Scoggins came for the day and Harry was cheerful, even joked with Joan, petite Joan, who thought she was overweight. "Don't just talk," he laughed, "if you want to loose weight get off the fence and do something about it."

"Not if it means giving up eating," Joan said, and everybody laughed.

When the Scoggins left, Norma and Mary Lee went to the evening service at the chapel, giving Anne and Charles time alone with their dad. His main concern was that they all go back to school tomorrow. They promised, but not Norma. "Maybe on Tuesday," she said. Monday was a day of silence; words were unnecessary. It was a day of listening to the heartbeat of the other. And hand holding. His touched hers so very lightly. Always it had been light and gentle, but today there was hardly more than the warmth of the touch, no pressure. Only his eyes were holding her to him, brilliant blue, alive, burning with love. Yearning, pleading, watching, giving. Had they said good-by when she left? Driving home she was burdened with the fight raging within her, she was nearly suffocating from the awareness that he was dying and still the denial of it. She felt him slipping away with only her will holding him. At home she faced her Gethsemane. She tried to comfort Anne and Charles, and they tried to comfort her, but she was alone...alone...

In the depth of her anguish a voice within, which often spoke, spoke now. *He's ready to go. Release him.* "No, I cannot," she argued. "He is my life." *It's his life and he's done the best he can for you. Let him go with grace, with love.* A giant light moved across her tired and grieving mind illuminating the words: "To everything there is a season, and a time to every purpose under the heaven: a time to be born, and a time to die."

And with the last of her strength, she let go, releasing him, totally, completely. Wearily, she rose from the floor where she had knelt beside the bed with her head on Harry's pillow, and then she lay upon the bed, where he had lain for so many years, and closed her eyes. His dear face passed before her sightless eyes in all the moods he had expressed to her during their years together and she felt his love engulf her.

Call him, the voice commanded, *Let him know.*

The clock said twelve-thirty and Glenn answered the phone. "Is it too late to speak with Colonel Kipp?"

"He's awake, Mrs. Kipp. I'll take the phone to him."

Her voice was calm and light now; no sign remained of the torment she had suffered over the past few hours, "Harry, darling!"

"Honeychild, you sound breathless, the same as the first time I heard you speak...in a phone call from San Francisco..."

"That was the beginning for us, wasn't it?" she whispered.

"Yes, it was the beginning ...of my life."

"Harry, I know it's late to call..."

"I was waiting."

"You were?"

"Yes, to hear your voice, to hear you say it again."

"That I love you? With all my heart and soul? You know I do! Sleep well, my Harry, and wait for me."

"Good night, dearest Norma, my love, my honeychild."

Norma held the telephone to her heart even after hearing its click. She couldn't be the one to hang up first. Slowly and deliberately, she returned the receiver to its cradle and, weary beyond description, gave herself to sleep. But at dawn she was suddenly awake. She called the sixth floor; Harley answered. "Is Colonel Kipp asleep?"

"He may be now, but I spoke with him earlier. He told me he'd had the best night in a long time. Do you want to speak with him?"

"No, Harley, thank you. Don't wake him. Just give him a message, please. Tell him I called and will soon be with him."

"I'll do that, Mrs. Kipp."

Tuesday, May 4. At eight Anne and Charles left for school. Mary Lee and Norma were leaving for the hospital when the ringing of the phone called Norma back. "Good morning. Mrs. Kipp speaking."

"Good morning, Mrs. Kipp. This is Doctor Sergeant on the sixth floor of the Naval Hospital."

"Yes, Dr. Sergeant?" She was impatient to get off the phone to go to Harry.

"Mrs. Kipp, there's no easy way to say this, and I'm very sorry to have to tell you, but...the Colonel's heart...has stopped beating."

Norma blinked, "What?" she shouted in astonishment, "Then what are you doing on the phone with me? Go start it again!"

"I can't, Mrs. Kipp....I mean, I used the wrong words. I was trying to tell you that...Colonel Kipp has died. I'm very sorry."

Norma shrieked one long wail, "Nooooooooooooooooooooooooooo" and Mary Lee took the phone from her.

Morning, May 5, Norma opened her eyes to sunlight on the acacia through the high bedroom windows. Golden blossoms and silvery green leaves almost hid the azure sky, and the sight lifted her from drowsiness to keen awareness. Harry was dead and the sun was shining. Harry was dead and the doves still cooed. Could it be a dream or was it real? What was real? Because she was seeing as plain as day Harry rising slowly upward to the heavens, well and happy, looking down at her, smiling his crooked smile. The magnetism of his blue eyes pulled her to him in one swift move, bridging the distance between, and she felt his spirit join with hers to continue the perfect union. She knew that no matter what happened to her from now to forever, she would not be simply Norma; she would be Eternally Norma and Harry just as the inscription inside her wedding band proclaimed. She understood as never before the meaning of his words written so many years ago:*Darling, you know I'll love you forever. My love for you is my life. It's greater than space, as true as the blue of heaven, and as eternal as time. If only I could hold you close to me and keep you in my arms forever!* She felt his arms around her now. If only she had known it would be like this!

June 30, 1965. Eleven-thirty. She sat alone in her bedroom listening to the silence of the night, looking at the bouquet of long stemmed pink carnations. Anne and Charles had said, "It's what Dad would do." Yes, he had brought carnations to her for their wedding, and when their children were born. And for Mother's Day and her birthdays. Never forgetting a special day and his thoughtfulness had influenced his children. They had done their best to make this a happy day.

She felt a compelling urge to touch something of his. From her jewelry case, she took his wedding ring and slipped it on her thumb; it was even too big for that. His big strong hands, so gentle, so accomplished. She recalled their wedding ceremony when she couldn't slip it past his knuckle. Later he had whispered, "Do you suppose we're only half married?!" So many things to remember, to make her feel his love.

She opened her cedar chest. There were his dress blues, the flag, which Dolly as postmistress had provided, his Marine Corps and Samurai swords, and a bundle of letters. His letters, smelling of cedar and yellowed with age, not disturbed since she tied them with a narrow red ribbon and put them there twenty years ago. She took them out to read, and her eyes went to his portrait hanging on the wall. She looked long at the portrayal of his majestic bearing, humor of smile, inclusiveness of eyes. Those vivid blue eyes that in real life had always closed out the rest of the world when they engaged hers. All through their years together, no matter what she was doing, she could look up to find his eyes, deep blue pools of wonder, waiting for hers. Now, there was only the memory of them, and his words. Words of a new life, a life Harry wanted her to have.

That knowledge would be the bridge across this wide river of sorrow to a far bank that must lie beyond the mist where grass smells sweet and dewdrops sparkle, where flowers dance and trees sway in a summer breeze. And perhaps on that distant bank in some future time, she might open her heart again to another love. Not ever a love to compare with Harry's great, encompassing love that would never leave her, a love as much a part of her as flesh and blood. No matter what path she walked, her eyes would forever see his tender, crooked smile in a cloud or a star-filled sky, in a rosy dawn or vibrant sunset, or in the ever changing phases of the moon. And her ears would forever hear in the sighing wind, the pounding surf, and the love calls of the doves, his voice coming to her in a soft, wondrous whisper, "Honeychild, my Honeychild!"

And always when she heard, her heart would swell with joy and answer back, "Oh, Harry, my Harry! Wait for me!"

About the Author

Norma Kipp Avendano is a retired elementary school teacher and active grandmother living in San Diego, California. Her hobbies are collecting Mexican folk art, gardening, painting, writing, and traveling. She enjoys a wide national and international correspondence. She and her present husband Tony Camilo Avendano have logged over a quarter million miles in motor homes during twenty-six years of marriage. He declares her to be the world's best travel planner and navigator.

On 2 October, 1989 the military papers and photographs, citations, and medals of Lt. Col. Harry E. Kipp, USMC, Retired, were presented to Dr. Stephen R. Wise curator of the Parris Island Historical Museum for its archives. Norma is grateful to Dr. Wise for including the medal and a photograph of Harry accepting *La Cruz de Valor* as part of the museum's Nicaraguan exhibit.